60

FARRAR
STRAUS
GIROUX

Also by John Hope Franklin

The Free Negro in North Carolina, 1790–1860 (1943)

From Slavery to Freedom: A History of Negro Americans (1947)

The Militant South, 1800–1860 (1956)

Reconstruction After the Civil War (1961)

The Emancipation Proclamation (1963)

Land of the Free (with John W. Caughey and Ernest R. May) (1965)

Illustrated History of Black Americans (with the editors of Time-Life Books) (1970)

A Southern Odyssey: Travelers in the Ante-bellum North (1976)

Racial Equality in America (1976)

George Washington Williams: A Biography (1985)

Race and History: Selected Essays 1938–1988 (1990)

The Color Line: Legacy for the Twenty-first Century (1993)

African Americans and the Living Constitution (editor, with Genna Rae McNeil) (1995)

The Diary of James T. Ayers: Civil War Recruiter (editor) (1999)

My Life and an Era: The Autobiography of Buck Colbert Franklin (editor, with John Whittington Franklin) (1997)

Runaway Slaves: Rebels on the Plantation (with Loren Schweninger) (2000)

In Search of the Promised Land: A Slave Family in the Old South (with Loren Schweninger) (2005)

Mirror to America

Mirror to America

The

Autobiography

of

JOHN HOPE FRANKLIN

Farrar, Straus and Giroux

New York

Farrar, Straus and Giroux
19 Union Square West, New York 10003

Distributed in Canada by Douglas & McIntyre Ltd.
Printed in the United States of America
Published in 2005 by Hill and Wang
First paperback edition, 2006

The Library of Congress has cataloged the hardcover edition as follows:
Franklin, John Hope, 1915–
    Mirror to America : the autobiography of John Hope Franklin / John Hope
Franklin.— 1st ed.
        p.   cm.
    ISBN-13: 978-0-374-29944-6 (hardcover : alk. paper)
    ISBN-10: 0-374-29944-7 (hardcover : alk. paper)
    1. Franklin, John Hope, 1915– 2. African American historians—Biography.
3. Historians—United States—Biography.   I. Title.

E175.5.F73A3 2005
973'.0496073'0092—dc22

                                                        2005007078

Paperback ISBN-13: 978-0-374-53047-1
Paperback ISBN-10: 0-374-53047-5

Designed by Abby Kagan

www.fsgbooks.com

1   3   5   7   9   10   8   6   4   2

A John Kluge Book,
Library of Congress

To all my students,

from whom I have learned more than they will ever know

Contents

Acknowledgments

Unfortunately, I kept no records of my life until I was a tenured professor and chair of the department at Brooklyn College. By that time my secretary, the first one I ever had, preserved records of my activities for the Board of Higher Education of the City of New York, and I was the beneficiary. For the earlier period of my life I have had to do a great deal of research, especially for my childhood and youth. Indeed, I was compelled to reconstruct my childhood—to the extent possible—not only from my own memory, but also from the unpublished census schedules for 1920 and 1930 and with the assistance of the few childhood friends I could locate. Clinton Robinson and Jeffie Price refreshed my memory of Rentiesville, while Kenny Booker, Zella Batson, and Goldie Williams helped me with the Tulsa years. Walter Hill of the National Archives not only facilitated my use of materials there, but also assisted me in securing State Department files as well as the files on me at the Federal Bureau of Investigation. The most that I learned at the latter institution was that in the files I was frequently confused with another John Franklin, about whom I knew nothing.

Many members of the senior staff of the Library of Congress, including the librarian, James H. Billington, and the director of the Office of

Scholarly Programs, Prosser Gifford, led the way for their gifted and experienced colleagues to facilitate my work and that of my research assistant, Rashad Jones, who was provided by the library. The fact that this is a John W. Kluge book bespeaks the immense generosity of the library in facilitating the work on this book at every stage, especially when I was a Kluge Senior Fellow at the library.

In doing the research for and writing this book I have benefitted from the assistance of many scholars and members of the staffs of several institutions. Among them were the New York Public Library and the libraries at Fisk University, Howard University, Atlanta University, Emory University, the University of Massachusetts at Amherst, Duke University, and the University of North Carolina, to which I am deeply grateful. Although I learned much from reading biographies and other relevant material, I learned even more, perhaps, from conversations with such masterful biographers as Arnold Rampersad of Stanford University, David Levering of New York University, and my Duke University colleague William H. Chafe. From time to time I have consulted various friends and colleagues whose suggestions and observations I greatly valued. Among them are Walter M. Brown, Sheila Flemming, Patricia Sullivan, and Barry Karl.

Among the research assistants who have been most helpful and accommodating were Richard P. Fuke and Loren Schweninger, when they were my students at the University of Chicago. Alfred Moss, also my student at the University of Chicago, now at the University of Maryland, was, in addition to being my coauthor for three editions of *From Slavery to Freedom*, generous in offering wise suggestions for organizing and writing this book. Indeed, I learned so much from these and my many other students in the various places I have taught that I am pleased to dedicate this book to all of them. At the six colleges and universities where I was a member of the faculty and the eight where I was a visitor, my colleagues contributed in many ways to my intellectual growth as well as to my understanding of the world, and for that I am grateful. For several years Terry Sanford, former governor of North Carolina and president of Duke University, and I had lunch once a month, ostensibly to "solve the race problem," and I profited greatly from the insights he shared with me.

Margaret Fitzsimmons, my secretary for more than thirty years, put order in my life, as well as in the records she kept. Subsequent valuable assistants were Nashani Frazier, Debi Hamlin, and Charity Greene, all of whom had much to do with collecting materials and preparing the manuscript and seeing it through the press.

Thomas LeBien, my editor at Farrar, Straus and Giroux, and his colleagues have been thoughtful and generous in their advice and assistance, for which I am deeply grateful.

After Aurelia died, I found a cache of notes and letters from me to her, many written while I traveled in the United States or abroad. These missives have been most helpful in my attempt to recount and evaluate my experiences. I even found letters to me, carefully written by her but never presented, that helped me recall and recount mutual experiences that I have used in this work. As in all things that I have attempted to do, she has been of inestimable help, for which I shall be ever grateful.

Mirror to America

I

No Crystal Stair

L IVING IN A WORLD restricted by laws defining race, as well as creating obstacles, disadvantages, and even superstitions regarding race, challenged my capacities for survival. For ninety years I have witnessed countless men and women likewise meet this challenge. Some bested it; some did not; many had to settle for any accommodation they could. I became a student and eventually a scholar. And it was armed with the tools of scholarship that I strove to dismantle those laws, level those obstacles and disadvantages, and replace superstitions with humane dignity. Along with much else, the habits of scholarship granted me something many of my similarly striving contemporaries did not have. I knew, or should say know, what we are up against.

Slavery was a principal centerpiece of the New World Order that set standards of conduct including complicated patterns of relationships. These lasted not merely until emancipation but after Reconstruction and on into the twentieth century. Many of them were still very much in place when beginning in the late 1950s, the sit-ins, marches, and the black revolution began a successful onslaught on some of the antediluvian practices that had become a part of the very fabric of society in the New World and American society in particular.

Born in 1915, I grew up in a racial climate that was stifling to my senses and damaging to my emotional health and social well-being. Society at that time presented a challenge to the strongest adult, and to a child it was not merely difficult but cruel. I watched my mother and father, who surely numbered among the former, daily meet that challenge; I and my three siblings felt equally that cruelty. And it was no more possible to escape that environment of racist barbarism than one today can escape the industrial gases that pollute the atmosphere.

This climate touched me at every stage of my life. I was forcibly removed from a train at the age of six for having accidentally taken a seat in the "white people's coach." I was the unhappy victim, also at age six, of a race riot that kept the family divided for more than four years. I endured the very strict segregation laws and practices in Tulsa, Oklahoma. I was rejected as a guide through busy downtown Tulsa traffic by a blind white woman when she discovered that the twelve-year-old at her side was black. I underwent the harrowing experience as a sixteen-year-old college freshman of being denounced in the most insulting terms for having the temerity to suggest to a white ticket seller a convenient way to make change. More harrowing yet was the crowd of rural white men who confronted and then nominated me as a possible Mississippi lynching victim when I was nineteen. I was refused service while on a date as a Harvard University graduate student at age twenty-one. Racism in the navy turned my effort to volunteer during World War II into a demeaning embarrassment, such that at a time when the United States was ostensibly fighting for the Four Freedoms I struggled to evade the draft. I was called a "Harvard nigger" at age forty. At age forty-five, because of race, New York banks denied me a loan to purchase a home. At age sixty I was ordered to serve as a porter for a white person in a New York hotel, at age eighty to hang up a white guest's coat at a Washington club where I was not an employee but a member.

To these everyday, ordinary experiences during ninety years in the American race jungle should be added the problem of trying to live in a community where the economic and social odds clearly placed any descendant of Africans at a disadvantage. For a profession, my father, Buck Franklin, proudly chose the practice of law. Depending as it did on the judicial system in which it operated, the practice of law in America could not possibly have functioned favorably or even fairly for a person who qualified as, at best, a pariah within it. My father, ever the optimist, persisted in holding the view that the practice of law was a noble pursuit whose nobility entailed the privilege of working to rectify a system that contained a set of advantages for white people and a corresponding set of disadvantages for black people. The integrity and the high moral standards by which he lived and that he commended to his children forbade him to violate the law or resort to any form of unethical conduct. And, as children, we had to adjust ourselves to dignified, abject poverty.

My mother, Mollie, shared these views, to which she added a remarkable amount of creativity and resourcefulness in her effort to supplement the family income and boost the family morale. She taught in public schools, made hats, and developed a line of beauty aids. To these creative skills should be added her equanimity, her sense of fairness, her high standards of performance, and her will to succeed. On many occasions she would say to me, "If you do your best, the angels cannot do any better!" These qualities became the hallmark of her relationship with her four children, giving us the strength and skills to cope with the formidable odds she knew we would encounter. If we did not always succeed, it was not the fault of our parents.

But the challenges I, my brother, Buck, and my sisters, Mozella and Anne, faced were always formidable. Living through years of remarkable change, the barrier of race was a constant. With the appearance of each new institution or industry, racism would rear its ugly head again. When the age of the automobile made its debut, there was the question of whether African Americans should be given the opportunity to acquire the skills necessary to find work within that industry. It was the same with the advent of the computer age. More than one company dragged its feet when it came to making certain that young people on "both sides of the track" had an opportunity to acquire the skills necessary to be successful participants in the new scientific revolution. Indeed, the expansion of numerous American industries caused debates or at least discussions regarding the abilities of African Americans to cope with new developments, whatever they were. Even at the end of the twentieth century, many Americans continued to debate nineteenth-century racial theories regarding the abilities of blacks to see at night, to make accurate calculations, and to learn foreign languages. These debates ranged from discussions having to do with the effect of African Americans on the growth of the gross national product to their ability to resist new diseases or their capacity to adjust to new educational or cultural developments. Throughout a life spent at the intersection of scholarship and public service, I have been painfully aware that superstitions and quaint notions of biological and even moral differences between blacks and whites continue to affect race relations in the United States—even into the twenty-first century.

In 1943 Gunnar Myrdal called attention to these discussions and debates over racial differences in his classic *American Dilemma*. And when the Committee on the Status of Black Americans, of which I was a member, took another look in 1989 while updating Myrdal's book, we saw much the same thing and set forth these and other views in *A Common Destiny: Blacks and American Society*. In our discussion of the problem of race, we declared that it could well create new fissures that might, in turn, lead to an increased level of confrontations and violence. The Rodney King riots of 1991 offered vivid testimony that there still persists much too much potential for racial conflict for anyone to be complacent.

Of the many recollections I have arising from my fifteen months as chair of President Clinton's advisory board on race is that of the black woman who screamed during a meeting her history of how she had been abused and mistreated because of her race. My memory of the white man who claimed that already too much was being done for African Americans, and it was he who needed protection from policies such as affirmative action, is no less vivid. The advisory board was troubled by these and similar competing claims, and it became clear that open dialogues and, if necessary, limitless discussions were the civilized approach to finding constructive ways of dealing with America's racial ills. It did and will require not only persistent diligence but also abiding patience.

During my life it has been necessary to work not only as hard as my energies would permit, but to do it as regularly and as consistently as humanly possible. This involved the strictest discipline in the maximum use of my time and energy. I worked two jobs in college and graduate school that made inordinate demands on my time, but there was no alternative to the regimen that circumstances demanded. And those circumstances included a refusal to check my catholic interests that have always prompted me to participate in activities beyond scholarship. Balancing professional and personal activities has resulted in a life full of rich rewards, a consequence deeply indebted to my near sixty-year marriage to Aurelia Whittington. My father called her the Trooper for her patient, good-willed, indomitable spirit. She was that and so much more. How do I calculate the influence of having spent two-thirds of my life living alongside an exemplar of selfless dignity?

Even before we were married, I learned much from Aurelia. She taught me to put others ahead of my own preference, as she did routinely. There is no more vivid example of her habit of self-sacrifice than when she abandoned her own career. She did so in order to be there for Whit, our only child, when our adult Brooklyn neighbors taunted him and sought in every way possible to convey that neither he nor his family was welcome to live in their previously all-white neighborhood.

My life has been dedicated to and publicly defined by scholarship, a lifelong affection for the profession of history and the myriad institutions that support it. A white professor at historically black Fisk University powerfully influenced my choice of a career, one I decided early on to dedicate to new areas of study, wherever possible, in order to maintain a lively, fresh approach to teaching and writing history. This is how I happened to get into African American history, in which I never had a formal course but that attracted an increasing number of students of my generation and many more in later generations. But I was determined that I would not be confined to a box of any kind, so I regarded African American history as not so much a separate field as a subspeciality of American history. Even in graduate school I was interested in women's history, and in more recent years I have studied and written papers in that field, although I never claimed more than the desire to examine it intensely rather than presume to master it entirely.

I could not work in the field of history without maintaining some contact with other historians and some affiliation with historical associations. Consequently, at the Library of Congress and in local libraries where I was engaged in research, I made a point of meeting other historians and discussing with them matters of mutual interest. I not only maintained an active membership in the Association for the Study of Negro Life and History but joined other groups, even where it became necessary to educate members, to the extent possible, that history knows no bounds, either in the human experience or in the rules governing who is eligible to record it. This would not, could not involve demeaning myself or in any way compromising my own self-respect. On occasion it did involve venturing into groups and organizations when it was not clear if their reception of me would be cool or cordial. Nevertheless, as a consequence I became active in the major national professional organizations long before most other African Americans joined them.

In much the same way, I became involved with historical groups in other parts of the world. My ever-widening contacts in the United States presented me with opportunities to become associated with historians in Europe, Asia, Africa, Australia, and South America. Each contact was instructive not only about the many things that peoples of the world have in common but also as to the intense interest other peoples have in problems and developments far removed from their own that would nevertheless assist them in understanding their own society. A remarkable and unforeseen result of my determination to pursue my profession wherever it led, be that into the halls of previously all-white academic associations or to the far-flung scholarly organizations scattered across the globe, were the contacts that released me from the straitjacket confinement of pursuing a career exclusively in historically black colleges and universities.

My life and my career have been fulfilled not merely by my own efforts but also by the thoughtful generosity of family, friends, and professional colleagues. I can only hope that they realize, as do I, how interdependent we all are and how much more rewarding and fulfilling life is whenever we reach a level of understanding where we can fully appreciate the extent of our interrelationships with and our reliance on those who came before us, kept us company during our lives, and will come after us.

2

The World of My Youth

THE SCHOOL BOARD of Rentiesville, Oklahoma, met in midsummer 1914 and after "due deliberation" voted to deny Mollie Parker Franklin's request for a maternity leave for one school year. Such denials were not especially unusual in those days, considering the fact that most school boards preferred young, single women as teachers. But this denial was special and pointed. Both Mollie and her husband, Buck Colbert Franklin, had incurred the wrath of Rentiesville's all-black, all-Baptist town fathers by revealing their commitment to Methodism shortly after their arrival from Ardmore, Oklahoma, in 1912. The couple having attended and met at Roger Williams University, Nashville's Baptist institution of higher learning for African Americans, it was assumed by the village leaders that they were "good Baptists." If there was any lingering doubt, it had been eliminated by the further local knowledge that after Mollie returned to her native town of Ged, Tennessee, to teach, Buck, having no strong attachment to Roger Williams, followed Professor John Hope who had moved to Atlanta Baptist College (later Morehouse College) in 1901.

My parents had enjoyed a lengthy and deeply committed courtship, based on common interests and constant association. Buck was from the Indian Territory, where his ancestors had fled with their Native American owners when Andrew Jackson expelled them from Alabama and Mississippi in the mid-1830s. In Mollie he found an ideal and attractive companion. They studied together, and she cheered him on as he drew admiration as a scholar-gentleman and varsity center and captain of the Roger Williams football team. And while they briefly went their separate ways at the beginning of the new century, they never lost touch with each other.

To bide her time until they could marry, my mother taught in Ged until her father, Harding Parker, died. She then secured employment as a teacher in Shelbyville, Bolivar County, Mississippi. Meanwhile, my father returned to the Choctaw Nation in the Indian Territory to be near his father in his declining and final years. By 1903, Buck's parents had both died and so had Mollie's. They could finally make plans for their own future. Thus, Buck journeyed to Mound Bayou, where he and Mollie were married on April 1, 1903. They went almost immediately to Springer, Oklahoma, in the Indian Territory, where Buck taught, farmed, and at a time when most advocated little more than "industrial education" for blacks, took correspondence courses in law and studied for the bar.

Awaiting teaching opportunities, Mollie became, for a time, a milliner as well as a seamstress. After they moved to Ardmore and after Buck passed the bar examination in 1908, she would pursue her trade alongside him in the same building. My father's practice grew, though not at a sufficient pace for him to cease looking for ways to supplement his income through writing, teaching, or journalism. Attracting clients was not easy. Few, besides African Americans, had any interest in engaging the services of a black lawyer. And many, black and white, were simply too poor to employ a lawyer of any kind. Regardless, those with economic resources viewed black lawyers with a wary eye, if for no other reason than they seriously doubted a black lawyer's chances in a court of law where a white judge and a white jury held him in such low esteem.

Buck learned this the hard way. In 1911, when a client's case pending in Shreveport, Louisiana, was called, Buck stood as a signal to the judge that he was present and ready to proceed. In disbelief, the presiding judge asked my father why he was standing. When Buck made the simple reply that he was representing his client in the case, the judge retorted that no "nigger" represented anyone in his court. With that pronouncement, my father was ordered to vacate the courtroom.

As he struggled against the odds during the next year or so, Buck kept his eyes open for a better opportunity. Soon, one appeared that seemed too good to be true. He heard of an all-black town, Rentiesville, in the northeastern part of Oklahoma, where people of his own color were in complete control of the schools, the judicial system, the post office, and all other public institutions and facilities. A score of such communities had arisen in the fledgling state, and many blacks sought refuge in them. Without any further investigation, my parents resolved to move as soon as possible; it could hardly be worse than their current situation. And so this adventuresome young couple, with their two young children, Mozella and Buck Jr., cast their lot with Rentiesville.

Finding a place that provided emotional security for themselves was one thing; finding a way to make a living in a village of a few hundred people was quite another. The Franklins soon discovered that Rentiesville provided neither. Rentiesville was torn by factionalism. The rivalry of the two principal churches, one Baptist and the other Methodist, was in part to blame. So too was the way the inhabitants sought to curry favor with the whites who lived in Oktaha, about six miles to the north, and Checotah, about five miles to the south. Buck Franklin soon referred to Rentiesville as the "Negro quarters" for the "big houses" that were Oktaha and Checotah. Within those quarters the Baptist pastor had assumed leadership over the entire community, including the school board and the town council. The Methodists were no match for him. And in Buck, the Baptist minister thought that he had a valuable ally. He was soon bitterly disappointed. A lifelong Methodist, Buck was quickly identified as a leader in the enemy camp.

Community-minded, the Franklins gave him cause. For though my parents were indeed Methodists by upbringing and inclination, their confrontation with Rentiesville's Baptist power brokers was not fundamentally theological. At its heart was my parents' resolve to pursue lives of dignified self-determination, and to instill that same resolve in their children and their neighbors.

Following the birth of my sister, my parents' third child, Anne Harriet, in 1913, Mollie secured a position as a teacher in the local elementary school. Buck practiced law locally as well as in Eufala, the county seat. He began to edit a newspaper, *The Rentiesville News*, and for a few months in

1914 he served as a justice of the peace. After waging a vigorous campaign through his congressman and some influential white lawyers, he was appointed postmaster. Postal service was dispensed in the front room of my parents' house, and when my father was away on some legal matter or attempting his hand at farming, my mother looked after the post office.

It was in the following year that Mollie, once again pregnant, requested from the school board a leave of absence until after her child was born. The board, under the Baptist pastor's influence, refused and, instead, requested her resignation. The white superintendent of the county schools disallowed the action and ordered that a substitute be employed until my mother could return to work.

Saturday, January 2, 1915, was not an especially eventful day in the world or, indeed, in Rentiesville. The war in Europe droned on, with that day's *New York Times* announcing the sinking by the Germans of the British warship *Formidable* in the English Channel. It would be another two years before the United States was drawn into the conflict. Buck Franklin himself noted in his diary simply: "The year 1915 was uneventful, except for the same grinding poverty caused by the continuous warfare [between the factions in Rentiesville]. This year's strain was agrivated [*sic*] by the birth of a child, John Hope." Forty years later, when I first read that entry, I realized here was poignant testimony of the family's circumstances from a man who never failed to make evident his love for and confidence in all his children.

I have astoundingly clear recollections of my early childhood, including my almost fatal bout with Spanish influenza in the fall of 1918. I can remember all too well Dr. Lowe calling to see me, and my mother sitting by my bed, day and night, until, finally, I recovered. And while it is not clear who looked after me during my first two or three years, my sister Mozella, nine years my senior, boasted until her death in 1986 that she was my first babysitter. Given my mother's success in retaining her teaching job, I suspect that some neighbor had a hand in looking after me during those first months and years. By the time I was three, however, my mother had charge of every aspect of my life.

There were few day-care centers anywhere in 1918, and certainly Rentiesville had none. Since the school board had lost its major fight regarding my mother's leave of absence when I was born, it left her to her own devices for the time being. Thus, it proved easiest for her to bring me to school with her. She placed me at a school desk, gave me a sheet of paper and a pencil, and admonished me to be quiet.

I was enthralled with the classroom, the pictures on the wall, the blackboard, and the animated responses of my mother's first-grade students. And there were letters and numbers that she wrote out in chalk. One day, as she visited the students' desks, she walked over to see what I was doing. She discovered that I had copied from the blackboard what she had written. I had, indeed, learned the alphabet and could write simple sentences. While my penmanship was poor, well before the age of five I could read and write.

My early memories are not solely of the classroom. When I was four, we moved from a small house on a road by the railroad to a larger house on the main road, evidence that my parents' steadfast efforts to escape poverty were increasingly succeeding. Here I had more playmates and for Christmas I got a tricycle on which I raced around outside.

Though we had moved farther from it, we remained dependent on the railroad, specifically the Missouri, Kansas, and Texas line, which we called the Katy. Two trains, one from the north and the other from the south, passed through in the early morning and again in the early evening. Except when they were flagged for oncoming passengers or when someone was aboard who wanted to get off, they did not stop. The mailbag was placed on a specially constructed pole from which it was snatched by a hook on the passing train. When my father was postmaster, I enjoyed going down to the track and watching him suspend the outgoing mail and pick up the mailbag that was thrown from the fast-moving train.

Besides the mail, the Katy brought news contained in the *Daily Phoenix* from Muskogee and the *Black Dispatch* from Oklahoma City. When it stopped to deliver them, the boxes and crates from the train invariably went to Brinson's store, a few yards up the main road from our house, where my parents purchased staples they had failed to buy in Checotah and where I spent my pennies on confections. Brinson's store was a large one-room emporium that, to my youthful eye, contained just about everything that one would ever need or want. Around the big wood-burning stove, customers and visitors gathered on winter days. The boxes displaying cookies and candies attracted me, but so too did the large wheel of cheese from which Mrs. Brinson cut thin slices that she served with crackers. Then there was the large barrel of pickles, a treat some children purchased for all-day suckers. Brinson's was a more than adequate substitute for those of us unable to go regularly to Checotah.

My father continued to receive public appointments that certain locals deemed he did not deserve. His legal practice, however, brought him into contact with influential men well outside the confines of Rentiesville, and a small number of our neighbors were suitably impressed with his probity, civic-mindedness, and the optimism inherent in his refusing to concede to the powers that be. In 1918 he was appointed industrial supervisor of rural Negro schools for McIntosh County. Later he was appointed deputy federal food administrator for the county. And while I grasped little concerning these appointments at the time, I knew, even as a four-year-old, that my father was bitterly hated by certain factions in the village. He seemed too ambitious, and some inhabitants viewed his education as excessive. His connection with Democrats was too much, moreover, for his fellow townsmen, most of whom were Republicans. Indeed, in August 1919, he received an anonymous letter ordering him to leave town within three days or suffer dire consequences. He and my mother outwardly ignored the threats, but it is not possible to measure their real toll. There was ample evidence that the threats weren't idle. Indeed, in that month, unidentified assailants fired shotguns at our home. No one was hurt, but one of our horses, Old Nelly, was hit with shotgun pellets. I vividly remember my father and a friend picking buckshot out of Old Nelly's buttocks while my brother held aloft a lantern.

This assault, and the continued threats, had something to do, I believe, with my parents' decision to move a mile from the village to a farm where, once again, they made an effort to grow cotton commercially and vegetables for home consumption. Without any means of transportation, we walked everywhere: to school, to church, to the railroad station, to visit, carrying a lantern at night.

Following the move, my world shrank considerably. Responsibilities, however, seemed to increase. My older siblings helped pick cotton, while my sister Anne and I were left at home to watch that the already picked cotton on the back porch did not blow away or catch fire. What was true for the children was exponentially true for my parents: The burdens of a farm merely joined the ongoing challenges of pursuing success in a town riven by faction.

The local feud had robbed the Rentiesville Trading Company, which my father had organized, of support and fueled the decline of his newspaper. These were the final failures that persuaded my parents that this so-called utopia, this bastion of racial unity, this Eden where all were supposed to be sisters and brothers, was a travesty. Having done absolutely all he could to survive and even improve this community, giving it everything he had to aid its development and prosperity, my father was now willing to acknowledge his efforts had failed and the time had come to seek a better life, even if it meant returning to a segregated community.

I do not remember the day in February 1921 when my father left Rentiesville to find our fortune in Tulsa, sixty-five miles to the north. I do recall that he failed to appear for dinner that night or the next or the next. Mother explained that our father had gone to Tulsa to live, and that at the end of the school term, when she was no longer teaching and Anne and I were no longer in school, we would join him there. That was small comfort for a six-year-old. It seemed that my world was suddenly crumbling. Buck Jr. and Mozella were off at boarding school in Tennessee, and nothing anyone told me would calm my fears that my sister, brother, and father had all abandoned me.

The railroad suddenly meant more to me than ever, for it brought not only packages and crates for Brinson's store but also the newspapers, with news of Tulsa, and an occasional letter from Dad. When he could break away from his fledgling law practice in Tulsa, it also brought my father. His visits were infrequent, just enough to give us hope. Sometimes, for want of something better to do, my sister and I would persuade our mother that all three of us should meet the train and give Dad the surprise of his life by greeting him as he stepped off. We managed to startle him not more than once or twice.

One day in early June 1921, shortly before we were to join my father in Tulsa, we learned that there had been a race riot there. A young black man, Dick Rowland, had been arrested and jailed for an alleged assault on a white woman. Rumors quickly circulated that a mob of white men intended to storm the jail, take Rowland away, and lynch him. Armed African Americans went to the courthouse where Rowland was detained, vowing to protect him from the lynch mob. An attempt to disarm these men, some of them veterans of World War I, set off sparks that escalated into one of the bloodiest and costliest race riots in American history.

The riot broke out the week that my father was to come to Rentiesville and move us to Tulsa. News of the violence reached us well before news of him. The black section of the town had been leveled, churches and residences burned, and a large but undetermined number of people killed. We got fragments of news from the newspapers and passengers who came on the morning train, but no specific details. For days we did not know if my father was dead, injured, or unharmed. Finally, we received a letter, in which he gave our mother some details of the tragedy and assured us that he was alive and well but was terribly busy seeking reimbursement for losses his clients had sustained. He was also suing the city for passing an ordinance that, in effect, barred blacks from rebuilding. The suit would eventually reach the Oklahoma Supreme Court, which finally declared the ordinance unconstitutional.

We were delighted to learn that he was unharmed, but the knowledge that he was conducting his law practice in a tent underscored the fact that we would not be leaving Rentiesville anytime soon. My father's rented house, all his clothes and most of his belongings, and his office and records had literally gone up in smoke. Our plans to move to Tulsa in June were postponed indefinitely and, almost as bad, due to the press of work and the lack of funds, Dad's visits to Rentiesville became less frequent.

A wait of four years ensued, during which life in Rentiesville began to press on me as never before. I was reading well at six years of age, but there was no library except that provided by my parents' limited resources. My father still had his Greek and Latin texts from college, but somehow they did not appeal to a six-year-old. My sister, mother, and I occasionally walked into town, but there excitement was confined to Brinson's store or, better, running into a few playmates. There were activities at the First Baptist Church, an imposing structure that was the most popular gathering place. But that was the "rival" church, and Mother, and at a distance Father, cautioned us against coming under the powerful influence of the "evil" forces there.

The nights were long and very, very dark. There was no electricity within miles of the village, and once night had closed in on its inhabitants, they had to depend on what little light they got from lamps and lanterns. Now and then, to break the monotony, a neighbor of ours from over the hill, Mrs. Sarah Bruner, would come over with the younger of her two sons, Edward, and "sit awhile." After an hour or two, often filled with long periods of silence, she would announce that they should be getting back "over the hill."

The only sound from the village that we heard at night was the occasional tolling of the First Baptist Church's bell announcing the death of a resident. I found it terrifying, for it seemed to come at some eerie hour and prove never ending. Once awakened, I could not to go back to sleep for wondering who had died. In so small a community, the deceased person was surely someone we knew. I tossed and turned and speculated, awaiting the chance to go into the village the following morning and learn the identity of the dead.

A rare pleasure, and a break in the monotony of village and farm, was visiting Muskogee, a town larger than Checotah, Oktaha, or even Eufala, our county seat. I had the opportunity to travel there during the first year of my father's absence. Perhaps because of my excessive reading, some done by poorly lit kerosene lamps, at six I began to have trouble with my eyes. Our local physician, Dr. Lowe, felt his expertise insufficient, and so there was nothing left to do but to go to Muskogee to see an eye specialist. Dr. Nagel examined my eyes, and immediately relieved us by his diagnosis. I had, indeed, suffered from eyestrain due to reading in poor light. This could be corrected by mild medication and eyeglasses. We were left with a day in which to explore the city.

That first visit to Muskogee was memorable. I marveled at the paved streets and sidewalks, of which I had seen so few on our infrequent visits to Checotah. Wafting out of the Nafziger Baking Company was the heavenly smell of freshly baked bread, one that I had never before experienced. At home, mother made cornbread, flour pancakes, and biscuits, but no yeast bread. Mother made a point of taking me by Manual Training High School, all-black, of course, and a future rival once we moved to Tulsa. As we toured the town, I was duly impressed with all the delivery trucks scurrying around and especially those that brought boxes and crates to the station to be loaded on our train. In one of those boxes, a few days later, my eyeglasses arrived, and I have worn glasses ever since.

From the time that I was seven or eight, I went each Saturday afternoon to the home of Mr. Nathan Bohanan, who was blind, to read to him. My mother had thoughtfully volunteered my services. He seemed grateful not only for my reading but also for my company. Although he had a wife, son, and grandson living with him, he was usually alone, and I read to him from recent issues of the *Muskogee Daily Phoenix*, the *Black Dispatch*, which was published in Oklahoma City and contained good coverage of nationwide news concerning African Americans, and the Sunday school lesson. I always left the Bohanan home feeling that I had done something worthwhile.

In the absence of my father, Mother strove to engage me in pastimes that she thought young boys would like. Thus, she taught me how to fish. We would dig for worms after a rain and keep them until the spare Saturday morning or holiday. She could take a straight sapling and trim and polish it down to a fishing pole as well as anyone. Our line was heavy thread or light string, and the only concession we made to manufacturers was in the purchase of hooks. We were on a serious mission when we went to Elk Creek and cast out our line for sun perch or catfish, intent on taking home our dinner. I have often wondered what Mother would think of a son who last summer on the Madison River in Montana cast out a dry fly, a Royal Wulff, that was taken by a nineteen-inch rainbow trout and, when I finally landed it, was immediately released. In Rentiesville that could have fed the three of us for two days.

Though I missed my father keenly, I never felt abandoned by him, and this in large part I attribute to my parents' love for each other and particularly my mother's strength of character. It wasn't simply that she covered the ground from teaching me to read and write to how to cast a fishing line; it was her ability to match my father's own spirit of courageous self-discipline and a resilience that in hindsight is all the more remarkable given the lack of fanfare with which it was so routinely mustered.

After my father left for Tulsa, my mother resigned from the Rentiesville public school in anticipation of moving to Tulsa at the end of the school term. When we did not move, there was no chance of her returning to her position, and she went to teach in Pine Hallow, about four or five miles east of our home. There was no rail transportation, and she had to go by horseback. Riding sidesaddle, with a pistol in her saddlebag to protect herself from wolves or some vagabond who might attempt to molest her, she generally was able to get home before dark. Anne and I had no problem getting there before her even if we dawdled during our walk from school, which we were prone to do, especially if we saw Mrs. Maggie Collins, our principal neighbor, on our the way from the village. Sporting a wig and marked by a rather strange pattern of speech, Mrs. Collins was a novelty to see and hear.

At home we had chores to perform before we settled down to do our homework. A major task was drawing water from the well for use that evening and the following morning for cooking, washing, and bathing. Another was to bring in wood and stack it in the kitchen or on the back porch. Yet another was to clean the chimneys of our kerosene lamps. We did this by crushing newspapers and carefully using pieces of them to rub all the soot out. We would then use clean pieces of paper to give the chimneys a good shine. We were not allowed to trim the wicks or to test the lamps by lighting them. Indeed, a cardinal rule was that we must never, ever use matches, and if the weather was cold we should remain at school or stop off at Mrs. Collins's house, coming home only after we were certain that Mother was there. With not even a volunteer fire department anywhere near, my mother was terrified by even the remotest possibility of a fire.

In those early years of the 1920s, we traveled by train a good deal, often to Checotah, a town of about two thousand, of whom two hundred were black, for supplies. We went a few times to Muskogee to check with Dr. Nagel about my eyes, and once or twice a year to Eufala for county-wide meetings with children from other all-black schools. I always found a visit to Checotah quite exciting. I liked to go in and out of the stores, Putter's being my favorite, merely to look and admire, for there was hardly anything I could afford to purchase. I was struck by the "elegance" of these small, one-story shops, though soon enough they would pale in comparison to the stores I would visit in Tulsa. Easily the most exciting thing to do in Checotah was to visit our cousin Henry Garland, a big hulk of a man who looked like an Indian chief and operated a small restaurant. I do not know the exact basis for our kinship, but my father had many Indian "cousins," especially among the Choctaws and Chickasaws. It was at Cousin Henry's place that I had my first hamburger, the most marvelous sandwich I had ever had, and it became the thing I most looked forward to whenever we went to Checotah.

It was on one of those trips that I had my first experience with crude, raw racism. On our way to Checotah, we flagged down as usual the southbound Katy train. As it moved away, we sat down in the coach where we had boarded. When the conductor came through, he observed that we were sitting in a white coach and ordered us to the Negro coach. My mother, as firmly as she could, refused to do so, observing that she would not take two small children from one coach to another in a moving train. She pointed out that it was not her fault that the train had stopped where she could not board the so-called Negro coach. The conductor then stopped the train, not to let us move to the segregated coach but to "teach us a lesson" by ejecting us from the train altogether. We trudged back to Rentiesville through the woods.

Just six years old, I was confused and scared. The uselessness of my mother's reasonable refusal to endanger her children, the arbitrary injustice of the conductor's behavior, the clear pointlessness of any objection on our part, and the acquiescence if not approval of the other passengers to our removal brought home to me at that young age the racial divide separating me from white America.

As I cried, my mother promptly reminded me that while the law required us to be kept separated from whites and usually placed in inferior accommodations, there was not a white person on that train or anywhere else who was any better than I was. She admonished me not to waste my energy by fretting but to save it in order to prove that I was as good as any of them.

There were the rare occasions when Mother, Anne, and I journeyed even farther south, to Eufala, the county seat. This was the scene of the annual spelling bee for children from the county's black schools, which I won for three consecutive years. On the return trip from one of these contests, a man passed by my seat and referred to me as that "spelling demon." And while it took me a moment to realize that "demon" was meant as a compliment, I was pleased, for I was proud of my accomplishment. My grades at school were generally good, and on several occasions I was skipped ahead a grade, which never seemed to bother me or my classmates. Thus, by the time I was nine years old, I was in the sixth grade.

I was not solely studious. I sang with the school chorus, was the catcher on the class softball team, and danced in the school's operettas and plays. I was especially happy to have as my dance teacher Mrs. Ethel Giddings, wife of the school principal. I loved dancing for dancing's sake but, already aware of the opposite sex, hoped that my prowess on the dance floor would bring me to the attention of girls. My male schoolmates and I even speculated on which girls might be sexually active, though the fact we needed to speculate in so small a community as Rentiesville, where little wasn't known about one's neighbors, spoke loudly to the conservative mores that governed our behavior.

While we were a churchgoing family, we were not particularly sectarian or even God fearing. In Rentiesville, we attended regularly the Methodist church for social as much as for religious reasons. There was one occasion, however, when I was forced to take religion quite seriously. I was nine years old when the Reverend Mary Blake, a black evangelist, came to conduct a revival at our church. It would be a long time before I realized the extent to which the conducting of a revival by a woman preacher represented an unusual example of female empowerment. My mother, my sister Anne, and I went one night just to see what it was like, and it soon became clear to me that Reverend Blake was both eloquent and persuasive.

After her sermon, she asked those who were not members of the church to raise their hands. I raised mine, and before I knew what was happening she was escorting me down to the mourners' bench. She began to pray for me as one who had not accepted Christ as his savior. She asked for divine intervention to save me before I moved to Tulsa where so many temptations would be placed in my way. (Since there had been talk of our moving to Tulsa for three years, I was not surprised that she knew of the impending move.) As the evangelist moaned and prayed over me and asked the congregation to pray that I be saved, I finally told her that I had been, to her great joy and to my great relief. At least when we finally moved to Tulsa the following year I would not have to go through that again.

Father's fortunes in Tulsa began to turn for the better, not dramatically, but somewhat so. By the summer of 1925, his plans for our move were sufficiently concrete that Mother did not accept a teaching contract for the ensuing year. Anne and I became so excited at the prospect of moving to the big city that we were virtually out of control. But in her inimitable way, Mother reined us in. Almost every day after school we discussed packing, although we did not have all that much to pack. Father came down several times during the autumn to see that things were going well. He put the place up for sale, and when the Randall family expressed an interest in purchasing it, the die was cast.

On Thursday morning, December 10, 1925, we flagged down the Katy going north. They loaded our trunks, suitcases, and boxes on the train. Within minutes, the whistle sounded, and the physical place of my birth was gone forever, thereafter to remain a congeries of precious memories, indeed too precious to be reduced to material things.

3

From Rentiesville to T-Town

MY FATHER MET OUR TRAIN and escorted us from Tulsa's old redbrick railroad station to the house that he had rented on Frankfort Place. It was scantily furnished, with beds and a few necessities. I assumed that this was in order to give my mother the widest latitude in furnishing and decorating it. I gradually learned that a new piece of furniture appeared only after my father had collected a fee from a client. During the postriot years, members of Tulsa's African American community were still using much of their resources to rebuild. Although W.E.B. Du Bois would visit Tulsa a few months after we moved there and would describe black Tulsans as people with grit, they were not yet in a position to pay legal fees *and* the expenses of rebuilding.

Our house was spacious enough—larger than any abode we ever occupied in Rentiesville, but there were only two beds, one for my parents, and one for Anne, although she was already twelve, and me, who would be eleven in less than a month. That arrangement did not last very long, for as soon as they could afford it they set up Anne in her own bedroom. And with every additional piece of furnishing, the house took shape as a home. It remained a modest establishment but served the family well until my parents purchased a home a few doors down the street where we would remain until I completed my high school education.

Christ's Temple C.M.E. Church, also on Frankfort Place, was presided over by the Reverend J. C. Colclough, a learned, imperious man more interested in the literary quality of his sermons than in rebuilding the church that, like every African American church on the north side of the city, had been destroyed during the race riot.

We did not get to Sunday school our first Sunday morning, December 13, but we were in our seats for eleven o'clock services. Reverend Colclough delivered a sermon more erudite than any I had ever heard. According to my father, whose knowledge of the Bible seemed limitless, it was a masterpiece. When new members were invited to come forward, our entire family went down as a group seeking affiliation. After our joining Christ's Temple, the next important affiliation for us to make was with Tulsa's black school system.

When Anne and I presented ourselves at the Booker T. Washington High School, though I was then not quite eleven years of age, we were both placed in the seventh grade. A letter from our mother attesting to the fact that Anne and I had been in the seventh grade in Rentiesville was accepted without questioning by our new principal, Ellis W. Woods. The high school was a two-story brick structure that adjoined the one-story brick elementary school. Both had been spared by the rioters of 1921 and were much more impressive than their Rentiesville counterparts. Booker T. Washington paled, however, when compared with the enormous all-white Central High School, which covered an entire city block and contained, as I would later learn, every facility that the nation's best high schools boasted.

What Booker T. Washington High School could rightly boast was a first-rate faculty dedicated to teaching and, perhaps more importantly, the development of their students' self-confidence. Charles S. Roberts, who taught Latin, entertained no excuses for our not doing our homework. Friendly and even personally generous, James T. A. West, the chemistry and physics instructor, was as demanding as any teacher I have ever had. Carrie Booker Person, who composed the school song and directed all musical activities, endeared herself to everyone by her warm personality and leadership. Our three English teachers, Mable Gates, Horace S. Hughes, and Gertie Berry, made us stretch our minds. They not only assumed that every one of us would go to college, but major in English as well. There were others: C. D. Tate and Horace Mitchell in mathematics, Beaulah Wims and Julia Huff in homemaking, Corinne Lythcott and Mamie Smith in art, Charles Graham in music, A. G. Rogers and William Graham in shop, James Foster in business and office practices, and H. C. McCree and Seymour Williams in history. Every faculty member took an interest in what I was doing and how I was doing. Mrs. Gates was my homeroom teacher, and all the others were my teachers away from home.

Presiding over this educational enterprise was one of the most remarkable men I have ever known. Quiet but efficient, friendly but demanding, Ellis W. Woods did not possess the talent to intimidate. And living in a segregated society with inferior facilities at the school and a curriculum that was inadequate by any standard, the last thing we needed was intimidation from within. Knowing better than we did the degree to which we suffered from inequalities that made a mockery of the doctrine of separate but equal, enshrined by the United States Supreme Court in 1896 in the shameful *Plessy v. Ferguson*, Principal Woods instilled enough self-confidence in us almost to compensate for them. Not quite, however. So he added to his preachments of self-confidence the argument that in any fair competition, the students at Booker T. Washington would perform not only creditably, but even excellently.

At Booker T. Washington, Mr. Woods spoke to all of us at the weekly assembly and, from time to time, with each of us individually. The conversation was always the same. "Can't you do better?" he would ask, then quickly add, "I believe that you can." Coming from him, his words convinced us that we could. He also instilled in us a strong appreciation for the rights of others as well as our own rights. In his straightforward request, "Keep to the right and keep going," that he made in the assembly and when we changed classes, we understood he was defining the importance as well as the limits of one's own space and what was involved in respecting others in an orderly, civilized community.

I know of no member of the faculty who did not subscribe to the general principles of conduct laid down by Principal Woods. Indeed, the faculty was as zealous as he was in urging students to cultivate self-confidence in the face of racist practices and policies that would deny them their dignity and even their humanity.

Within two years of my arrival, I was a full-fledged ninth-grade high school student and participating in numerous activities at school, at church, and in the Boy Scouts. I had joined Troop 42 of the all-black Boy Scouts at Vernon A.M.E. Church, exposing me to activities and people I would not have known otherwise. I reveled in the troop meetings, the periodic councils, and the summer camps that took us into the country, where we lived in tents, cooked our own food, and learned a great deal about outdoor life. In short order, I became a First Class Scout.

It is amazing how an unlimited amount of energy and a limited amount of talent can drive a person. Thus, I tried out for and won the leading role in the senior class play, *Dangerous Waters*. Even so simple an extracurricular activity laid bare our limited resources. Everything went well until we took the show on the road to Sand Springs, all of eight miles away. In an early scene, my chauffeur appears on the stage in his uniform and boots. Later, I was to meet the leading lady while elegantly dressed in a riding habit and riding boots. The problem was that we had only one pair of boots, and someone forgot to bring the bootjack that would facilitate the change. Consequently, in the quick change of costumes, I was unable to get my feet down into the stiff leather toes. Receiving the stage manager's cue, I had no alternative but to go on stage obviously standing on tiptoe, the boots precariously on my feet.

One of the high points of my high school days was my election as class president during my senior year. This was the first time I had been chosen for a leadership role, and although my parents were immensely pleased, I was ambivalent about this display of confidence on the part of my classmates. I fully appreciated the significance of the honor, and I did everything I could to fulfill my responsibilities, but the very things that had led to my election—my numerous extracurricular activities, friendships with most of my small class, and consistently high grades—would be further crowded by my new post as president. And almost immediately I found myself in a tight spot: the fierce competition among my female classmates for election to high school queen, Miss Booker T. Washington. It was won, amid unfounded charges of collusion, by my girlfriend, Ada Perkins, a junior representing her class.

When I was in high school I felt the weight of close parental supervision. One Friday, for example, I casually announced that some classmates were having a party that evening, I noticed after dinner that Mother was dressing as if to go out. I asked her where she was going. She said quite calmly that I had said that there would be a party, and since I had been unable to say where or who was giving it, she thought she should go along. I would have been embarrassed beyond words except that several other mothers had also decided to accompany their children.

Throughout my years in Tulsa, the legacy of the race riot remained a constant presence, and it was not unusual for some brush with racism to dampen my day. One in particular stands out. During my first year as a Boy Scout, age twelve, I was in downtown Tulsa and spied an elderly white woman hesitantly attempting to cross the street. It was obvious that her sight was impaired, and I rushed to help her, thus fulfilling the Boy Scout requirement to do one good deed each day. She eagerly accepted my assistance. However, when we were in the middle of the intersection and exchanging pleasantries, she asked me if I was white or Negro. When I replied that I was Negro, she shook my arm loose, commanding me to take my filthy hands off her. Realizing that for her my race defined my cleanliness as well as my ability to guide her safely across a busy intersection, I left her stranded in the middle of traffic. I cannot say that I was deeply hurt by the experience, for my mother's admonition when we were put off the train some years earlier remained with me. Although surprised, I did not fret. I would prove, in due course, that her color or race did not make her any better than me or my people.

Two or three years later, at almost the same location, I was again reminded of my place along the American color line. In the spring of 1931, a few months before I was to graduate from high school, Tulsa was host to the National High School Band Contest. It was an exciting event, with bands in attendance from across the country, including a few African American participants. John Philip Sousa himself was there to conduct the marches that he had composed and that we had played in the Booker T. Washington High School band. A few band members and I went early into downtown to secure good vantage points on Main Street from which to view the parade. As the crowds increased and decent viewing places decreased, a white woman asked me to move so that she and her party could have our spots. When we declined, she brusquely told us that she was from Texas, where they did not tolerate such insubordination from blacks.

She expressed the hope that someday we would visit her home state. There, she assured us, she would have had the pleasure of teaching us our proper place. We had no desire to visit Texas, but with Tulsa's separate and patently unequal schools, the still-visible scars of the 1921 race riot, Jim Crow laws dictating access to everything from swimming pools to water fountains, not to mention restaurants, cultural institutions, and many downtown stores, we also felt no need of any lesson a more southern state could provide.

At the time, American racism was endemic, even infecting so innocent a thing as my great love of music. Each spring, following the close of its season at home, the Chicago Civic Opera Company (now the Lyric Opera of Chicago) went on tour and spent several days performing in Tulsa. Perhaps because of the influence of our music supervisor, Mrs. Carrie Booker Person, members of the opera company, including Mary Garden, Richard Bonelli, Rosa Raisa, Claudia Muzio, and Tito Schipa, would visit our high school.

Several of us were interested in attending performances of this distinguished opera company, and through the good offices of Mrs. Person we were able to secure tickets. The problem for my parents, though, was that blacks were segregated in Convention Hall. They were forced to sit in a special section off to one side. Neither my mother nor my father would ever voluntarily accept segregation. They pointed out that if my friends and I cared to demean and humiliate ourselves by going to the opera under those conditions, it was a decision that we would have to make ourselves, without any encouragement from them. I chose to attend, and to this day I continue to reproach myself. Whenever I hear *La Traviata* or *La Bohème*, I still, more than seventy years later, recall the humiliating conditions under which I learned to appreciate those great musical masterpieces.

At the time, however, breaking the parental barrier that stood between me and segregated performances at Convention Hall left me emboldened to try it again. Paul Whiteman was coming to Tulsa with his world-famous band. Again from the hall's segregated seats, I heard Whiteman play George Gershwin's haunting *Concerto in F*. I was so mesmerized that I was tempted to play the melody on my own trumpet.

Aspiring to be in the all-white Whiteman band I knew to be totally unrealistic; not altogether out of the question, however, was a less known but rapidly rising African American musical group. One weekend Louis Armstrong brought his band to town, and for once there was not the usual problem of going to hear him, for he was playing in north Tulsa, primarily for African American listeners. Braced by my parents' stern warning to stay clear of persons who were drinking, arguing, or tending toward violence, I went to the dance. Such instructions were unnecessary, for all that I and my companions, Kinney Booker and Julius Moran, wanted to do was to listen to the music, watch the musicians, and take cues from them regarding their musical style. Armstrong was just beginning his meteoric rise to fame, but his immense talents were evident even to us neophytes. When he played "The Sunny Side of the Street" and "When You're Smiling," we were thrilled. When he put a towel around his neck to absorb perspiration, we adopted the practice. At the next rehearsal of our band, we each appeared with a towel around our neck.

In the spring of 1931, when I was sixteen years of age and in my final year in high school, I endured another Jim Crow experience, more deeply humiliating than going to segregated Convention Hall. Once a year, one of the leading service clubs had a luncheon to which it invited the outstanding male student from all-white Central High School and his counterpart from Booker T. Washington High School, each with his faculty sponsor. On the appointed day, Mr. Charles S. Roberts and I went to the elegant Mayo Hotel, where we were greeted most cordially. My attention was immediately drawn to the magnificent chairs and sofas in the lobby and the smooth-running elevator on which a Negro operator took us to the floor where the luncheon was held. When the time came for us to be seated, however, we were ushered to a table set apart from the others.

By intent or consequence, I never did have a chance to meet the student from Central High School. Years later I would think on the irony that it could well have been Daniel Boorstin, who that year was the valedictorian of his class at Central High and who would recruit me to be his colleague at the University of Chicago in 1964. At the time, while my table was resplendent with fine silver and beautiful linen, and the program was elaborate, I heard little of what was said, and the idea of tracking down my Central High counterpart didn't even cross my mind. I was physically close enough to have listened if I cared to, but I spent my time trying to determine who benefited from having Mr. Roberts and me, the only blacks present besides the service staff, seated some distance from the rest of the group. For me, it was a problem that begged an answer. For others, the thought that the arrangements could have been any different from what they were presumably never occurred to them.

Throughout high school I took great pleasure in going to my father's office to clean it, to sit and talk with him during his idle moments, or merely to gaze out his second-story window at the passing parade of people. It was as though I wanted to compensate for our separation during the critical years of my early childhood. He always treated me as his equal in discussing the most abstract matters, and I felt free to raise with him any question on any subject. If he was alone, he was never too busy to cease his reading or writing to talk with me, and because he never talked down to me I always felt secure raising whatever topic came to mind.

His office was located on "Deep Greenwood," the hub of the black business and commercial activity of north Tulsa. On the way to the modest two-story building that housed my father's office, I could view all of those small businesses that have recently—and inaccurately—been touted as "Black Wall Street." There were no banks or insurance companies such as those in Richmond, Virginia, and Durham, North Carolina. Even so, there was pride. Situated along the street were the New Welcome Grocery (owned by Uncle Henry Smith, my mother's brother); two drugstores, Thompson's and Ferguson's; two theaters, Dreamland and Dixie; the Greenwood Haberdashery; Hooker's Clothing Store; Neal's Jewelry Store; and the offices of physicians, dentists, lawyers, and Realtors, in addition to a few pool halls and recreation parlors.

I spent numerous Saturday mornings looking out my father's front windows while behind me my father was quietly intent on his work or reading. Before me was the heart of black Tulsa, which each weekend was memorable for the resilience conveyed in the simple fact that just over a decade earlier the riot had leveled this very neighborhood. The one act of near-violence I ever witnessed there, when a shot fired by a distraught wife missed her husband as he disappeared through the rear door of Picou's dry-cleaning shop, which was directly under my father's office, merely underscored the otherwise proud stability of the neighborhood.

Equally exciting and ever so much more routine was the Thursday night spectacle. On a pleasant evening, at any time of the year, the maids, chauffeurs, and butlers would leave the South End, where they worked for white people. Dressed in their finest and most stylish attire, they would "stroll down the avenue" from about seven to ten o'clock. The street lights were bright enough to make it easy for them to see and be seen, and they were as attractive as present-day models prancing down the runway at some exclusive fashion show.

My father was one of the most studious people I ever knew. If my visit to his office caught him without work, I usually found him reading and smoking his pipe. Upon my arrival, he would put down his book and we would talk. He answered my questions earnestly and conversed with me seriously, adult to adult. Among my proudest moments were when he and I went to the courthouse or city hall, where he transacted business. We had no automobile until 1929, and prior to that time we would walk the ten or fifteen blocks to downtown Tulsa. As we walked and talked, I looked up at him with pride. He was just over six feet tall, with a spare, athletic body. Though he could walk faster, his pace always accommodated mine. At the courthouse, he took pains to see that I was comfortable. Never wanting to yield even to voluntary segregation, he preferred that I not sit where blacks were expected to; though no law required us to sit in a designated place, longtime practice did. If there was no jury trial, he suggested that I sit in one of the jury seats. If there was a jury trial, he escorted me to the bar where he and the other lawyers, black and white, sat. On such occasions, especially when he introduced me to his fellow lawyers, and they indicated to me how much they respected him for his honesty and integrity, I would nearly burst with pride.

Perhaps my father's most significant expression of confidence in me came in 1928, on the eve of my thirteenth birthday. He had accepted an invitation to give the keynote address at the traditional observance of Emancipation Day, January 1, at Wesley Methodist Episcopal Church, about a block from our home. Subsequent to accepting the invitation, he discovered that he had urgent business out of the city. Instead of bowing out, he wrote his speech and asked me to deliver it. I was sent to the meeting with a note to the presiding officer introducing me and requesting an understanding for my father's absence.

I cannot recall all of the proceedings. Most memorable for me, Lou Holder and his Seven Clouds of Joy played. They were at the beginning of a spectactular career as a major jazz orchestra. When the time came for me to deliver my father's address I did so without difficulty. Apparently I read the speech quite satisfactorily, for when I concluded, the large audience was on its feet applauding and even cheering. But my true sense of pride and accomplishment came later, when my father returned and told me that many people had expressed their pleasure at hearing my recitation.

Acting as the unchanging backdrop to these specific events was the fact of my family's general economic privation. Broadly unaware of the collapse of the national economy during the Depression, it was my own view that our difficulties arose from my father's poor management of his law practice. Too lenient with his clients and disdainful of what he termed "ambulance chasers," he, in my opinion, never demanded his requisite legal fees. One of the principal reasons I had determined to go to law school was to return to Tulsa and join my father's practice, adding efficiency, vigor, and, above all, fiscal responsibility to the family enterprise. This would relieve my father of the onerous duties connected with the profession and leave him to pursue "the jealous mistress," as he always called the law. It was only much later that I became aware of the fact that my father's clients, virtually all black, were without the resources to pay their bills, and that many potential clients who could pay engaged white attorneys, feeling the latter had a better chance of convincing the exclusively white judge and jury.

I would have worked during my high school years even if we had not so desperately needed the income. I took odd jobs, cleaning offices other than my father's. One summer I even worked in a funeral home, illustrating the lengths to which I would go to make a few dollars. My friend Kinney Booker and I sometimes rolled our manual lawn mowers up and down the streets in Tulsa's white neighborhoods, seeking jobs to cut lawns that for the most part did not need it because of the heat and drought. I once worked for a house painter; and for more than a year I served as the assistant to Mr. D. Rippetoe. This amounted to delivering the Tulsa *Tribune*, the afternoon newspaper. Race dictated our association: Mr. Rippetoe was white, and the *Tribune* did not permit African American boys to have their own paper routes. He and I struck up a warm friendship, and each day after school and on weekends, I would meet him to fold and deliver the paper. The route took us through the business section of the Greenwood area and to nearby residences. Occasionally, we would stop and have some refreshments, a soft drink or a slice of pie, always, for obvious reasons, at an African American restaurant or snack bar. High points were the evenings on which championship boxing matches were scheduled; we would go to the *Tribune* building, listen to the fight on the radio, then wait for the extra edition. On warm summer evenings, all the paperboys gathered on the lawn and sidewalks outside the *Tribune* building to listen. Come winter, we listened in the lobby. Regardless, I was the only African American paperboy at such gatherings. When the fight was over and the paper was ready, Mr. Rippetoe and I would get our quota, dash to Greenwood, and sell them to scores of anxious readers.

Easily the most fascinating job I held in Tulsa was at King's Market, a fancy grocery store on South Boston Avenue, in a middle-class white neighborhood. When I began the job, Mr. Paul Iverson, the store manager, told me that I was to work two hours in the afternoon on school days and eight hours on Saturdays. I was to assist Newt, the full-time janitor, in keeping the place clean and neat. And I was to eat nothing from the store's stock, bringing my lunch on Saturdays. If I wished to purchase anything, I would receive a 20 percent discount.

Newt, the market's only other black employee, was shrewd, efficient, and thoroughly dishonest. On my first Saturday at the store, he led me into the basement at lunchtime, asking me what was in the small bag I had with me. I told him that it was my sandwich. He instructed me to throw it in the trash, for he had planned a meal of T-bone steaks, french fries, and a salad. Raised to be scrupulously honest, I was terrified, but I did not wish to offend. At fifteen, I was presented with my first "adult" moral dilemma. I held on to my sandwich, in part to use it in my defense if the manager came down to challenge us. But Newt clearly inferred from my silence that I would join him in the banquet he was planning.

In the next few minutes, I observed one of the smoothest operations I had ever seen. Newt got his bottle of window cleaner and a cloth and set out on a procedure that I would witness many times. The windows in the meat display cases needed cleaning, so he went upstairs to perform the task. Soon he returned, boasting that the display cases were glistening. He also brought with him two magnificent steaks and asked me how I wanted mine cooked. This was long before I knew that dishes could be prepared to order; rare, medium, and well done meant nothing to me. Unsure and fearful of being caught, I told him to cook mine the same way he was cooking his. Soon, the potatoes were in the deep fryer, and the salad he had previously prepared was placed before me. In due course, the steak and fries were ready, and we indulged ourselves in a classic American feast. The act was repeated with appropriate variations over the next several months.

King's Market had a most astonishing display of fresh fruits and vegetables, and one of Newt's duties was to remove the bruised and overripe peaches, plums, grapes, or whatever. It was 1930, and Prohibition was in full force, but Newt proposed to the manager that if he were provided with some sugar, he could take the bruised fruits home and make wine, sharing it, of course, with Mr. Iverson. The latter eagerly accepted. Day after day, Newt would go out the front door, where Mr. Iverson stood to bid the employees a good evening, and he would show Mr. Iverson the discarded fruits he was taking home for his wine making. There was just enough battered fruit to cover the pounds of butter, meat, eggs, and other items for Newt's larder. Meanwhile, Newt made the wine in the basement of the store, where the manager never went. While I played no role in this duplicity, I suppose that I was an accessory after the fact. That would have been an insufficient plea, if my mother had learned about it. Regarding a court of law, I can only hope that at this point, some seventy-odd years later, I am protected by the statute of limitations.

It was in Tulsa that, for the first time, I was truly able to view my mother and father as a married couple functioning in the role of parents. In Rentiesville, by the time I was old enough to notice such things, my father was already in Tulsa working for, among other things, our reunion. After we moved to Tulsa, I was able to discover the deep affection my parents had for each other. He seemed to take pride in doing small things for her, such as bringing modest personal gifts, or coming home and escorting her to the movies, or surprising her with our first radio. While my father was not very efficient in performing domestic duties, he seemed to delight in preparing the occasional breakfast. It was an amusing sight to see him cooking oatmeal or bacon and eggs with his right hand while under his left arm he held firmly to the morning paper, lest the children get to it first and leave it in disarray. For Mother's part, she delighted in occasionally dressing in her best clothes and going to his office just to return home with him, just as she delighted in cooking his favorite dishes and having a few of his closest friends in for dinner.

They treated each other as equals, discussing thoroughly every critical decision they had to make, and, having made the decision, they faced the consequences together. One matter on which they had a different approach, however, was in disciplining their children. Mother believed in corporal punishment, while my father could not bear to touch any of us in anger. Looking back on those years, even from the vantage point of more than a half century, I can reflect on a family that was stable and happy despite its poverty. And radiating out from my parents was profound hope for the future, especially for their children.

During the family's Tulsa years, my mother began to enjoy a life of her own. I also began to see her as a person in her own right and not just as "Mother." She was slightly above medium height, presenting a healthy appearance without being plump. She had a medium brown complexion and long black hair that was already beginning to turn gray. Most noticeable were her poise and carriage. I thought she walked like a queen, swinging her arms just enough to draw attention to the lilt in her step. Indeed, I always thought of her as queenly, perhaps because in addition to her physical appearance she occasionally sang bits from the cantata "Queen Esther," which she had sung in her college choir.

Mother worked all of her adult life. During the years we lived in Rentiesville, she was, when not teaching, a milliner, a seamstress, and manufacturer of hair and facial ointments. Her older sister, Aunt Bunch, would visit us, and together the two sisters would work in the kitchen, stirring several ingredients that constituted the hair ointment. My aunt would then take some back to her home in Guthrie, where her friends were pleased to purchase it, while Mother sold it in Rentiesville and Checotah.

Mother seemed much more interested in her not-for-profit activities, particularly once we moved to Tulsa. Observing an increasing number of African American women working outside the home, she became concerned about the well-being of their children. Many of them were essentially latchkey kids as, indeed, Anne and I had been when Mother was teaching. But those other African American working mothers could not take their children to white people's homes as my mother had taken me to school with her when I was three years old. She simply could not let this hardship pass without doing something about it. Inviting women to join her, in 1930 she planned a day-care center for working mothers. Within a few months the center was open and operating, providing Tulsa's African American working mothers the first opportunity to leave their children in a safe, healthy environment. She was enormously proud of the opening of this day-care center and always regarded it as one of her most important accomplishments.

My mother was also active in the African American branch of the Young Women's Christian Association. For several years she was chair of the Board of Management, which frequently met in our home. The YWCA on Archer Street was beyond walking distance from our home, and even after we bought an automobile she never did learn to drive. She therefore depended on public transportation, primarily taxicabs. On one occasion an assistant at the Y ordered two taxis, one for my mother and one for the white women who had come from the "other" YWCA to attend an Archer Street meeting. Agreeing to travel separately wasn't, however, a sufficient enough gesture. The white taxi driver refused to accept her as a passenger. Unfortunately, the assistant had failed to order one of Emerson's Blue Bird Taxis, an African American enterprise, and it was the policy of white taxi drivers to refuse service to black passengers. Mother was not very annoyed. Intent on never voluntarily conceding to segregation, my mother concluded that she should hold as many committee meetings as possible at our home.

Mother seemed to derive more personal satisfaction from her affiliation with the Women's Federated Club movement among African American women. While she was acquainted with it before we moved, it was in Tulsa that she became quite active at the local, state, and national levels and used this connection to assist in the support of the day-care center that she had founded. Now that her children could be safely left at home, she attended meetings in Oklahoma City, Little Rock, and on one occasion Charleston, West Virginia. Through her own club, named for Mary McLeod Bethune, she sought to improve working conditions for African American women in Tulsa's white-owned businesses and to secure better treatment of African American customers in those same businesses. I was deeply impressed with my mother's activism, and I have no doubt that a desire to emulate her inspired my own efforts to make sure my work, whether within colleges and universities or on the larger stage of public opinion and public policy, strove to improve society.

One of best things about being around my father was to hear him discuss the political issues of the day. He called himself a Jeffersonian Democrat and had been one all of his adult life. In the early years of Oklahoma statehood, an African American Democrat of any kind was an anomaly, but he was steadfast in his beliefs and loyalty. He got very little in return. Perhaps his affiliation had something to do with his securing the job as postmaster in Rentiesville during the administration of President Woodrow Wilson. Later, during the 1928 campaign, he worked hard to elect Democrat Al Smith as president. He was even in charge of a Smith campaign office located near his legal practice. I was paid to keep that office clean and pass out campaign materials at rallies, and my disappointment was acute when Herbert Hoover won the election.

I was sixteen during the final months before my high school graduation, a bittersweet period. It seemed clear to me that my commencement would constitute the most complete break that I would ever experience. Tulsa remains the only place I have ever called home. Though I had lived there only six years, it had seemed a lifetime; I had matured more than I would in any other six-year span. It was the longest period I would ever spend with my parents and siblings, and it was the period during which I learned the value of friendship and of loyalty to institutions and organizations, and a sense of civic responsibility. Already accepted as a freshman at Fisk University in Nashville, I knew the break would come soon enough and be painful enough, and so I savored each moment of those spring and summer days of 1931.

I cannot remember the valedictory speech I gave at my high school graduation. That day's program is long lost and my memory of the event clouded for having given so many commencement addresses in the last sixty years. But whatever I said, I hope that it was earnest, warm, sincere, and grammatical. I dare to hope that it was felicitous. I also prefer to imagine that whatever it contained and whatever the felicity of the language, it adequately conveyed my gratitude to the family, teachers, friends, and people of Tulsa who in so many ways were the formative backdrop of all that was to follow.

4

The Gold and Blue

W HEN MY SIBLINGS AND I WERE GROWING UP, our parents
had regaled us with stories about Nashville, the rivalry between Fisk and Roger Williams universities, and the subsequent decline of Roger Williams and steady rise of Fisk in importance and
influence. Named for a Civil War general, Clinton B. Fisk, the university
was founded in 1866 by the American Missionary Association and other
advocates of education and uplift for the freedmen. It achieved no real stability until students, led by George L. White, went north and then to Europe in 1874, giving concerts under the name of the Fisk Jubilee Singers.
They raised sufficient funds to assure the future of the fledgling institution. It weathered the Reconstruction years, perhaps by not challenging
the restoration of white rule. And while it cannot be said that Fisk was
thriving in the first quarter of the twentieth century, it was surviving,
thanks to support by the American Missionary Association and Northern
philanthropists.

The price of stability was the university's autocratic control of the student body and its administration's careful adherence to local white demands that the institution conform to the social and political mores that
had always governed the races in the South. Tellingly, its best-known
alumnus, W.E.B. Du Bois of the class of 1888, had in 1925 exhorted the

students to revolt against the president, Fayette Avery McKenzie, whom Du Bois described as "unfit and a detriment to the cause of higher education for our race."

When my sister Anne and I arrived in Nashville in September 1931, Fisk was enjoying a steady advance in virtually every way since McKenzie's unheralded departure in the spring of 1925. Thomas Elsa Jones, an energetic and spirited white educator who was considered "safe" in the eyes of the white citizens of Nashville, had attracted some of the leading African American scholars to join the Fisk faculty. He had also recruited a corps of white professors, including, most important for me, Theodore S. Currier in history. Financial support for Fisk was increasing despite the Depression, and a newly constructed library and a renovated memorial chapel gave every indication that the university was fiscally sound and educationally strong.

Viewing my undergraduate degree as merely a staging platform from which to launch a career in law, I was restless to get through it as quickly as possible. I informed my temporary adviser, Professor Dora Scribner, that I would major in English. Being in that department, she thought it a good idea but concluded that I should have a male adviser. She recommended that Professor Lorenzo D. Turner, chairman of the department, become my postregistration adviser. My first core requirement was Contemporary Civilization, presided over by Professor Charles S. Johnson but taught by an array of professors from the history, sociology, psychology, and education departments. This would be followed by a survey course in literature during the winter term, and a general science survey in the spring quarter. I selected German to satisfy my modern foreign language requirement, regretting all the time that no modern foreign languages had been taught at Tulsa's Booker T. Washington High School, this despite the fact that several were taught at Tulsa's all-white Central High School. Finally, physical education completed the list of required courses for credit. Chapel, held twice a week and offering no credit, was also required.

I had received only a tuition scholarship. My parents were able to provide limited assistance, there being my sister's expenses too. Consequently, I had to work. I secured on-campus employment to pay for most of my room, board, and laundry, working as secretary to the librarian, Louis S. Shores, a quiet, scholarly man who seemed to have the utmost confidence in me from the very beginning. The fact that I could type and take dictation in shorthand, learned in high school, thus relieving him of having to write his letters by hand, pleased him tremendously. I worked for him from the fall of my freshman year until the beginning of the final term of my senior year, when preparation for graduation claimed all of my time. My other job was in the publicity office, as clerk-typist for Ethel Bedient Gilbert, who became a close and admired friend.

Occasionally I also worked a few hours a week as a typist in the office of the student newspaper, the *Fisk Herald*, whose editor, the glamorous senior Lucybelle Wheatley, admonished me never to enter her office before knocking. In subsequent years I would work in the dining room, pulling up to the dining-room-floor level the dumb waiter once it had been laden with food prepared in the basement. Many of the cooks and other locals became good friends over the years.

My first week in college was hectic, settling into my room in Livingstone Hall, registering for classes, lining up jobs, and seeing to it, as well as I could, that my sister was making the transition satisfactorily. I was also becoming involved in activities outside of class. My roommate, whom I met on the train en route to Nashville, was Bob Glasco from Muskogee, Oklahoma. Concluding that since we had similar backgrounds and did not want to risk whom we would get by blind chance, we decided on the ride up to announce to the dean of students that we wished to room together. We ended up roommates for all four years, without so much as one argument or, indeed, any differences whatsoever. My sister Anne seemed happy enough living in Jubilee Hall, and with her jovial personality was making friends easily. Buck Jr. had graduated from Fisk a year earlier, and since there were three current classes who knew him as a fraternity president, member of the glee club, and a popular campus leader, we both benefited from his recent presence. Indeed, many students referred to me as "Little Buck," while Anne was known as "Buck's Little Sister."

Before going to Fisk I could not have imagined that, assembled in one place, there could be so many class valedictorians and bright, articulate leaders as were in my freshman class. I discovered this during the week of orientation when the dean of the college announced that there would be an early election of the freshman class president. Of the dozen or more who responded to the dean's invitation, at least six or seven were high school

valedictorians, including myself, while most of the remainder were saluta-
torians or very high-ranking members of their graduating classes. Some
were women, but most of them were men. Asked to give their first impres-
sions of Fisk, we were all well-spoken and thoughtful, but one person
stood out. He was L. Howard Bennett, a graduate of Avery Institute in
Charleston, South Carolina. Articulate and charismatic in a way that won
over the dean as well as all of his classmates, he remained class president
for four years and became my best friend. During our freshman year we
vowed, prematurely it turned out, that someday we would practice law together.

During that first week I was delighted to read an announcement that
the director of the Fisk Choir would hold auditions for several vacancies
in that premier singing group. Successful candidates would be announced
during the second week of the term. Having sung in high school and able
to read music scores quite handily, I decided to try out on the very first
night of the auditions. Ray Francis Brown, professor of music and director of the choir, and Alice Grass, university organist and professor of
piano, were the admissions committee. The audition was businesslike and
straightforward. Professor Brown selected a hymn from the University
Hymnal and asked me to sing the bass/baritone part as he played the piano. I sang it with ease. Brown eyed me suspiciously and asked if I had
ever heard the hymn before. When I replied that I had not, he took care, it
seemed to me, to search for a hymn that he felt certain I did not know.
When I sang that hymn as well as I had the first, he closed the book,
looked directly at me, and said that he had already decided that I should be
in the choir. I was to report for regular rehearsal later that same evening.
Thus, on the very first Sunday of the new academic year, I sang in the
choir with the regular members, to my great delight and to the surprise of
my classmates, who seemed to wonder how and why I was the only freshman up there with the veterans.

On a Saturday afternoon early in that first term, I went by streetcar,
with some male classmates, to downtown Nashville. Before leaving the
campus, I went by Jubilee Hall to ask Anne if she wanted anything. After
she told me, she asked the classmate with whom she was talking if there
was something her brother might get her. And so I was finally introduced

to Aurelia Whittington, whom I had seen a few days earlier but had not met. Aurelia requested chocolate-covered peanuts. Since my cash reserves were limited and were to last me for a very long time, I was in no position to be gallant. I readily took the fifteen cents that she pressed into my hand.

When we had completed our shopping, including a great deal of mere window-shopping, we went into the transfer station to purchase tickets for the return trip to campus. When I asked for a ticket for the Jefferson Street car, I presented the ticket agent with a twenty-dollar bill and apologized profusely, saying that it was all the money I had and that if he chose to do so he could give me my change in one-dollar bills. He almost leaped through the ticket window and shouted to me that no "nigger" would tell him how to make change. He then proceeded to count out my $19.85 in nickels and dimes. I was stunned. In all my six years in Tulsa I had never encountered so rawly racist an outburst, and I spent many subsequent months with no thought of going again to downtown Nashville.

Shaken, I returned to campus and gave my sister and Aurelia the items I had purchased for them, telling them of my ordeal with the ticket agent. Aurelia, from Goldsboro, North Carolina, said that she had never heard of such outrageous conduct. She ventured the opinion that the agent was teaching me a "lesson," since I was obviously a Fisk student from another part of the country and he wished me to know I could not expect to be treated in Nashville as I had been at home.

A tragedy that befell the dean of women and some Fisk students in Georgia taught all of us what we could expect in the American South. Juliette Derricotte was an esteemed young officer in the national office of the YWCA, with a solid reputation for leadership, when in 1928 she accepted the position of dean of women at Fisk. She quickly became a very popular administrator. One weekend, in the fall of 1931, she and three students took a motor trip to Athens, Georgia, to visit parents and relatives. En route, while she was driving on a rainy afternoon, they had a head-on collision with a white couple near Dalton, Georgia. Though Derricotte and one of the students were seriously injured, they were denied admission to the local tax-supported hospital. Instead, the two were treated in the office of a white physician and sent to the home of an African American woman who provided beds for sick or injured black patients. The student died there during the night. Miss Dericotte was eventually transported to Walden Hospital in Chattanooga, Tennessee, where she died the following night, November 7, 1931.

When the news of their deaths reached Nashville, the entire campus was plunged into a period of mourning and outrage that the university had lost a student and its young administrator to segregationist practices. There was, indeed, national outrage, with Dr. Du Bois writing of the incident in the *Crisis* and the nationally prominent Howard Thurman delivering the eulogy in Athens. Ms. Derricotte's death was magnified by the racial violence then routine throughout the South. At least twenty blacks had been lynched in 1930, and in March 1931, just months before Ms. Derricotte's death, nine black teenagers, who would become known as the Scottsboro Boys, were accused by two white women and found guilty of rape in Alabama. Despite inconsistencies in the women's testimony and the fact that one recanted, eight of the youths were sentenced to death, the ninth avoiding that sentence only by virtue of being a minor. In 1931, the decades-long successful fight to overturn those convictions was barely visible.

I did not turn to scholarship in search of tools to confront America's racial injustice. In a way, there was no turn to take. Since following my mother's chalk marks on the blackboard when I was three, I had enjoyed the determined effort to excel at my studies. A part of that pleasure no doubt traced to my parents' injunction to all of their children that, so long as they tried their hardest, no white person was any better than they. But that very injunction underscored the fact that Jim Crow America was set on confronting any black determined to excel. I hardly needed to seek a way to confront American racial injustice. My ambition was sufficient to guarantee that confrontation. My decision to focus that ambition on a career as a scholar, as opposed to a lawyer or some other pursuit, was not a response to the racial injustices that marked my freshman year, but can be directly attributed to a single individual.

Professor Theodore S. Currier's lectures on history for the course on contemporary civilization immediately impressed me. First, he was quite young, a mere twenty-eight, to be the senior person in Fisk's history department. Second, he was so animated that he was in constant motion before the class, pacing from one side of the room to the other. Finally, without any notes that I could see, he gave riveting lectures on European and American history. Embellished with anecdotes concerning real, live characters, ranging from kings and queens to prime ministers and presidents to industrial giants to common laborers, his lectures raised and answered questions of how and why events occurred. Only as he wound down did his listeners gradually return to the real world from which he had transported them for an hour or two. I quickly concluded that I should take a course exclusively taught by him.

Thus, in my second year I elected to take Currier's course in United States history. As it happened, he was then teaching all the university's history courses. The department's other historian, Alrutheus A. Taylor, already well-known for his studies of Negroes during Reconstruction in Virginia and South Carolina, had become dean of the college and would not teach at all during my four years at Fisk. I considered this my good fortune, for I found Currier's courses in history so exciting and satisfying that I took every one that he offered. I switched my major from English to history and gradually reached the decision not to study law. Currier promptly advised me to prepare to go to graduate school for a PhD in history, and he began to offer a variety of courses that would well prepare me, including seminars, colloquia, and reading as well as lecture courses. He never questioned where I should go for that PhD: Harvard, of course, where he had studied but never completed his doctoral work. It was an exciting prospect that I thoroughly embraced.

My life beyond the classroom continued to flourish. From the time that Aurelia accompanied me to the homecoming game and evening prom on October 31, 1931, she was my regular date for the next four years.

In the spring of my freshman year I joined the debating team, coached by Professor Currier, which soon gave me an opportunity to travel to the North and East for the first time. Traveling by automobile allowed me to see the countryside, and stopping at points of historical interest and spending nights in towns and cities added much to the journey. Debating also gave me my first opportunity to be in intellectual competition with white college students. That I could more than hold my own added immeasurably to my mounting confidence, an asset that would prove essential in graduate school and during the years that followed. Each time I debated students from predominantly white Notre Dame or New York University, or for that matter from predominantly black Howard University, I did so with increased self-assurance. Here was tangible evidence of the truth of my mother's early admonishment that were I to apply myself on a level playing field I could prove that I was as good as, if not a bit better than, anyone else. Whether my debating counterparts were white or black, I quickly felt equal to the task.

Although my brother had been extremely popular at Fisk and was polemarch (president) of his fraternity, Kappa Alpha Psi, and although I admired him greatly, I did not follow him into his fraternity. In the spring of my freshman year, along with the closest friends I had made, I pledged Alpha Phi Alpha, to the dismay of the Kappas. In the autumn of my sophomore year, December 1932, I was initiated. In my junior year I was elected president of the Fisk chapter and, with the assistance of the interfraternity council, immediately launched a drive to eliminate hazing and reduce the intense rivalry among the fraternities and sororities. The drive was not altogether successful, but the harshest and bitterest feelings were considerably reduced.

Certainly one of the most exciting events during my second year was the student and staff choir's extensive concert tour to the Northeast. We performed in Cincinnati, Cleveland, Hartford, Boston, and New York. In Cleveland, Jane Hunter, the legendary head of the Phillis Wheatley YWCA, not only opened up a floor for male members of the choir so that everyone could be housed in the same building, but she also invited Fisk alumni in the Cleveland area to a reception at the Phyllis Wheatley House. She immediately became one of the choir's most beloved patrons of the entire tour. Comparatively in Boston, where President Jones had charge of the arrangements, the male students were to stay at a hotel that was little more than a flophouse. Balancing costs with the restricted housing choices available to African Americans, he insisted that it was the best the president could do. A former Fisk student, Eddie Matthews, already on his way to stardom in such stage productions as *Four Saints in Three Acts* and *Porgy and Bess*, fortunately volunteered to find us a more suitable place.

Perhaps the high point of the tour came in New York City, where we performed at Carnegie Hall. Given my lifelong love of music, I was thrilled to be on the stage of one of the world's greatest performance centers in the greatest city in the nation. Several of us decided that rather than waste our time sleeping, we should see as much as we could, including

Harlem. It was memorable, right up to when the wealthy philanthropist John D. Rockefeller Jr. greeted all of us backstage with a warm smile and a vigorous handshake during intermission.

Debating, along with singing and traveling in the choir, crowded my undergraduate schedule. There were dances staged by fraternities and sororities and by social groups such as the Tanner Art Club and the Decagynians. Nor did I socialize solely with my fellow students. The Wranglers, a group of students dedicated to arguing the merits of an announced subject, offered participants an opportunity to become better acquainted with members of the faculty. A few of those, such as Professor Currier and his friend Frances Yocom on the library staff, frequently invited Aurelia and me to lunch or dinner. John Knox and his wife had students in for tea and refreshments, and those of us who were unable to go home for the Christmas holidays found the Knox residence to be literally a home away from home.

None of these activities, delightful as they were, obscured the new focus Ted Currier had given me, and I worked as diligently as I could to make the most of the academic opportunities Fisk presented me. As my courses continued to go well and as my grades held up, I gained confidence in myself. Despite flattering overtures from Professor Elmer Imes, the chair of the Department of Physics, and the distinguished composer Randall Thompson, I assured them that history was my chosen vocation. Meanwhile, I enrolled in beginning French in my senior year in order to satisfy the Harvard prerequisite that all entering graduate students command two modern foreign languages. I was also writing my first research paper for Professor Currier's seminar. Taking a cue from him, I began to work on free Negroes in the antebellum South. One of the benefits of the subject was the opportunity it provided me to do research in the newspaper files and the manuscript collections at the Tennessee Historical Society, training in research that I would deeply appreciate when I finally enrolled in graduate school.

Throughout my four years at Fisk, I remained committed to the highest scholarship that I could achieve. Everyone seemed aware of my commitment, and they respected it. Indeed, I became known as the person who had disciplined himself to the point of letting *nothing* interfere with his studies. I once heard someone in the dormitory remark that there was no need to knock on John Hope's door after ten o'clock, for if the light was on and he had not yet gone to bed, he would undoubtedly be studying. And in that case, there was no way that he would answer the door. At one point it was rumored, quite inaccurately, that if I were escorting Aurelia to her dormitory in the evening and the time arrived in my schedule to be studying, I would bid her good night and proceed to my room, leaving her to return to her building unaccompanied.

Almost as important as formal classes was what my father called our "larger education," or the lectures, concerts, and campus visits of persons who shared their experiences with the Fisk students. A central event in this "larger education" was the annual Festival of Fine Arts. Participants were the Jubilee Singers, if they were available. The visiting dignitary in 1933 was Maggie Porter Cole, one of the original Jubilee Singers, who was then living in Detroit. Another visitor was the celebrated tenor Roland Hayes, a former Fisk student. He thrilled his listeners with his rendition of spirituals as well as classical works. In other areas of the fine arts, there was Langston Hughes and, of course, faculty member James Weldon Johnson, both of whom recited from their works to the delight and enlightenment of their audiences. The festival was an occasion for many people, including local white residents, to visit the Fisk campus and experience the only racial integration in the entire city of Nashville.

There were times, despite my immersion in my studies, when I wondered if my career would take a turn toward activism and a deep involvement with people. Again and again I was pressed by one group or another to assume still another leadership role. I was content to be president of my fraternity and to serve as the nominal leader of the varsity debating team. Others, however, wished I would do more. Without any prompting on my part, there was in the spring of my junior year a successful drive to elect me president of the student council.

When Dean Taylor learned of the election results, he summoned me to his office and explained that they had someone else in mind to preside over student government. By "they," I assume that he meant the administration, consisting, perhaps, of the president and his advisers. He informed me that he thought that L. Howard Bennett would be an ideal president, with his charisma, his strong leadership qualities, and his experience as president of his class for three years. I actually had no interest in the position, but I was not prepared for a blunt request that I step aside. I told him that I would think it over and give him my response the following day.

That evening I informed Aurelia of my conversation with the dean and of my inclination to step aside and make room for my best friend to become president of the student council. She asked me if I was prepared to tell the students who had elected me that I was abdicating and give them my reasons for rejecting their selection of me as their leader. I admitted that I had not thought about what I would say to them. She suggested that if I rejected their choice of me, I would owe them an explanation, even an apology. I had no answer for her or for the students. And in this fashion she helped me decide that I should accept the results of the election. The following day I informed the dean. Although he was obviously disappointed, he accepted my decision.

Even before my senior year, my family's economic situation was so bleak that I was determined to earn more in the summer of 1934 than I had earned during previous summers, when I had returned to Tulsa and worked in my father's office and for various African American professionals. Following the stock market crash in 1929, the national economic picture had steadily worsened. We lost our home in 1932, by which time the urban unemployment rate among African Americans ran as high as 30 percent. The worsening economic picture contributed to the election that year of Franklin D. Roosevelt, who gave most Americans some hope for a better future; the present, however, remained grim, particularly so for African Americans. Given my options, I decided that, perhaps, I could find better employment at Fisk or in Nashville than I could in Tulsa.

Soon I learned that Professor Charles S. Johnson was conducting an ambitious study of the economic and social conditions among Negro cotton farmers in the South. I also learned that he was in need of student assistants. I went to see Dr. Johnson and bluntly asked him for a job on the study. Despite being the source of my only grade of C, given me in my first quarter in college, Dr. Johnson and I had subsequently become better acquainted. He said that he could find a place for me as an assistant to the agricultural economist Giles Hubert. Johnson was going to need someone who could assist Hubert interviewing farmers and preparing the report that would become a part of the book that Johnson was writing, *Shadow of the Plantation*. As soon as classes ended in the spring of 1934, the study commenced.

Our first stop was in the Mississippi Delta, where I saw a population density of African Americans that I had never witnessed before. As we visited Negro cotton farmers, many of whom were sharecroppers, the rumor spread that we were employees of the federal government, part of a New Deal program launched by Roosevelt's activist administration and intended to incite opposition to white planters who were allegedly exploiting black farmers. While there was not a shred of truth to the rumor, we realized that we needed to be careful lest we incite white farmers against us. After getting a picture of conditions in the delta, we were ready to move on. A brief visit to Jackson, where Giles Hubert lived and worked at Jackson State College, prepared us for the hill country in eastern Mississippi.

We made our headquarters in Macon, the seat of Noxubee County, and found lodgings with a very hospitable woman in the Negro part of the town called "Sweet Potato Hill." On our first morning there, we visited the town square, where "Chief Hubert," as I called my supervisor, approached a prosperous-looking white man, telling him of our project and his wish to interview some of his Negro tenants. As the man cast his steely blue eyes on "Chief," he replied brusquely that Hubert should not go on his plantation. Shortly thereafter, "Chief" went out to interview other farmers and I returned to the room to work on the reports of counties we had already visited.

That evening, following a delicious dinner served by our hostess-landlady, I volunteered to go to the variety store on the town square and get some ice cream for dessert. With an air of confidence, I drove to the square, entered the store, and ordered two half-pints of ice cream. There was no ready-packed ice cream in those days, so I had to wait until the clerk prepared the order. I knew that I should not take a seat, so I stood until the two half-pints were ready. Then I paid the clerk and headed for the exit.

As I walked out onto the store's porch, a crowd of white men formed a U shape in front of the building. They blocked every avenue of escape, unless I was willing to provoke them by attempting to breach their line.

There was nothing for me to do but wait until someone said, or did, something to me. The evening was warm, the ice cream heavy in my hand, and I stood in silence for what seemed to be an eternity. Finally, their spokesman asked, in what was presumably his best hill country drawl, what we were doing in Noxubee County. I said something about examining the economic condition of Negro cotton farmers. There was another long silence. Then, he pointedly asked if I feared that I would be lynched. There was no safe answer. Any reply would have been a challenge. Mute, still, I waited. One of them finally said something that I did not hear but it must have been an order or a suggestion that they should not bother with the likes of me. The line broke, I walked slowly to the car, got in it, and raced back to Sweet Potato Hill.

Breathless, with no taste for ice cream, I told "Chief" that I could not possibly stay in Macon another night. He quietly told me that he was already packed and was waiting for me to return to tell me that he had indeed visited the plantation he had been warned away from that morning. By the time the man learned of his transgression, he had hoped to be safely in Jackson. In less than a half hour we were on our way.

The remainder of the summer went peacefully enough. We spent several weeks in Texas, and although there was much activity among the Negro cotton farmers, the entire atmosphere was quite different from what it was in Mississippi. In the area around Rosenberg, many of the planters were of German descent, and their relationship with their tenants seemed to be quite different from the relations of planters and tenants in Mississippi. While the Brazos and Trinity rivers provided rich lowlands for the cultivation of cotton, the climate and general topography were so different from Mississippi's as to render Texas an unlikely place with which to compare it. Nevertheless, the study continued more or less to Johnson's expectations, and by the end of the summer, broadly more experienced and with money in my pocket, I was ready to begin my most arduous year in college.

When the term opened in the fall of 1934, several matters claimed my immediate attention. High on the list were my efforts to enter graduate school. Mr. Currier gave no thought of my going anywhere except Harvard. Consequently, we sent for the catalog, application forms, and other materials relevant to my matriculation, and in due course I submitted my application. The other principal matter was the student council and plans for my administration. I projected a series of meetings of the entire student body to consider such items as faculty-student relations, the improvement of scholarship, and the place of intercollegiate athletics in a liberal arts college.

By far the most important business facing the student body and, for that matter, the entire university was the murder of Cordie Cheek. In mid-December of the preceding year, Cordie Cheek, a teenage African American boy, had been taken from his uncle's home at the edge of the Fisk campus and lynched. It was alleged that while chopping wood for a white family in Maury County, Tennessee, Cheek had taken a load of wood into the house and accidentally tore the dress of the white girl, whose brother then gave her a dollar to claim that Cheek had raped her. After his arrest, the grand jury refused to indict him on the basis of flimsy evidence, and he was set free. He left Maury County and went to live with relatives in Nashville. The mob, determined to bestow retributive justice on Cheek, followed him, seized him, and returned him to Maury County. He was castrated and lynched, his body riddled with bullets as the barbaric participants passed a pistol from one to another.

Those of us who had remained in Nashville over the Christmas holidays were obsessed with discussing the Cordie Cheek lynching. Indeed, the entire remainder of our junior year was shadowed by this tragic event. There were investigations, interviews, and other actions. The conclusion that many of us reached was that if it could happen to Cordie Cheek, who had been seized within three blocks of the Fisk Chapel, it could happen to any of us.

That was the sentiment expressed over and over from December 1933 to June 1934. It was the same when we returned in the autumn, as students searched for some means to express to the general public as well as official Nashville how they felt. I met with groups of students and presided over meetings of the entire student body. Members of the faculty and other interested persons met with us, and some made suggestions. For example, Grace Nail Johnson suggested a silent protest parade down Church Street in downtown Nashville, similar to the famous 1917 parade down Fifth Avenue in New York led by her husband, James Weldon Johnson, and

W.E.B. Du Bois. A good idea, perhaps, but someone observed that Nashville was not New York.

Then, without warning or preparation of any sort, the White House announced that President Franklin D. Roosevelt's annual visit to Warm Springs, Georgia, would include a stop in Nashville to visit two places he had always wanted to see, the Hermitage, home of Andrew Jackson, and Fisk University. Many white citizens could not believe that the sitting president of the United States would come to Nashville and ignore such landmarks as George Peabody College, Vanderbilt University, and Centennial Park. Obviously, FDR had his own priorities, and as the Fisk students learned of the impending visit, they began to plan and organize. They would lay a petition before the president, asking him to speak out against the barbaric practice of lynching and specifically against the horrible murder of Cordie Cheek. We had only to make certain that the petition, which as president of the student council I would present, was in its thrust and language worthy of the Fisk student body.

As the day of the president's visit approached, the excitement on campus and in the city rose to fever pitch. The Secret Service personnel arrived several days ahead of the president. They conferred with me at length, pointing out my responsibility in helping to inform the students about the routine security measures to be taken wherever the president went. Since he would arrive at Jubilee Hall, where the University Choir would sing, all windows were to be closed and the building was to be entirely vacated. They also wanted me to assist in instructing ushers who would be selected to seat the visitors in the bleachers that had been installed on the grounds near Jubilee Hall.

In the midst of the preparations for the presidential visit, President Jones called me in to discuss the conduct of the students during the historic visit. Upon learning that we planned to present the president with a petition calling for action in the Cordie Cheek lynching, he expressed sympathy with our plan but observed that the president of the United States was honoring Fisk with a visit and we should take care not to press our case when he was our guest. Declaring such a gesture unbecoming and impolite, he offered an alternative. Since many Fisk students would be accompanying the football team to Atlanta for the homecoming game with

Morehouse College the following week, he hoped that I would go. If I could arrange the trip, he would arrange an appointment for me to see the president at nearby Warm Springs. Reluctantly, I agreed.

The day of the presidential visit, November 18, 1934, finally arrived. Despite the fact that the local radio station, in describing the visit, had failed to mention FDR's stop at Fisk, the visitors, black and white, began to come to the campus early for the noontime event. Shortly before the president's arrival, I was walking near the bleachers when a white man approached me and asked where white people were to be seated. I told him that at Fisk we never practiced racial segregation, and he was free to sit in any of the bleachers. He accepted the information calmly and then quietly informed me that he had voted the Democratic ticket all his life as had, indeed, all of his kinsmen. But if the Democratic president could come to a school that did not separate the races, he could not ever vote the Democratic ticket again. He even shook my hand and found a seat in the desegregated bleachers to await the arrival of the president of the United States.

The visit went off very well. In the open sedan with the president were Mrs. Roosevelt and Secretary of the Interior Harold Ickes. Fisk President Jones delivered some remarks of welcome, the choir sang several spirituals, the members of the presidential party expressed delight and gratitude, and they were off.

I spent much of the week studying and preparing for the trip to Atlanta. Two other members of the student council went with me, and our faculty escort was the Reverend W. J. Faulkner, the new dean of men and future dean of the chapel, who had recently moved from Atlanta to Nashville. Along with passing on to President Roosevelt our statement, I wished while in Atlanta to meet the person for whom I was named: Professor John Hope, then president of Atlanta University. Tall and erect and having the physical appearance of a white man, he briefly adjourned a meeting to ask about Fisk, when I would graduate, and what I would do then. He was pleased that I intended to begin graduate studies at twenty years of age. He inquired of my mother and father and expressed his admiration for them, and asked me to send them his warm and affectionate best regards. With that he wished me well and returned to his meeting.

Other than that brief sojourn, I stayed put, awaiting the call from

Warm Springs. As time passed, I told my colleagues that they should go on to the Morehouse-Fisk game without me. The afternoon dragged by slowly. Suddenly, it dawned on me that I would not receive a call, that very likely President Jones had never contacted President Roosevelt, that it was all a charade. In the days and weeks that followed, Dr. Jones never mentioned the matter, and in the absence of an explanation, an excuse, or even an alibi, I could only conclude that from the time he first suggested the arrangement back in early November, Dr. Jones never intended to make an appointment with President Roosevelt for a committee of Fisk students. I took from my disappointment one lesson: Jim Crow America was skilled at deflecting or ignoring appeals to justice and equity. I would soon learn an easier way to ensure the attention of Jim Crow America. All it would require would be my ambition, determination, and willingness to excel.

Life went on, even with no campus resolution of the Cordie Cheek case. Classes continued, and even the French class during my senior year was not as much of a bore as I feared. I was spending more time with Professor Currier, soon to be "Ted" to me, as we plotted and planned for my admission to Harvard Graduate School. It was something of a boon to learn that Fisk had been placed on the list of colleges approved by the Association of American Universities, the first historically black institution to receive that distinction. With my application, transcript, and other materials already at Harvard, I needed only to take the Scholastic Aptitude Test, which was to be administered at Vanderbilt University.

Having never been on its campus, I went to Vanderbilt rather early on that spring Saturday morning in order to find the correct building and room well before the examination was to begin. When a professor entered with a bundle of papers, I concluded that this was the right place and that he was in charge of the examination. As I reached that conclusion, the professor saw me and asked me what I was doing there. I told him that I was a senior at Fisk and was required to take the Scholastic Aptitude Test for my admission to the Harvard Graduate School. Incensed, he hurled the examination at me, and, unable to catch it, I had to pick it up from the floor. The experience was so unnerving that I doubted I would perform well on the examination. When I had written what I could, I turned in the paper and departed. As I left, a black janitor asked me what I had been doing in that room. When I told him that I had been taking an examination, he remarked that he was asking out of curiosity. He had never seen a person of our color seated in a room at that all-white university.

To my elation, I shortly received a letter from Harvard informing me that I had been admitted to the graduate school in good standing. The letter pointed out that this was the first time that a student from a historically black institution had been admitted without condition, a consequence of Fisk having been placed on the approved list of American universities. That, I suppose, should have been a great consolation; I felt more immediately the fact that I had been denied financial aid. Clearly, I would have to prove that I was deserving of it. That would depend, of course, on whether I would have sufficient funds even to get to Harvard. In the spring of 1935, that looked exceedingly unlikely.

As I completed my undergraduate course work and prepared to take the comprehensive examinations and finals, the future did not look promising. My father's law practice was no better and was, perhaps, worse than it had been. Anne had been out of school for a year because of poor health and was now a junior at Talladega, majoring in physical education. Aurelia's fortunes were no better. She had ceased taking piano lessons because of the expense, and she had instead begun a job cleaning glassware in the university dining room. Since limited funds kept us on campus even during long holiday periods, we saw much of each other and began to discuss our plans for the years ahead. We knew quite well that the end of the academic year would mean our separating for an indefinite period of time. I hoped to be going to Massachusetts for graduate school, and in all likelihood she would teach in North Carolina for a while in order to assure her continued education and that of her younger sister, Bertha, who was already completing her freshman year at Fisk.

The examinations were at hand and graduation was approaching. I had given up my job in the library, and I was reducing the time I spent with the debate team, the choir, and the fraternity. With a grade point average of 3.79 I would graduate magna cum laude, along with Marian Minus of Dayton, Ohio, and Louis Roberts of Jamestown, New York.

Unfortunately, my parents could not afford the trip for both of them to attend commencement, so my mother came alone. The same was true of Aurelia's parents, so her mother likewise came alone. Seventy-five of us were graduating and there were many sad farewells, for it was inevitable that some of us would never meet again. From the beginning, however, we had insisted that the class of 1935 was exceptional, and many of us were convinced that some classmates would achieve so much and enjoy such high visibility that it would not be difficult to follow their careers. Even our first year was one of achievement, as L. Howard Bennett led us on insisting that our twelve-point program for the improvement of Fisk was all that was needed for the institution to become *the* leader in higher education. In our final year it was not too much to insist that the world would hear from many members of that small class of seventy-five, and it did.

5

Fair Harvard

THE SUMMER OF 1935 was one of uncertainty. I returned to Tulsa shortly after commencement and began to look for a job. The Depression was in full force, with national unemployment rates at just over 20 percent and my prospects dim. But that was not the only reason I spent as much time as I could with my family. My mother was not in the best of health, and I was delighted to be able to visit with her after my long absence. I also accompanied my father on his rounds at city hall and the county courthouse. I wondered aloud, one day, how he felt about my not going into law and becoming his partner. He reminded me that even when I was very young he had always placed great confidence in me. He had followed my various activities with loving admiration. He and my mother were proud of what I had been able to accomplish thus far, and he regretted that he had not been able to do more for me. He was confident that I would continue to bring credit to myself and the family. That is all that he wished of me.

It had been at least a dozen years since I had seen much of my older sister, Mozella, who was always simply known as Sister, and my brother, Buck Jr. They had been away in boarding high school at Lane College during our late Rentiesville and early Tulsa years, after which Mozella went to West Virginia State College, while my brother went to Fisk. By

1935 they had graduated and were back in Tulsa, where Sister was an elementary school teacher and married to her longtime friend Waldo E. Jones. My brother was already a highly respected principal of a county school in Bixby, some twenty miles from Tulsa, and was married to Bessye Wilson, a member of an old Tulsa family. Though content, both of my siblings spoke about continuing their studies at some future date. With Anne also at home, all of us were together for the first time in years and we made the most of it, enjoying not only each other's company but that of our parents.

Securing employment was difficult, and once again the only job that I could find was at a funeral home. Inherently unpleasant, it also yielded little income. When alone, I kept to the funeral parlor's large veranda, where I could still hear the telephone but was well away from the slumber room and the smell of death. As the summer droned on and my finances failed to improve, graduate school seemed more attractive and more unattainable than ever.

Although I had received letters from Ted Currier during the summer months, they were largely news dispatches about his sojourn to his home in Maine. When he returned to Nashville in September, he called to see how my summer had gone and inquire if I had rounded up the resources I would need to enter Harvard. I recounted my humdrum summer, admitted I had earned little income, and concluded that the entire future looked bleak. Without even teaching credentials, I had no hope of competing for the few jobs that might materialize. I told him that Aurelia was doing better on that score. Already certified, she had secured a position in Garysburg, North Carolina. Ted asked if I could secure train fare to Nashville. When I answered in the affirmative, he suggested that I pay him a visit, and he would see what he could do. With Harvard's semester set to begin, either a solution would be found or my graduate school career would have to be, at best, delayed.

A few days later, Ted Currier hosted me for the night in his modest home, where I had spent so many pleasant hours during my years at Fisk. The following morning he went into downtown Nashville alone, his purpose unannounced. Within a few hours he returned and informed me that he had been to his bank and had borrowed five hundred dollars. He placed the entire sum in my hand, and in a voice I can still recall, he declared,

"Money will not keep you out of Harvard!" With that gracious declaration from one of the most generous people I have ever known, I began to prepare to depart for Boston that very evening.

When Ted Currier requested that I come visit him, I suspected that he had in mind some maneuver to get me into Harvard, but I had no idea that he would borrow the money I needed and make a loan of it to me. After all, his income was modest, even for a young single man with a secure position during the Great Depression. Now, he was doing something my parents would have done, had it been within their means. Had he been my real brother, I could not have felt closer or more grateful or, indeed, more challenged. His expression of confidence merely added to my determination to succeed in graduate school. Having come to Nashville prepared to either return home or continue on, I set my sights on Harvard.

Arriving in Boston the following morning, I located 415 Broadway in Cambridge, where I was greeted by my gruff but friendly landlord, John W. Clark. He showed me to my room, for which I was to pay five dollars per week, and recited to me the rules of the house. Roomers were to be quiet at all times. There were to be no female guests, and male guests should be kept to a minimum, so that quiet would prevail for those who wished to study. There were three other people living there, besides the landlord's two maiden sisters. One was Charles Quick, a very able and self-confident first-year law student from Talladega, whom I knew from my undergraduate years at Fisk. The other student was Hosea Campbell, a sixth-year graduate student in history who spoke more frequently about his plans for a preparatory school for Negro boys than about the completion of his graduate studies. The other roomer was a veteran of World War I from Accomac, on the eastern shore of Virginia. To state the obvious, all the boarders were African Americans, as, of course, were the Clarks.

The following morning Mr. Clark invited everyone to a traditional Sunday breakfast, consisting of baked beans, codfish cakes, rolls, and coffee. Nothing more emphatically confirmed that I had indeed reached Boston than those beans on Sunday morning.

The very next day I went to see my adviser, Professor Arthur M. Schlesinger. He looked much younger than I had expected, perhaps because I assumed that anyone attaining such an eminent position required a corresponding ripe old age. He advised me to take his seminar in American social and intellectual history. My other courses would include the history of England and world economic history. The latter was the only course in which there were women, because its professor, Edwin Francis Gay, refused to cross the street and repeat at Radcliffe College the lecture that he had just given at Harvard. Finally, I would audit the lecture course on American diplomatic history. To close our consultation, Professor Schlesinger invited me to tea on any Sunday afternoon, when he and his wife welcomed his students into their home. Very little during that first day made me feel so much a part of Harvard as that invitation.

Following that first successful interview at Harvard, I strode with confidence over to the Harvard Trust Company to pay the first hundred-dollar installment on my tuition, which was four hundred dollars per year. On that very same day, I went to the university employment office. My goal was a job provided by funds from the National Youth Administration or one of the Depression-era federal agencies financing student employment opportunities at so many colleges and universities. Unfortunately, Harvard University refused all federal funds, leaving only a handful of employment opportunities to be had at the university. I dutifully filled out the application form, hoping that my stenographic qualifications would give me a leg up.

Meanwhile, I learned from Hosea Campbell that one of Harvard's undergraduate societies was looking for someone to wash dishes after the evening meal. I indicated my interest, he gave me the address, and I went over to the Pi Eta Society in Boylston Street and introduced myself to Louis Zucker, the resident manager. The job indeed existed for someone to wash the dinner dishes in exchange for his own dinner. Preparing to sit down to eat, Zucker invited me to join him. I quickly learned it was much better fare than I could afford and accepted the job. Soon I was a part of the family at the Pi Eta Society, vacationing with Louis's family several weekends in nearby Scituate and becoming friendly with its members. Best known of those was Joseph P. Kennedy Jr. who, after I found his misplaced train ticket to Bronxville one evening, took to seeking me out.

Within days of the start of classes I realized that I had been well prepared by Ted Currier to meet whatever academic challenge Harvard might present me. Indeed, when I was told that Professor Schlesinger was rumored to give out only one A in any given class, I glibly responded that one A was all that I would need from him. I can explain such brash conceit only as evidence of my desperate need to affirm my confidence in myself.

A day, and often an hour, didn't go by without my feeling the color of my skin—in the reactions of white Cambridge, the behavior of my fellow students, the attitudes real and imagined struck by my professors. However well Currier had equipped me to meet the demands of Harvard's course work, race precluded my enjoying the self-assurance to which most of my colleagues, along with affluence and influence, were born. As had been true all my life, being ambitious and black guaranteed that I would stand out. I was also keenly aware that, unlike the vast majority at Harvard, I had only determination and a corresponding work ethic to fall back on.

At the first meeting of class, Professor Schlesinger indicated that each of us would be expected to write a paper on some aspect of American social or intellectual history in the late nineteenth century. He suggested several topics, including Lyman Abbott, who had been a white minister active in the social gospel movement. He then asked each of us if any of the topics were appealing. I said that I wanted to write on Abbott. A few minutes later another student, who perhaps had not been attentive, said that he wanted to write on Lyman Abbott. Mr. Schlesinger noted that I had taken that topic unless, he inquired, I wished to write on some Negro leader, like Booker T. Washington. I declined. Although I did not indicate it in class, I was eager to write on a non-Negro subject and compete with the students on material where it was not perceived that I had some inherent advantage. In any case, I wrote a paper on Abbott that Professor Schlesinger praised at length and on which I received an A, though if it was the only A awarded I do not know.

Professor Edwin Francis Gay, who had a long and distinguished career in government as well as in the academy, was a regal presence in his class and spoke as though he was delivering a Sermon on the Mount. He was also the only Harvard professor ever to tell a "darky" joke in a class I attended, something about a person of color who "moped and moped about a problem and before solving it went to sleep." I have always wondered if the silence that followed his delivery was because of my presence.

Easily my most animated and dramatic lecturer was James Phinney Baxter III. Since I was to be in his seminar during the second term, I elected, at his urging, to attend his lectures on American diplomatic history during the first term. Sporting a topcoat, overcoat, or fur coat, he would enter the room and throw the garment toward a chair, on which it sometimes landed. He was, for the next hour, engaged in the narration and analysis of some diplomatic venture that was in all likelihood a life-and-death struggle for the United States. One day it could be the battle of the ironclads and its implication for foreign policy; another day it could be the sinking of the *Maine* and how that led to the war with Spain. He would almost weep as he told of the various ways the very life of the nation depended on some turn of diplomatic events. For his subsequent seminar, I chose to write on "The Movement to Annex British Columbia to the United States, 1868–1880," an effort that he awarded with an A minus.

Several weeks after I registered with Harvard's employment office, I received a call from Elliott Perkins, the senior tutor at Lowell House. He was writing his dissertation in English history and he needed a person familiar with the field who could type various drafts of his manuscript and help him prepare it for submission to the Department of History. I happily accepted, especially since the work could be done whenever I found the time to go down to Lowell House and type out what he had written. When I took the job I knew neither that he was descended from America's famous Adams family nor that his father was the influential banker Charles Elliott Perkins, who sat on the Harvard Board of Overseers. Elliott was delighted that I could correct his spelling and on occasion even his grammar, and in time we developed a lifelong friendship.

During the fall term of that first year, yet another employment opportunity arose. Professor Wilbur Cortez Abbott, nearing retirement, announced that he would like to see Mr. Franklin at the end of his lecture. When I presented myself, he said that Elliott Perkins, for whom Abbott was an adviser, had informed him that I could take shorthand as well as type. He then said that publishers had expressed an interest in his lectures, and since he did not write them out he wondered if I would be good enough to take them down in shorthand and give him a draft, for which he would pay me. I was pleased to do so. On subsequent days, before Professor Abbott began his lectures, he would address me, asking if it was all right for him to begin. The sight of this venerable Harvard professor seeking my permission to speak engendered not a little confusion.

Despite these varied jobs, a near-emergency arose when it seemed that I would not have the money to pay my last tuition installment, due in April. This gave me the opportunity to test the university's stated policy of advancing students short-term loans. True to its word, Lawrence S. Mayo, the associate dean of the Graduate School of Arts and Sciences, on learning that I had not received money from home but expected it soon, wrote me a check for three hundred dollars. I was in arrears on rent, food, and laundry and this money proved a lifesaver.

The most serious difficulty I encountered that first year was sheer loneliness. The extremely long hours of work and study ensured that I returned to my room late each night, coming from Widener Library or Pi Eta. I had scant time to relax with my fellow boarders, and while association with the other Harvard students was satisfactory, it felt cold and distant after the excessive togetherness at Fisk. I attempted to fill the void in several ways.

At the university, I affiliated with two departmental organizations. One was called, quite simply, the History Club. It was large, unwieldy, and impersonal; every history student and faculty member was eligible for membership. It held monthly meetings, and the topic for discussion was as likely to be a problem in Turkish history as in North American history. Reflecting my waning interest, I attended irregularly. The other club, called the Henry Adams, was composed of students in the history of the United States. It was, of course, much smaller, and its members were people I saw regularly in classes or seminars. The speaker tended to be an advanced student who was writing his dissertation or, better still, a member of the faculty. In those cases, we had a chance to become better acquainted with the men who held our future in their hands.

I seldom, if ever, missed a meeting of the Henry Adams Club, and I learned a great deal from the speakers. They were all accomplished scholars, whether just starting out or long established, and for that reason the exposure to them was valuable. It was also in the Henry Adams Club that I witnessed anti-Semitism for the first time.

Toward the end of the term I was asked to serve on the committee to nominate the club's officers for the following year. When the committee met, I was quick to recommend Oscar Handlin, a second-year student from Brooklyn who was quite active in the club and had made a straight-A record in his first year. After I made the nomination, there was dead silence in the room. Eventually, one of the members spoke up and said that although Oscar did not have some of the more objectionable Jewish traits, he was still a Jew. I was appalled. I regarded my nominee as merely a white man who was brilliant, active, and deserving. Growing up, I had necessarily spent time and energy dealing with racial bigots, and I had learned to identify them by their skin color and degree of ignorance. I had never heard any educated white person speak of another in such terms, and I lost respect not only for the individual who made the statement but for the entire group that tolerated such views. Handlin went on to win a Pulitzer Prize and become director of the Charles Warren Center for American Studies and the Carl M. Loeb University Professor at Harvard University. I only hope his detractors developed some respect for him both as a Jew and as the scholar they never could become.

Replicating in Cambridge the social life to which I had grown accustomed at Fisk proved extremely difficult. There was no opportunity to see Aurelia during vacations or holidays. She was absorbed in her work in North Carolina, and we simply did not have the financial resources to travel. There were some substitutes, however. Many of the homes in Roxbury, an area where there was a concentration of African American families, warmly welcomed Harvard's black students. There were also the League of Women for Community Service at 558 Massachusetts Avenue, and Estelle's, a restaurant on Tremont Street that specialized in fried chicken dinners. Harvard's African American students frequently met the young women of Roxbury at Estelle's, permitting the rare evening of relaxation from our studies. Pivotal to any social evening in Roxbury was the McCree family. Wade McCree Sr. was a member of the celebrated Fisk University Class of 1911, and his wife was also a former Fisk student. Their son, Wade Jr., who would become a distinguished attorney and United States Circuit Court judge, was already at Fisk, and their two daughters, Betty and Catherine, would follow in due course. Their home was, literally, my home away from home. Unable to travel, I celebrated Thanksgiving and Christmas there and frequently enjoyed long and enlightening conversations with the senior McCrees.

Boston was not Nashville, but I discovered quite early in my first autumn in Cambridge that it was hardly free of racism. One Sunday, following an afternoon concert, I went with a young lady to Child's restaurant for a light meal. We took our seats and waited for a server to take our order. We waited and waited. Servers passed by our table, pointedly ignoring us, and after more than an hour we obliged them by leaving.

Shortly after that, Juanita Jackson, the youth director for the NAACP whom I had met the previous year, came to Boston to organize a young people's branch. She called a meeting at 558 Massachusetts Avenue and requested that I attend. After she made her appeal, she asked me to speak. I told of my experience in the restaurant, arguing that this underscored the need for young Bostonians to organize a branch. When I had concluded my remarks, an older African American woman took the floor. Boston did not need a youth branch of the NAACP, and it certainly did not need a Southern Negro to come up there and tell them how to live, she retorted. She then invited me to go back south and appealed to the young people of Boston to ostracize me until I left the city. The young people did not follow her advice, but I learned from that senior citizen of Boston how African Americans can buy into a system that gives them a sense of belonging without bestowing on them the rights that others enjoy. Many, like this "proper Bostonian," could not even see the obvious similarities between racism in Boston and, say, Charleston.

One afternoon, in the early autumn of that first year in Cambridge, there was a light tap on my door. It was a fellow boarder, John Wharton, who lived on the third floor in a small room. I knew that he was a veteran of World War I and that he did not enjoy robust health. He did not work and he lived, I believe, on a pension, presumably from the military. He politely said he did not wish to disturb me, but he had received something that he was having difficulty reading. He complained that the writer had not made the words clear, and he hoped that I would assist him. When I took a look at the letter and saw how clearly it was written, I concluded that John Wharton was unable to read. Pretending that I too found the letter confusing, all the while wondering to myself who previously had been reading his letters for him, I did as he asked.

When I had finished, he thanked me. Before he could leave, I suggested that perhaps he and I could work together to "brush up" on his reading. He thanked me but said that he was certain that I did not have the time. I persisted, saying that I could make the time in my schedule. Besides, I assured him, I would enjoy the time spent with him. We agreed that he should come to my room at five o'clock each afternoon, at which time we could work for a half hour, just before I went to the Pi Eta Club to wash dishes for my evening meal.

At the appointed time each day, Wharton would make his appearance at my door, notebook in hand. We worked on words, their spelling and their use in simple sentences, taking notice of the parts of speech. He was very serious and hardworking and yet remained considerate of my varied commitments. Indeed, he was so eager to learn that he would improvise his own work routines beyond those that I had assigned. Within a short time he was writing sentences and composing brief letters to relatives back home in Accomac, Virginia. By the end of my first academic year, when I received my MA, John Wharton was ready to receive his certificate in elementary reading and writing. And I was more pleased with his accomplishments than I was with my own.

By the spring of 1936, I had decided to leave the university for a year in order to earn money with which to repay Ted Currier's loan. Further, the way I intended to do it was by replacing him at Fisk for a year. That is why I applied for the MA, which I felt sure would look better following my name than BA. Besides, this was the tercentennial anniversary of Harvard University, and commencement promised to be a festive occasion. With no friends or relatives in attendance, I went to the commencement exercises alone and later picked up my diploma. I had not given up the goal of my PhD, but I enjoyed the feel of that parchment. It was a relief to have tangible proof that Harvard had not taken much of a risk in admitting unconditionally a student from a historically black college.

Knowing that it would be at least one year before I would return, I did not hurry away from Cambridge. Indeed, I was already contemplating what my course work would be in the fall of 1937. En route home I stopped in Nashville to visit with Ted Currier, seeking suggestions regarding my course work at Fisk and housing for the following year. He had already arranged for me to have a room at the faculty club and to take my meals in the dining hall, where I had worked during my undergraduate years. Such clear evidence of my transition from student to teacher, all in a matter of twelve months, pleased me, I confess. With things arranged for the autumn, I made my way to Tulsa and family.

My very short visit was somewhat overshadowed by my mother's health. Suffering from what was described as a nervous condition brought on by high blood pressure, she had been ordered by her physician to remain as quiet and inactive as possible. He urged her to relax and not to worry about anything. Under these constraints, the family made the most of our time together. My visit was so brief, and my days were so full seeing family and friends, that I did not even seek employment.

In September I settled into what was to be merely a year's interruption of my studies at Harvard. That year at Fisk, however, promised to be challenging. The juniors and seniors had been my student colleagues just a year earlier. Now, I was their teacher and mentor. I made the same demands of them, as well as of my freshman and sophomore students, that had been made of me as an undergraduate, and I was impressed with the manner in which they all adjusted to me as their teacher. Not only did the upperclassmen show me the respect due a faculty member, but they responded to my demands for high performance in their course work.

I experienced my first and only significant difficulty as a member of the faculty when I received my first check. When I was hired, I had signed a contract indicating that my salary would be $1,400 per year, which meant that I was to receive $140 per month over the ten-month school year. My first check was for $126. I went to see Dr. Jones, still Fisk's president, and said that there had been an error regarding my salary. He replied that I had received a 10 percent reduction in pay, as had all the other members of the faculty. By 1937 the still-faltering economy was giving only grudgingly to President Roosevelt's federally orchestrated New Deal, the benefits of which were even slower to reach African Americans. Dr. Jones claimed the pay cut a necessity. I replied that there had been no indication, when I signed my contract, that I would receive a reduction in pay, and that I could not possibly work for less than $1,400 because of my debts and current obligations. When I adamantly refused to work for the reduced salary, he capitulated with ill grace.

Early in the term, Dean Taylor asked me if I would like to attend the annual meeting of the Association for the Study of Negro Life and History, convening at Virginia State College in Petersburg, with the university paying my transportation and expenses. Founded by Carter G. Woodson and others in 1915, the association was by 1936 the premier organization of scholars and laypersons committed to the study, research, and dissemination of information on the history of black people. Because no so-called white hotels would accommodate national meetings of African Americans, the association's annual convention usually met on a black college campus.

On Friday, October 23, I left for Virginia State College, located in Petersburg, Virginia, in order to be present for the opening session on Sunday. This was the first time I had attended a historical association of any kind, and the presence of so many African American historians deeply impressed me. The remarkable thing about this meeting, although I did not know it at the time, was how schoolteachers and laypeople were as much a part of the organization as the professionals. Dr. Woodson, serving as executive director, cultivated the teachers, for he was as determined to see Negro history taught in the schools as he was devoted to scholarship in the colleges. Thus, several schoolteachers read papers on the inclusion of Negro history in their school's curriculum as, indeed, did several college professors.

Dr. Woodson likewise emphasized the importance of making the association racially inclusive. Virginia's white superintendent of education, Sidney Hall, as well as W. Herman Bell of Hampden-Sydney College, Garnett Ryland of the University of Richmond, and other white scholars were in attendance.

Still another way Dr. Woodson sought to extend the reach of the association was by encouraging nonhistorians to assume leadership roles. At the Virginia meeting, Mrs. Mary McLeod Bethune, then on leave from the presidency of Bethune-Cookman College to serve with President Roosevelt's National Youth Administration, was elected the association's president to succeed John Hope who had died earlier that year. On the morning before her election, she was to have breakfast with Rayford Logan, who had just completed the work for his PhD at Harvard. To my great delight, Logan also invited me. I was in awe of her, one of the leading women of the nation. I doubt that I spoke a word as she talked about her work with the Roosevelt administration and as a college president and her struggle to decide between a career as an educator and one as a politician.

At the conclusion of one of the sessions, Dr. John M. Gandy, president of Virginia State College, handed me a telegram. While I read it, he realized that it contained unsettling news. He inquired, and I told him that my mother was gravely ill and that I was urged to come home immediately. His prompt response was to ask if I had my fare home. I told him that I did not, and he took out his wallet and without ceremony handed me sufficient funds to travel to Tulsa. I thanked him, promised him a prompt reimbursement, and looked for Dr. Woodson. When I found him, I told him why I was rushing away, at which point he put an arm around me, expressed his concern, and asked if I needed any money. When I told him that Dr. Gandy had already provided the fare for my journey home, he bade me farewell.

I arrived in Tulsa late on Saturday, October 31, after what was easily the longest train ride I had ever taken. On reaching home, I was informed that any excitement might cause my mother to have another convulsion. She had experienced several already, any one of which could have taken her away. As we began the all-night vigil, I could, therefore, only look at her from a point where she could not see me. The following morning, November 1, All Saints' Day, she died peacefully. The funeral, presided over by the Reverend T. M. Gatewood, longtime friend of my parents and the person closest to being a family chaplain, was held the following Thursday. My sister Anne and I left the same day, she for Talladega, where she was in her senior year, and I for Nashville, which I had left almost two weeks ago.

When people on campus learned of the reason for my long absence, there was not only indulgence but deep sympathy expressed by colleagues and students. When Aurelia learned of my mother's death, she called me, our first long-distance telephone conversation, and it was not only comforting but reassuring. My life was soon consumed by office hours, student papers, and examinations, and, perhaps gratefully, I spent what spare time I had planning for the following year.

At Harvard I had been encouraged to apply for a fellowship, and although nothing had been promised, I was optimistic. Even a Harvard fellowship, however, would be insufficient, especially if I received one that forbade me to engage in any outside work to supplement my finances. So when that autumn I learned that two representatives from the General Education Board, a philanthropic initiative of John D. Rockefeller, were visiting the Fisk campus to meet with any faculty members who were seeking financial support for further study, I sought an interview. They seemed quite interested when I told them what I had done and what I planned to do. When they learned that I was twenty-one, however, one of them remarked that there were many college professors more than twice my age with nowhere near my breadth of training and experience. They frankly admitted an obligation to assist such persons before getting around to young people like me.

One well-publicized source of support for ambitious students was the Julius Rosenwald Fund. Established in 1917 by the great Jewish philanthropist, the fund was merely one of several major benefactions by Rosenwald. He had supported hundreds of rural Negro schools in the South, had contributed to a model Negro housing project in Chicago, and had demonstrated the extent of his vision by contributing to both the YMCA and the YWCA. The fund was established, Rosenwald said, for "the well-being of mankind," and into it he poured a fortune that by 1929 amounted to some $30 million. The president, Edwin R. Embree, boasted that the fund chose recipients so carefully and with such confidence in their futures that it would not disturb its board if some of its recipients decided to go fishing. I decided to apply and was pleased to receive a full fellowship. Soon thereafter I learned that I was also the recipient of an Edwin Austin Fellowship from Harvard University. Long before the end of the academic year at Fisk, I could plan confidently for my return to Cambridge.

The late autumn was greatly brightened by Aurelia's Christmas visit to see her sister, Bertha, now a junior at Fisk, and me, by now a "veteran" teacher of four months at our alma mater. That there was little to do for recreation was no hardship; after eighteen months of separation we were very happy simply to talk and talk. I had much to tell her about Harvard, Cambridge, and Boston. She had much to say about what was lacking in Northampton County, North Carolina, "peanut land," as she called it. The days passed quickly, and she did much in that brief holiday period to cheer me up in what would otherwise have been a bleak time, for I was much reminded of my departed mother.

The remainder of the year was uneventful. I lived on a very tight budget, especially since I was determined before the end of the academic year to pay my debts in full to Ted Currier and to President Gandy. I enjoyed the teaching much more than I expected, especially since I was carrying a full five-course load and had so many preparations that I sometimes worked almost around the clock. I was determined to be as well informed and as carefully prepared as I possibly could be, and it is not hyperbole to say that I learned at least as much during my year of teaching at Fisk as I had learned in my first year at Harvard.

6

A Published Author

THE SUMMER OF 1937 was split between Tulsa, visiting with family, and Nashville, passing the baton back to Ted Currier and preparing for my return to Harvard. Upon arriving in Cambridge, I immediately felt that I was returning to familiar territory. I rented my old room at 415 Broadway and sailed through registration, since Professor Schlesinger and I had planned two years of course work for me when I first entered the university. I would take his general course on the social and intellectual history of the United States, which I ordinarily would have taken before taking his seminar. I believed then, as I do now, that he reversed the order to discover, firsthand, how well I could perform and whether it was worth his and my time for me to be there at all. I also took the course on the history of the nation's westward movement, taught by Professor Frederick Merk and known as "Wagon Wheels" to future generations of students.

Early American history was usually taught by Professor Samuel Eliot Morison, whose recently published history of Harvard during its first three centuries had been favorably received. That year, however, he was off on the widely discussed Columbus voyage in which, using the explorer's fifteenth-century journals, Morison and his crew would retrace that early Atlantic crossing. Meanwhile, the history of the thirteen colonies and the history of the American Revolution would be taught by Professor Curtis Nettels of the University of Wisconsin, who proved to be precise and exacting, emphasizing the economic aspects of American colonial history much more than Morison would have, as I would discover.

Since I needed another outside field, along with Professor Gay's World Economic History, I opted for the constitutional history of England to the sixteenth century, taught by Professor Charles Howard McIlwain, Eaton Professor of the science of government. This turned out to be an unanticipated delight. McIlwain, a balding man with a mischievous, cherubic smile, enjoyed his course more, perhaps, than any of his students. The course text would be Stubbs's *Select Charters of English Medieval History* in the original Latin. Several students walked out, one grumbling that he had only two years of college Latin. I had had one year in high school, but I quickly decided to stay and, if I had to, teach myself Latin; Professor Schlesinger expected me to take McIlwain's course, and I had no intention of telling him that it was too much for me.

As the course commenced, with Professor McIlwain lecturing on some aspect of the Norman Conquest or the rise of Parliament or the meaning of the language in the Magna Carta, my smattering of Latin returned. It was not sufficient, so I began to teach myself what else I needed. For the required paper, I chose "The Constitutional Position of the Norman Queens," a piece calculated to make me one of the pioneers in women's history. Although the reader in the course was not as impressed with my achievement as I was, I had done sufficient work to pass the course with ease, which is more than the dropouts could say. And while I felt a justifiable pride in having achieved my goal in the course, the boastfulness that had punctuated my first year at Harvard had mellowed. I never could abide the clubby, insulated world that cocooned so many of my fellow Harvard graduate students, and I will admit it often honed an edge on my own ambitions. But a year of teaching at Fisk and having attained my master's degree left me confident that I could earn a Harvard PhD; the challenge I saw before me was not whether I would succeed, but how far my determination and hard work might take me.

One day, as I was looking up some items in the card catalog in Widener Library, Professor Schlesinger approached me and wondered in jest if I was boycotting his Sunday afternoon teas. I assured him that I was not—I had been simply too busy. I then told him of my emerging interest in Edward Bellamy, the nineteenth-century novelist and social critic, and that I was considering writing a paper on some aspect of his life and work to fulfill the requirements in Schlesinger's course. He expressed delight, adding that he thought Bellamy's widow was still living, perhaps in Springfield, Massachusetts. Encouraged, I plunged into the Bellamy saga.

After I had reread Bellamy's utopian novel *Looking Backward*, I decided to try to contact the Bellamy family. Since he had died in 1898, I could not imagine that his widow would be living some forty years later. Hoping merely to uncover living kin, I wrote the postmaster in Springfield, inquiring if any descendants of Edward Bellamy lived there or in Chicopee Falls, the place of Bellamy's birth. Within a few days I was astounded to receive a letter from Mrs. Bellamy herself, expressing her pleasure in my interest in her late husband and inviting me to come to visit. She further promised that I could read any materials that she had. Over the next several weeks I journeyed to Springfield, where Mrs. Bellamy and her daughter, Marian Bellamy Earnshaw, proved most hospitable. I took it all in and returned to Cambridge, where I wrote "Edward Bellamy and the Nationalist Movement."

Professor Schlesinger was so pleased with my paper that he suggested I send it to the *New England Quarterly*, where it was accepted for publication. My great joy was complete when Professor Schlesinger, at a subsequent meeting of the Henry Adams Club at which he was the speaker, began his talk by announcing to the group that one of its members was a "published author." On his identifying me, the utter surprise of the members merely added to my pleasure.

The remainder of the year passed without any other significant event. Indeed, nothing could have occurred to surpass the fact that I, as a second-year graduate student, had published a research paper in a reputable journal. It gave me the focus and confidence that I needed for the next phase of my studies, the preparation for the general oral examination.

Professor Schlesinger was aware of some of my concerns, especially about choosing a field in which to write my dissertation. I told him of my interest in English history, but because of my limited resources I could not imagine myself ever trekking to London to check materials in the British Museum. My second interest was in Christian socialism, but that field had been preempted by a student who was already publishing a book on the subject. I then mentioned my interest in free Negroes, which I had done some work on as an undergraduate. He thought the area needed extensive research and encouraged me to pursue it. He then indicated to me that while he would be pleased to continue as my adviser, he had a large number of graduate students in the dissertation stage and his ability to offer individual attention was limited. He wondered, therefore, if I would be willing to "take on" a younger member of the department, Paul Herman Buck, who was working on the history of the South, the area of my expressed interest, and who had just won the Pulitzer Prize for his book *The Road to Reunion*.

I had seen Paul Buck in the stacks of Widener Library but had never met him. Professor Schlesinger said that he would be happy to introduce me to him but reiterated that if I was not interested he would understand and would supervise my dissertation himself. I told him that I would be pleased to meet with Buck and, if he was willing to do so, would be happy to have him supervise my dissertation. Indeed, I decided that I would look him up myself and request that he serve as my supervisor. Having a subject worth pursuing and one that I could discuss at length, I was ready to track down Professor Buck.

When I went to see my prospective adviser, he greeted me cordially, immediately putting me at ease. I told him that I was generally familiar with the history of the South and would like to write a doctoral dissertation on free Negroes in North Carolina. He said that he would be pleased to advise me during the writing of my dissertation but on one condition, about which he was quite firm. I had to agree that I would never attend his lectures on the history of the South, because he was certain that I knew more about the subject than he did. I replied that much as I would like to hear his lectures, I would respect his wishes. With that, he became my adviser. His first task was to get me through the general oral examinations, and I promised him that I would devote virtually all of my time studying for the tests, which we agreed should be held in February or March 1939.

Upon the completion of my course work in the spring of 1938, I had fulfilled Harvard's PhD residence requirements. I had passed the two language examinations, in French and German, that were required of all candidates for the degree. Ahead of me lay the general oral examination, the dissertation, and the final oral examination. I took the summer off, went to Nashville to teach summer school at Fisk, and then continued on to Tulsa to visit my family.

In late August I was back in Cambridge for my final year of residence. I would audit the course in American constitutional law taught by Professor Henry A. Yeomans, to satisfy an outside field, and I would audit the course on the history of the American colonies and another on the American Revolution, both taught by Professor Samuel Eliot Morison, back from the Columbus voyage. For the history of the South, I would prepare myself as best I could since I had promised Professor Buck that I would not audit his course.

I had learned from experience that it was wise to inquire of the professor of an audited class if he wished me to do anything other than attend the lectures and read the assignments. Professor Yeomans, a courtly elderly gentleman, was gracious in offering advice. When he learned that constitutional law would be a field for my upcoming oral examination, he suggested that I augment the class work by visiting him from time to time to discuss any points of the law that I found confusing. Those sessions with Professor Yeomans proved very helpful.

Professor Morison's teaching assistant suggested that I call on Morison as early as possible in the year, to tell him that I had taken Professor Nettels's course and would be offering American colonial history as a field for my general oral examination. Following Morison's first lecture of the term, I was second in line to see him. The young man ahead of me followed Professor Morison into his office; without closing the door, the professor asked him what he wanted. The student replied that he was from the University of Chicago, where he was a graduate student and was trying to decide on a dissertation subject. His interest was in an area Professor Morison was expert in, and his adviser at Chicago had urged him to seek Morison's advice before proceeding. Morison then asked what he wished to know. When the student hesitated in his response, Morison asked him to go home, write it out, and return and read it to him. The student blanched, saying he had to register at Chicago the following day. Morison replied that was not his problem and bade the unfortunate student good-bye.

Concluding that Professor Morison was out of sorts that day, I departed along with the Chicago student. Following the next lecture, I again went to see Professor Morison. He greeted me with a smile, invited me in, and asked how he could be of assistance. I spoke rapidly, without hesitation. I told him that I had taken the Nettels course and planned to offer colonial history as a field for my orals. I asked him what else I should do aside from auditing his lectures and reading his assignments. He replied that he had seen me in his course, and he encouraged me to continue to do what I was doing. He assured me that if I did that I should have no difficulty with the orals. I thanked him, pleased not only with the answer but with the successful interview.

As I left, he called out to me that he descended from "good abolitionist stock." That patronizing remark stopped me in my tracks. How was I to understand it? Was it intended to put me at my ease, assure me that I could rely on him to understand any shortcomings I might have? Was I to expect different treatment from him, different grades, different expectations? Did he anticipate different behavior from me? I did not turn around, said nothing at all, and departed his office. I can only attest that Professor Morison's remarks not only led me to judge him more critically, but further led me to decide that, absent a transparent meritocracy, I must ever more decidedly demonstrate my abilities as a scholar.

The biggest event of the fall had nothing to do with Harvard. It was the great New England hurricane that struck on September 21, casting a shadow over the next several months. Heading home from Widener Library, I found myself walking into the strongest wind I had ever faced. As I went down Broadway I could hardly make my way, and the going became more and more difficult. When I saw a tree come out of the ground, I realized that I was in physical danger. I ran the remaining distance to my rooming house and did not venture out until the next afternoon.

There was no effective hurricane warning system in 1938, so the entire east coast of the United States was caught unawares. While the damage in the Boston area was extensive, it was not nearly as great as in the rural portions of New England. A class-A hurricane, it killed 600 people, felled some 275 million trees, seriously damaged 200,000 buildings, and left an estimated $600 million in damages. After the scattered, uprooted trees were cleared in the Harvard area, we students returned to our normal, if rather humdrum, existence.

Life went on. Professor Yeomans was as helpful as ever, and if his ex-

planations were not always clear, his efforts to make them so won my admiration. Meanwhile, Morison wound up describing in great detail the
problems of sailing in the fifteenth century but rarely spoke of America's
early history. The common quip among his students was that while we celebrated our own Thanksgiving in November 1938, Morison's Pilgrims had
not yet reached the Bay Colony! And in my spare time I audited courses in
the law school.

In addition to having befriended several law students, I had a deep interest in constitutional law, taught at Harvard by the renowned Thomas
Reed Powell, and I also wanted to hear some of the other great law school
faculty. Among them were Roscoe Pound, the former dean, who would
lecture on jurisprudence, and Erwin Griswold, a future dean, who taught
conflict of laws. Surely the professor who excited the most interest during
my year of auditing was Felix Frankfurter, lecturing on jurisdiction and
procedure of the federal courts.

This was the year that President Franklin D. Roosevelt nominated
Frankfurter to the United States Supreme Court. From the time the Senate
took up his nomination to the day of his confirmation, some of us kept a
vigil by attending each meeting of his class in order to be present when he
made his farewell speech to his students. On January 17, 1939, Professor
Powell came to the door of the lecture hall with a slip of paper in his hand.
From our seats in the last row, we could see Powell as he descended the
steps of the amphitheater. When he handed the slip to Frankfurter and
whispered something to him, Frankfurter, who had been badgering a student with one question after another, became silent. By that time the newspaper reporters and photographers were crowding into the rear of the
room, near us. Only then did Professor Frankfurter inform the class that
word had just come to him that he had been confirmed by the Senate for a
seat on the Supreme Court. He announced to the gathered crowd that
though he would be soon leaving for Washington, his heart would remain
in Cambridge. And he wished his students success in their studies and in
their careers.

As he departed, so did we, electing to audit no more lectures on jurisdiction and procedure of the federal courts.

Throughout the winter I continued to study for my general oral examination, which was now set for February 15, 1939. On the appointed day,

Paul Buck presided over his first general examination. In addition to him, there were Professors Morison; David Owen, who had succeeded Professor Abbott; and Benjamin Wright in the place of Professor Yeomans, who was indisposed. The examination went well enough until Professor Wright began to examine me. He asked simple, elementary questions that I had not expected: the date of the Dred Scott decision, the dissent in *Plessy v. Ferguson*, and the membership of the first Supreme Court. While they were questions I should have known, they were not calculated to plumb the depth of my understanding of the field, and I was completely thrown off. By the time Wright had completed his questions, I was exhausted and not a little fearful.

When the examination was over and I had been congratulated—for what, I wondered—Professor Wright made it clear to me that I was a competent student of constitutional law. The reasons for his unorthodox questions only slowly became clear. He wondered why I had audited Yeomans's course and had not even bothered to consult his own reading list. He left no doubt as to the superiority of his approach to the field over that of Yeomans. In time it became clear to me that the department would have long since dropped Yeomans's course if he had not been one of President A. Lawrence Lowell's oldest and closest friends. Wright had taken my orals as an opportunity to further demonstrate that Professor Yeomans was redundant, a fact everyone seemed to appreciate but me. If there was a silver lining to this inappropriate exercise of inner-departmental competition, it was this: It was so typically Harvard. Though Professor Wright's behavior had accrued nothing to the glory of the institution, I could honestly read it as evidence of the even-handed approach the committee had taken toward my examination.

Paul Buck was pleased with my performance and advised me to make plans for the research stage of my dissertation. He wondered if I would like to apply for another fellowship or even a coveted traveling fellowship. I did not. I wanted to get away from Cambridge and Boston as soon as possible.

In a great many respects, the two and a half years I had spent there had been stifling. I was greatly disturbed by Harvard's prevalent anti-Semitism so blatantly evident in Oscar Handlin's rejection as a possible officer in the Henry Adams Club, an event that awakened me not only to the fact that whites discriminated among themselves, but to the extent of that discrimination throughout Harvard. I had also begun to wonder why I had never been offered a teaching assistantship, especially since I had performed at the very top of both of my seminars and in some of the lecture courses. I was grateful for my fellowship, which gave me much more time for my studies, but I had taught only one year and a summer at Fisk and one summer at A. and T. College in Greensboro. I needed more teaching experience, which, it was hard for me not to conclude, Harvard had denied me because of my color.

There were other reasons for my desire to quit Cambridge. I had been greatly offended by Professor Morison's hint that I would receive preferential treatment on account of his descending from "good abolitionist stock." The potential capriciousness of the faculty was underscored when I heard of a doctoral committee flunking a Southern white candidate whose drawl and unprepossessing appearance convinced them that he did not *look* like a Harvard PhD. Finally, I found the pretension of some of the students reprehensible. I did not so much mind the spoiled undergraduates who came to the Pi Eta Club seeking release from their boredom. They were acting in the manner to which they had been raised—in Bronxville, the Hamptons, or the North Shore. However, I did mind the graduate students who attempted to emulate the habits and conduct of the professors, walking and talking like them, as though that would establish their intellectual worth and win their admission to nirvana, a teaching post at dear old Harvard.

I would, somehow, support myself in my dissertation year, perhaps by finding a teaching job and getting more experience in the classroom. Regardless, I was determined to go.

As I said my farewells at Harvard, Cambridge, and Boston, I was ready to depart for North Carolina to begin my research on free Negroes during the antebellum period. First, however, I would stop at Hampton Institute in Virginia, where Aurelia had, at long last, enrolled in the Library School the previous autumn. It was a source of great pleasure to both of us that she had been finally able to go to graduate school. Her sister Bertha had graduated from Fisk the previous spring, and her brother Sam had graduated from Johnson C. Smith University and was now employed. The siblings being settled, Aurelia no longer felt that she had to "be there" in the event of a family emergency; at long last she could leave her teaching job and her parents' home to continue her studies. Her father, whom I had never met, continued to work as a supervisor in the railway mail service, and her mother, an alumna of Livingstone College and a talented musician, continued her duties as homemaker and seamstress for her daughters.

Able to get away from Cambridge a few days earlier than expected, I rushed to Hampton. It was a joyous reunion after more than fifteen months of separation, though Aurelia was somewhat embarrassed to tell me that she had a dinner and dance date planned for that first evening. When she stated her wish to cancel, I would hear nothing of the kind. Long ago we had agreed that until the time came when we could commit ourselves to each other, we were free to go out with a friend or friends. She kept her date while I rested and thought on my plans for tomorrow.

From the moment I purchased an engagement ring from a Cambridge jeweler, my excitement increased. On the one hand, Aurelia and I had for so long understood that we loved each other and intended to marry that I was supremely confident, so much so that not only did her dinner date that evening not concern me, but I had purchased a wedding ring especially designed to go with the engagement ring. On the other hand, having both rings in my possession gave me a sense of premature elation. The dual purchase made the wedding seem imminent, thus adding to the significance of the moment when I would offer Aurelia the engagement ring.

Thus the happiest moment of my brief visit came that subsequent evening after an excellent dinner in Magnolia Cottage, where I was staying. Finding a quiet place in the lounge, I suggested to Aurelia that we could now plan for the future if she was at all interested in doing so. Soon, I proclaimed with confidence, I would complete my doctorate and could settle into a decent job. At the end of the current year, I continued, she would obtain her degree in library science. And at that point I offered her the engagement ring that I had brought, asking her to wear it as a symbol of our commitment. Overjoyed, she accepted it. While we postponed making specific plans until we were clear on what we would be doing the following year, I left for Raleigh feeling happier than I had ever been and highly motivated to earn my doctorate and secure a job as quickly as possible.

Upon my arrival in Raleigh, I went to the Arcade Hotel, operated by Plummer and Cora Hall. It was widely known as one of the few places, if not the only place, between Richmond and Atlanta where African Americans could use a restroom and be served a decent meal. Greeting me warmly, the Halls regretted that they could not accommodate me for an extended stay and recommended a place where I could secure a room. I thanked them and promised that I would see them for dinner.

The Cabarrus Street residence of Mrs. Alice Carrington Jones, recently widowed and a teacher in the public schools of Raleigh, was very pleasant. I could stay as long as I wished, Mrs. Jones assured me. Furthermore, she proclaimed her home was my home, and I was therefore not confined to my room. I unpacked, had "a sociable cup of tea" with Mrs. Jones, and explored the neighborhood. I was delighted to realize that I was within walking distance of downtown Raleigh and Capital Square, where I would be doing my research.

On the following Monday I walked to the state education building that housed the State Department of Archives and History. I asked to see the director, and when Christopher C. Crittenden appeared, I introduced myself and told him my research subject. Crittenden, a PhD in history from Yale, assured me that the archives had relevant materials but admitted quite frankly that in planning the building the architects had never anticipated that any African American would ever do research there. He readily granted that I had a right to do so and suggested that I return within a week, during which he would make some arrangements. When he saw my astonishment and disbelief, he cut the waiting time in half.

The following Thursday, I was escorted to a small room across from the large whites-only research room. It had been outfitted with a table, chair, and wastebasket and was to be my private office for an indefinite period of time. Crittenden also presented me with keys to the stacks of the manuscript collection, this to avoid my requiring the white assistants to deliver manuscripts to me. So situated, I began my work. The stacks were a veritable gold mine. I would emerge from them with my cart overloaded with boxes, rolling it through the whites-only research room en route to my private room across the hall. The arrangement lasted only two weeks, after which the white researchers, protesting discrimination, demanded keys to the manuscript collection for themselves. Rather than comply with their demands, which would have created chaos in the stacks, the director relieved me of my keys and ordered the assistants to serve me.

Over time I would come to realize that nothing illustrated the absurdities of racial segregation better than Southern archives and libraries. In Raleigh, the state library had two tables in the stacks set aside for African American readers. The state supreme court library had no segregation at all, while the state archives solved the problem on an ad hoc basis. I had already seen that the state archives in Tennessee did not segregate users, and Alabama had a similar policy. In Louisiana, in 1945, I was permitted by the director of the archives to use the collection, from which African Americans were usually barred, simply because they were otherwise closed in celebration of the United States' victory over Germany and Japan.

As my research progressed satisfactorily, I began to venture out into the city and in time became acquainted with people at St. Augustine's College, one of Raleigh's two African American institutions of higher learning. A Fisk classmate, Louis Roberts, taught physics there, and it was through him that I learned St. Augustine's was seeking a history teacher. Miss Jessie Guernsey, who had been the only person there in that field for the past thirty years, was retiring, and they were looking for someone to take her place. Securing a teaching job in Raleigh, where I was deeply immersed in my research, would be ideal. I made an appointment with the Reverend Edgar H. Gould, the president, who was white, as for that matter was Miss Guernsey, and presented him with my credentials. In due course, he offered me the job, which I accepted immediately. Pleased, Miss Guernsey, who implied that it would be good for the students to have one of their own as their history teacher, graciously gave me books and briefed me on the courses she had taught for such a long time. I was deeply grateful.

Having secured a position in Raleigh, I thought that I should do as much out-of-town research as possible before the beginning of the term in September. In order to compile all the names of free Negroes in North Carolina, a visit to the Library of Congress and the Bureau of the Census was high on my list. That year, 1939, was well before the widespread use of microfilm, and the bureau was the only place where I could secure the complete inventory of names. So after a very profitable spring and summer, I went to Washington in late July.

I knew what a treasure trove the unpublished census schedules would be, and I resolved to work on them as soon as I could. So, armed with some surplus funds from my Rosenwald fellowship and a very favorable rental arrangement in Washington secured with the assistance of Mrs. Alice Jones, I enlisted the aid of Roy Wilson, my boyhood friend from Tulsa and a fellow graduate from Fisk, to assist me in reviewing the records. While Roy awaited the start of his teaching job in the fall at Delaware State College in Dover, I agreed to provide him room and board in Washington in return for his help. For several weeks Roy and I worked each day, all day, at the Bureau of the Census, guided graciously by Joseph Houchins, the specialist in Negro statistics at the bureau. It is virtually impossible to describe my feelings as I worked through the records in Washington. Not only was I doing research for the first time among some of the country's finest resources, but I was making my way as an independent scholar. While Roy was my constant companion and helper, I took the initiative in deciding on what we should do, where we should go, where we should look, and whether the sources were worth our time. These activities were most satisfying and were a foretaste of the career that awaited me. After a very rewarding summer, it was back to Raleigh not only to continue my research but also to prepare for my classes at St. Augustine's.

I was assigned a room in the men's dormitory and a place in the teachers' dining room, where I could take my meals as part of my compensation. Several other faculty members and university staff likewise took their meals in the dining room, and without question it was an economical arrangement that introduced me to life on campus. Given my meager salary, which I was determined to stretch as far as possible even while setting something aside in expectation of marrying Aurelia, I was grateful for the room and board. But I missed seeing Mrs. Alice Jones, our occasional sociable teas, and particularly the easy walk from her home to the state archives. From St. Augustine's I would have to take a bus, which was, of course, segregated. That was of little consequence, however. The bus to the archives went through black neighborhoods. Only the very rare white person ever boarded it, though the first seat was generally reserved for him or her. Yet another illustration of Jim Crow absurdity were those routinely empty bus seats awaiting their white passengers.

While the teaching load at St. Augustine's was no heavier than what I had at Fisk, it was still heavier than one person should have been expected to bear. In addition to the survey in Western civilization and the year-long course in European history, I taught the history of the United States from the colonial period to the present and an advanced course for seniors on various topics of United States history. Except for the survey course, which was required, the number of students attending each class was not very large. Thus, although the preparation was quite demanding, the burden of grading papers was not. My students seemed eager to learn, and I encouraged them as much as I could to read extensively in each subject, and while not as sophisticated or as worldly as those at Fisk, the students were earnest and hardworking.

In the autumn of 1939, what kind of future they were preparing themselves for was an open question. As of late August, it was already clear that Europe was, once again, readying for war. By September, in rapid succession Germany invaded Poland, England and France declared war on Germany, and President Roosevelt declared American neutrality. But the memory of American involvement in World War I, the increasing signs of American military preparedness, and our ever sharper confrontations with Japan in the Pacific left little doubt in my mind that American participation in the world war just then breaking out was a possibility. I found myself very much disturbed, even agitated, for I not only opposed wars in general, but I felt quite vulnerable. At twenty-four years of age and very eligible for any military draft, there was no doubt in my mind that it was quite feasible that I could be called to some kind of military service.

I allowed neither the heavy class load nor the fretting about the possibility of being drafted to deter me from pushing ahead with my doctoral dissertation. With the exceptionally able assistance of one of my more mature students, Robert Clarke, I made steady progress. For her part, Aurelia completed her work on schedule and graduated in May 1939 with a bachelor of science degree in library science. Moreover, she had the good fortune to secure the job of librarian at Dillard High School in Goldsboro, from which she herself had graduated. Her parents were overjoyed to have her once more living at home and employed in a position to which they attached great importance. Indeed, from their point of view she could not possibly have found a better post. I too was pleased. Goldsboro was only fifty miles from Raleigh. Although I would have to conform to the train schedule, I would be able to visit Aurelia regularly, although by then it was slowly becoming clear to me that Aurelia's parents were not entirely pleased with my increasingly regular visits.

Unwilling to depend on the train, I began to think seriously of purchasing an automobile, which would assist me, moreover, in arranging my research schedule. I soon found a Chevrolet that I could afford, but obtaining insurance was much more difficult. Very few insurance companies would insure the automobiles of African Americans, for the simple reason that in case of an accident, the car's owner was unlikely to receive equal justice in the courts. After some diligent effort, I was finally able to secure liability insurance and to drive my recently purchased automobile. Suddenly, I was free to spend a few hours on the occasional Sunday or holiday with Aurelia.

Aurelia's parents seemed not to smile on the ease with which I could now visit their daughter in Goldsboro. I persisted, however, eager that Aurelia and I be able to discuss our marriage and even possible dates for our wedding. All the while Aurelia insisted that there be no discussion with her family about such matters. She would handle that herself. In hindsight, this should have clearly indicated to me that there was mounting resistance to our engagement from her parents, but at the time I simply refused to reach that conclusion. Forced to be content with her proviso, I pressed us to make plans for the upcoming summer and the following year.

Then, the bombshell dropped. In early April I received a letter from Aurelia informing me that she could not go through with our marriage. She could not, she insisted, leave her parents, and consequently she would retain her job at Dillard High School and make the most out of life in Goldsboro. I was stunned. The confidence that had guided my steps from the Cambridge jeweler to the moment of my proposing to Aurelia at the Magnolia Cottage had evaporated. In its place was bewilderment: Since we had first known each other as undergraduates at Fisk, Aurelia and I had expressed our love and intention, once the opportunity to do so arose, to live our lives together. Her letter and explanation were insufficient. I immediately drove to Goldsboro, arriving there in the late afternoon.

When I rang the bell, her mother answered the door. I told her as calmly as I could that I wished to see Aurelia. She called Aurelia, who came into the living room; her mother and father assumed seats on the stairs just off the living room. From there they could listen to our conversation and, better still, ensure that my upset did not turn violent. I truly hope that they were not apprehensive, though I am sure I must have worn on my face the depth of my disappointment and the shock of having the life I had so long anticipated upended. Seeing that Aurelia was firm in her determination, I arose to depart. She offered me the ring that I had given her at Hampton. I declined, managing in what I hope was a steady voice to suggest that she keep it for old time's sake.

Heartbroken, I returned to Raleigh, allowing my work to consume me as never before. My family was also attempting to come to terms with my sudden break with Aurelia. When I had initially announced our engagement, they had been delighted that at twenty-four years of age I would soon abandon the life of a bachelor. Sister was especially pleased, and had offered her assistance in any way possible. My father had been overjoyed that there would soon be another member of our family. When I informed them that the engagement had been ended, they offered their sympathy and sought an explanation. I struggled to provide them with one, but being uncertain as to what had caused Aurelia to write her letter to me in April I could only offer general answers. Sister felt the break was a family rebuff, and she was not pleased. My father, however, was more concerned for me. He had sensed some incoherence in my letter to him announcing my changed expectations and he had replied that while he regretted the break, he was anxious that I not let it get the better of me. In part following his advice, and in part to keep myself busy, I allowed the dissertation and the college to preoccupy me.

Then, in mid-May, I received a call from Aurelia. Could I come down? she asked. The following day, a Saturday, I went to Goldsboro and met Aurelia away from her parents' home. She told me simply that when the Dillard High School contract for the next year had been offered to her, she could see herself signing such contracts for the next fifty years. That was not the life she wanted. What she wanted was a life with me.

We began then and there to make our own plans. She said that she would announce to her parents that we would be married on June 11, 1940, and that she wished the ceremony to be held in their living room, if they would permit it. They accepted her decision, and we planned a very simple wedding with fewer than a dozen friends present.

I arose very early on Tuesday, June 11. We were to be married at seven-thirty in the morning, and so, armed with Aurelia's corsage, I drove to Goldsboro. I arrived shortly before the scheduled service, to be performed by Aurelia's pastor. She had made no request of her parents for a repast of any sort, but there was punch and cake. After the ceremony, we said our farewells and were off to Washington for a honeymoon of sorts.

We were never happier than in the hours immediately following our departure. A bridal suite was never more spectacular or beautiful than the room at the Rappahannock Hotel in Fredericksburg, Virginia, or the one at the Whitelaw Hotel in Washington, D.C. This was one of the few places in the nation's capital where African Americans could find accommodations in 1940. It was far from opulent, and, indeed, some referred to it in a jocular vein as the Outlaw Hotel, but that made no difference to us newlyweds. With our brief honeymoon over, I was ready on the morning of June 17 to complete the task of listing the free Negroes of North Carolina from the manuscripts in the Bureau of the Census. With Aurelia at my side, working at least as hard as I was, we completed the task shortly and soon we were on our way to Cambridge, where I would begin writing my dissertation. If ever Aurelia regretted the transformation of our first days as husband and wife into a working honeymoon, she never made mention of it.

7

Newly Minted

WE WERE WARMLY RECEIVED in Cambridge by my new land-lady, Mrs. Rosa Carter, the widowed sister of my former next-door neighbor. Mr. Clark, my former landlord at 415 Broadway, had passed away, and his surviving sister no longer lived at that address. Mrs. Carter opened her entire home to Aurelia, who felt very much at ease in our new quarters.

Once we settled in, however, I was ready to begin writing my dissertation. The principal reason for our being in Cambridge that summer was to give me ample opportunity to consult with Paul Buck as I began to write. Beyond advising me, Dr. Buck and his wife, Sally, welcomed us into their home several times during the summer, as did the Schlesingers. On one occasion, when we were having dinner at the Schlesingers', along with the Bucks, Paul wandered off with Aurelia, and they became involved in a protracted and animated conversation. Much later and after some prod-ding, Aurelia told me what they had talked of. Professor Buck was already convinced that I was headed for a significant career as a historian and public servant. Confessing to being rather presumptuous, he ventured the opinion that I was worth watching, especially from the vantage point of a spouse. He hoped that Aurelia would do everything to encourage me and work to remove any obstacles she found in my path. She assured him that not only would she do everything she could to assist me but that she was already long in that habit. I was deeply grateful to her and to him for their confidence in me, even as I questioned whether it was deserved.

From the time that we were undergraduates, I knew that Aurelia had great faith in me. She had indicated it on more than one occasion. It was, nevertheless, sheer optimism on the part of Buck, I thought, to have the opinion that I possessed bright prospects on the basis of a few conversations and what I deemed a less than stellar performance on the preliminary oral examinations. I was more determined than ever not to disappoint Aurelia and to live up to Buck's expectations.

For the next two months I worked virtually every day, outlining my dissertation and writing the first two chapters. At times I worked in our own room, though much of the time I went to Widener Library, usually accompanied by Aurelia. She either worked alongside me or visited some exhibit in the library or at the Fogg Art Museum, only a few steps away. As a newly minted librarian, she was keen to observe the organization and administration of a vast enterprise such as Widener. There were breaks for our social life. We particularly enjoyed the Charles River Pops concerts by the Boston Symphony Orchestra, but overwhelmingly my time was spent feverishly working on the first draft of my manuscript.

In early August, as we began to say our farewells and prepared to leave for our new home in Raleigh, Paul Buck promised that he would read my manuscript as quickly as I could get it to him. Indeed, he would read it chapter by chapter, if I so desired. I could not have been more grateful to him for his enthusiasm and support.

After making stops at the Whitelaw Hotel in Washington and, for sentimental reasons, the Rappahannock Hotel in Fredericksburg, we made our way to Raleigh to move into our new quarters. St. Augustine's College had provided us with a three-room apartment on the first floor of the men's dormitory, the Lyman Building, in which I had lived during my first year there. We had our own separate entrance and were just across from the Cheshire Building in which the faculty dining hall was located. Though I had not received a raise at the end of my first year, my "in kind" raise was substantial: We were given the use of the apartment, and Aurelia was permitted to take her meals in the faculty dining room, all at no cost.

Before arriving in Raleigh from Cambridge, we had heard that the librarian's position at the Washington High School in Raleigh was open. Aurelia immediately applied and was appointed almost as quickly. Although the high school was across town, that presented no difficulty, for she could use our car; by then my research required me to go to the archives or the state library only infrequently, and I had already become accustomed to riding the bus downtown.

Though my teaching load remained five classes and five preparations, I was determined to complete the dissertation with as much dispatch as possible. By then, my habits of disciplined work were ingrained, but it was not habit alone that had me pressing myself so hard. I had two powerful impetuses to push myself even harder. The first was how near I was to securing my doctorate from Harvard. Whatever mixed opinions I had of the school, I was keenly aware of what the degree would mean. It was a mark of distinction, without question, and for a black man in the 1930s all the more so. That a host of people, from my parents and siblings to most particularly my dear friend Ted Currier, eagerly expected that distinction to be conferred on me was never far from my mind. My second impetus, however, was much more pragmatic. I was newly married in a world increasingly at war and in a country where my race put me at routine disadvantage. My ambition to succeed at Harvard was increasingly an ambition to do all I could to attain the skills that would better protect me and Aurelia in an unsafe and racially unjust world.

I set up a writing schedule of two hours in the evening and eight hours each day on weekends. I adhered to it, with virtually no exceptions. My student Bob Clarke had become so adept at looking up materials at the archives and the library that I frequently sent him to obtain information I needed so that I could write without interruption. Soon I was taking Paul Buck up on his offer to read my work chapter by chapter. In the twenty-first century, it is difficult to appreciate how efficient the train service was some sixty years ago. In the fall and winter of 1940–41, I could send a chapter to Paul Buck on Monday morning, he would receive it on Tuesday, read it on Wednesday, mail it to me on Thursday, and I would have it back, with his corrections and/or suggestions, by Friday morning. The train schedules and the fact that Paul Buck was burdened with no other dissertation students to oversee all worked in my favor.

Only once during the autumn did I break my intense work schedule and engage in an activity that was for pure pleasure: I made Aurelia dinner. She was off paying her parents her first visit since our return from Cambridge, and I decided to greet her with a home-cooked dinner by candlelight. Though we had one hot plate and a small electric oven that permitted me to prepare only one item at a time, I was determined to serve the meal in our apartment. The menu was relatively simple: spinach soufflé, which I had never prepared before; macaroni and cheese, which I had never prepared before; and a small beef roast, which I had never prepared before. Dessert would be a fresh fruit compote, which I also had never prepared before. The wisest thing I did on that Monday morning was to rise early. By the time I was to meet Aurelia at the railroad station, the meal was taking shape. Upon our return to the apartment, I had only to arrange the flowers on the small table and light the candles. A five-star restaurant maître d' could not have been as proud as I was of that production, particularly given Aurelia's compliments to the chef.

Another pleasant interlude occurred that late autumn. Paul and Sally Buck paid us an unexpected visit. During the Thanksgiving holidays, which they spent exploring a part of the South, they decided to look me up as they passed through Raleigh. I was greatly surprised—and honored. Unfortunately, they did not have time to see Aurelia or stay for more than a midday visit and I led them to the only public place in Raleigh where the three of us could sit down together for a meal. Mr. and Mrs. Hall, at the Arcade Hotel dining room, were so delighted that I had brought my guests to their place that they insisted on providing the meals with their compliments. The Bucks had at long last witnessed real Southern hospitality, and they could not have been more pleased.

Otherwise, the work on my dissertation proceeded apace. My teaching, however, was an ongoing struggle. I was not distracted by the dissertation as much as I was by my having to shift from medieval to modern European history, from colonial to recent American history, from a survey of civilization to a survey of Latin American history, from large lecture courses to small reading courses or seminars. I hit up against the limitations not only of my training but also of my capacity to fulfill the needs of the students, whose backgrounds and education differed so significantly. My time, talents, and capacity to work were sorely pressed.

Once I got past administering and grading the final examinations for the fall semester, however, there were no obstacles to my completing the dissertation, getting it up to Paul Buck and the graduate school office, and preparing for my own final examination. Aurelia and I managed to send the completed dissertation to Cambridge in mid-April, nicely ahead of the May 1 deadline. That gave Paul Buck and his colleagues ample time to schedule the test so that the paperwork and all requirements could be completed well before commencement. After Paul announced his satisfaction with the manuscript, he advised me to make plans for the final oral examination, which he and his colleagues set for May 19, 1941.

The moment that date was fixed, Aurelia and I began to make our plans. By this time, the St. Augustine campus, and especially my colleagues, was abuzz regarding the possibility that the faculty might soon have its first PhD in the history of the college. Given the mounting attention directed at me, Aurelia and I decided to keep my travel plans to ourselves. The fear was that I might not pass. Since the examination was set for a Monday, I would go up to Cambridge on Sunday, after the final meal in the faculty dining room, which was always at midday. Aurelia would then avoid the dining room until Monday evening, at which time she could honestly say where I was and what the outcome of the examination had been, for I would call her by telephone the moment it was over.

The examination, set for two o'clock Monday afternoon, would cover the period in which my dissertation was set—and much more. The dates for which I was responsible extended from 1789 to the present. The prospect was daunting, to say the least. For some reason I concluded that it was important for me to be quite familiar with Thomas Bailey's just published *Diplomatic History of the American People*. The problem was finding a copy of the book. No bookstore in Raleigh, Durham, or Chapel Hill had a copy. No copies were available at any college in Raleigh. I tried Duke and the University of North Carolina, but their copies were out. By this time, the search for Bailey's book had become nothing short of an obsession, and I concluded that if I was unable to find and read it before the examination, I was sure to fail. My final ploy was to go quietly into Cambridge, avoid the university until moments before the examination, go to the Boston Public Library as soon as it opened on Monday morning, and read the Bailey book, or as much of it as I could. Alas, that Monday morning I discovered that the Boston Public Library's copy was out. All that I could then do was to go to Widener Library, steal quietly into the stacks, take down a copy of Bailey, find a quiet, secluded place, and read until two p.m. There, at last, was the book! Although I did not have much time, I sat down to read.

At that point I heard a voice calling my name. It was Professor Schlesinger. He had been looking everywhere for me. He had expected a call. He said that if that was a book in my hands, I should be reading nothing since my examination was less than two hours away. In any case, he wished to take me to lunch and talk about my dissertation and other things. Feeling helpless, I accepted his gracious invitation, Bailey went back on the shelf, and off I went with Schlesinger, certain that in doing so I had sealed my own fate.

As a jovial "Professor S" spoke of how delighted he was that I had completed the work for the PhD degree, I thought of the impending examination and of my ignorance of the contents of Bailey. He spoke of my dissertation, which he had read in its entirety and declared was publishable without any revisions at all. He stood ready to recommend it to any publisher that I would suggest. He then asked me quite candidly if I had had any notion, at the outset, when, if ever, I would receive a PhD. I answered in the negative, the specter of Bailey before me. He then declared that during my first semester at Harvard he had known that I would receive the degree. Based on my performance in his seminar, he had been certain of it. I said to myself that I only wished that I had known as much.

Paul Buck presided over the final examination. The other members of the committee of three were Professors Schlesinger and Richard W. Leopold. The latter was a junior member of the department who had been enlisted to lecture in American diplomatic history when James Phinney Baxter left to become president of Williams College. Buck opened the examination by indicating that he had supervised my dissertation and that I already knew of his enthusiastic approval of what I had done. He then asked for other opinions. Professor Schlesinger indicated that over lunch he had told me that the manuscript was worthy of publication and that he had no further comments. Leopold indicated that he had not read the manuscript and would have no comments. That left almost two hours to be filled; my only thought was that I had not read Bailey, and the disaster would begin.

As I thought of that dire possibility, Richard Leopold made a proposal that would take up considerable time. He asked me hypothetically to accept an invitation from Oxford University to give six lectures on American labor history. What would be the subjects of the lectures, how would they be organized, and what would be the principal sources on which I would rely in writing them? Since I regarded that as a playful question, I saw no reason why I should not "play" with it. This was the beginning of a delightful conversation between Leopold and me that must have lasted for the better part of an hour and in which the other members of the committee joined. Other questions had to do with my plans for further research and what I hoped to do in the way of writing and teaching. The entire exercise was most pleasant. Two hours later, I had survived the entire examination without Bailey or his book having been mentioned. My committee made it clear that I had more than survived—I had done credit to myself and to Harvard.

When Aurelia went to the dining room on Monday evening, May 19, she was immediately confronted with questions about my whereabouts. She answered calmly that I had gone to Cambridge to take my final examinations. When asked if I had passed them, she said even more calmly that I had indeed. Immediately, there were celebrations and congratulations. By the time I returned the following day, word had spread over the city, to the friends with whom I lived when I first came to Raleigh, to colleagues not only at St. Augustine's but at Shaw University as well. One would have thought that some great and good fortune had visited large numbers of people, but it was merely that a friend had qualified for the highest degree at the oldest university in the country. No African Americans in Raleigh or, indeed, in North Carolina had previously reached that point, and it was a time for rejoicing all around.

Not everyone was delighted. When the Reverend Edgar H. Gould, the president of St. Augustine's College, learned about my recent trip to Harvard, he sent for me. He asked if it was true that I was about to receive the degree of doctor of philosophy from Harvard. I answered in the affirmative. He then asked, in a tone of incredulity, what remained for me to do in order to receive the degree. I answered that I merely had to be present for the conferring of the degree on June 19, but if I chose not to be present, the degree would be mailed to me. Then, to my great astonishment, Reverend Gould launched into an admonishing lecture. He reminded me that no one at St. Augustine's College held such a degree from any institution, and the holder of the PhD degree at St. Augustine's College would have to be extremely careful, even modest, in his conduct and relationships with others. It would be entirely possible, in Reverend Gould's estimation, that I might now be overbearing and intolerant of those who did not possess such credentials, and such conceit and impatience with others on my part would be, at best, reprehensible. I should be careful, he sententiously continued, to make certain that I showed the proper patience and forbearance with my colleagues who may not have as many degrees as I but who had qualities that made them just as valuable to the college.

When I told Aurelia of my "audience" with President Gould, she could scarcely believe that any person, and surely not a man of the cloth as well as an educator, could be so harsh and critical in his strictures. While she was correct in her judgment, I was not quite so put off. Indeed, I was already aware that at least some people tended to belittle the achievements of others, particularly when they were fearful that an individual's accomplishments might overshadow the standing of the institution to which they were affiliated. Indeed, the president had said nothing about the credit that having a PhD on faculty brought to the college, and I had to conclude that he had no interest in celebrating that fact. How much my accomplishment, and the effort and ambitions that clearly stood behind it, personally bothered President Gould I could not fathom, and at the time I ascribed his response solely to an administrator shortsightedly worrying about smooth relations among his faculty. Aurelia and I "considered the source" and, while being careful not to dismiss his tirade out of hand, tended to regard it as one person's reaction, about which we should be mindful, but hardly reason not to fête the event quietly. Aurelia's parents struck the right chord, perhaps, when in their note of congratulations they commented that this was one bridge that we had crossed, but in the future there would be many more.

Once Aurelia had completed her work at Washington High School and I had completed the spring semester at St. Augustine's, we could concentrate on the trip to the Harvard commencement and then to Oklahoma to visit my family. For the graduation ceremony itself, Aurelia's mother had made Aurelia a black silk faille suit of designer quality, with appropriate accessories. As a graduation present for me, Aurelia ordered a cap and gown of black silk bengaline cord, with the Harvard insignia in the proper place.

Any Harvard commencement is an exciting event, although rarely well organized or smoothly run. But the one held June 19, 1941, showed clear signs of the war fever gripping the university. Most of the day's attention was lavished on recipients of honorary degrees, especially those who were, in some way, connected with the incipient preparations for war. University President James B. Conant conferred on Clarence Dykstra, president of the University of Wisconsin, the degree of doctor of law and praised him for being the director of the Selective Service, while he conferred on Ernest O. Lawrence, the director of the Radiation Laboratory at Berkeley, and Vannevar Bush, chairman of the National Defense Research Council, the degree of doctor of science and praised them for their work in fields whose wartime value was obvious. Then he conferred on Lord Halifax, British ambassador to the United States and chancellor of Oxford University, the degree of doctor of law, describing him as an "eminent public servant, representative of a stalwart nation, unyielding before the blows of tyranny." Then he added these words to the citation: "A slowly awakening America acknowledges her debt to the heroism of his countrymen."

Not to be outdone, toward the end of the Harvard commencement, Lord Halifax sought permission to hold a special Oxford convocation for the purpose of conferring on the president of the United States the degree of doctor of civil laws, in absentia. With permission granted, Lord Halifax, attended by a young English page who held up the train of the chancellor's black and gold robe, reentered the outdoor theater and presented the degree to General Edwin Watson, representing President Roosevelt. In conferring the degree, Halifax declared that nothing would make him believe that "the abiding values which Oxford and Harvard shared could go down before so foul and so vile a thing as Nazism has shown itself to be." The message that President Roosevelt sent contained the following words: "In days like these we rejoice that this special convocation, in breaking all historic precedent, does so in the just cause of preserving the free learning and the civil liberties which have grown stone upon stone in our land through the centuries." Thus was my commencement converted into a war rally. Despite the bellicose nature of the Harvard commencement, I could not permit it to dampen the realization that I had completed the first stage of my journey as a scholar-historian. While my mother did not live to see it, my father and the other members of my family fully appreciated what I had done and rejoiced in it. Aurelia, moreover, celebrated the fulfillment of the prophecy that she and Paul Buck had made the previous summer. No one was more pleased than Ted Currier who, while having talent enough to deserve several PhDs but not the discipline to earn one, saw my graduation as the fulfillment of his fondest dream.

After witnessing the ceremonies, I could not help but feel some apprehension about the future. That provided yet another reason for our visit to Oklahoma: It was high time I introduced Aurelia to all my family and friends. Visiting Tulsa in late June 1941 was a unique experience. Having completed my studies at Harvard, I was in a celebratory mood. Aurelia, for her part, well tolerated what at times must have felt more like a public inspection than a friendly introduction. It seemed that everyone wanted to have us to breakfast, brunch, lunch, or dinner, and our greatest burdens quickly became the enormous varieties and quantities of food offered us. An intensely hot summer added to our discomfort. It was not at all uncommon, during the weeks that we were there, for the temperature to reach 110 degrees, and on one occasion it reached 115 degrees!

It was my family I brought Aurelia to visit, and it was my family that I was eager to have her like. My mother, whom she had met at Fisk graduation, had long since passed away. Anne, the other member of the family she knew, was already in graduate school at Howard University and would remain in Washington after graduation. Brother Buck was married to Bessye Wilson, and they were living in their own home some distance from my father. Sister Mozella was married to Waldo E. Jones and had come to live with my father following our mother's death. In a sense, then, Sister was the official hostess, and she took pleasure in seeing to it that

Aurelia was comfortable, that is, as comfortable as was possible in an apartment that was not air-conditioned.

My entire family liked Aurelia immediately, showering her with attention. My father was especially taken with her, and it was almost immediately that he began to call her his favorite "trooper" as she bore up under the scrutiny and heat. In early August we were prepared to take our leave, after thanking many friends, old and new, for their unmatched hospitality.

The trip back to North Carolina took us across Arkansas and Tennessee to North Carolina, our first time traveling due east from Oklahoma. We left Tulsa quite early, and by the middle of the day we were approaching Little Rock, Arkansas. Suddenly, a huge storm arose. There was much thunder and lightning and, perhaps with memories of the 1938 hurricane in mind, I chose not to drive in such weather. At the first house that appeared able to hold more than its inhabitants, we stopped. I was not distressed that the person who answered the door was white. I said to her, quite simply, that I was afraid to drive in such a storm, and I would appreciate it if she would permit me and my wife to come in until it had subsided. Without demur, she cordially welcomed Aurelia and me into the living room. She asked who we were and where were we from. Then she told us that she was the sister of Senator Joe Robinson, the unsuccessful candidate for the vice presidency in 1928. We had managed to pick the home of one of Arkansas's first families. I indicated to her that I was quite familiar with him and his career, and I recited a few incidents in his life that persuaded her that this was indeed true. She offered us lemonade and cookies, which we accepted, and she wondered if Aurelia would like to take a nap. Aurelia assured her that she was well rested. Anyway, by this time the storm had passed over and we were expected in Memphis that evening. We thanked her and bade her farewell. It was a unique experience, and we would never forget it.

We were back in Raleigh in adequate time for Aurelia to return to her duties at Washington High School and for me to resume my course load at St. Augustine's College. The first thing I did upon my return, however, was to call on Christopher Crittenden, the director of the State Department of Archives and History. Just before I went up to Cambridge for commencement, I had dropped off a completed copy of the manuscript on free Negroes and requested that he read it. As I entered his office he congratulated me not only upon receiving my degree but also on the manuscript. He pronounced it ready for publication and expressed the view that it was a "natural" for the University of North Carolina Press. He wondered, therefore, if I would object to his sending it there, where he knew the director. I told him that I would be honored and I assured him that he could get support from Professors Paul Buck and Arthur M. Schlesinger, both of whom thought it worthy of publication. I may be entirely wrong in this calculation, but I have always believed that Christopher Crittenden was pleased to assist me in seeing the book published because of the conditions under which I had had to work at the archives.

I continued to entertain apprehensions about the possibility of the United States becoming involved in a shooting war and what the implications of that would be for me. I had complied with the requirements of the Selective Service Act by registering. In the national lottery, I received a low number, indicating that in case of a draft I would likely be called up early, this despite the fact that I was married. Rather than ponder that possibility, I focused instead on the real likelihood that the newly minted PhD would soon become a published author again. I was already busy, moreover, on another research project that would become at least an article.

Throughout my dissertation research, I had sought an ordinary free Negro, one who had problems, economic and social, and who could, therefore, stand as a case study for the vast majority of free persons of color. In the fall of 1941, while browsing through the card catalog of the archives, I saw a reference to one James Boon, free person of color. I sent for the documents and found that there was sufficient information to make this an intriguing story. Soon, I was deeply involved in the fascinating and satisfying attempt to reconstruct a life and, based on the sources, to endow James Boon with a work ethic, some integrity, and even some emotions.

Toward the end of that paper, which was published in 1945, I made the following comment: "That James Boon lived for at least forty-nine years has great significance for the student of antebellum history. To have the opportunity to know rather intimately the life of a person of his capabilities and his adroitness is a privilege all too frequently denied us by the scarcity or inadequacy of the records. Boon reminds us once more that the history of a nation is to be found not only in the records of victorious battles and in the lives of notable personages but also in the lives of the most humbly born, the most consistently despised, and the most miserably improvident." In 1946, the Boon paper won the Bancroft Prize, having been judged to be the best article published in *The Journal of Negro History* the preceding year.

8

Days of Infamy

THE APPREHENSION THAT I FELT in 1939 was greatly increased as the United States began to express its support for the Allies that were fighting the Axis powers. The Selective Service became a reality in 1940, forcing men of draft age to seriously question their support, neutrality, or opposition to the war effort. Suffice it to say, it was a far more complicated question for African Americans to answer, for every day brought some evidence of our incomplete inclusion in the country we might be called upon to kill and die for. In the fall of 1941 I was not alone in brooding about the possibilities, nor was I indifferent. The war in Europe was broadening to involve, by this time, virtually the entire continent. What was even worse, United States–Japanese relations were deteriorating to the point that war in the Pacific seemed imminent even if we were able to steer clear of a European involvement. And as a historian, I was painfully aware that, going back to the American Revolution, black participation in America's wars had never brought African Americans any meaningful change in their status as second-class citizens. In 1941, nothing suggested this war would be any different.

These were matters about which we chatted during the weekend of December 5, as Louis Roberts, my Fisk classmate and now my colleague at St. Augustine's, and his wife, Mercedes, Aurelia, and I journeyed to

Charleston, South Carolina, to visit another Fisk classmate, Howard Bennett and his bride, Clae. While the international crisis lingered in the background, we had much to discuss about our respective experiences in graduate school and subsequent careers, and conversations were lively, protracted, and wide-ranging. It was a joyous reunion, with some joking as the weekend came to a close that we would meet again on the front lines.

It was not until we reached the St. Augustine campus, however, that Aurelia, Louis, Mercedes, and I learned of the early morning bombing of Pearl Harbor and the inevitability of war. Cecil Haliburton, the chairman of the Social Science Division and soon to be dean of the college, met us as we arrived on campus and broke the news. Over our customary improvised Sunday dinner, the four of us reacted to the war and spoke of what our individual chances were of going into the armed services or remaining at the college. As a physicist, Louis had no immediate worries. He could always go into some war-related industry and make his contribution in that way. As for me, with a low draft number and no war-related civilian skills, the prospect of remaining out of the military was not very bright.

That Monday, many of us listened to President Roosevelt's message to the joint session of the Congress that began, "Yesterday, December 7, 1941, a date which will live in infamy . . ." Later, several of us at the college decided that we should do everything possible to teach our students about the war and to alert them to their responsibilities as citizens in a country at war. The dean asked me to chair a committee of faculty and students that would decide what the college should do and then follow up with concrete plans. Deciding to make an ongoing study of the war, we concerned ourselves with problems of peace and with matters of postwar adjustment. Obviously, we could not neglect the impact of the war and the war aims on the status of African Americans, especially since that group was fighting not only tyranny abroad but racism at home as well. The students on the committee enthusiastically took the initiative in communicating with other St. Augustine students the importance of remaining not only loyal but also critical. Students wrote relevant papers, publishing them in the campus newspaper. They also made posters about various aspects of the war effort, especially the importance of conservation. None expressed criticism that could have been fairly regarded as disloyal.

With a low draft number and with my draft board indicating that it would begin to call up men as soon as the volunteers failed to fill the quotas, how best to serve became the question uppermost in my mind. Although I was already passionately nonviolent, I was not inclined to assume the role of a pacifist. I decided that I would serve in some capacity where my talents and my training could be fully utilized. The navy, having taken the worst hit of any of the armed services, was literally begging for volunteers. There was a shortage of personnel to handle the crush of office work, and men who could type and take shorthand and who had some office experience could look forward to early promotion. Consequently, I rushed down to the navy recruitment office to volunteer my services.

By the time my interview with the navy recruiter began, I was eager to do my part and aggressively "sold" myself. I reeled off my qualifications in the hope of overwhelming the youngish lieutenant. I was the winner of three gold medals in typing, I told him, and even then could do at least seventy-five words per minute. I knew shorthand and had racked up about six years of experience as a secretary at the semiprofessional level in college and graduate school. I had taken a course in accounting in high school, and although I had not worked in the field recently, I still had a grasp of the principles. And, oh yes, I had a PhD in history from Harvard University. The recruiter looked at me with what appeared to be a combination of incredulity and distress. He was briefly speechless.

Finally, it was out. He did not say that I was overqualified, a euphemism invariably used when the employer is reluctant to resort to greater candor. He said simply that I was lacking in one important qualification, and that was color. The navy had long restricted black enlistment, and as a matter of policy limited blacks serving to menial positions; even as late as 1943, 37 percent of African Americans serving in the U.S. Navy did so as stewards. I mumbled something to the effect that I thought there was a great national emergency, but I was obviously mistaken. I left with the same feeling that black volunteers must have had when George Washington rejected them in the Continental Army in 1775 or when Abraham Lincoln sent them home when they tried to enlist in the Union Army in 1861. There were different kinds of days of "infamy," I thought.

I next turned to the War Department, which was assembling a staff of historians to write the definitive history of the great conflagration. I knew that several white historians who had not obtained their advanced degrees—some had even flunked out of graduate school—had signed on as historians in the War Department. That knowledge gave me hope. I applied and sent along my qualifications, proudly including information about my book in press. As far as I can determine, the War Department did not even consider my application. Although I watched the mail for weeks that stretched into months, no response one way or another ever arrived. I asked Dr. Frank Porter Graham, president of the University of North Carolina, to write on my behalf, and he assured me that he had done so. I even wrote to Mrs. Eleanor Roosevelt and called her attention to my desire to serve in the area where I was best qualified. Perhaps the War Department's historians were too busy to respond to a fellow historian's expression of interest in their enterprise. Perhaps once again I lacked that one essential prerequisite.

Among the many things the war affected were the calendars of institutions such as St. Augustine's. The college was to have celebrated its seventy-fifth anniversary in 1942, but the impact of the war rendered this impossible. Consequently, it was set for January 1943. President Gould thought it would be good to have a distinguished African American to visit and speak. He asked me if I knew Ralph Bunche. I replied in the affirmative, recalling our having met when he visited Cambridge. The president asked me to invite him for the anniversary observance; I did so, and Bunche was delighted. He came and gave an excellent talk. Aurelia and I spent considerable time with him, and he was pleased to read the galleys of my forthcoming book and congratulated me for it.

In the 1940s, there were some of us who sought not only to give our country every opportunity to distance itself from the barbarism of Adolf Hitler but to adhere truly to the principles of egalitarianism with which America had long flirted but had never really embraced. I was among them. We pledged ourselves to a "Double V," or victory over Nazism abroad and racism at home; and no one more devoutly wished for success on both fronts than myself. With these twin goals in mind, I was as patriotic as any American. There is, however, a point beyond which even the most patient, long-suffering loyalist will not go. I reached that point in 1943, when I was invited to give the commencement address at the Tulsa high school from which I had graduated.

As the war continued and as the casualties mounted, the local draft boards began to increase the pressure on conscripts. If one was likely to be in the next draft call, as I was in 1943, he could not leave the jurisdiction of his draft board without permission. When Booker T. Washington High requested that I speak at its commencement that year, I sought permission and it was granted with the condition that before departing I should get a blood test, so that if I was called up during my absence, I could report for induction immediately upon my return. Fair enough, I thought.

When I went to see the draft board's physician, as directed by the clerk, I was not permitted to enter his office and was directed to a bench down the hall near the fire escape. There I was to wait until called. I refused and went back to the draft board office, requesting a physician who did not think I was vermin. I added that if I was to be drafted, it had to be done with due respect to my humanity. The clerk said that there were no other physicians on duty that day and that, with her intervention and assistance, the doctor would see me. When I returned to his office I was immediately ushered into his consultation room. He was all smiles, very cheerful, and ready for a "friendly" conversation. I was not so ready. I rolled up my sleeve, turned my head from him as he drew my blood, and returned his cheerful, brainless banter with stony silence.

This last experience forced me reluctantly to one irrevocable conclusion, that the United States, however much it was devoted to protecting the freedoms and rights of Europeans, had no respect for me, little interest in my well-being, and not even a desire to utilize my professional services. If I needed any further proof, it was in the treatment given my older brother, a college graduate and high school principal, who was drafted when white high school principals were not. He was abused by his uneducated, white staff sergeant and consigned to the kitchen brigade. This was the kind of segregation and discrimination that my parents had decried years earlier. This time, however, I saw it much more clearly than I had before. Not only was I older and better able to appreciate its consequences and the toll it could take on people and on society, but I was witness to the damning effects it had on Buck, who struggled hourly against its erosion of his humanity and sense of dignity.

The blood test behind me, my visit to Oklahoma in May 1943 was filled with pleasure despite the fact that my brother had already been drafted and was stationed in Alabama and my sister Anne was away in the School of Social Work at Howard University. It was the first time that I had made an official visit to my high school since graduation twelve years earlier. Many of my teachers were still there, and many of my classmates were living in Tulsa or had returned for a reunion. My commencement address was the first that a Booker T. Washington graduate had ever delivered, and it was warmly received.

Upon my return to Raleigh, I learned that I had been reclassified by the draft board to 1A, which meant that I could be called up almost immediately.

I was by then prepared to use any tactics I could to avoid being drafted. When I was called up for induction, I appealed the decision. When I met the draft board, the members asked me on what basis was I making the appeal. I replied that there was a shortage of people in my field with my qualifications, to which the chairman replied that the only shortages with which he was familiar were in the fields of science and mathematics. I calmly called his attention to the fact that, as in all such matters, that determination had been made by white people. I then asked if he knew the number of black historians in North Carolina with a PhD degree. He confessed ignorance. I told him that there were two, and if he drafted me, the supply would be cut by 50 percent. He found it difficult to argue with my statistics or my logic, and I was without shame in pressing my point. The board granted another deferment, perhaps to placate me but doubtless with every intention of getting me the next time around.

Because my situation was so precarious, I decided that I should stockpile my deferments, as one would stockpile any items needed in an emergency. I had not asked President Gould for any assistance with the draft board. If I could get him to write a letter when the current deferment expired, that would take me far into the next academic year. With that in mind, I went to see him and asked him to be prepared to request the next deferment.

He said that he would do nothing of the kind. Indeed, in tones reminiscent of his lecture that I not be overproud of my PhD, he volunteered that a stint in the armed services would be good for me. It would teach me to be more disciplined, to be neat, and even to hang up my clothes. I have always prided myself on my ability to hold my temper. This, however, was almost too much. As calmly as I could, I told him that he knew *nothing* of my personal habits. As for hanging up my clothes, my mother had taught me to do that when I was a child. I did not even dwell on the discipline it took to maintain my teaching schedule at St. Augustine's while at the same time completing my doctorate. I left immediately, and though I have no recollection of it, I hope I slammed the door. I intended never to see President Gould again.

Dr. James E. Shepard, the founder and president of North Carolina College for Negroes in Durham, had earlier expressed an interest in hiring me. I called and asked him if his invitation was still good. He said that indeed it was. I told him that I would accept under one condition: If he was still a member of the draft appeal board, he would see to it that I would be deferred if the request ever came. He said, in a jocular tone, that it would be disastrous to the American cause if I was drafted because I would make such a poor soldier. I agreed and then asked when he wished me to report at the college. He replied that he would expect me at the beginning of the fall term. I thanked him and said I would be there, reminding him, meanwhile, that my wife would also need a job. A few days later I resigned from St. Augustine's College, and we made our plans to move on.

Aurelia and I had already accepted the invitation of President H. Council Trenholm, of Alabama State College in Montgomery, to work there during the summer. I would teach and Aurelia would assist in a massive reorganization of their library. It was a pleasant if largely uneventful time, marvelously capped by a visit from my father. He had been successful in settling the legendary Lete Kolvin case, which had slowly made its way through the courts for at least a decade and had dealt with a huge oil estate worth several fortunes. A large number of lawyers and laymen were involved, and although the settlement was divided many ways, my father's share was more than he had ever made in a single legal action. He elected to take some time off and, among other things, visit us as well as my brother, who was stationed nearby.

My father had done very little in the way of traveling since his college days in the first years of the twentieth century when he had worked in Chicago and Milwaukee during the summers. A break was long overdue, and it was a joy to see him relax. After he arrived at our home in Montgomery, our first trip was to Tuskegee, only a short distance away. He had been a great admirer of Booker T. Washington and was thrilled to visit the institute that Washington had founded, to tour the laboratory of George Washington Carver, whom my father had met when the "Wizard of Tuskegee" visited Tulsa in 1927, and to see the great expanse of farmland in the area known as the black belt. Our next trip was to Camp Dothan to visit Buck. Bessye, his wife, had come to spend the summer with him, and that added to the joy of the occasion. My brother was, on the whole, content, but we could see that what he had been experiencing was affecting him deeply. Only later would it be clear just how deeply. During the several days we visited, my brother's distress, disappointment, and anger came through in flashes, and we were consoled by the fact that Bessye would remain with him until she returned to Tulsa to resume her position as a teacher in Dunbar Elementary School, where Mozella also taught.

My father, who had not been in the Southeast since he left Atlanta Baptist College in 1903, seemed content merely to accompany us wherever we went. Wartime travel tested the mettle of us all, and it was during these trips that my father finally bestowed on Aurelia the permanent title of "Trooper." The trains were crowded beyond belief, frequently with large numbers of people utterly unable to obtain seats. Many passengers could find space for themselves and their luggage only in the aisles and between coaches. South of Washington, D.C., moreover, the situation for African Americans was exacerbated because they were confined to seating in the "Negro coach," usually just behind the baggage car and sometimes being no more than one half of the baggage car. One had to be patient and good-natured about the entire experience; otherwise misery would be inevitable. In due course, we arrived in Raleigh, where we were able to get splendid accommodations for my father at the Arcade Hotel and where he especially enjoyed the food. After unpacking and repacking, we were prepared for the next stage of our travel plans: the momentous journey to New York City.

The railway coaches to Gotham were even more crowded than they had been from Montgomery to Raleigh. My father had never been in the Northeast, and the anticipation of visiting New York more than compensated for any inconvenience in getting there. In those days, as far as hotel accommodations were concerned, African Americans traveled by faith. There were few hotels where we could be certain to get rooms, and if the hotels accepting black guests were filled, the proprietors relied on a list of homes whose owners were willing to take visitors. Happily, we secured rooms at the Hotel Theresa, on 125th Street and Seventh Avenue, where Aurelia and I had stopped twice en route to Cambridge. We spent little time at the hotel, however, for there were tours, museums, movies, restaurants, and various stores worth visiting, and we were intent on seeing as much as possible in the few days we had.

My father was astounded to see the long lines of people, stretching for two or three blocks, waiting to get into Radio City Music Hall. He had trouble imagining that such large throngs of people could idle away their morning just to see a show. I reminded him that he was doing the same thing. Perhaps most of all, he enjoyed the food and drink. Before that trip I did not know if he ever drank anything stronger than lemonade. During Prohibition, Tulsa was dry, because of both the Eighteenth Amendment and the city fathers' determination to keep alcohol away from Native Americans. Raids on people's homes were conducted regularly, and if any alcohol was found it was brought out and very publicly smashed on the sidewalk. After my initial surprise at my father accepting a drink, we fell into the habit of enjoying cocktails before dinner. After a pleasant week in New York, we saw him off on the train for Tulsa, and we returned to North Carolina and my new job in Durham.

There was plenty to do upon our return, starting with finding a place to live. We knew no African American real estate dealers in Durham, but we learned through friends of a small, one-bedroom apartment upstairs in the home of Mr. and Mrs. James Bruce, on Linwood Avenue eight or ten blocks from the college. We went over to see it and promptly took it. We then went by to see Dr. Shepard, and he informed us that if Aurelia would present her résumé, including her college and library school transcripts, she would become librarian in the law school. Realizing that this was merely a procedural matter, we thanked him and placed her salary in our budget.

Surely almost as exciting as moving to a new community and to new positions was the appearance, in September 1943, of *The Free Negro in Carolina, 1790–1860*, published by the University of North Carolina Press. Copies of the book arrived on the day we were moving to Durham, and as I drove, Aurelia read passages to me even as I persisted in looking over at the book. The weaving automobile drew the attention of a highway patrolman, who pulled us over. While we honestly explained the cause of our excitement, he saw the book, congratulated us, and suggested that we put it away until we arrived at our destination.

Whereas Raleigh had seemed more like a colonial village, Durham was bursting with energy. Business was what the city was all about. At the great private university, Duke, one felt the posthumous presence of the business tycoon James B. Duke; and at the public North Carolina College for Negroes, one felt the living presence of the consummate pragmatist James E. Shepard, the founder and current president.

To be sure, Durham was not New York, but as soon as we had unpacked our sparse belongings, we set out to see the town. We were impressed with the fact that although there was an African American business section of the town, Hayti, the black businesses were by no means confined to that section. We had the feeling, moreover, that Durham's middle-class African American community, with its bankers, insurance executives, and investment moguls, was more secure in its place than the one in Raleigh, which was composed largely of lawyers, clergy, physicians, dentists, and other small entrepreneurs. Consequently, blacks in Durham seemed more at liberty to express themselves on various economic, political, and social questions. The Durham Committee on Negro Affairs, a remarkably diverse segment of the black community, was quite active politically, and its voice was heard and respected at every level, especially during political contests.

Once we became better acquainted with its leaders as well as the rank and file, we regularly attended the meetings of the Durham Committee, and in that way we learned a great deal about Negro affairs in Durham. Despite the fact that the city had an easily identifiable black upper middle class, that group seemed to work well with the black working class, many of whom were employed in jobs related to the tobacco industry, where independent unions were unknown. It also worked well with the white community, some of whose leaders were said to have family ties with local blacks.

Perhaps the most impressive thing about the African American community in Durham was its strong business base. The North Carolina Mutual Life Insurance Company, still the oldest and largest African

American—owned and —operated insurance company in the United States, was the flagship business, having been founded by two unlikely collaborators, A. M. Moore, a physician, and John W. Merrick, a barber. Its great success was due to the leadership provided by Charles C. Spaulding, who joined the company in its early days and brought with him vision, ambition, and creativity. Spaulding was also president of the Mechanics and Farmers Bank, which by the time we arrived in Durham enjoyed the patronage of a considerable number of whites. In the offices of the bank's downtown building, which also housed the insurance company, Spaulding, attractive in appearance and charming in personality, greeted throngs of customers in his ceremonial offices just inside the entrance. Many descendants and in-laws of these founders were still in those businesses when we arrived in 1943. Other black-owned businesses, including the Bankers Fire Insurance Company, presided over by Rencher Harris, and the Mutual Savings and Loan Association, headed by H. M. Michaux, were emerging.

North Carolina College for Negroes, renamed in 1942 North Carolina College at Durham, was a lively, intellectually stimulating place, despite its limited resources. The endemic disparity of public support between black and white institutions of higher education was aggravated by wartime austerity. Dr. Shepard was aggressive and successful, with the assistance of his able business manager and legislative lobbyist, C. C. Amey, in building a strong faculty. He knew of the very limited job opportunities available to African American scholars, no matter how highly trained and productive, and he intended to collect at his institution as many as he possibly could. In 1938 he brought William E. Farrison, an authority on nineteenth-century African American literature, to chair the English Department. Pauline Newton, Julia Harris, Ila Blue, and Charles Ray, who would become my closest friend, would further strengthen the college. Zora Neale Hurston was there briefly but soon moved on. The college's other PhD in history, Joseph Taylor, and I, along with Helen Edmonds, soon to receive her PhD degree, shared the responsibility of handling the offerings in history. All in all, the college was a marvelous place to work and teach.

A few members of the faculty were not African Americans. The most prominent was Ernst M. Mannassee, a Jewish refugee from Germany, who taught German as well as philosophy, his own discipline. It was Mannassee who took the initiative in bringing several of us—Farrison, Albert Turner, Charles Ray, and myself—and several professors from Duke University—Edgar Thompson and H. Shelton Smith—together regularly to discuss papers or topics of common interest. We always met in a classroom at our college, to avoid embarrassment to anyone who might have felt unable to entertain the multiracial group at his home or at Duke. In its own way, that group was as important in bringing people together as the so-called secret basketball game between North Carolina College and Duke University that was played in 1945 but not widely known of until fifty years later.

Charles Ray and I became fast friends. It was, perhaps, our relationship with Dr. Shepard and our determination to bring distinction to the college that bonded us more than anything else. While most members of the faculty stood in awe of the president, our attitude was quite different. We were always respectful, but we would engage him in friendly banter, which he thoroughly enjoyed. When Dr. Shepard would inquire about our ability to survive during wartime scarcity and rationing, we would suggest to him that he share with us some of the butter and other rare items that we knew he had. It seemed to amuse him that we would even hint that he was hoarding, and on occasion he would indeed pass on to us some items that were painfully scarce. Regarding racial segregation, he would accuse us of accepting it and would boast that he had never ridden in a Jim Crow railway car, whereupon we would say that if he would but share more of his resources with us, we too could ride in style, in a Pullman car, as he did.

Each quarter I taught three courses, usually one or two sections of the first year of American history and perhaps one advanced course. Alternatively, another course would be a section of the freshman survey of European civilization. I always assumed that the students were intellectually curious and mentally alert. And usually I had no difficulty in stimulating them to do the work and complete their assignments on time. Occasionally, I had students of remarkable ability and industry who would go far beyond my general expectations for the class.

Even as I carried a heavy load of courses, I was determined to continue my research and writing. In addition to the appearance of my book on free Negroes, I published several articles in professional journals and began to write book reviews for various historical journals. Nevertheless, by the time we moved to Durham, I was ready for a new research project. The

The law office of my father, Buck Colbert Franklin, in Ardmore, Oklahoma, photographed in 1910. Buck Sr. is the first from the right.

My parents, Buck and Mollie Franklin, photographed in Tulsa, Oklahoma, around 1927

This photograph of me was taken in July 1915, when I was six months old.

A photograph of the sixth grade in Rentiesville, Oklahoma. I am third from the left in the front row and my sister Anne is on my right.

An early photograph of my father, Buck Sr.

My mother, Mollie Franklin, in 1935

By 1927 we had joined my father in
Tulsa, Oklahoma, and I had joined
Boy Scout Troop 42.

In Tulsa my sister and I attended Booker T. Washington High School,
called a separate school, where I joined the band.
I am sitting in the second row, third from the right, holding a trumpet.

Spring 1932, on the steps of Fisk's library. Pictured (from bottom to top) are Adelaide Lewis and William Sapp; Aurelia and me; Cora Brown and E. Yerby Lowe; and Elizabeth Ryans and Jerry Bradford.

Aurelia and me on a date during our senior year at Fisk

My mentor and best friend, Ted Currier, standing outside his Fisk campus home

Aurelia's mother, Bertha Kincaid Whittington, stands between the newly minted Fisk graduates, Aurelia and me.

Ted Currier shaking my hand at Fisk's 1935 commencement. He would soon play a singular role in ensuring that I was able to continue my studies at Harvard University.

My mother, Mollie Franklin, visiting Fisk for my graduation. In 1935, neither my father nor Aurelia's could afford to attend the ceremony.

*Aurelia and me in Cambridge, Massachusetts, in 1941, on the day
I was awarded my PhD from Harvard University*

*My older brother,
Buck Jr., at the
Bixby, Oklahoma,
school where he was
principal until
being drafted into
the Army in 1942*

ABOVE: *My first book-signing party, for* The Free Negro in North Carolina, *held in the Richard B. Harrison Library in Raleigh, North Carolina, September 1943*
BELOW: *I am leading a class at my first Salzburg Seminar in American Studies, 1951. Opportunities to teach overseas would help open doors to me back in the United States.*

Aurelia and me on our first visit to London, 1951

After much effort, we bought and moved into our Brooklyn, New York, home at 1885 New York Avenue, where we lived from 1957 to 1964.

The proud new parents in 1952: Aurelia and me admiring our son, Whit, then four months old

*My father, Buck Sr.,
and Whit in Tulsa, 1955*

ABOVE: *With several of my Brooklyn College students on campus in 1963*
(COURTESY OF BROOKLYN COLLEGE)

BELOW: *The 1960 class reunion at Fisk. Whit, wearing a striped jacket in the center of the first row, stands in front of Aurelia, who stands before me.*

Aurelia and me in the rear garden of 21 Chaucer Road in Cambridge, England, where I spent the year as Cambridge University's Pitt Professor of American History and Institutions

Whit and me boarding the Queen Mary *in September 1962, en route to England*

*Confrontations over civil rights occurring back at home during 1962
and 1963 lent a unique backdrop to my discussions with Cambridge University students.*

*In December 1963 I was appointed a member of the American
delegation to the independence ceremonies in Zanzibar.*

ABOVE: *The civil rights march to Montgomery, Alabama, in April 1965 was memorable.*
None of us were certain how the locals would respond to our being there,
and I took the hand of the woman beside me for support and solidarity.
BELOW: *The swearing-in of the Fulbright Board in 1963. I am second from the left,*
and to my right stands Oscar Handlin, my friend and onetime fellow Harvard graduate student.
(COURTESY OF THE U.S. DEPARTMENT OF STATE)

At Ambassador Patrick Moynihan's invitation, I delivered a lecture in New Delhi, India, in 1974.

Former president of Turkey Ismet Inonu and me in Ankara in 1967

I am leading a seminar at the University of Chicago in 1971. Pictured (from left to right) are my students Paul Finkelman, Nancy Grant, and Woody White.

archives in Raleigh were no longer convenient, especially since gasoline was rationed and an application for additional fuel for the purpose of engaging in historical research would likely be dismissed. There was the Duke University Library, however, just across town. It had an excellent collection of materials, including manuscripts, on the history of the South, and there were many questions in my mind regarding the region's history. Perhaps the one uppermost was the South's bellicosity and the reasons for it. The more I looked into the question, the more important it became, not only to me but for anyone interested in a clear understanding of the South and its history. I was soon doing systematic research on a project that would consume a decade.

Early on I discussed my interests briefly with Professor Charles S. Sydnor of Duke, with whom I was becoming professionally friendly. We worked in similar fields, and whenever I encountered him we would discuss his and my research. Although our conversations always took place in the corridors of the stacks of the Duke library and not in his office, to which he never invited me, I found them, even if intrusive, to be informative and stimulating. One in particular stands out in my memory.

Professor Sydnor had heard that I was opposed to racial segregation and he wondered aloud if this was true. I assured him that I was opposed to racial segregation in all of its forms. He confessed that he did not understand how or why I could hold such a view. I had a "good job" out at the Negro college, and if segregation ended, he concluded, I would be out of a job. Then what would I do? I no more thought that the end of segregation would jeopardize my job, I countered, than it would jeopardize the jobs of others at all-white and all-black institutions. I said that if racial segregation was outlawed, which I fervently hoped it would be, then the University of North Carolina and Duke University would no longer be segregated. It might mean that black students would attend formerly all-white institutions and that white students would attend formerly all-black institutions. The same would be true as far as teaching personnel was concerned, and in that case, I could be competing for a job at Duke. He did not present a counterargument and merely remarked that he had not previously thought of it like that. We continued to have our chats in the corridors of the stacks, but the subject of racial segregation never came up again.

As the months passed, Dr. Shepard and I became more friendly, and soon he was expressing a quiet confidence in me that was deeply flattering. One day he outright told me that I could have any position at the college I might want—except his! He then expressed the hope that he could persuade me to join his administration in some capacity, perhaps as dean or vice president. The invitation—or challenge—forced me to think seriously about the future. Then I tried, as best I could, to describe to Dr. Shepard my goal in life. I pointed out that at present North Carolina College was known as Dr. Shepard's institution. Even as people drove along the street, they referred to it that way. I then told him that I wanted to do my teaching and research so well that at some future time people would pass along the street and look over at the college and say, "That is where John Hope Franklin teaches." It was not the response Dr. Shepard anticipated. By that time, he knew me well enough to realize that I was disciplined and determined, but that my ambition would lie in teaching rather than in administration baffled him. In 1940s America, he had reason to be baffled. Put simply, the most prestigious research and teaching schools in America did not hire blacks. Academic organizations did not accommodate black members, access to research materials required a fight, and refereed academic journals and publishing houses were hardly bias-free. There was no evidence that the Professor Sydnors of the academy had any interest in acknowledging the achievements of an African American scholar, no matter how talented. Shocked, Dr. Shepard's only remark was, "Franklin, I simply do not understand you."

No matter his opinion concerning my ambitions, Dr. Shepard soon had another opportunity to express his confidence in me. The seventy-six-year-old W.E.B. Du Bois, who had been teaching at Atlanta University for a decade, and the president of that university, Dr. Rufus Clement, came to a parting of the ways. Dr. Shepard and Dr. Du Bois were longtime friends, and during a visit to Durham in the spring of 1944 the latter sought Dr. Shepard's counsel. On the spot, President Shepard offered the distinguished author, professor, civil rights activist, and editor a position at North Carolina College. Taken aback, Dr. Du Bois asked his host what on earth could he do at the college. Dr. Shepard replied that he could do anything he wished to do and for starters suggested he might like to edit a magazine such as *Phylon*, which he had begun at Atlanta University. Dr.

Du Bois found the suggestion intriguing but countered that at his age it would be irresponsible to initiate a periodical without some able assistant who would continue it when his time was up. Dr. Shepard then indicated that perhaps he would find one John Hope Franklin able to assist him and assume the responsibility for editing the magazine upon his retirement. At that point Dr. Du Bois said that he would like to meet me; Dr. Shepard was only too happy to arrange it.

I had, of course, seen Dr. Du Bois numerous times, first in 1926, when he visited Tulsa and spoke before the Oklahoma Negro Teachers Association. I also saw him on his several visits to Fisk during my student days, and I heard him speak at the Ford Hall Forum in Boston, when I was a graduate student at Harvard. I had never met him, though once in the Arcade Hotel in Raleigh in the spring of 1939 I had come close: Seeing Dr. Du Bois dining alone and reading, I decided that this was an opportunity that I would not let pass. Crossing the dining room, I approached his table and spoke to him, giving him my full name. Surely he would recognize the fact that I was named for one of his closest friends and hearing it would embrace me. He did not even look up. Then I told him that I was a graduate of Fisk University, class of 1935. That, I assumed, would bring him to his feet singing "Gold and Blue." Again, he continued to read and eat, without looking up. Finally, as a last resort, I told him that I was a graduate student in history at Harvard and was in Raleigh doing research for my dissertation. Without looking up from his book or plate, he said, "How do you do." Dejected, I retreated, completed my dinner, and withdrew from the dining room.

That incident was fresh in my mind as I waited in Dr. Shepard's living room for Dr. Du Bois to make his appearance. He entered the room shortly and greeted me warmly. He seemed to remember me, not from any past personal encounter but from an article I had submitted to *Phylon* some weeks before he left Atlanta. He remembered the piece, "History, Weapon of War and Peace," and would have published it had he remained the editor. He then asked me about my work at the college, what my research interests were, and whether I had any interest in editorial work. I told him of my research on the militant South and my lack of experience but real interest in editorial work. He appeared satisfied with what he saw and heard, but it was obvious that Dr. Shepard's invitation would be one of several he would entertain, and it would be some time before he would reach a final decision about his future.

Subsequently, while in New York, Dr. Du Bois was warmly welcomed by Walter White, the executive director of the NAACP, who offered him the position of director of special research. Dr. Du Bois accepted, and he joined the staff for one of the wildest rides of his long career. In his second autobiography, he described this as the worst decision he had ever made, and he regretted it deeply. Had Dr. Du Bois returned to North Carolina College, founded a magazine, made me his assistant, and subsequently retired, leaving the periodical in my hands, I can only surmise that my future would have been quite different.

By the spring of 1945, I had succeeded in remaining free from military service. The war in Europe was moving toward a climax, with the successful invasion of the Continent following D-day. As American casualties mounted, some people on the home front became increasingly anxious, even paranoid as they observed the restlessness and presumed disloyalty of segments of the population. African Americans, insulted by the continued segregation in the armed forces, widespread racial discrimination in war-related industries, as well as the nation's endemic racism, threatened to withdraw their support of the military operations in Europe and Asia. The evermore widely adopted motto "Victory at home and abroad" indicated their impatience with the United States holding Germany and Japan to higher standards than it set for itself. The restlessness and disillusionment of African Americans were reflected in their response to insults and blatant acts of discrimination in the armed forces and in the workplace. There were numerous riots during the entire period of the war, including outbreaks such as the one that roiled Detroit in 1943, leaving twenty-five blacks and nine whites dead. President Roosevelt responded in a variety of ways, including issuing executive orders to end discrimination in the defense industry, but African Americans wanted more, and they continued to press him. When he died suddenly in April 1945, many thought that their last best hope for racial equality had died with him.

On Thursday afternoon, April 12, I learned from Aurelia that the president was dead. My first question, after expressing shock and grief, was if the funeral would be in the college auditorium or at White Rock Baptist

Church. Aurelia then said that it was President Franklin D. Roosevelt, *not* Dr. Shepard. While it was sad to learn of the death of President Roosevelt, anyone who had seen pictures of him upon his return from Yalta or had heard him address Congress after his return should not have been surprised. Having already been president for twelve years, he was only a few months into his fourth term; the nation had become so accustomed to him that it was difficult to think of anyone else as president. Perhaps Mrs. Roosevelt herself was thinking about that when the newly sworn in President Harry S. Truman called to ask what he could do for her, and she replied by asking what she could do for him.

By the beginning of the summer in 1945, the end of the war was clearly in sight. Even though fighting continued in Asia, many of us felt that it was only a matter of time before Japan would surrender. It was now clear that I would escape the draft. Buck remained in the service, and it was my fervent hope that he would be speedily discharged without further damage to his psyche. That damage had been done was evident: My brother was no longer the self-assured, dignified man who had been a respected civic leader in Tulsa before the war. How dire his need for rehabilitation, however, was only then dimly apparent.

At the end of the summer session, I went to Baton Rouge to work in the state archives, located at Louisiana State University. I did not know until my arrival that African Americans were not permitted to use them. Fortunately for me, the war's end yielded a very practical and immediate benefit. The state was celebrating a week's holiday in observance of the return of peace, and the director of the archives, Edwin A. Davis, was kind enough to invite me to work in the archives while it was otherwise closed. He alone would be there during the week's holiday to note facism's demise and so could circumvent the state's ban on persons like me. I was deeply grateful, and thanks to his generosity I was able to examine a large number of valuable manuscripts.

My work at the archives in Baton Rouge completed, I met Aurelia in New Orleans. It was our first visit to the city, and we took advantage of the free time we had. No hotels would receive us as guests, so we found accommodations in the home of a black minister, who provided us with a large room at the back of his house. We were thankful that it had an abundance of windows, which remained open, though in truth this did little to alleviate the high humidity of which New Orleans proudly boasts. We visited Dillard University and walked the French Quarter but hesitated to enter any shops because of our limited budget. We also walked through the streets of an area that can best be described as the Negro Quarter. Short of traveling abroad, this visit to New Orleans, with its strange sounds, stretches of homes behind walls, mixtures of French and patois, exotic markets and foods, was the next best thing to a grand tour.

Aurelia returned to North Carolina to visit her parents before the fall term began at the college. I went on to Montgomery, where I did research for several weeks at the State Department of Archives and History. It was here that I concluded it was quite impossible to make any generalizations about the South. I requested manuscripts from the attendant, and when they arrived I was in a quandary as to where to sit. It was clear that they would not be preparing a special room for me. After surveying the research room, I walked toward a quiet place where no one was sitting. At that point, the elderly white female attendant informed me that I could not sit over there. It was too warm in that corner, she explained. The coolest part of the room was where the fan was and where the other researchers, all white, were sitting. Besides, she said, the others needed to meet me, whereupon she stopped everyone at the two tables and introduced me all around. The other researchers all greeted me cordially, after which we proceeded with our work.

After I had been there for about two weeks, I requested the papers of Governor John Anthony Winston, the chief executive of the state at the beginning of the Civil War. The attendant informed me that since those papers had not been completely processed, only the archivist herself, Mrs. Marie Bankhead Owen, could grant permission to see them. At the first opportunity, I went to Mrs. Owen's office and asked the secretary if I could see her. With the secretary's authorization I went in, and as I did I learned two important lessons of Southern etiquette. The first was that the door should not be closed when a black man is ushered into the presence of a white woman. The second was that I should not expect to sit down in the presence of a white woman, unless she told me to do so.

When Mrs. Owen looked up, she asked me quite graciously what she could do for me. I asked permission to see the papers of Governor Winston. She said that she was pleased to grant it, and was there anything else

I wished? I replied in the negative, thanked her, and was about to leave when she said, "I hear that there is a Harvard nigger here. Have you seen him?" Before I could recover myself sufficiently for a reply, a voice reached us from the outer room. It was the secretary, who could hear everything, since the door was open. "That's him, Mrs. Owen, that's him."

Mrs. Owen looked up at me and exclaimed, "You don't look like a Harvard nigger to me! Have a seat." As I took the seat close to her desk, she remarked that neither did I act like a "Harvard nigger." Then she asked me where I was born and raised. When I told her I was from Oklahoma, she shook her head. She declared that I could not have received my "nice mannerly training" in that wild country. Then she inquired about my college education. When I told her that I was a graduate of Fisk University in Nashville, she exclaimed that she now knew where I got my good manners: "in a good old Confederate State!" Then she rambled on and on, taking up subjects as they came to mind. She spoke of the end of the war and how relieved she was that the "boys" would be coming home. She hoped that peace would last forever. It was equally obvious that she hoped that the segregated South she was so enamored of would last forever too unaffected by peace or war.

Days of infamy had passed. More days of infamy yet remained.

9

From Slavery to Freedom

Although I had taught Negro history at St. Augustine's and at North Carolina College, I thought of it, from the outset, as a corrective or as a supplementary revision of United States history. I had published a book on free Negroes, and I thought of it as a part of Southern history. Similarly, I thought of the militant South as a revision of United States history. Until we understand clearly the psychological underpinnings of Southern conduct, I thought, it would be impossible to understand the complete history of the South and its relation to other parts of the country. The breadth of the question was why I felt some urgency to pursue it in all of my spare time and why I went into the sweltering South to conduct research in the summer of 1945. There was more yet to be done, and I intended do it as thoroughly and as quickly as possible. Duke and the University of North Carolina at Chapel Hill, just ten miles away, held valuable materials, and I meant to plumb them before the summer of 1946, during which I hoped to complete my research in more distant archives.

I did not then know that there were plans afoot that would interfere with my own. I later learned that a highly trained, well-known African American historian had submitted a manuscript on the history of American Negroes to Alfred A. Knopf for possible publication. I do not know if that publishing house had already thought of bringing out such a work or of soliciting one. But it soon became clear that the editors were not impressed with the nearly complete delivered manuscript's organization and style.

The principal editor in the College Department at Knopf was Roger Shugg, a PhD in history from Princeton and author of a well-received book, *The Origins of Class Struggle in Louisiana*. From the time the manuscript in question reached his desk, Shugg was convinced that Knopf should publish such a history and that the submitted manuscript needed a thorough revision before it could be considered for publication. He inquired among historians at major graduate institutions about African American historians who might be able to work on such a book. Professor Schlesinger recommended me, and on the basis of that recommendation, Shugg got in touch with the person whose manuscript they had been considering, asking its author if he would be willing to collaborate with me in the rewriting of his manuscript. The historian replied that although he knew and respected me, he saw no reason why he needed a coauthor at that stage.

I knew nothing of Knopf's interest until Roger Shugg wrote me at the end of November 1945. He asked about my current research and wondered if I had ever thought of writing a history of the Negro in America. I told him of my work in progress, that several university presses had expressed an interest in it, but if he was at all interested, I would be pleased to tell him more about it. I also stated that while I had thought seriously of writing a history of the Negro in America, someone else would likely get to it before I did because my primary interests were elsewhere. Early in January I sent Shugg an outline of "The Martial Spirit" and indicated that I might be able to get to the history of Negroes in the next eighteen months or two years.

Later that month, Shugg came to see me in Durham, and we talked about the martial spirit project as well as a history of Negroes. He mentioned my collaborating with another person on the latter project, but later wrote that it was no longer a possibility. Instead, he urged me to consider writing a history of Negroes on my own. The great problem for me, as I told him, was whether I should "sidetrack" my study of the Southern military spirit to make way for a history of the Negro. By this time I was inclined to agree with him that there was some urgency in getting out an up-to-date history. I even implied that if I could take some time off, I would proceed with it, but as things stood I simply could not afford to do so.

By this time Roger Shugg and I were exchanging letters weekly, sometimes even more frequently. On February 25, 1946, he outright stated his hope that I would write a work about 150,000 words in length, emphasizing "the cultural heritage of the Negro in Africa . . . his history in South as well as North America, and give sufficient attention to his history since the Civil War." He then said that if I submitted an outline and several sample chapters, they might be able to offer a small advance on royalties "provided that such an advance assisted you in taking six months off to complete the book." He concluded by stating he was confident that the "eventual rewards would fully justify your doing so."

In early March I wrote Shugg that I had decided to write a history of the Negro, and I would do so without delay. I told him that I had already begun to outline the work and was planning the beginning chapters. It would be a straightforward narrative and analytical account of the Negro in the New World with three or four introductory chapters on Africa and several on the Caribbean and South America. I told him quite frankly that while the scholarship in the work would not suffer, I fully intended to ensure a high-quality literary style. I promised that within a few weeks I would send an outline and some initial chapters in order for them to offer me a contract. Shortly thereafter, one of Shugg's colleagues in the College Department, Madge Pickard, indicated to me that they were preparing the spring catalog, and she thought it might be well to make at least a brief announcement about my forthcoming book. This was before we had even signed a contract, let alone settled on a delivery date for the manuscript, facts I duly pointed out.

In early May I sent Shugg the first five chapters and an outline of the remaining book, indicating to him that these chapters, dealing with the African background, would be the weakest since I had no special training on Africa. He said that the chapters were enough to persuade them that they would like to publish the work. "It promises to be a book of genuine distinction," he wrote, "not only as a useful text but as an interesting and authoritative reference work for a good many years to come, and you are to be congratulated upon the very lucid and judicial style in which you present the findings of the latest researchers." He was prepared to sign a contract, the terms of which he spelled out in the letter. The advance against royalties amounted to five hundred dollars, half to be paid on the signing of the contract and half to be paid upon delivery of the finished manuscript. "We realize," he said, "that it is not going to be easy for you to meet a delivery date of April 1, 1947." They would extend it if they had to, but he hoped to take advantage of the fall market of 1947. He added in a postscript that the work was "so good that we should like to list it in our Summer and Fall catalog, beginning the publicity essential to promoting it well." To meet his deadline, I had less than two years to write the book.

Naturally, I thought of the career of George Washington Williams. While reading the spines of the books shelved in the stacks of the North Carolina College library, I had come upon his *History of the Negro Race*. Published in 1882, the work was in two volumes and included much material on earlier African history. It was, in virtually every respect, a remarkable piece of scholarship for its time. So began my forty-year involvement with George Washington Williams. As I dug in to concentrate on writing my own history of the Negro people, I could not refrain from using Williams as an inspiration. If a person who did not learn to write a full, grammatical sentence until he was nineteen and who never had a course in any kind of history until he went to the Andover Theological Institution could produce a work that was widely admired in Europe as well as the United States, then I should be able to write a work of some merit. As soon as the spring term was over, I turned my attention exclusively to working on *the* history.

Even with all of my spare time during the summer devoted to working on the book, it was clear that if I was to deliver the manuscript on or before April 1, 1947, I would need to work harder yet. Aurelia saw how difficult it was for me to work in Durham, where our small apartment meant I had to write in the stacks of the Duke library or the empty classrooms at North Carolina College, which provided no faculty offices. It was she who suggested that I use my fall term off to go to Washington and work at the Library of Congress for a few months. The advance of $250 arrived in August, but that was not sufficient to sustain me during the autumn, especially since my leave of absence was without pay. Aurelia continued to work as librarian in the law school, and she said that if I went to Washington and got a study room at the Library of Congress, she would supplement the advance in order to make it possible for me to work in Washington. Her loyal and generous support I would later refer to as a subvention from the "Aurelia Franklin Foundation."

As soon as summer school ended, I left for Washington. I secured a room at Howard University's Carver Hall, which would be my home for the next four months. Willard Webb, who presided over study rooms and stack privileges at the Library of Congress, was very cooperative, and I soon settled into a routine of having breakfast in the Lucy Slowe Hall, around the corner from my dormitory, taking the bus to the Library of Congress, working there all day, with time out to eat in the cafeteria of the Supreme Court or the Methodist building, the only two places near the Library of Congress where African Americans could have lunch, and then working until late afternoon or early evening and returning to my room in Carver Hall to prepare for the following day. The speed with which my research and writing progressed was not only satisfactory but quite surprising even to me who had long wanted such an opportunity to work without interruption.

By early December I had completed ten chapters and had outlined the remainder. Moreover, I had begun to work on the bibliographical notes and possible illustrations—charts, maps, photographs, and the like. Unfortunately, I had to return to Durham the second week in December to teach during the second quarter. Pleased with what I had accomplished but greatly distressed that I had to cease my focused writing schedule, I determined to use the Christmas holidays and any other days and even spare hours to move toward completion. Shugg kept pressing—for more chapters, for a tentative introduction, for bibliographical notes for the first ten chapters. When on behalf of Mr. Knopf and himself he invited me to a buffet luncheon during the postholiday annual meeting of the American Historical Association, to be held that year in New York City, I thanked him but told him that the pressure of work prevented my attending the meeting. I took advantage of every waking hour during the holiday period, with the result that before the end of January I had completed twenty chapters of the manuscript and had complied with most of Shugg's numerous requests.

Even as I moved toward completion of the manuscript, we still had no satisfactory name for the book. For a working title, we called it *A History of the Negro*, realizing all the time that we would choose something different before publication. For a while, we toyed with *Toward Freedom*, but that title was "too tendentious for a book of this nature," Shugg thought. *Freedom's People* was satisfactory, but no one had any great enthusiasm for it. Someone thought of the title *From Slavery to Freedom*, but there was some hesitation because a book with that title, though on an entirely different subject, had appeared about twenty years earlier. Roger Shugg concluded it was too apt a title to allow the previous book to dissuade us, and we adopted it for our own.

Years later, when we were both at the University of Chicago, Roger Shugg would remark how shocked he had been when I arrived in New York in early March 1947, with the bulk of the remaining manuscript. For the first time he realized that I would make the deadline of April 1. There were still numerous details to be attended to, yet it was sufficiently close to the end to see the end. Indeed, by the time I was writing the last few chapters, I was also reading galley proofs. We held galley proof parties in our small apartment, with people like Charles Ray, Eric Moore, and the blind sociologist Joseph Sandy Hines. It was remarkable how Hines, who sat and listened to me or one of the others read from the galleys, would stop us and suggest that we begin the sentence over again. He could not see the typographical errors, but he could hear the awkward and ungrammatical sentences. In that way, he contributed greatly to the improvement of the text.

Knowing that the analogy is more than a bit presumptuous, but on the completion of *From Slavery to Freedom* I was reminded of how Edward Gibbon described his feelings after completing his monumental *Decline and Fall of the Roman Empire* and still to this day paraphrase him thus: In the planning and writing of my work, I had witnessed more than five hundred years of human history pass before my eyes. I had seen one slave ship after another from Portugal, Spain, France, Holland, England, and the United States pile black human cargo into its bowels as it would coal or even gold had either been more available and profitable at the time. I had seen them dump my ancestors at New World ports as they would a load of cattle and wait smugly for their pay for capture and transport. I had seen them beat black men until they themselves became weary and rape black women until their ecstasy was spent leaving their brutish savagery exposed. I had heard them shout, "Give us liberty or give us death," and not mean one word of it. I had seen them measure out medication or education for a sick or ignorant white child and ignore a black child similarly situated. I had seen them lynch black men and distribute their ears, fingers, and other parts as souvenirs to the ghoulish witnesses. I had seen it all, and in the seeing I had become bewildered and yet in the process lost my own innocence.

The spring and summer of 1947 were filled not only with the stressful task of completing the big book, now some 240,000 words, and seeing it through the press, but also with a serious, tragic family matter. My brother had not been stable since his discharge from the army in 1945. He had no interest in resuming his work in the public schools; indeed, he had no desire to remain in Tulsa. He and Bessye moved to St. Louis, where he secured employment in the Veterans Administration, a very unfortunate development in view of his several unhappy years in the armed forces. He suffered from periods of depression, resulting in his inability to perform the tasks his job required. There were times when he wept as he denounced the army and what it had done to him. He recalled to me how a white sergeant had vowed to devote his life to seeing that so long as Buck was in uniform he would do nothing better than peel potatoes. Clearly, my brother's education and attainments, already nullified by a segregated army that would never meaningfully promote him, were also enough to draw vicious cruelty from this racist officer. In his anguish, Buck wondered how this country could give up the lives of so many young Americans to save Europe, all the while humiliating African American soldiers and treating them as less than human. His situation was so desperate that in March 1947 Bessye called me and asked me to come and talk with him. I went immediately, of course. He told me that he wanted to start over again, first by locating in another part of the country and then by going into business, using the skills he had acquired when he majored in that field at Fisk. He wanted to come back with me to North Carolina, which he had never visited. I told him of the area's dynamic business interests and thought, perhaps, he would find something to his liking there. The result was that he returned to Durham with me, and Aurelia gave him a warm welcome.

After visiting with us, he planned a visit with our sister Anne in Washington. She had, by this time, graduated from the Howard University School of Social Work and was an inspector in the Women's Bureau of the Metropolitan Police of the District of Columbia. En route, Buck thought that he would like to visit Richmond, Virginia, where there were several thriving businesses operated by African Americans. I agreed and suggested that he stay at the Slaughter Hotel, which had a good dining room and where he would meet many of Richmond's black businessmen and -women. So off to Richmond he went. Two days later, I received word that he was in the McGuire Veterans Hospital in Richmond. I rushed up to see what had happened. He had either fallen or jumped from a second-story window of the hotel and suffered multiple fractures, including a skull fracture. After he regained consciousness, he could not or would not tell exactly what had happened to him. During the next several weeks Aurelia and I were commuting to Richmond from Durham, and Bessye had come over from St. Louis to be with him.

While in Richmond we secured accommodations in a private home in the vicinity of the hospital. Our hostess could not have been more understanding and helpful had she been a relative. I particularly recall one occasion when I returned from the hospital and was visibly agitated; she asked me what had happened.

I had gone to the hospital to give blood for a transfusion for my brother. Returning on the bus, I sat down in the first vacant seat I saw. The driver, a white man, told me that I would have to move back to the Negro section. I told him that I had neither the strength nor the inclination to move. I had been to the veterans hospital to give blood to my brother who had served in the United States Army so that someone, certainly not he, could enjoy equality. Now, the bus driver wanted me to accept unequal treatment, and I was not going to do it. From the rear of the bus, the black riders began to call out, "Stand your ground!" and when it was clear that I was going to do precisely that, the driver said nothing more to me. If he had stood *his* ground, I frankly do not know what I would have done, but I had had enough.

Whenever I went to Richmond, between reading galley proofs and performing other chores in connection with the production of the book, my convalescing brother wanted to know how things were going, what remained to be done, and how long it would be before it was all finished. I answered him as best as I could. One day, when I was in Washington to do some last-minute checking of bibliographical materials, I went to see Anne. She said that they had been looking for me to inform me that our brother had passed away the previous night. Aurelia was already driving up from Durham to Richmond, where we met and went to the hospital morgue to claim my brother's body. The physicians expressed their wish to do an autopsy to confirm or disprove their suspicion that he had lung cancer. I called my father, seeking his advice. In one of the few bitter statements I ever heard my father make, he said that they should not touch his son. They had butchered him enough, he declared, and the only thing to do now was to send him home.

Aurelia, Anne, and I returned Buck's body to my father, to Bessye, and to the rest of the family. Funeral services were held at the family's church, and he was buried in the family plot in the Booker T. Washington Cemetery.

The entire family felt the tragedy of my brother's death. He had been drafted by a segregated army and had served his country more honorably than that country had served him. And he had emerged from war and military service to an America still shaped by racist laws and customs. We each in our own way struggled to deal with his passing and the larger injustice within which it had occurred. For my part, I can only attest that I was ever more determined not to waver in my own ambitions, sadly aware of how my brother's had been subverted by racial injustice.

I have never been busier than in the summer of 1947. I was reading galley and page proofs, compiling the index, and seeing to dozens of matters related to the publication of *From Slavery to Freedom*. With the illness and death of my brother, I had assumed the role of the only male family member of my generation, and I found myself striving to aid all of us in withstanding the devastation resulting from his tragic passing. I was also negotiating for a new position as professor of history at Howard University.

That possibility had been brewing for some time. I first met Rayford W. Logan, head of Howard's History Department, at the general convention of the Alpha Phi Alpha fraternity. We were both members, he prominently so; Logan would become a future president. Subsequently, during my first year at Harvard, he came to Cambridge to take his final oral examinations for the PhD, and I had the opportunity to have a meal with him. I next saw him in Petersburg, Virginia, in 1936 during a meeting of the Association for the Study of Negro Life and History. In 1938 I visited with him at Atlanta University, just before he moved to Howard. He always seemed genuinely interested in my work, and in December 1946 I suggested to Roger Shugg that Professor Logan should be added to the list of readers for my manuscript. Logan accepted the invitation and consequently was in a good position to make a decision regarding my merits as a prospective colleague. In the late spring he invited me to become a professor at Howard University, and I accepted.

As we prepared to leave North Carolina College at Durham, I thought to evaluate the variety of relationships that I had cultivated there. There was my early experience with a white couple, Guion and Guy Johnson, which occurred shortly after my arrival in the state in 1939. Guion had written a monumental work on antebellum North Carolina, which I found indispensable in preparing my study of free Negroes in North Carolina. When I had gathered sufficient courage, I decided I should call on her and solicit suggestions about my research. I took the bus to Chapel Hill and phoned her from Sutton's Drug Store on Franklin Street. When I was finally able to tell her who I was and what I was doing, she told me to wait at the drugstore; she would come down, pick me up, and take me to her home. It was clear that she knew that I was not white, but that did not seem to matter. The moment we arrived at her home, she went through her files and pulled out all of the material in which she thought I would be interested. When her husband, Guy, a professor of sociology at the university, arrived, she stopped long enough to prepare lunch. At the end of the day she wished me well, urging me to be in touch whenever I wanted to discuss my topic. That was the beginning of a friendship that would last for the rest of our lives.

Nor could I fail to recall my friendship with Howard K. Beale, professor of American history at the University of North Carolina. There he was, one day in 1940, standing just outside my room in the men's dormitory at St. Augustine's, in his chesterfield topcoat, white silk scarf, and bowler hat, with his calling card in hand, perhaps looking for a silver tray in which to drop it. Paul Buck, whom he knew at Harvard, had told him to look me up. He wanted to invite me to his home in Chapel Hill to have lunch or dinner and to meet his family. From that point on we saw each other regularly.

After I moved to Durham, he invited me each year to give a lecture on "The Negro in American Social Thought" in one of his classes. One day when I was en route to Beale's class, I encountered one of his colleagues, who greeted me and inquired where I was going. I returned the greeting and told him that I was going to Howard Beale's class to give a lecture. After I began the lecture I noticed that Howard was called out of the class. He returned shortly, and I did not give it another thought. Some years later, after we both had left North Carolina, Howard told me that he had been called out to answer a long-distance phone call from a trustee of the university who had heard that a Negro was lecturing in his class. The trustee ordered Beale to remove me immediately. In recounting this story, Beale told me that he had said that he was not in the habit of letting trustees plan his courses, and he promptly hung up. Within a few years Howard accepted a professorship at the University of Wisconsin. A favorite comment from Chapel Hill was that upon his departure from North Carolina, blood pressures went down all over the state.

Then there was Arthur S. Link, who was teaching part-time at North Carolina State University in Raleigh while completing his doctoral dissertation at Chapel Hill. Arthur, a North Carolinian by birth, was so strong in his Presbyterian faith that if he was commanded to love his brother, of whatever race, he did so with fervor. We saw each other regularly when I was in Raleigh and Durham. After I married, he expressed his affection for Aurelia as if she was his sister. When he married Margaret Douglas at Davidson College, where her father was a professor, he invited us to the wedding. When we were unable to attend, Arthur brought his bride of two days to our apartment in Durham and said simply that since we were going to be friends for life, we should meet the fourth link in the friendship chain as soon as possible. Arthur and Margaret remained our loyal friends after they moved on to Northwestern and Princeton, throughout their retirement, and until the end of their lives.

It was equally difficult to leave my friends and colleagues in Durham: Charles Ray, who would soon marry Eva Frazier, the registrar at Shaw University; the Farrisons, who had become a part of the inner circle; Joe

Taylor in the Department of History, who was my "colleague" in every sense of the word; and Helen Edmonds, who carried more than her load after completing her doctorate at Ohio State University. But it was most difficult to say farewell to Dr. Shepard, with whom I had developed a special bond and affection. Once the moving van had been loaded, Aurelia and I felt free to go by his office. He was gracious as he bade us good luck and godspeed. He was also humorous. Did we have a very large moving van, he inquired. We did, we replied. He then expressed both relief and pleasure, adding that we would need it when our old automobile broke down. As he turned to leave, he ordered us to keep in touch. Sadly, before we could even send a letter, we were back in Durham for his funeral. He had died suddenly, of natural causes.

While I did not hesitate to accept the invitation to Howard University, I had mixed feelings about moving to the so-called Capstone of Negro Education. It was regarded as the "final" institution for Negro scholars. After making that club, there was nowhere else to go. It was 1947. I was thirty-two years of age, with most of my career ahead of me. Was I ready to take the very last position that I could ever secure? I felt certain that whatever else I accomplished, if I created an absolutely new school of historical studies or a revolutionary way of thinking about the historical process, there was nowhere for me to go beyond Howard. However, the opportunity had come, to be sure, somewhat unexpectedly and even prematurely, and it was clearly not an opportunity to reject. So off to Howard we went that autumn.

I knew enough Southern history and culture to realize that in moving to Washington I was not leaving the South. I had visited Washington enough to know that the stamp placed on it by Mr. Jefferson and his contemporaries in 1800 was one of racial segregation and discrimination, which still existed. In that sense, we were making no radical social changes in our lives by moving to the District of Columbia. Thus, in looking for somewhere to live, we knew that there were limits to the hospitable places we could find, and we acted accordingly. There were newly constructed apartments in the far northeast, designed by Albert Cassell, a distinguished African American architect, and available in various sizes. My sister Anne was already living there, and we sought and obtained an apartment in the same complex. I do not believe that there were many white residents in Mayfair Mansions, as the complex was called, although there was no policy against their living there. It was convenient to public transportation and to Howard University by car.

We had scarcely become settled in Washington before we had to turn our attention once again to *From Slavery to Freedom*, which was soon to ship from the printer. I had proudly dedicated it to Aurelia, the CEO of the "Aurelia Franklin Foundation," and when it arrived we were pleased with its design and appearance. Like performers on the Broadway stage, we needed only to wait to read the reviews. They were not long in coming, and we devoured them voraciously. All of them had at least one thing in common. Not one noticed that the book's publication date on September 22, 1947, coincided with the anniversary of Abraham Lincoln's issuance of the preliminary Emancipation Proclamation.

Roi Ottley's review in *The New York Times* stung, perhaps primarily because its appearing in the "paper of record" accorded it undue influence. Ottley called it a "bulky, unwieldy, conventional history, with the studied scholarship of doctoral thesis . . . There are neither the sharp, crisp, incisive observations expected of a first-rate journalist, nor the perspective, balance and interpretation expected of the historian." Nowhere did the *Times* identify Ottley as the author of a forthcoming book in the same field or, indeed, as a historian or reporter. Nor did the newspaper print any of the rejoinders it received, copies of which their authors forwarded to me. I did not write *The Times* but poured out my disappointment to Roger Shugg. "I cannot see by what standards the editor of the Book Review judged [Ottley] to be competent to review a book that lies so clearly outside his domain," I complained. "I take serious exception . . . to a responsible press placing the book in the hands of an irresponsible person who deals with it arbitrarily, whimsically, and capriciously."

I was not consoled by others who praised the book. Benjamin Quarles wrote Roger Shugg that it was "a work of compelling excellence." Rayford Logan, my new chairman at Howard, had praised the book in a lengthy critique that he sent to Roger Shugg. One of my new colleagues at Howard, Alain Locke, the philosopher and close student of the Harlem Renaissance, welcomed me to the university by sending me a copy of his comments in the *Saturday Review of Literature*. "With this significant volume," Locke wrote in his review, the author "has made several constructive and timely contributions to the history of the American Negro. . . . the most welcome and important, is to have integrated the story of this minority group with the general context of American history."

Other reviews began to offset my disappointment with *The Times*. William Harrison, an African American scholar in American literature who was a contemporary of mine at Harvard, declared in the *Boston Chronicle* that he was struck by "the impressive grandeur of the total achievement." The reviewer in the *Chicago Tribune* said that of the nine histories of the Negro written since 1887, "*From Slavery to Freedom* . . . is by far the best." Meanwhile, the other leading New York newspaper, the *Herald Tribune*, proclaimed it "a rich, absorbing book, with clarity of design which all readers will appreciate." There were reviews and notices in such papers as the *Register* in New Haven, the *Southern Packet* in Asheville, North Carolina, the *Post-Dispatch* in St. Louis, the *Sentinel Mist* in St. Helena, Oregon, and the *Star* in Winnemucca, Nevada. There were also reviews in such durable sources as *Survey Graphic*, *The American Mercury*, and *Commentary*.

If I had misgivings about some of the reviews, Roger Shugg and I shared our apprehension about the sales of the book. I felt strongly that a big New York publisher, however knowledgeable it might be about the book market in general, had not the slightest inkling about how to promote a volume dealing with the history of Negroes either in the general market or in the Negro market. Consequently, I made suggestions about advertising in the Negro media, about having sales personnel target the Negro market, about using me to publicize the book with appearances around the country. I provided Knopf with lists of Negro newspapers and magazines, lists of bookstores and other possible outlets, and the names and addresses of hundreds of people who might wish to purchase the book.

As Shugg looked at the sales figures and as he talked with the sales personnel in the field, he became apprehensive, even as he tried to console me. When I complained that there were many bookstores that were not stocking it at all, while others did not reorder when they sold out, he reminded me that not every bookstore would take the book and there was nothing they could do about that. "In the South, after talking with our Southern salesman I am inclined to think that there is less support than you might expect for your book." Even if they made no attempt to suppress it, the bookstores in the South "are apt to be a little diffident in promoting its sale. There is no conspiracy, I am sure, but it is in the North that we must find our chief sale to the public," he concluded.

During the first six months, 1,001 copies were sold to the general public while only an additional 263 were sold as textbooks. The royalties for that period did not quite repay the advance. Over the second six months, things improved somewhat, with 976 copies being sold as trade books and 1,158 as textbooks. In subsequent periods, the trade sales fell sharply, while the textbook sales declined but not as much. It became quite clear that the author's and publisher's enthusiasm for the book was not immediately shared by the buying and reading public. Fortunately, both were prepared to await the public's change of attitude.

I did not have to wait very long to learn what the professionals thought of the book. The first critical review in a major academic journal came when my new Howard colleague Williston Lofton gave his public assessment in *The Journal of Negro History* for April 1948. After several criticisms, he stated the book to be "one of the most scholarly contributions of recent years to the field of literature dealing with the American Negro." *The Journal of Southern History* called it "praiseworthy for its comprehensiveness," written in a style that was "unusually felicitous." This reviewer had complaints, stating, for example, that I had failed "to achieve a high degree of objectivity," but I had reason to be grateful that a journal believed in some quarters not to be friendly to African Americans would print so favorable a review.

The fallout from writing a general history of Negro Americans that was, on the whole, well received was considerable. As early as 1944, Carter Woodson had added me to the board of editors of *The Journal of Negro History*. Now, to the surprise of almost everyone, he paid more public attention to me, graciously indicating a collegial relationship between us that was both flattering and rewarding. At the annual meeting of the Association for the Study of Negro Life and History held in New York at the end of October 1949, I read a paper, at Dr. Woodson's invitation, on "Charles Sumner and Civil Rights: A Reappraisal." Notes on the book and notices of its availability seemed to appear virtually everywhere. Letters of congratulations came from all parts of the country, ranging from

Edwin R. Embree, president of the Rosenwald Fund, to Edward T. Garrett, a New York bibliophile. Answering the letters, together with making up still more lists of names and addresses to which Knopf should send notices of the book, took up much of my time.

In the spring of the following year, Woodson called together a group of his loyal supporters, in which I was included, and solicited suggestions regarding the long-delayed African and American encyclopedia of which he had dreamed for such a long time. The suggestions were halfhearted, poorly structured, and discouraging. Dr. Woodson appeared unusually depressed by the inconclusive results of the meeting. He had been unwell, and the slow pace of change—within the scholarship and the nation—left him dispirited. Within a few days he was dead. At his funeral, where I served as honorary pallbearer, I was urged to take up Woodson's torch. I demurred. I was certain that I could not make the sacrifices that Woodson had made to assure the association's success. By this time my commitment to scholarship and teaching was much too deep to regard such an offer as an attractive alternative.

10

A Hilltop High

THE ADJUSTMENT to Washington, D.C., and Howard University was not easy. Both the city and the institution were quite different from anything Aurelia and I had experienced. Washington was large, government-centered, and very impersonal. So was Howard. Getting settled presented its own set of problems. Complicating matters, there was no office space in Douglass Hall, where Howard's Department of History was located. I was assigned to one of the World War I barracks, whose title of Temporary B belied its virtually permanent status. I was "in exile," as my colleagues called it; such basics as requisitioning office supplies, from paper clips to a telephone, were a struggle.

My pleasures in being at Howard were twofold. One was the opportunity to associate with a faculty whose roster read like a *Who's Who* of black scholars. There were James Nabrit, secretary of the university; Thurgood Marshall, already with the NAACP; and Charles Houston, who gave courses in the law school. In the College of Liberal Arts, there were Frank Snowden in classics; Sterling Brown, Charles E. Burch, Charlotte Crawford, and Ivan Taylor in the English Department; Alain L. Locke and Eugene Holmes in philosophy; Rayford Logan, Leo Hansberry, and Merze Tate in history; and E. Franklin Frazier, Harry Walker, G. Franklin Edwards, and Mark Hanna Watkins in sociology and anthropology. It also had more than its share of distinguished theologians and scientists, both in the college and the medical school.

While most of them were cordial, few beyond my immediate associates in the History Department became intimate friends. The nucleus of this small group was known as the "Thinkers and Drinkers." It was not that we did a great deal of drinking, but that all members were vigorously opposed to the poker playing that preoccupied the leisure time of others. We met about once each month in members' homes and spent the evening talking, largely about what was wrong with the university, and eating and drinking. The membership seldom increased, but when it did, a main requirement was that the new recruit forswear poker playing.

The other great joy in teaching at Howard came from my students. I taught seminars and colloquia to graduate students as well as fairly large classes of undergraduate students. This was the first time I was able to teach graduate students. Howard did not have a doctoral program, but it had a rigorous program leading to the master of arts degree. Some of the best students I ever taught were at Howard University. Many of them went on to graduate and professional schools, while others taught at the elementary and secondary levels in public and private schools.

Shortly after we arrived in Washington, I resumed my research on the martial spirit in the Old South and was a regular attendant at the Library of Congress. It was there that I made contact with historians at neighboring universities and developed close ties with some of them.

I had previously met C. Vann Woodward, who in 1955 would publish *The Strange Career of Jim Crow*, a book Martin Luther King Jr. would call "the historical Bible of the Civil Rights Movement," but I got to know him much better when I was at Howard and he was at Johns Hopkins. During my first year in Washington, Vann invited me to meet with his seminar at Hopkins to talk about my own research. That was a refreshing and exhilarating experience, the first time I had been with an all-white group of scholars since my own graduate school days. The students were very interested in what I had to say, and several became lifelong friends, including Louis Harlan, who was then just beginning his important work on Booker T. Washington. Harlan later told me that his encounter with me in the Woodward seminar was the first time that he had met an African American with more than a rudimentary education.

Meanwhile, a group of Southern historians launched a new series designed to provide up-to-date volumes on the history of the South. The first to appear was *The South During Reconstruction* by E. Merton Coulter, a respected professor at the University of Georgia. The editor of *The Journal of Negro Education*, published at Howard, had asked me to review the entire series. When I examined the Coulter volume, I was shocked. Here it was in the middle of the twentieth century, and a scholar with the full weight of academic approval—his book had been vetted by scholars, series editors, and its scholarly publishers—was presenting views current in 1880. He told how drunken black former slaves displayed their ignorance in the state legislatures and betrayed their brutish lusts by chasing white women with the intention of raping them, and throughout, his treatment of the period was strikingly similar to that revealed in Thomas Dixon's *The Klansman* and in D. W. Griffith's infamous film *Birth of a Nation*.

Despite this, several reviewers praised Coulter's work. I began my review by criticizing them for it. I then pointed out that Coulter grossly misrepresented and distorted his sources. I described the post-Reconstruction careers of several black officials to prove that they did not all return to their old positions of "street sweepers, waiters, and field hands," as Coulter claimed. I concluded by noting that the Coulter work was more valuable in the history of history than "it was in the history of Reconstruction." Since the journal was not widely read among historians, and I was determined to alert the wider profession to the flaws in Coulter's work, I distributed two hundred offprints to influential historians. Almost unanimously, they praised my essay and thanked me for what I had done. Several requested copies to use in courses they were teaching. My willingness to publicly and vigorously confront the damning presumptions of accepted scholarly wisdom would prove to be more important in advancing my reputation than I could have anticipated.

About the time the Coulter article appeared in the autumn of 1948, Vann Woodward came to my study room at the Library of Congress and asked me to make him a promise. *If* he became chair of the program committee of the Southern Historical Association and *if* the next annual meeting was not held in one of the more racist towns in the South, would I be willing to read a paper at the meeting? No African American had ever been on the Southern Historical Association's program and most historians in the South regarded the association as equal parts social club and professional organization. Put succinctly, African Americans were not expected to attend. But if they had the temerity to appear, they would accept segregated seating wherever a paper was presented and would never presume to attend the members' luncheons, dinners, or other social gatherings, which were understood to be for whites only. Indeed, some African American historians referred to it as the Confederate Historical Association, and few if any ever attended. Vann's proposition was just uncertain and mysterious enough to encourage me to accept.

Shortly thereafter, he was made the committee chair and announced that I had agreed to read a paper on "Slavery and the Martial South." Caught completely off guard, the program committee was thrown into a state of panic, for I presented them with unsought and unwished-for problems. The committee wondered where I would stay, where I would eat, even where I would stand when reading my paper. Vann countered with the claim that Franklin was quite resourceful. He just might bring K rations and a pup tent, Woodward told a dejected committee.

He did not tell them that Douglass Adair, editor of *The William and Mary Quarterly*, had already invited me to be a guest in his home, which was conveniently near William and Mary College and Colonial Williamsburg where the meeting was being held. Regardless, when the materials for the meeting, including forms for hotel reservations arrived, Vann asked me to fill them out just to see if the Williamsburg Inn or Lodge would accept me. My application went ignored. Meanwhile, my friend Howard K. Beale, by then affiliated with the University of Wisconsin, was in Washington doing research for a biography of Theodore Roosevelt. Delighted to be in on the "intrigue," he announced his intention of attending the conference and insisted that I ride with him to Williamsburg.

I was warmly welcomed by Douglass and Virginia Adair and their young children, though I necessarily spent much of the time at the college or with colleagues at one of the convention hotels. I vividly recall one incident in a hotel room. I was visiting a friend, along with several other historians. We decided to order room service, and when the African American waiter arrived with our food, he promptly dropped his tray on seeing me comfortably lounging in the hotel room. He apologized, and with that was off to the kitchen to replace the order. Despite that incident, however, no one else seemed surprised at seeing me in the corridors of the hotel or, indeed, in the rooms. Then and now, what the hotel gained by refusing to accept my reservation eluded me. Perhaps the management would have resorted to the excuse that it was, after all, "the law." Vann knew, as he would later establish in his *Strange Career of Jim Crow*, that laws requiring segregation were not nearly as old as many Southerners claimed. One of my roles in Williamsburg was to demonstrate that the laws were not only rather recent but demonstrably absurd.

By the time I read my paper to the meeting on November 10, all of the questions raised by the members of the program committee had been answered. The chair of the session, who had volunteered his services, was Henry Steele Commager of Columbia University, while the other person to read a paper was Bell Irvin Wiley of Emory University. The problem of where I would sit or stand was settled by the decision that there would be no change from the customary practices—I would be treated no differently. In his official report as committee chair, Vann called the audience "large"; I recall the crowd as having filled the oversized first-floor room, with many people looking through the windows. The presented papers were warmly received, questions were few, and several members of the audience came up and congratulated me.

I published the paper the following year in *The Journal of Negro History* largely because I wished to indicate to the members of the Southern Historical Association that the official journal of the Association for the Study of Negro Life and History, established in 1916, was not only more venerable than their own *Journal of Southern History*, launched some twenty years later, but was arguably the more respectable, with an interracial editorial board consisting of distinguished professors at Harvard, Columbia, and other universities of similar standing. The reaction to my article was such that I was encouraged to push ahead with my research and to complete the book-length manuscript as quickly as possible.

In due course, Dr. Alfonso Elder was named to succeed Dr. James E. Shepard as president of North Carolina College at Durham. In February 1949, Elder wrote to me to inquire of my possible interest in becoming dean of the graduate school. By that time it was not difficult for me to respond to such queries. I assured Dr. Elder that while I would always be interested in the future of the institution, I thought it best that I not encourage him to expect that I could ever become a candidate for such a position. I was steadfastly determined to dedicate myself to teaching and original scholarship. Perhaps not surprisingly, therefore, North Carolina College's director of the summer school persuaded me to teach there over the summer term.

Even as we prepared to go to Durham that summer, my duties and responsibilities broadened in yet another way. Thurgood Marshall of the NAACP Legal Defense Fund asked me to assist him in a case that had arisen in Kentucky. Lyman Johnson, a history teacher in the public schools of Louisville, had applied to pursue graduate studies at the University of Kentucky. He was denied admission and informed that he should consider instead the Kentucky State College for Negroes at Frankfort, where, it was asserted, he could secure the same graduate training. It was clear that the institutions were not at all equal, so Marshall sued the University of Kentucky, demanding Johnson's admission. In preparing his argument, Marshall asked me to make a study of the two institutions, comparing the library facilities, the offerings in the respective departments of history, and the qualifications of the teaching personnel. I was only too happy to do so and completed my comparative analysis just before the case was to be tried in the Federal District Court before Judge H. Church Ford.

In the first hour or two, the University of Kentucky, in an absurd poison-pill defense, attempted to establish the fact that it was no more able than the state college for Negroes to provide graduate study for Lyman Johnson or, indeed, anyone else. Rather than accept an African American, they were prepared to argue their inability to accept anyone. At the morning intermission, Marshall was so disgusted with the university's feeble argument that he informed his colleagues that he was prepared to ask Judge Ford to make a summary ruling in Johnson's favor. Following Marshall's request, the judge did precisely that. After chastising the University of Kentucky for even attempting to make such a plea, he directed the university to admit Johnson and closed the case. Everyone was delighted with the verdict except, perhaps, me, who had worked assiduously to make the case for Johnson and wished, more than anything else, to testify against the university. I quickly recovered from my pique and celebrated Marshall's significant victory.

In the autumn of 1949 I was invited to be a member of the Harvard faculty for the summer term of 1950. I was shocked and excited. I had never thought of Harvard's having any African Americans on its faculty, ever! In the recent past there had been a token one or two, and as graduate students we all knew of but never met the distinguished syphilologist William A. Hinton, who had served on the faculty of the medical school. Yet he had taught as an instructor from the time of his appointment in 1918 until 1948, the year before his retirement. Only at that very late date was he promoted to full professor. That appointment seemed the joke it was, and none of us took seriously the possibility that Harvard would ever have another African American professor, even on a temporary basis. Aurelia, once past her disbelief, agreed: This was a matter not to be debated. I accepted promptly.

We had never lived in Cambridge except marginally, in one room and with an automobile that constantly threatened to cease running. During our summer sojourn, we intended to move up just a notch or two. Immediately, we began searching for housing, and we were offered the home of Dr. Bernice Brown Cronkhite, dean of the graduate school at Radcliffe College. Dean Cronkhite was off doing research of her own that summer. It was a lovely, spacious home, tastefully decorated and furnished, and right in the middle of things on Appian Way in Cambridge. We had already purchased a new automobile, and long before the trek to Cambridge, we had become accustomed to its comfort as well as the increased cost of transportation the new car brought with it.

I am certain that Harvard's invitation came on the recommendation of my supporters in its Department of History, among them Paul H. Buck, Arthur M. Schlesinger, and Frederick Merk. Upon our arrival, they all welcomed us warmly, and Aurelia and I settled into a summer of pleasant work and refreshing relaxation. I never suffered any sense that faculty or students were shocked or disturbed that an African American scholar was in their midst. Indeed, the faculty, many of whom I knew personally, made it clear that they hoped Aurelia and I found the summer both relaxing and stimulating. It also goes without saying no one made any mention of my seeking a permanent position there, let alone that I be asked to teach students other than those signed up for summer school courses. I had one lecture course, American history since 1865, and a seminar on the history of the New South. For the lecture course I had a teaching assistant who graded the papers and looked after other details connected with the course. Student performance ranged widely, thanks to the disparate students who enrolled for the Harvard summer school. Even so, there was a sufficient number of interesting students to make the experience worthwhile.

During the evenings and on weekends we saw a good deal of Paul and Sally Buck, David and Louise Owen, Arthur and Elizabeth Schlesinger, Oscar and Mary Handlin, and Elliott and Mary Perkins. We had a delightful time with Ralph and Ruth Bunche when they passed through Cambridge in consequence of his work. Ralph was widely and well-known for mediating the Middle East conflict, for which he would be awarded the Nobel Peace Prize later that year. He had been appointed to a professorship at Harvard but had postponed taking up the chair because of his United Nation duties. Two years later he would resign his chair for the same reason, without having ever taught. The addition of an African American to Harvard's full-time teaching faculty still eluded the university.

One of the reasons we so enjoyed our summer in Cambridge was that in the previous April I had been awarded a Guggenheim Fellowship for the following academic year. Consequently, we were in a celebratory mood. The additional funds meant that I could, at long last, complete my study of the militant South. We were so pleased that we overlooked, for the moment, the fact that the executive committee of Howard University's Board of Trustees had amended my sabbatical to a "leave of absence without pay."

This was emblematic of my less-than-smooth working relations with Howard. I had had to contest my omission from a list of promising young professors who had received a special raise. I had been on that list, since my chairman and my dean both recommended me, but the president of the university vetoed their recommendation. I confronted the treasurer, telling him that I was familiar with the records of the approved young professors, and as far as I knew none of them had written two books, edited another, and written eleven articles as I had. I bluntly announced that if I was not awarded the salary recommended by my chairman and dean by the following Monday morning, I would, rather than teach under such obviously unequal compensation, leave the university and go to Oklahoma and sit on my father's porch. On the following day, the dean of the university called me at home to inform me that a check, based on the new salary scale for the promising young professors, was already in my office mailbox.

I always regretted having to take a stand against certain administrative policies and practices at Howard University, but I never wanted anyone to interpret my silence as acquiescence. It was a habit ingrained in me since childhood. Consequently, whenever I felt it imperative, I called attention to things that I regarded as inimical not only to my interests but also to the best interests of the university.

On the other hand, I also did whatever I could to contribute to Howard's growth and strength. Such efforts ranged from working with the Howard University chapter of the American Committee on Human Rights to helping the registrar improve conditions during registration periods. I made various suggestions to the dean of the College of Liberal Arts regarding the scholarly activities of faculty members and how that information could be used to encourage and improve the performance of the faculty, and I prepared a working paper on how to enhance the university's intellectual and professional atmosphere.

Within two or three years of our moving to Washington, Aurelia reached the conclusion that with a first-rate library school at nearby Catholic University, she would be remiss if she did not take advantage of it and enhance her learning. Consequently, in 1950 she resigned her job, applied, and was admitted for graduate studies. I had always known Aurelia to be a dedicated and gifted scholar and thinker and as a graduate student she once again made her talents abundantly clear. She did not lack for the disciplined focus to details that inevitably determines who extracts everything they can from their graduate, or for that matter undergraduate, instruction. As she had been numerous times in the past, Aurelia was once again an inspiration. For a while she was so busy writing her MA thesis that I assumed the lion's share of the household duties. Remembering those days in Washington when she financed the writing of *From Slavery to Freedom*, I readily accepted the fact that it was "payback time," and I felt greatly rewarded at her commencement in 1951, when I sat with the families of the graduates. Almost immediately, she became the librarian of the new Spingarn High School in northeast Washington, a position she would hold for the remainder of the time we were in the city.

We could not have imagined a more fitting way to celebrate Aurelia's graduation than a grand tour of Europe, which is precisely what we wound up doing. It all began in the summer of 1950 with our developing friendship with Dexter and Wilma Perkins. In addition to being a professor of diplomatic history at the University of Rochester, Dexter was president of the Salzburg Seminar in American Studies. The seminar had been founded just after the war by three Harvard graduates who wanted to provide an "academic rest center" for young European students and scholars who needed more than the standard fare of war relief. The project, established in Max Reinhardt's eighteenth-century castle, Schloss Leopoldskron in Salzburg, Austria, succeeded from the very beginning in attracting and bringing together European students and American professors. In the fall of 1950, Perkins invited me to be a lecturer at the fourth annual summer session, which would convene the following summer. I enthusiastically accepted.

For our transatlantic crossing, we chose the French line, wanting to escape from American racism as quickly as possible. Thus, we booked passage on the *Île de France*, sailing from New York in June 1951. Never having been on an oceangoing vessel, we knew little about the procedures for reserving a table in the dining room or which serving time was best for us. When I heard it announced over the public address system that if anyone had yet to register for a table, kindly see the maître d' at once, I got in line. When I reached the maître d', he said that he had just the table for two, table 34. I accepted it with the same grace that he offered it to me.

The table was the worst in the entire dining room, just by the door to the kitchen. Each time waiters burst through the swinging door, Aurelia and I instinctively dodged. We had learned our lesson and swore that it would not happen to us again.

In London, we were met by our friend from Raleigh, Emory Johnson, who had begun to visit England annually, though he had not yet taken up permanent residence there. He had booked a room for us at a hotel that was within walking distance of Marble Arch and London's West End. Although the war had ended almost six years earlier, the damage that London had sustained was still evident almost everywhere. We began to understand what the British had endured and how sensitive they were to those of us who had not experienced war's suffering, privation, and devastation. Even rationing persisted. The other thing that impressed us was the British curiosity about color. This was before the great influx of immigrants from Asia and the Caribbean, and the British were not yet accustomed to seeing black and brown people walking about the city and engaged in the workplace. Some stared at us as if they were experiencing an apparition.

On this first trip to Europe, we did the tourist routine extensively, traveling throughout France, Italy, and Germany. The French manifested no curiosity about our race, acting coolly indifferent. Indeed, they were barely cordial, evidencing much more interest in what we were willing to spend than in how we looked or, indeed, how we responded to them when they ignored our poor French and spoke to us in English. Italy was quite different. Wherever we went, the locals were excessively polite, flattering us about our fluency in their language even though it was limited to a greeting. The Germans were pleasant but seemed as curious as the British about our appearance. They would follow us for blocks, just to get a better look at us and to observe our skin color and to hear us speak. I had more than a smattering of German, and when I spoke to them in their language, they reacted in disbelief.

The Salzburg Seminar, which had been operating regularly since 1947 had already acquired a reputation. Students came from most of the countries in Western Europe, from Scandinavia, and from the Balkans. In due course they would come from behind the Iron Curtain as well as from the Near East and South Asia. From the beginning, a limited number of American students, primarily from Harvard, attended to facilitate interactions and to share with European students their own experiences as students in the United States. Among the professors I joined that summer were Alfred Kazin, who gave that session's opening address; Henry Steele Commager, with whom I team-taught a course in recent United States history; Howard Higman of Colorado; Jean McKelvey of the Cornell School of Labor and Industrial Relations; and R.W.B. Lewis, dean at Salzburg and on the threshold of a distinguished career as a professor and scholar at Yale.

As American professors, we adhered to two principles that we hoped would indicate how different the entire American academic system was from Europe's. While we did not search for disagreement among ourselves, we did not flinch from it. We also encouraged a level of informality to which the Europeans were certainly unaccustomed.

There were numerous pleasant diversions to our classroom labors. On weekends there were trips to the Grossglockner, Salzkammergut, and even Vienna, which had all the excitement of travel behind the Iron Curtain, since the Russians were in charge of that area at the time of our visit. I keenly recall that at one of the rest stops, a waitress had a small son who regularly greeted the bus. When he first saw me, he was terrified and ran to his mother. She explained as best she could that I was a friend and would not harm him. Upon our return, he came looking for me. When he found me, he embraced me and presented me with an edelweiss, which I continue to cherish after almost sixty years, and he waved to me as long as our departing bus was in sight.

At the end of the seminar I was invited to visit Frankfurt and Berlin to deliver a few lectures. The devastation in England paled by comparison with what we encountered in Germany. The only structure we saw that had not been touched was the I. G. Farben building, which, we were told, the Allies declined to bomb, having decided that it would be a very satisfactory headquarters for them once the war was over. I gave a talk in Frankfurt, then Aurelia and I went by U.S. Army plane to Berlin, where I gave a talk on problems of the postwar world. We also saw a memorable performance of Wagner's *Parsifal*, in which Kirsten Flagstad sang, the one and only time that either of us would hear her in person.

The summer passed rapidly, and very soon we had to take the train for Cherbourg, where we would take the *Île de France* for the return trip to the United States. Only one matter consumed me as we embarked—to claim satisfactory seating in the dining room. As the ship left the harbor, I was first in line for a table. It was the same maître d' I had encountered on the crossing from New York. I told him that I wanted a table for two at the second, or slightly later, seating. He replied that he had just the spot. I could not believe it when he indicated table 34. I told him that I had served my time there on the eastward crossing three months earlier. I wondered aloud why the table next to the kitchen was such a suitable one for me. I then took the seating chart, which was still quite blank, and pointed to the table where we would sit. He merely replied with a meek "Mais oui, monsieur." I returned to Aurelia, persuaded that we could not get away from discrimination merely by changing the flag under which we traveled. The United States line, which we had avoided, could hardly have been any worse about such matters than the French line had been.

Our return from Europe was marked by the fact that for the first time since our marriage, we would not be living in an apartment. E. Franklin Frazier had been appointed chief of the Division of Applied Social Sciences at the United Nations Educational, Scientific, and Cultural Organization in Paris. He and his wife, Marie, would be leaving Washington for two years, and he wondered if we would like to live in their home, where our sole financial responsibility would be to pay the utility bills. It was an offer too good to refuse. One of the many joys of living in the Frazier home was the use of their library, which was considered a prize collection, and to enjoy the art that they had collected over many years. The Frazier home was not far from Howard University, in a neighborhood of middle-class African Americans and near an area that was zoned for small businesses, restaurants, funeral homes, and convenience stores. It was an enviable location. Most members of the Howard University faculty lived in the upper northwest neighborhoods or in the northeast, out near Catholic University, which is where I would live during my last two years at Howard.

My academic work continued to go well, and my research and writing were moving ahead. I regularly attended meetings of the learned societies and reviewed my share of new books. I also reviewed manuscripts for publishers, including one that Knopf was considering. When the manuscript came to me I read it quickly but very carefully, concluding that it in no way merited publication. In a critique of fourteen pages, I laid bare its many faults, and I was unequivocal in my letter to the editor at Knopf, Harold Strauss.

I thought little more about my harsh critique of the manuscript until some months later I received a letter from Harold Strauss categorically rejecting my manuscript on the militant south. Among other things, he said, "You have completely missed your chance to write a colorful and dramatic book," and he concluded, "It has the stamp of a university press book, I hope that it finds a welcome from one of them."

This appraisal, however, did not disturb me. I had worked on the manuscript for such a long time that I had supreme confidence in the merits of its argument and I had no doubt that it would be properly published. I did wonder, just a bit, if Harold Strauss was exacting some measure of retribution for my earlier harsh critique, particularly in view of the fact that my editor, Roger Shugg, was just then leaving the house to take a position with the National Committee for a Free Europe. The politics of publishing seemed no more transparent than those governing book reviews. No matter; I set my sights on seeking the interest of other publishers.

Happily, I learned that I would have the time to put the finishing touches on the manuscript. A friend from my Harvard days, Edmund Morgan, was professor of history and dean of the graduate school at Brown University. There was a fund at his disposal to encourage research and writing by anyone he determined to be worthy. He invited me to apply. Nothing was required, not even residence at Brown. Appointed a Brown University President's Fellow in 1952, I would have the opportunity to prepare my long-in-progress work for publication.

II

Legacies

A FTER A DOZEN CHILDLESS YEARS of marriage, in the early winter of 1952 Aurelia began to experience some physical discomfort. Her physician gave her some medication for indigestion, and she continued her work at Spingarn. Soon, she and I realized to our great delight that she was pregnant. Since she was quite comfortable and happy, she continued her work throughout the year without interruption. Even when she was in the full bloom of pregnancy, with a late August delivery date, she graced the Howard University commencement in mid-June to hear President Harry S. Truman deliver his address. I continued work on preparing the martial South manuscript for someone other than Knopf's Harold Strauss and anxiously awaited the end of August.

Aside from a stint of writing, it was a leisurely, almost lazy summer, during which we had ample time to make plans for the great event. I marveled at Aurelia's happiness and her joyous anticipation, never betraying the slightest apprehension of having her first child at age thirty-seven. I, however, experienced at least a tinge of apprehension. The fact that the birth proved moderately difficult (memorably, at one point her physician expressed concern about Aurelia's survival) meant that I was all the more relieved on Sunday morning, August 24, 1952, when I was informed that she had "pulled through" the ordeal and that our son was healthy.

Since there was a real possibility that he would be our only offspring, we decided to pack as much of his heritage as possible in his name. My first name and Aurelia's family name became his first and middle names. Since my brother had died childless, the burden of passing on the Franklin name rested squarely on young John Whittington Franklin's shoulders. Indeed, since Aurelia's sister had three girls (the fourth and final child would also be a girl), and with her brother at the time unmarried, the Whittington name was also in danger of disappearance, at least from that branch of the family.

Within four days of our son's birth, my father arrived from Saratoga, where he now regularly spent his summers in an effort to cope with his allergies. He was delighted with his newest grandson but thought that he should not be called John or John Whittington, but Whit, for ease and convenience. Whit he remained throughout his childhood. Within a few weeks, Aurelia's mother and father, who had never visited us before, journeyed to Washington to see their first grandson. They too were overjoyed, and Whit soon became the object of universal lavish attention and affection.

Whit's good temperament vastly helped us navigate a busy year. A growing list of supportive friends and my ever stronger list of publications and public lectures meant I was the recipient of more generous offers. One of them, greatly due to the determination of Howard K. Beale, resulted in my being offered a half-year appointment at the University of Wisconsin.

Even before we went to Wisconsin, Paul Gates, chair of the Department of History at Cornell, approached me about teaching there during the 1953 summer term. I was happy to do so, and long before our arrival, Gates had secured housing for us: A physics professor would be away and was pleased to rent his home to us for the six weeks that we would be there.

Once Wisconsin's final examinations were over and the seminar papers had been graded, the Franklin family prepared to take a leisurely, unstructured trip from Madison to Ithaca, New York. Aurelia's mother, who had joined us for our final weeks in Madison, would travel with us. She could become well acquainted with her grandson and help Aurelia with him, since Whit was beginning to crawl everywhere. Our loose travel plans called for us to go up to the tip of Wisconsin and come down on the Michigan side, making our way across the Canadian border at some point to travel across Canada, returning stateside near Buffalo. Having been warmly embraced by the University of Wisconsin's faculty and students, we were not prepared for what we encountered almost from the time we left Madison. By midafternoon after an early morning departure, we decided to find a motel, engage two rooms, prepare and heat Whit's food, have dinner, and go to bed early in preparation for an early start the next day.

At the first motel, the proprietor said that he had no vacancies, although the posted sign clearly indicated that they were looking for customers. At the second, third, and fourth motels, it was the same response: no vacancies. At the fifth motel, the woman in charge frankly said that she was sorry but they did not accept Negro guests. I immediately retorted that I was also sorry that as a law-abiding and loyal citizen of the United States I could not secure accommodations for my family anywhere in the state of Michigan. I reminded her that it was June 18, 1953, the day of the execution of Julius and Ethel Rosenberg for treason. I then told her that there were various forms of disloyalty, including discrimination and the denial of equal rights to all citizens regardless of race. I suggested that she examine her own policies and practices and raise the question of whether she was also guilty of treason to the principles for which this country was supposed to stand. I then departed, and at the first opportunity we made our way across the border into Canada. The very first Canadian motel we stopped at offered us lodgings for the entire family.

My mother-in-law, having lived in a segregated community all of her adult life and grown used to the implicit rules that, when followed, avoided direct confrontations, was frightened not only by the realities of explicit discrimination but by the frankness with which I spoke to the proprietress. I assured her that I did not believe that I was endangering our safety or well-being by speaking out unequivocally to people who were themselves guilty of violating the spirit and the letter of our laws. If my outburst did not change their thinking, it at least gave me the opportunity to vent my feelings. The remainder of the trip to Ithaca went off well, except at Niagara Falls, where Grandmother placed Whit in his stroller and walked near the falls on the United States side. At one point, a white woman looked down at him admiringly and asked how old he was. When she learned that he was ten months old, she smiled and said, "What a sweet little pickaninny," whereupon I thought that Grandmother would have a stroke.

We were pleased with our Ithaca home. It was quite commodious, with sufficient bedrooms for Grandmother, who would remain for about two weeks, Whit, and us. The grounds were attractive without being oversized and burdensome. The neighbors, all white, were cordial and helpful. When we went to buy groceries and other supplies, some African American shoppers, observing that we were strangers, approached us and wondered if they could assist us in any way. They also wanted to know where we were living; when I gave them our address, 627 Hudson Street, they said that I must be mistaken. They were certain that no Negroes lived in that part of the city. Then, without our having to insist that the address was correct, they suddenly seemed to realize that I was the new visiting professor about whom they had heard, and that explained why we were temporarily living in that part of town.

This was my third visiting appointment at a predominantly white university, and since the first two apparently had given no thought to the possibility of my joining the regular faculty, this despite the fact that each was actively recruiting candidates to teach the history of the South, I gave none of them credit for being courageous in inviting me for a part-time, temporary stint. My having been a temporary member would look quite good for the department's record if it was ever challenged about its racial policies. Indeed, I don't doubt a reason I was invited to each department was so that they could remind any and all that they had pioneered in having had Franklin on their faculty, albeit briefly.

My classes at Cornell were small and conducted informally, with a great deal of interaction between the professor and the students. I enjoyed them immensely. One day, as I entered the classroom, I noticed that the students were reading over a paper that apparently someone had drafted, and as each student read it, he or she signed it. I was naturally curious but made no inquiries. At the end of the class, a student remarked to me that he would be interested to see how the faculty would "squirm" out of this. He then said that the circulating letter was a petition from the students to the Department of History, requesting that I be invited to join the department. No invitation came, but I was long struck by this overture of support from the all-white students I had come to admire and appreciate.

Before we departed Ithaca for Washington, I received a telephone call from Thurgood Marshall, with whom I had been in irregular contact since our triumph in *Lyman Johnson v. the University of Kentucky*. He began by inquiring of my plans for the autumn. I informed him that my leave of absence was expiring, and I would be returning to Howard University. In blunt language he told me that I would also be working for the Legal Defense Fund, since he was preparing to reargue the case of *Brown v. Board of Education*. He expressed serious doubt that I would survive his wrath if I dared to decline. Getting down to business, he reminded me that in June the United States Supreme Court had ordered that the case be reargued in the fall term, 1953, to answer the questions propounded by the Court following the initial hearing of the case on December 9, 1952. The inherent inequality of the separate-but-equal precedent might finally be established; the stakes could not have been greater.

The principal question was what evidence was there that the Congress that passed the Fourteenth Amendment and the state legislatures and conventions that ratified it understood that the amendment would abolish segregation in the public schools. If the answer was in the negative, the Court asked if it was within the power of Congress to abolish segregation nationwide. The Court examined every variation and wondered if it was at all possible to interpret the Fourteenth Amendment as empowering any federal agency to abolish segregation in the public schools. Finally, the Court asked if it should remand the case, and those related to it, to the lower courts with directions that they frame appropriate decrees. The attorney general of the United States was invited to take part in the oral argument and to file an additional brief if he so desired. Answers to these questions required a knowledge of the legislative history of the Fourteenth Amendment that few lawyers possessed or had the skills to acquire. Indeed, most lawyers seemed helpless in the face of the contextual issues raised by the Court. Historians, to the rescue!

By early September, with Howard's fall semester under way, I had developed a regular schedule for work at the New York office of the NAACP Legal Defense Fund (LDF), where Thurgood expected me each week. On

Thursdays I would take an early afternoon train from Washington, check in at the Algonquin Hotel, and then report for duty at the Legal Defense Fund offices around the corner. Thurgood was always there working at his desk. Somewhat disheveled in appearance—shirt open at the neck, necktie loose, a lighted cigarette in an ashtray or dangling from his lips—he would greet me, tell me what they were doing, and tell me what he wished me to do. He would ask me if I had any news, as if during the week I had found the answers to all the questions raised by the Court. When I would reply in the negative because I knew what "news" he wanted, he looked just a bit dejected. I would tell him what my most recent study of the legislative history of the Fourteenth Amendment had revealed and report how far along I had come on any writing assignment he had given me or that I had given myself. I would then work until about midnight, when Thurgood would say, "Why don't we take a fifteen-minute break," whereupon I would return to the hotel for my night's rest. I do not know how long he remained at his desk. He was usually there when I returned the following morning. After working Friday and Saturday, I would leave for Washington on midday Sunday.

Since the LDF staff wished to be fully informed about every aspect of the history of Reconstruction that might even remotely affect the Court's decision, it had engaged the services of historians, political scientists, even psychologists who might provide some insights into the case. I was working along with Rayford Logan of Howard University, C. Vann Woodward of Yale, Alfred Kelly of Wayne State, and Herbert Gutman of the University of Rochester. These and other scholars were on call and did much of their work at their places of residence. They would come to the New York office, but not on a regular basis. Whenever they were present, it was evident how much the lawyers appreciated what the historians could offer. Some of our discussions took the shape of seminars, when the dependence of the lawyers on the historians was much in evidence. In discussing the views of members of Congress such as Thaddeus Stevens or Benjamin Butler, the legal staff appeared to be in awe: "Let's hear what Vann has to say," one of them would ask, while another might want to hear from Al Kelly, the great constitutional historian. It was obvious that they would take whatever morsels we had to offer and be grateful for them. For me, and I suspect the same was true for the other scholars, it was exhilarating.

At times I would conduct the seminar and call on my fellow historians to talk about what they had discovered in their studies of Reconstruction. At other times, one of us would distribute a paper on which we had been working and that, we hoped, would shed some light on the subject. For example, I prepared a paper with the intriguing title, "Jim Crow Goes to School: The Beginnings of Segregation in Public Schools," which provoked a lively discussion, leading to a more searching examination of the positions of some members of Congress on segregated schools. Regardless of how pointed our questions were or how significant our discoveries might be, the one thing that Thurgood would not tolerate was speculation about possible opinions of the Court. Our task, he would say, was to present a case so persuasive that the Court would be compelled to rule in our favor. We should, therefore, work on the case and not on the Court's opinion.

It was in early November when drafts of the LDF's brief began to appear. We were all invited to comment on it, to offer suggestions, corrections, criticisms, or whatever came to mind. It was at this point that the tables turned. While a few weeks earlier we historians had regarded ourselves as authorities on Reconstruction and the legislative history of the Fourteenth Amendment, we were now awed by the very appearance of the brief—its formality, its legalistic wording, and its deference to the Court. It was not altogether new to me, since I had seen some of my father's briefs in cases before the Oklahoma Supreme Court. Even so, I was very impressed with what Thurgood Marshall and his colleagues had done with the material we had provided and the vast amount of information they had generated on their own. None of us on the nonlegal staff could qualify for admission to hear the arguments before the Court on December 8, 1953. We had to content ourselves with secondhand reports and the long wait until the decision was handed down.

On May 17, 1954, I was in my office at Howard University, giving little thought to the possibility that this would be a historic day in the life of the nation. Aurelia called me from her office at Spingarn High School. She wondered if I had heard the news. I had no idea what she was talking about. Then she told me that the decision in *Brown* had just been handed down and that it was unanimous in favor of Brown. I am certain that I let out a shriek, the beginning of my extended celebration. Recalling not only my own experiences at Tulsa's Booker T. Washington High School but the more recent comments in Duke University's stacks of Charles S. Sydnor, who could not fathom anyone's questioning the wisdom of segregation, I read the Chief Justice's words with an odd sense of disbelief: "We conclude that in the field of public education the doctrine of 'separate but equal' has no place . . . we hold that the plaintiffs and others similarly situated . . . are, by reason of the segregation complained of, deprived of the equal protection of the laws guaranteed by the Fourteenth Amendment." It was a sweet victory, which we savored and celebrated until the wee hours of the morning. We would not know until later that the decision's many opponents were also awake that night and already plotting its reversal.

While the *Brown* decision was historic, even revolutionary, it did not mean that black and white children would be going to school together in the fall of 1954. Indeed, resistance began to build, and the reaction against the decision was so fierce that the Court sought to rein in the notion of rapid desegregation by requiring compliance "with all deliberate speed." The word "deliberate" permitted a great many to do little or nothing at all. The imagination and creativity of those resisting any kind of change would be revealed in the succeeding generation, thus giving the warriors of 1954 reason to wonder if the time would ever come when peaceful desegregation of the public schools of the South and North would enjoy anything resembling widespread support.

In the few conversations I had with Thurgood after *Brown*, he seemed to be in a mood bordering on depression. His wife, Vivian (affectionately known as "Buster"), had been ill for some time and died the year following the decision. As the years passed, he grew ever more angry and frustrated over the snail's pace of desegregation in the public schools, particularly after he took his seat on the United States Supreme Court in 1967. He seemed to regard the Court's 1978 decision in *Regents of the University of California v. Bakke*, that race could be one factor in admitting students but quotas were not permitted, as unfortunate. During the time that the Court was reaching that decision, he called me to inquire about some references that he wanted to use. I asked him why he sounded so glum. His only response was that soon enough I would understand. When the decision was handed down, the euphoric days of 1954 seemed distant indeed.

Two years before Bakke he had sent me the draft of the speech he would deliver before the American Bar Association meeting in Hawaii. In it he had called the United States Constitution a "flawed" document. I congratulated him on the speech and encouraged him to read it as written. Afterward he was criticized in some quarters for being both a sitting Supreme Court Justice and critical of the Constitution; in urging him to deliver the speech, I took the position that the Constitution was not sacrosanct and calling attention to its flaws was a sign of civic health. By the *Bakke* decision, I could not help but feel its health had taken a turn for the worse.

The United States is frequently in the position of awkwardly attempting to address its major social and economic problems even as it announces to the world what these "special problems" are as well as its "courageous" attempts to solve them. This was essentially what the United States Educational Commission in the United Kingdom (the Fulbright Board in England) had been attempting to do in the summer sessions at Cambridge University that began in 1952. In 1954 I was invited to participate in the conference scheduled for that July and August. I accepted and announced that I would give a series of lectures on ethnic and regional influences in American history.

At the outset, I fully intended to have Aurelia and Whit accompany me, but the executive secretary of the commission indicated that there were no accommodations for families at Peterhouse, the oldest of the Cambridge colleges (established in 1284), where the conference participants were to be housed. If I lived outside with my family, that would defeat one of the purposes of the conference, since maximum contact between professors and participants could be achieved only if they lived together. Aurelia graciously said that she would be very pleased to remain in Washington with Whit.

The voyage across the Atlantic was pleasant. I made friends quickly in the dining room—where my seating was perfectly acceptable—and we arrived at Southampton on schedule. After visiting acquaintances in London, I settled into Peterhouse, and by July 12 I was ready for the Fulbright Conference on American Studies to begin. The director of the conference was William R. Brock, a scholar of nineteenth-century United States history at Selwyn College, Cambridge. The other historian was Denna Fleming from Vanderbilt; lecturing in the field of government were David

Truman of Columbia, Easton Rothwell of Stanford, and Clarence Elliott, the city manager of Kalamazoo, Michigan. George Stoddard of New York University lectured on the American educational system. The two lecturers in American literature were Arthur Mizener of Cornell and Eudora Welty of Jackson, Mississippi. John Fischer, the editor of *Harper's Magazine*, would present a lecture on writing for a major American journal, while the journalist and author Virginius Dabney would lecture on the daily newspaper. Lowell Harriss of Columbia presented lectures on the American economy, while Andrew Clark of the University of Wisconsin lectured on problems in American geography.

Given the people involved, the conference sessions were stimulating and, at times, exhausting. We had vigorous discussions concerning racism, social change, and the economic disparities among sections, races, and ethnic groups. There were also meaningful opportunities to participate in events that allowed us to impart our knowledge of the United States to the British public. In August, for example, I was invited to join the Daily Express Anglo-American Study Group Forum in Liverpool, along with Lord Hailsham, a former Tory MP for Oxford, and Sir Victor Raikes, Tory MP for Garston. In Manchester there was a conference on "Aspects of Life and Politics in the U.S. and the U.S.S.R." at which I was invited to speak on "Life in the U.S. Today: Problems of Liberty and Equality." In attendance were several hundred senior grammar school pupils, most of whom expected to go to some university upon graduation.

Due to the arrangements under the Fulbright Act, I could not take my earnings, which were in pounds sterling, out of Great Britain. Consequently, at the end of the Cambridge conference, I found myself spending a great deal of time in London shops making decisions about matters to which I had never previously given much thought. I purchased one china dinner service for twelve, one coffee service for twelve, a carving set and serving spoons in sterling, and some clothing for Aurelia and Whit. While uncertain how my choices would be received back home, I had succeeded in spending nearly all my earnings and arranged for shipment of the purchases before I departed for New York on the *Queen Elizabeth*.

Aurelia and Whit had come up by train to greet me when I disembarked. While I had been away, Whit had learned to talk, proudly greeting me with, "I love my daddy." I was thrilled. As we boarded the train for

Washington and as I attempted to pack our things in the overhead racks, Whit said, in what was clearly an unrehearsed statement, "Sit down, Daddy, the train is moving." I could not have been prouder.

Returning to Washington this time was quite different from any other. In the spring we had purchased a home, our very first, on Monroe Street in the northeast section of the city. It was a Dutch colonial, four-bedroom house, sitting in the middle of a fairly large lot. We did not know or care that our neighbors would be white. Our attention was called to that fact, though, shortly after we moved in. Whit saw an elderly white man in the adjoining yard and he rushed out to exercise his newly discovered capacity to speak. When the man turned his back on him without a word, Whit ran back into the house and announced that the man out there could not talk. I did not explain to him what the man's trouble was. I was certain that soon enough my son would discover too many people like our next-door neighbor. In the meantime there was our yard in which he could play, and there were our friends' and colleagues' children with whom he could play.

I seemed to be busier than ever. I had accepted an invitation to teach in the summer session at North Carolina College, and I was booked to give a lecture at Harvard immediately after that session ended. From Harvard I would go to New York, from where I would sail on August 10 on the *Queen Mary* for Southampton, England, only to proceed to Braunschweig, Germany, to attend a conference on the writing of textbooks. The United States was especially interested in the types of textbooks that were being developed for West German students in the postwar years and specifically their treatment of Nazism and the crimes of the Third Reich. I was interested in learning more about what techniques could be transferred to the writing of textbooks in the United States. It was clear to me that better American textbooks would encourage more enlightened attitudes as far as race and class were concerned. With my interests coinciding with those of the United States government, the Department of State was eager to have me attend and, indeed, was willing to defray the costs of the trip. The memory of E. Merton Coulter's misrepresentations in *The South During Reconstruction* still fresh in my mind, I realized how necessary it was to revise textbooks in the United States, particularly regarding the Civil War and its aftermath, to challenge their uniformly uncritical approach to American history. What the Germans were doing to overcome the nationalist propaganda rife in the textbooks written during the Hitler era offered examples to anyone interested, as I was, in seeing that better books were written for students in the United States.

Long before my arrival in Braunschweig, Professor Donald McKay of Harvard, the American representative on the Executive Committee of the International Conference of Historical Sciences, informed me that he had noted with regret my failure to offer to read a paper at the next meeting of the conference to be held in Rome in 1955. He was writing to ask if I would reconsider. I replied that since I had other business that would bring me to Europe, I would be pleased to read a paper on "Sectionalism and the American Historian." My proposal was accepted immediately, and I made plans to go from Germany to Italy.

At the conclusion of the textbook conference, I duly proceeded to Rome and was there for the conference opening on September 4. An impressive group of scholars attended the conference, including Howard Beale and his family, and an interesting group from Brooklyn College. Upon the completion of my presentation, Hans Kohn of the City College of New York sent me a note requesting a copy, which he proposed using in his forthcoming book, *The Age of Nationalism*. The Brooklyn group also made a point of complimenting me on my paper; I was flattered but attached no further significance to the New Yorkers' interest.

12

A Change of Venue

WHEN I FINALLY RETURNED to the United States at the end of September 1955, I could not have predicted that I was on the threshold of the busiest academic year of my life. I had already become more active on the Fisk University Board of Trustees, to which I had been elected in 1952. That same year I had been elected to the board of the American Council of Learned Societies. Meanwhile, earlier in 1955 I had been appointed to the program committee of the Southern Historical Association; already, for six months or more, its chair, James W. Silver of the University of Mississippi, and its vice president, Bell I. Wiley of Emory University, were dispatching letters almost weekly urging me to offer suggestions for sessions or requesting the names of possible program participants. My promise to help make the program so attractive that no Association member could fault the fact that an African American was on the committee was made contemporaneously with the national outrage over the barbaric murder of fourteen-year-old Emmett Till, bludgeoned and shot simply for having supposedly whistled at a white woman in Mississippi. It was also particularly ironic in that I had already ruled out my own attendance. There were times when I had to say enough is enough. The conference was to be held at the Peabody Hotel in Memphis, which barred blacks from sleeping or dining there. Once again, my participation would have demanded unique housing and eating arrangements, again would require creativity in getting to the conference and around the city, again would have meant overcoming or ignoring the passive to active resistance of conference attendees. While I was prepared to help organize the conference, I made the principled decision not to attend it.

My work with the program committee did not incite a revolution in the Southern Historical Association, but an increasing number of its members did feel free to voice their dissatisfaction with its backward-looking racial policies. Both Jim Silver and Bell Wiley were ready for change as, indeed, were others, such as LeRoy Graf of the University of Tennessee and Bennett Wall of the University of Kentucky, who offered me suggestions and encouragement. Over the next decade the leading members of the association would argue with hotels and convention centers about their racial policies, here and there gaining small concessions and laying the groundwork for greater change. As Southern cities yielded to the pressures created by the Civil Rights Act of 1964, the attitudes of the association's members further changed. Slightly more than a decade after the meeting in Memphis, I was elected president of the association, long before the other two predominantly white national historical associations made a similar move.

Even as I helped design the conference program, my usual heavy teaching load at Howard continued, with perhaps more than my share of MA theses to supervise. There were also my regular courses in nineteenth-century and African American history that had large enrollments. If that was not enough, I shared with Osborn Smallwood of the Department of English the responsibility of coaching the university debating team. In this I could not help recalling what debating did for me under Ted Currier's tutelage.

Unfortunately, my willingness to serve numerous causes was interpreted by a great many as license to request more of my time. A Louisville high school teacher, for example, asked me to send her a bibliography for a new course she was to teach. Another high school teacher asked me to read a fifty-page manuscript and offer suggestions for improvement. A foundation executive requested me to assist him in planning a conference on Negro life. One university urged me to address the plenary session of a conference on "Freedom to Dissent." I was even asked to contribute to a

Festschrift for a historian with whom I had neither studied nor been a colleague.

The autumn passed too quickly. I was pleased to learn that the Memphis meeting of the Southern Historical Association went off without any hitches. My greatest regret in not being there was that William Faulkner spoke, and I missed this one opportunity to hear the South's Nobel laureate deliver what everyone said was a memorable speech. In part, he said:

> It is our white man's shame that in our present southern economy, the Negro must not have equality; our double shame that we fear that giving him more social equality will jeopardize his present economic status; our triple shame that even then, to justify ourselves, we must becloud the issue with the purity of white blood; what a commentary that the one remaining place on earth where the white man can flee and have his blood protected and defended by law is Africa—Africa: the source and origin of the people whose presence in America will drive the white man to flee from defilement.

If anything was needed to add excitement to Faulkner's address, it was the remarks of African American scholar Benjamin Mays, president of all-black Morehouse College. Mays, one of the most eloquent speakers of his time, declared, "As this country could not exist half slave and half free, it cannot exist half-segregated and half-desegregated." The session followed a dispute between association officials and the Peabody Hotel, which had insisted that no Negro could sit on the raised platform in their grand ballroom, which would have meant his speaking down to whites seated in the audience. Before the session, however, the hotel reluctantly relented, thus giving Mays an opportunity to deliver his exhortation from the podium.

That hectic year continued on, right up to my presentation of a paper at the December meeting of the American Historical Association in which I undertook to show how Southern historians, long on the defensive due to Northern criticism, were finally bringing a new and more objective view to the study of the region's past. This, I concluded by saying, increased the chances for history finally to play an important constructive role in the South's understanding of its current problems.

Before I delivered my paper, I noticed that the three people from

Brooklyn College—Jesse Clarkson, Madeline Robinton, and Frances Childs—whom I had met in Rome that summer were sitting near the front of the room. Presumably they were there to cheer their new friend along. Otherwise, why would scholars of Russian, British, and French history be there at all?

At the end of the session, they greeted me warmly, complimented me on my paper, and introduced me to several of their colleagues, some of whom specialized in U.S. history. One of them inquired if the rumor that Aurelia and I were giving a party in the late afternoon was correct. I answered in the affirmative, and to my astonishment they asked if they could attend. I said that we would be immensely pleased, recalling once more the delightful times I had spent with them in Rome. The party, augmented by a number of unanticipated guests, went off quite well, with the five or six from Brooklyn College apparently enjoying themselves.

Early in January of 1956, the reason those New Yorkers had taken particular interest in me became clear. That month I received letters from several historians at Brooklyn College, including my three friends, indicating their interest in having me join their faculty as a professor and chair of the Department of History. This came not only as a complete surprise but also as a real shock. In 1956 it was almost inconceivable that a group of white scholars at a predominantly white institution would seriously entertain the possibility of having me join them as their tenured colleague *and* their chairman. My brief teaching stints at Harvard, Wisconsin, and Cornell were fresh in my mind, and I was quite certain that most of the historians at those institutions never gave a second thought to my affiliation with them except on a most temporary basis. Brooklyn College's overture was of a different order entirely. Their invitation was that I join the faculty, not for a summer or a semester, but permanently!

It was the first such offer I had received from a predominantly white institution, and I was obliged to take it seriously. Aurelia and I discussed the matter thoroughly, viewing it as objectively as possible, attempting to look at it from every angle. We concluded that this could be good for us and good for higher education; I should at least seriously entertain the offer. That the president of the college was rumored to have promised to veto any current member as department chair because of bitter internal conflicts deepened the mystery. Why turn to me? I could only conclude that the search committee had not been satisfied with any of the outside candidates who had applied for the job and that the members of the department whom I had met in Rome belonged to one faction and had "sold" my candidacy to the other. Very likely, and without my knowledge, my AHA presentation had been not unlike a first job interview. Having made that first cut, it was my responsibility to "sell myself" to the department as a whole.

When I visited Brooklyn College several days later, I was graciously received by President Harry Gideonse, other members of the administration, and members of the department. Everyone was cordial, although I sensed immediately who was in which faction. No one raised hostile questions, but several department members evidenced enough skepticism to indicate that they were on their guard when considering any candidate recommended by the "other side." My personal reaction was favorable, and I indicated my willingness to join the faculty if I was elected by New York's Board of Higher Education, a necessary formality.

With the possibility that a move to New York was becoming more likely, Aurelia and I revisited the matter. I was struck then, as I had reason to be both before and after, by her willingness to view the matter without any thought for her own career. The fact that she had an attractive position as librarian at the new Spingarn High School in Washington seemed not to influence her consideration of our decision. Just as when we had left Raleigh, then Durham, she was quite willing to leave Washington. As the myriad reasons the offer held such appeal became clear, she never hesitated or protested, and her very acquiescence merely heightened my sense of guilt over always uprooting her for the sake of my own career. Rather, she was as firm in her insistence that I grasp this new opportunity as she had been a decade earlier when she insisted that I leave Durham and go to Washington to write *From Slavery to Freedom*.

In the early afternoon of February 14 I received a call from Benjamin Fine, the education editor of *The New York Times*. He quickly came to the point. He stated that he knew that on the following morning, New York's Board of Higher Education would elect me to a full professorship at Brooklyn College and that I would also become chair of the Department of History. While he appreciated the confidential nature of the matter, *The Times* intended to run its story on the proceedings *before* the meeting. If I was willing to talk with him, he would like to verify a few factual matters. If I was unwilling to talk, he would still write the story and hope it was accurate. I agreed to clarify any factual matters.

On the morning of February 15, 1956, I was teaching my regular eight o'clock class at Howard. I had not gone far beyond some introductory remarks when Harold Lewis, my colleague in European history, came into my classroom. Exclaiming, "Look!" he held up *The New York Times* for the students to see. There was a photograph of me on the front page under the headline, "Negro Educator Chosen to Head Department in Brooklyn College." The students were so surprised and excited that the remainder of my lecture went ignored. Indeed, rather than discuss nineteenth-century history, they wished to discuss what they felt was a rather important development in the middle of the twentieth century.

I described to them the appointment process at an institution such as Brooklyn College, and I pointed out that the newspaper was reporting this to be the first such appointment in the country. They wanted to know about the other states, and I replied that I knew of no comparable appointment anywhere else. By the time the class ended, other news reporters were on campus looking for me and I was told that I had received numerous telephone calls. I was finally assigned a temporarily vacant office in Douglass Hall where I could receive visitors as well as answer the phone. Except for some time out for lunch, the barrage of attention kept me in that office until late afternoon. In the days and weeks that followed, many Howard colleagues whom I knew only casually sent me messages of congratulation, as did friends, closer colleagues, and even casual acquaintances from all over the United States.

The problem with cutting my ties to Howard was that Aurelia and I would say our farewells in two stages. I had agreed to teach at the University of California at Berkeley that summer, and so we would leave first for California only to return to Washington one last time before making our final departure for Brooklyn.

Even with a small seminar on post–Civil War history and a class of several hundred students on late nineteenth-century social and intellectual history, my stay at Berkeley felt celebratory. Fortunately, for the large survey course I had as my assistant an advanced graduate student, Leon Litwack, who was to have a distinguished career largely spent at Berkeley.

In between classes, Aurelia, Whit, and I did a great deal of sightseeing in the Bay Area and even ventured to Los Angeles so that we could introduce Whit, then almost four years old, to Disneyland.

The two months in California passed quickly, and in late August we returned to Washington to make preparations for the move to Brooklyn. There were the farewells to our friends at Howard, the endless packing, and finally the move. A couple of our new colleagues volunteered to assist us in finding housing, with at least one of them ominously concluding that it would "not be easy." After some preliminary investigation, we made a firm decision to postpone the purchase of a home until we had accumulated more capital and, perhaps even more important, were better acquainted with the neighborhoods. Meanwhile, we had the good fortune to meet the person who would be our landlady for the next two years.

Rose Abdou, an attractive and personable African American woman, was married to an Egyptian, a member of the merchant marine who was at sea most of the time but whose three-family flat on Eastern Parkway was his pride and into which he was investing most of his earnings. Mrs. Abdou managed the property and was pleased to rent the second-floor apartment to us. Childless herself, she was especially pleased to have Whit in the house, entertaining him with snacks and his favorite television programs. Overall, our living situation was satisfactory, particularly since Aurelia elected not to work, thus allowing her to become acquainted with our entirely new environment and to spend more time with our son. She had not taken any significant time off since his birth, and, more important, all of us realized that with this move we were confronting very different circumstances.

Indeed, the world we were now navigating was new to all three of us, and Aurelia and I moved carefully. We had both grown up in all-black neighborhoods and had secured our pre–graduate school education in quite small, historically all-black institutions. We had both worked at black schools where the student and faculty composition was roughly equivalent to Fisk's and the curriculum was traditional. Brooklyn College, on the other hand, was large by the standards of the 1950s, with more than ten thousand students and a faculty numbering in the hundreds. But despite its size it was truly a neighborhood college, with very few students from New

York boroughs other than Brooklyn and virtually none from any other part of the United States.

The governance of Brooklyn College was also quite new to me. While the president was clearly in command, and had become legendary because of his opposition to Communist Party influence on campus, he shared considerable authority with his colleagues in the administration and with the very powerful Committee on Personnel and Budget, consisting of department chairs and administrators such as the deans of administration, the college, and the school of general studies. The P. and B. Committee (the Committee on Personnel and Budget), as it was called, acted on every recommendation for appointment and promotion, thus giving me an excellent opportunity to become acquainted rather quickly with the quality of the faculty and the other personnel at Brooklyn College. Meanwhile, the bylaws of the Board of Higher Education of the City of New York determined the nature of the college's operations, including such mundane details as when departments should hold regular meetings.

The Department of History was large, consisting of approximately fifty full-time faculty at all academic ranks. The very size reflected two important considerations that were central to the philosophy of the college. One was that every student, regardless of academic interests and concentration, was required to take a two-semester course called the History of Western Civilization. Teaching materials and, indeed, the philosophy of the course, were the responsibilities of a departmental committee. The other consideration was that the college was committed to small classes, none to number more than thirty-five students. It took a large faculty to discharge the department's obligation to achieve this objective alone. Add to this the personnel needed to staff strong undergraduate majors in several areas of history, and the need to maintain a large department becomes urgent.

Brooklyn College also enjoyed a reputation for rigorous scholarship and the top-flight performance of its students. This was in the period before the college adopted open enrollment, and students who were admitted routinely placed above the ninetieth percentile of their high school graduating class. It was a reputation that administration, faculty, students, and parents guarded jealously.

Not only would the faculty go the extra mile, but the students asked for extra assignments and sought satisfactory explanations from faculty for their eventual grades. Even parents entered the fray. They were often on the telephone seeking information about their children's performance and requesting appointments with teachers if the responses they received were disappointing in any way.

I was quite aware of the fact that my primary responsibility as the newly appointed chair was to quiet the troubled waters in the department. While the majority of the history faculty had agreed to our coming, they agreed on little else. The content of courses, the role of students in the department and on campus, and President Gideonse's aggressive efforts to "root out the Communists" all tended to divide the department. Eventually, I sensed a deep division along what I considered to be class lines. Some members of the department seemed to be more privileged than others, or at least their detractors felt so. Those who spent summers in Europe or were among the recruited faculty that had been a part of the pre-Hitler regime in Germany or Austria seemed to have a leg up, including exercising greater influence with students. For all of these reasons, members of the department were being driven in opposite directions, and at times the rage was only slightly below the surface. My task was to appraise those feelings and work to assuage them.

I maintained an open-door policy, especially as I realized that everyone was eager to talk with me. I also moved quickly to make certain decisions, such as appointing a deputy chairman to work out the class schedules and to assign teachers to courses. I appointed Arnold Broggi, the leader of the faction that seemed most opposed to those who had principally engineered my being hired. In our initial conference, I told him he had my utmost confidence, but if I ever discovered that he was using his powers to get revenge or curry favor, his powers would revert to me and I would appoint a new deputy chairman. He assured me that he would carry out his duties in a thoroughly professional manner.

Jesse Clarkson, whom I had met in Rome, was a leader of one of the factions and an advocate of my becoming department chair. He immediately told me that my appointment of Arnold Broggi was a big mistake. Broggi, Clarkson was certain, would use his new position to injure his enemies. I predicted the opposite, and by the end of the year Clarkson was the first person to acknowledge that my appointment of Broggi was the best initial step that I could have made. True to his word, Broggi discharged his duties with a fair and even hand.

Such successful administrative jockeying, however, merely freed me up to turn to more important concerns. I encouraged scholarship by urging members of the department to attend professional meetings and to get on with their own research. Departmental meetings became opportunities for faculty to discuss their research projects, and soon members of the department were coming to me not to discuss the faults or weaknesses of their colleagues but to discuss their own professional futures.

While I was not expected to teach more than one course, I opted from the beginning to teach two. Committed to teaching and scholarship, I knew that I could not remain abreast of my field unless I maintained a real presence in the classroom.

Despite my preoccupation with teaching and administering the department, I was determined not to neglect my family. I was hardly unaware of the extent of Northern racism and was not a little apprehensive of our introducing Whit to not only so large a city but one in which racial tensions were often harder to discern. I was fortunate in that I could be with him even as I discharged my duties at Brooklyn College. The college had a first-rate Early Childhood Center, headed by Rebecca Shuey and staffed with capable psychologists and other teachers. Each morning, when I took the subway from our home to the office, Whit went with me, and I would drop him off at the center before I took up my duties for the day. And if I was unable to do so, Aurelia would take him to the center and pick him up at the end of his day there. We were deeply gratified when it became clear he thoroughly enjoyed the school and made friends easily. What was more, this arrangement not only allowed me to remain very much a part of Whit's early years but eased our introduction to New York tremendously.

13

On Becoming New Yorkers

THOUGH CONSTRAINED BY FINANCES and commitments, Aurelia and I, often with Whit in tow, made as many trips to the Brooklyn Museum, the Museum of Modern Art, and the Metropolitan Museum as we made to the opera, concert hall, and theater. Al Martin, who had taught physics at Fisk since the middle 1930s, had moved back to New York and assumed responsibility for seeing to it that Aurelia and I became acquainted with Harlem, despite our Brooklyn residence. Dr. and Mrs. Ernest Alexander, ardent Fiskites, took an almost proprietary interest in us, and since Ernest sat with me on the Fisk Board of Trustees, he and I had much to discuss from time to time. Among my colleagues at Brooklyn College, old friends such as Hugh and Mabel Smythe and Charles and Margaret Lawrence kept us busy with their generous hospitality, while new colleagues such as Jesse Clarkson, Sol Bloom, Joseph Shulim, and Abe Eisenstadt entertained us, as indeed did President Harry Gideonse and the dean of administration, Francis Kilkoyne.

Aurelia became quite active with the Faculty Wives of Brooklyn College, and her consequent friendship with Pat Withner led to my own friendship with Pat's husband, the botanist Carl Withner, who was as responsible as anyone in my becoming interested in the cultivation of orchids. My citywide reputation, signaled by that front-page *New York*

Times article, meant that I was frequently asked to speak before various groups, from the New York branch of the Association for the Study of Negro Life and History to such informal gatherings as that hosted by Lester Granger, executive director of the National Urban League. He had invited approximately twenty New York men to meet at his home with Nelson Rockefeller, at the time chair of the Rockefeller Brothers Fund, to give their assessment of the needs of African Americans in the community.

Following that meeting, I realized as never before that I could speak out and advocate changes in human and race relations and be heard. I had always wondered how far my academic work could take me in the larger world. In my ever-widening New York activities and connections, I saw that it was indeed possible to function in my chosen field as a scholar and command an audience when addressing practical, everyday affairs. My increasing public stature and my affiliation with major national groups, such as the American Council of Learned Societies, brought to me almost more invitations to participate and be heard than I could handle. I keenly recall, for example, my opportunity to represent the Council in India for the observance of the centennial anniversaries of the universities of Calcutta, Madras, and Bombay. The public I was being allowed to address was increasingly an international one.

One New York acquaintance deserves special mention. Shortly after we arrived in Brooklyn, I received a note from Dr. W.E.B. Du Bois, in which he congratulated me and wished me well in my new position. A bit later we received an invitation to dinner from him and his wife, Shirley. We accepted with pleasure. By this time I had met him on several occasions, but he seemed not to remember me from one encounter to the next. But as he greeted us at his door, the stern "persona" was gone and he was at his cordial best. He was so relaxed that I ventured to recall my failed attempt to introduce myself to him in the Arcade Hotel in Raleigh almost twenty years ago.

He seemed greatly amused by my recounting the incident and attributed his earlier abrupt behavior to a preoccupation with other thoughts and his lifelong shyness. Though these seemed to me an insufficient explanation, I did not pursue the matter. Despite the fact that I would later be regarded as having close ties with Dr. Du Bois, that was not the case. I did, however, enjoy a cordial relationship, and whenever he called me, I answered with pleasure. On one occasion he asked me to speak to a class that he was conducting at City College, and I shall never forget the sight of Dr. Du Bois sitting with his students and taking notes as I lectured.

As relations between the United States and the Soviet Union became increasingly strained and anticommunist sentiment in this country reached a new level of hostility, Dr. Du Bois only became more critical of American foreign policy, speaking out more vigorously than ever. Anti–Du Bois sentiment in the Department of State similarly reached a new level, and for a time he reached the status of a pariah, with his passport taken to render it impossible for him to travel outside the country. Thus, as his ninetieth birthday approached in February 1958, how it might be acknowledged was a serious question. A few stalwarts sent out invitations. When I received mine I promptly replied that I would be present, and I sent a check to become a part of the purse that the committee was preparing for him. Surprised that I would attend, the committee asked if I would make some remarks, speaking for Fisk University as well as for myself. I replied that I would be delighted.

A decade earlier there had been a huge Fisk-sponsored celebration of Dr. Du Bois's eightieth birthday at the Hotel Roosevelt in New York. Then too I was honored to be asked to give the principal address. For his ninetieth birthday, also at the Hotel Roosevelt, there was no dinner, only a modest reception, made notable for the many congratulatory messages sent from left-wing groups throughout the world. When I was called on to speak, a shudder of disbelief went through the audience, so much smaller than it had been a decade ago. I made my way to the podium and offered greetings from Fisk University as well as myself, making it clear that Dr. Du Bois remained our mutual alma mater's most distinguished and most beloved alumnus. At the end of the reception, a man came over to me and said that he was shocked that President Gideonse had given me permission to speak at such a gathering. I brushed him aside, declaring that no one at any point held sway over where I would speak or on what.

While Aurelia and I enjoyed our apartment on Eastern Parkway, we knew we would never feel like settled New Yorkers until we had a place of our own. After spending several weeks with my father, who had suffered a debilitating stroke in the spring of 1957, I suggested to Aurelia that we should look in earnest. A prerequisite was a home within walking distance of Brooklyn College, which was, after all, located in a quite attractive residential section of the borough. We began to scan the real estate sections of the daily newspapers and were soon going to look at properties advertised by one broker or another. Quickly, a pattern emerged. The Realtor or the home owner would notify us, upon our arrival, that the property was under contract or that it had been informally committed. If negotiations fell through, he would promise to be in touch with us. Only after we had heard the same story several times did we begin to suspect the truth: The Realtor was unwilling to be the first to damage the "integrity" of the neighborhood by selling a home to an African American. Going through newspapers day after day and encountering the same Realtors who persisted in offering the same lame excuse, we concluded that if we depended on Brooklyn real estate brokers, we would never acquire a home.

Our next move was to respond only to those advertisements in which the *owner* offered the property. Up to a point the strategy worked, and we began to see houses that Realtors would certainly not have shown us. But numerous experiences conveyed the clear message that we were not welcome in the neighborhood. One Sunday afternoon, we were told that the house we had come to see was under contract. We were also shocked to discover, upon our leaving the property, that residents on both sides of the street were out on the sidewalk to observe us and presumably offer a silent message that we would not be welcome. As always, I was left wondering who benefited from such behavior? As it happened, not that home owner. Six months later, when we finally moved into that neighborhood, the home that was supposedly under contract was still for sale.

One Saturday afternoon in the early fall of 1957, I read of a home for sale by the owner on New York Avenue, five blocks from Brooklyn College. I called him and he invited me to come and see the property, bringing my family if I had one. Aurelia, Whit, and I went immediately. It was a modest-appearing, attractive brick home, free-standing with a garage in the rear and a driveway shared with the next-door neighbor. The owner came to the front door and asked if we were the prospective buyers he had invited. When we answered in the affirmative, he left us at the door and went back to the kitchen. After pouring himself a drink and knocking it back, apparently in one swallow, he returned and invited us in.

At some point, early in the visit, the owner must have decided that we were likely purchasers and that he would promote the sale in every way possible. He began to tell us what he had done to improve each room, how much money he had invested in this mirror or that fireplace. There were laundry facilities that he would pass on to the new owner, and there were other amenities that he would leave. Within an hour we were all getting along quite well. As we departed he told us that we could return for a second look whenever we saw fit, and that if we had any questions, he would be pleased to answer them.

Within two or three days, Aurelia and I indicated to him that we would be pleased to acquire the property if we could secure the financing. I took up the latter with my lawyer, Murray Gross, whose office was on Nostrand Avenue, just around the corner from where we lived. Murray wanted to know if I had any life insurance. I told him that I had a twenty-thousand-dollar policy with a major New York company. When I gave him the name of the company, he said that the problem had been solved, for that company had set aside millions of dollars for loans to its customers who sought assistance in purchasing a home. He asked the name of my insurance agent and told me not to worry, he would have a loan for me in a matter of days.

On the following day, I received a frantic call from my insurance agent, blurting out that his company had done a great deal for my people, and he hoped that I would understand. When I asked him what he was talking about, he replied that his company could not lend me the money to purchase the home. Our purchase of that New York Avenue property with a loan from his company would mean that he would have helped Negroes "jump" over the line into a "white" neighborhood. His company's standing rule was never to directly facilitate such a jump. I promptly informed him that I was canceling my insurance with him, and if I needed any in the future I would seek it with a company that had the courage to loan me the money to purchase a home where my family wished to live and not where the insurance company wished us to live.

When I reported the conversation to Murray Gross, he expressed dismay and asked me to give him a few days to look around and see if he could find the money. The following week, after having been flatly turned down by most of the banks in New York, he called me to say that my loan application had been approved by the South Brooklyn Savings Bank, on whose board Murray's father sat. Meanwhile, the home owner apparently had become convinced that I should be the house's next occupant and had taken the property off the market with the understanding that I would purchase it once I had secured a loan. Indeed, he seemed to be as enthusiastic to sell to us as we were to buy from him.

Moving day is always important, even exciting, and this one particularly so. New York Avenue presented its own problems. It is a narrow two-way street, with parking on one side only. Our large moving van could not conveniently double-park, yet when the van's driver asked my next-door neighbor if he would move his car so that he could park curbside, our new neighbor refused to do so. Thus, with the van almost blocking traffic, our furniture and belongings awkwardly made their way into our new home.

By late morning, everyone on the block knew that we were moving in. Passers-by stopped to look at us. Our neighbor on the other side brought flowers, introduced himself, and offered his assistance, for which we were grateful. Soon, the movers had completed their tasks and were off, leaving us to get acquainted with our new home. By dinner time, we realized that our own company was what truly distinguished it as ours.

It was less easy for some of our neighbors to reach the same conclusion. When I decided to paint the tiny, rusty wrought-iron fence that circled our small front lawn, a group of neighbors gathered across the street to watch, likewise observing Whit playing outside as I painted. Sometimes in the evening the telephone would ring and a voice would denounce me, promising that I would find it impossible to remain there. Yet not all of our neighbors were hostile. Each time I appeared on local television or my name appeared in the newspapers, my "fans" increased. Even the next-door neighbor who would not move his car was no longer a problem. In time, he came around, to the point that his family would visit and share dishes, and our children would play in our shared driveway.

There were others, people of goodwill who wished us well in the neighborhood. At the intervention of two sisters of advanced age who lived three doors down from us, the Reverend Chester Hodgson, pastor of Kings Highway Methodist Church, which was just a few blocks away, welcomed us, and invited us to visit his church and to worship there whenever we wished. Several weeks later we attended Sunday morning service at Kings Highway, were introduced by the pastor, and were greeted by some of the members at the end of the service.

Soon, Aurelia and I found ourselves engaged in a rather serious conversation regarding a possible church affiliation. Neither of us was especially religious, but we both thought it important to provide Whit with a religious experience and leave it to him to become as active or inactive as he wished. We decided to join Kings Highway, where two African American families were already members. Soon, Whit was attending Sunday school, serving as an acolyte, and going to classes that, in some way, served as a rite of passage. I spoke to the entire congregation one Sunday morning, and Aurelia and her friend Pat Withner were active in women's groups. When it became clear to us that not all of the members were enthusiastic about our affiliation, we decided to regard the recalcitrant as possible recruits to our larger crusade to see to it that all members of the human race lived as brothers and sisters.

The appearance of *The Militant South* during my first year in Brooklyn provided the credentials I needed to indicate that I was a scholar as well as an administrator. Published by the Harvard University Press, it was widely reviewed. Some raised questions about my argument that Southern culture was deeply affected by its bellicosity, that even its educational system leaned toward the military, and that the region's emotional and militant response to criticism prevented its constructive and healthy development. But the mere fact that reviewers argued with the book's thesis indicated that my work was taken seriously and that my standing as a professional historian was increasing. As rewarding as I found my expanding public role, I was, I admit, fiercely interested in my scholarly work and standing. Indeed, both aspects of my professional life seemed interwoven, and I was determined never to allow my scholarship to suffer even as my public commitments multiplied.

Early in 1958, I had received yet further evidence that the academy was following my progress. I was invited to be visiting professor for the summer session of 1959 at the University of Hawaii. From the outset, however, it was clear that the department was interested in a longer commitment if I was at all open to the idea. Two years earlier, the very thought of leaving Howard for any nonhistorically all-black university would have struck me as revolutionary and attractive. Having made the transition to Brooklyn, however, such an overture was no longer an obvious decision for me. Far easier was the choice to commit to spending a summer in Hawaii, which had Aurelia's clear support.

Upon our arrival at the Honolulu airport Aurelia, Whit, and I were greeted by the chair of the department and his young son, who placed the traditional leis around our necks as tokens of welcome. They took us to lunch and to the faculty home that we had rented for the summer. Our next-door neighbors, David and Helen Bell and their two children, Judy, a teenager, and David, who was six, or about the same age as Whit, gave us a warm welcome and offered to assist us in any way possible. They volunteered Judy to babysit for us and David to show Whit the neighborhood. The contrast to our shaky acceptance into our Brooklyn neighborhood could not have been starker.

Honolulu was not the tourist attraction that it would become a decade later. Today, it is difficult to imagine it as a sleepy small town, but it was hardly more than that in 1959. Our home, located on a kind of faculty row, was near the university farm from which we had milk delivered each day. The island didn't even have a car rental agency. Unfortunately, we desperately needed transportation, not to go to and from classes, which were within walking distance, but to see and appreciate the island of Oahu. At Aurelia's suggestion I went to one of the island's few car dealerships and inquired of its owner if he had any automobiles that I could rent for the summer. Forty dollars wound up renting us a car with insurance. He did not even require a deposit. An automobile made all the difference, since we were able to see the entire island by day and make it to our favorite restaurants or luaus in the evening. Toward the end of our stay, a colleague let us have his house on the big island, Hawaii, to which we flew for a weekend. The Kona coast, with its mercifully quiet volcanoes and lush undeveloped stretches of land, was stunningly beautiful.

One Hawaiian experience changed my life forever: becoming acquainted with and attached to the cultivation of orchids. I had seen orchid flowers on the mainland, but I had never seen the plants themselves. On the part of faculty row where we lived, several neighbors had orchids blooming on their patios and porches. On late afternoon walks, Aurelia and I would inspect them carefully, and with each inspection, my fascination grew. Soon I concluded that I should begin cultivating orchids. So began in earnest a lifelong obsession.

Nothing that I experienced, however, could have been more life transforming than Whit's learning what real freedom was like. It could not have come at a better time. He had recently experienced the taunts, from adults as well as children, as he rode his bicycle around our Brooklyn neighborhood. He had watched as local children gave him the cold shoulder whenever he approached. And the implicit weight of racism was rarely at more than one remove.

Our neighbors in Honolulu were nothing like this. Judy Bell became more than a babysitter. Her simple, easy friendship increased Whit's confidence in himself and in others. But it was David Bell, Whit's age, who showed Whit what it meant to be truly free. Each morning after breakfast David would appear. Wearing a strange-looking hat or with a cape draped over his shoulder, he would rap on the door or at a window to indicate to Whit that it was time to begin their day's adventure. After a morning of exploring the neighborhood or playing in the sand or visiting a friend, they would return for lunch at the Bells' or at our home. They would then be off for the afternoon. We never worried, for there were no adults to harass him or animals to harm him, and David and Whit continued that routine day after day.

As Whit was making known his reluctance to return to Brooklyn, I expressed to my Hawaiian colleagues and friends that I too regretted having to leave. They assured me that I was welcome anytime, and, indeed, a more permanent arrangement was a possibility. It was an invitation that struck me all the harder as I watched Whit weep bitterly at the airport when we departed for Brooklyn. It was as though he was being returned to the place where the authorities had meted out to him a miserable sentence. Soon after we returned to Brooklyn and I had resumed my duties at the college, I received a cordial letter from the dean at the University of Hawaii inquiring of my availability and assuring me that they were prepared to offer me a professorship.

As I weighed the pros and cons, I recalled the six-month delay in receiving books from the mainland and how far the journey had been by propeller plane, this being well before the introduction of jets. Very quickly, I realized that I did not wish to consider seriously leaving Brooklyn. Not only was Honolulu far from my and Aurelia's families, but I remembered too how in 1956 Brooklyn had pioneered in offering me the position as chairman of the department. I had been in Brooklyn only three years, and I did not wish to be seen as deserting one place just because another seemed more attractive. Hawaii was physically lovely, and it was peaceful, even protective, but it was too far from the center of the fight that I continued to wage both within the academy and without and too far from the places where I hoped to exert some influence. Under the circumstances, I felt that I had to decline, and I sent the dean my regrets.

14

Way Down Under

IN THE AUTUMN OF 1958, just as I was completing the agreement to teach at the University of Hawaii the following summer, I received an inquiry regarding my possible interest in lecturing in Australia for the same period. I respectfully declined but indicated my willingness to do so at another mutually convenient time. The delay gave me the chance to step back and evaluate what certain outside forces—higher education as well as governmental agencies—were encouraging me to do and how I might fit into their larger plans. While I appreciated the opportunity to see the world, so long as it did not seriously affect my family life, I was mindful of the need to understand fully to the best of my ability what those public and private institutions had in mind for me.

I did not want to be used merely to paper over or mislead the world regarding the state of race relations in the United States. On the other hand, if the government wished to use me as an example of what was possible, I had no objection so long as I could speak as I wished and my involvement was genuinely in the interest of improving the racial climate in America. With the United States fully aware of its vulnerability abroad regarding the race question, a wide range of individuals and agencies were hopeful that I would be willing to travel and speak out about conditions here. I quickly set myself the rule that so long as there was no effort to dictate what I would say, I was amenable to any overture, and I am pleased to say that no one ever asked of me anything that would compromise my professional or scholarly integrity.

In November 1959, Francis Young, executive secretary of the Conference Board of Associated Research Councils, again inquired of my availability for two or three months in the summer of 1960. I authorized him to proceed, with the understanding that the maximum length of time that I could spend in Australia would be two months, from mid-June to mid-August. Soon thereafter, the United States Educational Foundation in Australia (the Fulbright Board) expressed its pleasure in nominating me as a "distinguished American lecturer," and the Department of State authorized a grant to cover my expenses. It was understood that I would visit and lecture at any Australian university that expressed an interest in learning more about any facet of American life and history.

I was, of course, reluctant to be away from Aurelia and Whit for two months during the summer, and as usual Aurelia was understanding. Without it needing to be discussed, she realized that my accepting the foundation's invitation was not only in the family's interest but, indeed, was of a piece with what I was attempting to do as a scholar and civic leader. She was willing, once again, to manage things at home while I was away.

After the arrangements became final, I began to hear almost weekly from interested groups in Australia, and my summer's itinerary began to fill up. So it was that on June 10, 1960, the day before our twentieth wedding anniversary, I departed San Francisco on Qantas Empire Airways for the long trip to Sydney. As I stepped off the plane, from which I had been requested to disembark first, photographers began taking pictures of me. I was then ushered into a lounge where I held an impromptu press conference. Yes, I was pleased to be in Australia. No, I was not born in New York but had lived there for four years. Yes, I would lecture on a variety of subjects, mostly about American history. And so the press conference went, for about thirty minutes. This was, indeed, a new experience for me; I had never before experienced celebrity status. Of course, I realized that all the attention carried with it an added burden of being honest, fair, and accurate in what I said about myself and about the interests, both academic and public, that I represented.

Upon my arrival in Canberra, I began two exceptionally busy, strenuous months. The Australians responded to my willingness to give freely of my time by taking virtually all of it. From the moment my photograph appeared in the *Sydney Morning Herald* the day following my arrival, and the Canberra reporter for the *Sydney Sunday Telegraph* secured an interview that became the basis for a feature article in his newspaper, my time was not my own.

From Canberra I journeyed to Melbourne, where my days were filled with lectures, radio and television appearances, and meetings with various interested groups. In the evenings, there were receptions, cocktail parties, and dinners. It became clear during those first days in Australia that the press, radio, television, and general public were interested in me both as a scholar and as an African American. They seemed to have no preconceived notions about me as a scholar or, as the Europeans had, about the status of blacks in the United States. They also did not seem to draw any analogies between blacks in the United States and Aborigines in Australia. They seemed perfectly willing to accept me as an American who had made it to the upper reaches of his profession and deserved their esteem accordingly.

Zelman Cowan, dean of the law school at the University of Melbourne, interviewed me on a television program called *Spotlight*. On a radio program called *Guest of Honor*, I spoke about race relations in the United States; the response was such that the United States embassy made arrangements to print and distribute transcripts. When I left Melbourne for Adelaide, requests were still coming in for me to lecture or be a dinner guest.

While my schedule in Adelaide was not as hectic as what I had faced in Melbourne, I managed to remain busy. At the university one day I led a lively discussion at a joint seminar with the law school and the Department of History on "Problems of Segregation and Desegregation in the United States," and on another a joint seminar with the history and politics departments on "The Tradition of Reform in American History." The problems of race in the United States did not go neglected, and while in Adelaide I led a discussion with university students on "The Negro." I also delivered a public lecture on "The American Negro in the Twentieth

Century." My experiences in Sydney and New South Wales were more of the same.

All of this had done a great deal to dispel my initial misgivings over the wisdom of giving a summer to a country whose racial policies, in my opinion, left much to be desired. Prior to accepting the invitation to visit Australia, I had discussed this opportunity with African American friends, who declared that they did not have time to expose themselves to a country where they understood the "white Australian policy" meant that they were not welcome. I had also discussed it with two white friends, both of whom were surprised about my sensitivity to the matter of race where Australia was concerned. It was their understanding that the Australians were indeed sensitive to *Asians* coming there, since their very proximity posed an immigration threat given the relatively weak barriers that the country had erected. As far as African Americans or Africans were concerned, however, the Australians had, as far as these friends knew, not given them a thought, perhaps because of their distance, if nothing else, from Australia's shores. Balancing these two reactions, by the time I had accepted Francis Young's invitation I was resolved to do what I could to counter any Australian bias against people of African descent.

What I encountered relieved me of any such burden. It was not simply the professional courtesies extended to me by fellow scholars, or the excited interest of the Australian press. Literally upon my arrival I was promoted to a status usually reserved for a person with immediate, national celebrity. It was not only that my presence in Australia was announced far and wide, through the numerous newspaper, radio, and television interviews that occurred wherever I visited. It was also the fact that I was known to most adult Australians.

One morning, when I hailed a taxi, the driver greeted me with, "Good Morning, Professor Franklin. Where can I take you?" On another occasion, when I was standing in a bank line awaiting to cash a traveler's check, a clerk invited me to wait more comfortably in the manager's office. The manager visited with me, offered me a drink, and then, with my business complete, a lift back to my college in a Rolls-Royce. On yet another morning, when I was out for a stroll, I stopped at a boutique after spying an opal ring that I thought Aurelia would like. I went in, and the sole attendant was talking on the telephone. She looked up, saw me, and said to the person on the other end of the line, "I'll call you shortly. Professor Franklin has just walked in."

In Melbourne, I was honored when a delegation of eight or ten Aborigines, the first Australians, came to call on me. I had never seen such people, and I was interested to discover the similarities and contrasts, if such comparisons were at all in order, with Native Americans. I found them to be intelligent and articulate. They complained that they did not enjoy equal opportunities and that Aborigines as a people could ascend much higher in Australian society and culture if only they had a chance. One of my visitors was Minister Paul Hasluck, who would become governor general of the country that year. He very much wanted more for them, and he suggested that African Americans as well as Native Americans should join hands with the Aborigines of Australia and work together for the common good. Later, in a spirit of cultural exchange, another of my visitors, who happened to be Australia's champion boomerang thrower, not only taught me the rudiments of throwing the boomerang, but gave me one that he had made.

While there were many things about Australia that I did not understand, the practice of not staring at strangers was easily the most difficult. When Aurelia and I visited England for the first time in 1951, numerous Britons had stared at us. In Austria, that same summer, scores of local men, women, and children followed us as we walked from the bus station to a restaurant. I was not offended, for I understand that when people's inhibitions are not under control, their curiosity takes over. That was not the case in Australia, however. If I was walking on the street alone and encountered a group of children, not one of them stared at me. Even if they were playing and did not see me approaching, they might bump into me on the sidewalk, look up and offer apologies, but they did not take a second look and seemed to treat me as just another Australian. Having spent all of my life in some measure aware of my appearance as a black man, it was revelatory to be met with Australia's courteous disinterest.

To cap off my Australian visit, I had planned what would be my first circumnavigation of the globe, but as my first trip from Sydney to Hong Kong commenced, I was not at all certain that I would survive the return trip. I was so thoroughly exhausted that I thought I was ill, perhaps with something incurable. Having never experienced this level of discomfort, having grown accustomed to protracted periods of intensive work, and not regarding eight cups of coffee a day as unusual, it never occurred to me that I was merely tired. In Hong Kong I did a minimum of sightseeing and spent much of the time in my hotel room. My visit to Bangkok was just a tourist stop, and I did not leave the city, though I did a fairly thorough job of sightseeing despite the congestion. By the time I reached Cairo, my very first time on African soil, I was prepared to ignore my exhaustion to see the wonders of Egypt, where I was to spend several days.

The sphinx, grand and majestic, was followed by the pyramids, even grander and more majestic. But the suggestion that I climb to the pyramid's top drove home the realization that if I even attempted one step toward that goal, I would be unable to lift my other foot up to the next stone. I was unabashedly afraid that I was nearing the end. Therefore, I spent long stretches of time tired and frankly fearful, sitting on a bench by the Nile River, gazing silently at the water as it rushed quietly by. Fulfilling a small list of obligations and the occasional visit to a museum, I spent my remaining days in Egypt torn between my desire to see as much of the country as possible and what I presumed to be some vague illness I could not identify that sapped my strength.

Eventually a new jet plane, being used to transport the Egyptian Olympic team to Rome, carried me as well. From Rome there were only three brief stops before returning to New York. The first was in Copenhagen, which was only to visit the Tivoli Gardens, Andersen's Mermaid, and the zoo, always a favorite attraction regardless of the city. Much more important was Stockholm for the Eleventh International Congress of Historical Sciences, the high point of which was a reception at the royal palace with His Majesty the king of Sweden. The third and final stop was in England, where I visited friends, undertook to shop for Aurelia and Whit, and eagerly looked forward to returning home.

The first thing I did after my reunion with my family was to visit my physician. When I told him how I felt, he asked me to describe a typical day in Australia. When I did so, he observed that had I not been strong and healthy, I might not have escaped with only nervous exhaustion and caffeine poisoning.

15

Glimpses of the Motherland

ONE OF THE MOST remarkable developments on the world scene, even as we were making the adjustment in Brooklyn, was the emergence of independent states in Africa. We watched with awe and admiration as Ghana, under the leadership of Kwame Nkrumah, educated in the United States, led the way. As a token of its independence, it was admitted to membership in the United Nations in March 1957, a historic event we celebrated. While Aurelia and I were not among the considerable number of African Americans who attended the independence ceremonies, we followed developments there with enthusiastic admiration.

If possible, the emergence of Nigeria as an independent state in 1960 was even more loudly heralded among African Americans. I followed the unfolding of events, as I made my way back from Australia through Asia and Europe. The splash of Nigeria's independence was greater than Ghana's, in part because it was the largest African nation in sub-Saharan Africa. American interest in Nigeria was also generally greater than in Ghana for very practical reasons: Nigeria's immense mineral and agricultural resources made it much more attractive to European and U.S. investors.

Sensitive Americans were shocked to learn that the delegation that President Dwight Eisenhower appointed to represent them at the independence ceremonies of the largest black nation in the world was all-white. African Americans were deeply offended, and some members of the Department of State were clearly embarrassed to be sending a lily-white delegation to Nigeria. At about this time, one of them, with whom I had become acquainted during my various contacts with the department, asked me if I would like to visit Nigeria for the simple purpose of observing the new nation's institutions of higher education. I had never been in that part of the world and my interest in it was substantial. Despite the fact that I had so recently returned from Australia and needed time to catch up on my work as well as rest, I indicated my willingness to go. I had no idea then that my proposed visit would be planned to coincide with the inde-pendence ceremonies when thousands of visitors from all over the world would be present. Had I been aware of this, I would have declined. When I became aware of it, I had no doubt that my visit, to which I was by then committed, was designed to mitigate the nation's embarrassment for send-ing an all-white delegation. Perhaps I should have been more prescient, but I confess that my desire to see Nigeria was greater than my better judgment.

I was to depart for Nigeria on September 25. On the evening of the twenty-fourth, while I was out doing last-minute errands, my sister Mozella called to say that my father had died of a heart attack. She sug-gested that Aurelia urge me to complete my visit to Nigeria; the funeral service and burial in the family plot could await my return. Aurelia simply informed Mozella that we both would be there immediately. Of course, I grieved my father's passing, but I was also haunted by a specific guilt—my failure to help him secure a publisher for his autobiography that he had typed laboriously with the index finger of his left hand after a debilitating stroke in 1957. Selfishly busy with my own career, I had procrastinated. Now it was too late for him to enjoy the response to his first and only ma-jor publication, and it was my fault. My penance over the next several years would take many forms, but it was never sufficient to make up for my dereliction.

When we arrived in Tulsa on the evening of September 25, there were many friends and neighbors keeping vigil at my father's home. Among them was Samuel Boorstin, father of my friend and fellow historian, Daniel. A distinguished member of the Tulsa bar, Samuel and my father had been friends for years. Growing up, Dan and I, of course, were separated by segregated Tulsa, even though we were the same age and both first in our respective high school classes. Mr. Boorstin had come, as had dozens of others, to pay his respects and to extend his sympathy, for which the family was deeply grateful. Three days later, with the funeral and burial over, we returned to New York and I left immediately for Nigeria, where the independence celebrations were already under way.

The new, large hotel that had been constructed to house guests during the independence ceremonies was completely filled. The Department of State, however, had secured a room for me in the home of Elsie Austin, an African American lawyer who had been in Nigeria for several years helping to establish the new government infrastructure. Shortly after my arrival, I encountered Nelson Rockefeller, chairman of the U.S. delegation, with whom I by then had a nodding acquaintance. He wondered why I had not been there at the beginning of the celebration. When I told him of my father's death, he put his arms around me and offered his sympathy. He then invited me to all social and business meetings of the U.S. delegation. I thanked him, but did not accept. I was determined to do nothing that would dispel the fact that the U.S. delegation was all white and stayed as far away from it as possible. I meant to stick to matters of higher education, taking my assigned task seriously.

On the first full day of my visit to Lagos, I went for a walk, eager to observe the people as much as I could. One man, about my age, walked up to me, extended his hand, and said, "Welcome home, brother." I had never previously regarded Africa as "home," and this greeting gave me the opportunity to think on the idea of "motherland" and what its significance was to me and the millions of others whose distant past was rooted in the land south of the Sahara. I rapidly came to a firm decision: Even if that gracious, handsome Nigerian was not my brother, I was prepared to adopt him and to view the soil under our feet as my home away from home. At that moment, I became determined to assimilate as much of Africa's culture as I possibly could.

This was not as difficult as I feared it might be, for I had already assimilated more African culture and history than I had realized. The exercise of self-tutoring in African as well as African American history over several years, beginning more than two decades earlier while I was still in college, prepared me for a process that was, at that point, moving me to another stage. Writing *From Slavery to Freedom* gave me the orientation that I needed. Standing on African soil south of the Sahara for the first time and facing this young Nigerian on a basis of a genuine fraternal feeling persuaded me that, more than I had realized, I had already adopted Africa as my true motherland. All of a sudden, the feeling I had when I completed the writing of *From Slavery to Freedom* and saw several centuries of African and American history unfold before my eyes seemed more authentic and real than ever before.

On another morning when I was out for my usual stroll, I went by an artist's studio and paused to view the displayed sculpture. My eyes were drawn to a remarkably well-sculpted woman, austere in appearance, even as she was most attractive. There was a certain modesty about her, perhaps because she held her hands straight down, close to her sides. I tried to persuade myself that I should make no inquiries, that I should squelch my desire to acquire the work. Nevertheless, several days later, I not only went again to view the sculpture but entered the studio to talk with the artist. Felix Idabour welcomed me. The piece that had claimed my attention for the past several days was called *Benin Woman*. Carved from mahogany, it was already several years old, and he was reluctant to part with it. He would let me have it, at a reasonable price, only on my promise that when he had a show in the United States, he could call on me for permission to display it. I immediately acceded to that condition. When I left Lagos a few days later, *Benin Woman* was on its way to Brooklyn.

This piece of sculpture became the cornerstone of the art collection that I soon began to build. It was not the first piece of art that I had collected, but *Benin Woman*, a major work, was a turning point. It became a symbol of the motherland I increasingly came to respect and revere. In future years, whenever I considered adding to my art collection, whether it be a work by Souleyman Keita of Senegal or by Jacob Lawrence, I would invariably ask myself if it was worthy to be in the company of *Benin Woman*.

Upon my return from Nigeria, I expected a request from the Department of State for a report or at least a debriefing. I received neither. It was difficult not to conclude that my understood reason for being there, to discuss problems in African and American history with local educators, was superficially the reason the department had urged my visit. I concluded that my presence in Nigeria at the time of the independence festivities had been sufficient, and if there were those who had concluded that I was a member of the U.S. delegation, as far as State was concerned, all the better. I have no idea how many Nigerians, if any, believed that I was a member of the official delegation. I denied such membership to anyone who asked, and I had avoided all delegation functions. The thought that perhaps I caused some to infer that I had knowingly assisted the United States in conveying a false impression was and remains deeply disturbing.

As I reflect on the reasons that should have kept me from taking the trip to Nigeria at that time, my commitments at home alone were sufficient. I had scholarly meetings to attend, for which I needed to make preparations. There were books to review for journals and papers to write. Perhaps the heaviest responsibility was my extra assignment at the college. President Gideonse had asked me to chair a subcommittee on personnel and budget that would oversee the candidates for promotion to associate professor. Interviews needed to be conducted, and files, including articles and books, were to be read. Following that, my committee had to deliberate and make recommendations. It was an awesome and challenging responsibility, for careers depended on our conclusions. In due course, the committee completed its assignments and made its report, which was duly accepted.

My greatest personal responsibility was the completion of a manuscript on which I was already working. Back in 1955 I had signed a contract with Daniel Boorstin to contribute a concise volume on Reconstruction to the series that Dan was editing for the University of Chicago Press. Roger Shugg, who had persuaded me to write *From Slavery to Freedom*, was the new director there. He was enthusiastic, promising me that I would "suffer no pressure" to complete the book at the frantic pace he had demanded while at Knopf. Further, he was certain that on Reconstruction I would write a "new history, a true history, and one that will set a mark for other historians to shoot at."

As year after year passed, Boorstin and Shugg, keeping to their promises, restricted themselves to gracious expressions of their desire to see the completed book. Finally, the manuscript was ready, or at least I had grown weary of working on it and even more weary of providing Daniel

Boorstin and Roger Shugg with excuses. So in November 1960, I sent the manuscript to Dan. After he had read it, he wrote, "I think we are extremely lucky to have it and in my opinion it is by far the best treatment on the subject yet available." Following slight revisions, the manuscript was on its way to copyediting and publication.

Although some historians agreed that there was a need for a new and revisionist review of Reconstruction, none had attempted to meet that need. With the exception of Kenneth Stampp, whose book on the subject would appear two years later, no one, as far as I knew, was actively writing a generally revisionist approach to the subject. The need was urgent, and I undertook to meet that need. I could no longer endure the claim that Negroes were ignorant dupes of white radicals whose sole interest was amassing wealth for themselves. I would insist that most freedmen were desperate for an education and extremely eager to participate in the ongoing development of their communities. Their institutions, among them religious and social organizations, were serious, responsible agencies of stability as well as change. It would be difficult to find, I argued, anywhere at any time a more serious and responsible group of people so recently in bondage.

Subsequent to the appearance of *Reconstruction After the Civil War* and several months before there were any academic reviews, historians wrote to me commenting on the book. Henry Steele Commager wrote from Amherst, "I can't resist sending you my congratulations on your Reconstruction volume. It beautifully combines all the latest scholarship, originality, judiciousness, and literary charm. That you have been able to put all this into 40 thousand words or so is something really remarkable." David Donald wrote, "I say without qualification that this is the best thing in print on the subject. It is an admirable book—concise, lucid, beautifully written, accurate." Bernard Weisberger wrote that the book "is as good and useful as I knew it was going to be."

The reviews in the press were not so universally favorable as the appraisals sent by friends. It was as if those with a vested interest in the earlier, traditional interpretation of Reconstruction could not sit idly by and see their world crumble before my attack. I had said my piece, originally, in my review essay of Coulter's *The South During Reconstruction*. I had refused then to see a nineteenth-century interpretation of the Reconstruction restated as though it was not only a fresh new look but one that was already widely accepted as gospel truth. I have no doubt that there were those who had read my essay on Coulter's work with displeasure and had waited to see my larger treatment of the subject. T. Harry Williams said it was written from a "Northern Negro-liberal vantage point," while Eric McKitrick called my treatment "diffuse, unconcentrated, and somewhat casual." I could not resist the amusement that Avery Craven provided me in *The Journal of Southern History*, when he resorted to inventing a quotation attributed to me and then attacking me as though I had made the statement in the book. That degree of desperation persuaded me that I had truly said something worthwhile. Within less than six months, *Reconstruction After the Civil War* had sold more than three thousand copies, and the supply was sufficiently near depletion that the press was planning a second printing.

My father, who had studied and practiced law day and night, had referred to it as a "jealous mistress." I was learning that history was no less covetous. The work at the college seemed never ending, and my work, from research to related public service outside the college, made inordinate demands on my time. The trick was to prevent the cumulative pressure from keeping me awake at night or interfering with maintaining a wholesome, healthy family. I worked assiduously at the latter, seizing every opportunity to include Aurelia and Whit in my expanding world. Thus, when I was invited to receive an honorary degree from Virginia State College in the spring of 1961, we made it a family outing and combined it with a visit to Aurelia's parents in Goldsboro. Later that summer, when I was invited by Fred Rath, a Harvard graduate school friend, to participate in a summer seminar conducted by Louis Jones at the Farmer's Museum in Cooperstown, New York, I accepted not only because of my professional interest in rural and local history but also because it was a magnificent opportunity for Aurelia, Whit, and me to enjoy living closer to nature. Whit, I am proud to report, caught his first fish on the pier at Lake Otsego and was thrilled to have the hotel's chef prepare it for his dinner that evening.

My largest professional obligation following the completion of the book on Reconstruction was to the United States Commission on Civil Rights. Having been created by congressional legislation in 1957, the commission hoped to draw attention to its existence and its function by reviewing the history of civil rights since the nation's founding. The staff director, Berl Bernhard, engaged me to write such a history. Here again was a request for service by the national government, and once again I had to weigh a decision to accept it despite my other obligations and to make as certain as possible that I was not being used to further some ulterior motive of the federal government. Despite the fact that my commitments were already burdensome, I accepted the commission's invitation with the hope that the history of civil rights that I would write would contribute to a better understanding of the current status of race relations in the United States.

The commission requested that the history be completed in time for the observance of the centennial of the Emancipation Proclamation, January 1, 1963, and so provided me with the resources to engage two research assistants. It also requested that three consultants read the completed manuscript and indicate where it should be edited or revised. I suggested Allan Nevins, C. Vann Woodward, and Rayford W. Logan, and when I asked them to consult, they agreed enthusiastically. Most of the material was familiar to me, since I had used much of it in *From Slavery to Freedom*. By working diligently on the manuscript during the academic year, 1961–62, I was able to deliver it to the commission in June 1962.

The commission was sorely disappointed with what I submitted. The members were distressed that, in their estimation, there was no "analysis of the factors responsible for progress in civil rights and those factors and techniques which may have relevance for future progress." They were also disturbed that I had not given sufficient attention to the Negro's contribution, "taking into consideration factors of social, economic, and political significance." Put simply, anticipating a story in a celebratory key, they were thrown by my darker history of civil rights that indicated how much remained to be done. The commission had also solicited, without my knowledge, comments from my three consultants. Vann Woodward seemed completely satisfied, merely asking that a subtitle indicate that I had dealt primarily with Negroes and civil rights. Rayford Logan's suggestions were primarily editorial, which he sent to me and not to the commission.

The response that Nevins gave to the commission was obviously different from the one that he had already sent me. Observing that my manuscript needed tightening and, in some places rewriting, Nevins, on August 22, wrote to me that it was a "remarkably able piece of work, and reflected . . . long immersion in the subject." He "found the book well organized, and well integrated. You have done well in compressing so great a story into 325 pages." However, after the commission had expressed some displeasure about the manuscript and solicited further comments from him, Nevins wrote to me again on September 8. He now stated his assumption was that I would completely rewrite the book, not only tightening it but striking "a note of greater tolerance and moderation, and to give more emphasis to the contributions of the Negro to American life."

In my reply to Bernhard's letter informing me of the commission's dissatisfaction, I reminded him of what I had said much earlier, "that the history of the Negro and civil rights in the United States is not a pretty picture." If I now rewrote what I had written in order to clean up the story, "I would be writing a tract, but not a history." Bernhard claimed that the commission had anticipated that "heavy emphasis would be placed upon significant developments in recent times, but more than half of the manuscript covers the period prior to 1930." I responded by saying, "I had no way of knowing that the Commission had anticipated heavy emphasis on the recent period. As a historian, I am of the opinion that the past cannot be sacrificed . . . for the sake of the present . . . Little or nothing is known of the history of civil rights during the first seventy years following the Civil War. I felt fully justified in giving a balanced history, with due attention to the early years."

Bernhard and the commission also seemed distressed that I had not done more to underscore "Negro contribution and achievement." I gave examples of the attention I had given to the matter, but noted, "It is difficult to make a connection between the achievements of Booker T. Washington, George W. Carver . . . or Charles Drew or Carter G. Woodson and civil rights . . . There are hundreds of instances, many of which must be known to you, where achievements and contributions were not the result of civil rights but were, indeed, in spite of the denial of civil rights." I promised to work on the manuscript, but I was not optimistic. I wrote to Bernhard, "I am afraid that I cannot 'tidy up' the history that Americans themselves have made."

Subsequently, I learned from Paul McStallworth, chair of the Department of History at Central State University in Ohio, that the commission was searching for some historian or group of historians to rework my manuscript or to begin anew. McStallworth, who had been my colleague at St. Augustine's College during the early war years, told me that Bernhard had asked Charles Wesley, president of Central State and a distinguished historian, to assist them in reworking what I had done. In his letter of October 4 to me, McStallworth said that Wesley had urged the commission to accept my manuscript as it was. When the commission balked, there was some hope that Wesley and McStallworth would assist the commission in its "plight." Later, the commission dispatched a Mr. Cornelius Cotter to Ohio to talk with historians there. When Wesley again urged the acceptance of my work for publication, Cotter said that was not possible.

I continued to work on the manuscript despite the discouraging comments by the members of the commission and its staff. On November 19, 1962, I sent Bernhard a final set of revisions. They included a large number of corrections and editorial changes, a new preface emphasizing the evolving concept of civil rights during the previous century, and a new first chapter dealing with a significant enlargement of the concept during and after the Civil War. I also added a chapter, "A Century of Progress," that undertook to highlight some of the more significant areas in which African Americans had made advancements and had contributed to the general improvement of civil rights in the United States. I also requested information on what the staff had done to the manuscript I had submitted prior to this one and whether the commission had succeeded in securing the services of other persons in revising it. I ended by requesting a copy of the final draft of the manuscript.

Bernhard replied that he very much appreciated what I had done. He added, "I cannot pretend that we have been able to produce a manuscript which has the verve and character which one might expect of a book written by a single author free to express his personality upon it." At the end of November, Bernhard sent me a copy of the "staff report," as he called it, with a request that I send by cable, from Cambridge where I had gone to serve as Pitt professor for the year, my approval of their acknowledgment of my help. I was incensed, and I could not refrain from observing that the committee's report was "lacking in style, character, and movement." Its lackluster prose was the least of its sins; much of the writing evidenced a "remarkable innocence of interrelationships of various historical events and developments, to say nothing of the historical facts themselves." I conceded that it may well be too late for general observations that addressed basic concepts and approaches. Instead, I provided Bernhard with four pages of corrections of facts, spelling, and rather elementary interpretations of the significance of events.

Copies of the finished book, *Freedom to the Free*, were ready for the White House celebration of President Lincoln's birthday on February 12, 1963. I was invited, but my presence then in England fortunately made it impossible for me to attend. Copies were distributed to approximately eight hundred guests. In commenting on the report, President Kennedy said that while Negroes had suffered many setbacks, they could take "some satisfaction in the record of the last 100 years." I do not know if Allan Nevins attended and, if so, in what capacity. Rayford Logan was not invited, perhaps because he was to attend a White House luncheon for the king of Laos a few days later. I do not know if Vann Woodward attended or was invited. Writing to Woodward from her home in Montgomery, Alabama, Virginia Durr, a white civic leader and wife of Clifford Durr, a powerful force in New Deal politics, reported that the newspaper there had run a front-page story about the White House reception and had noted that "you and John Hope had produced an historical account of what happened in the field of Civil Rights and what was going to happen, both accounts being glowing indeed and prophesying continued progress and advance."

Of the many instances in which it appeared that I was used by the United States government, this is the clearest, most unequivocal example. Whether there was manipulation on the part of the State Department to serve the ultimate needs and ends of the government when they dispatched me to Australia, there is room for debate. If there was question about the government's use of me to study higher education in Nigeria, while an all-white delegation represented the United States at the independence ceremonies of that large African nation, there is considerably less doubt. However, there can be no question that the United States, through the Commission on Civil Rights, attempted to make blatant and crude use of me in its effort to present a false picture of "Negro progress" for the centennial of the Emancipation Proclamation. Its effort was so transparent and its procedure so crude that it would have been difficult for the most naïve person, historian or lay, not to have seen through it. I can only say that the United States Commission on Civil Rights did not do honor to itself or to the country. If I became a party to its machinations, it was only because I sought, as I had and would in numerous other instances, to contribute to the positive development of the nation as a whole.

16

Hail Britannia

TWO CHAIRS in United States History are reserved at Oxford and Cambridge universities for visiting professors from the United States. While the one at Oxford, the Harmsworth, is older, both are equally coveted by professors in this country. The committee overseeing the Pitt Professorship of American History and Institutions at Cambridge approached me shortly after I went to Brooklyn College to see if I was interested in holding the chair and, if so, when I would like to do so. After consulting with Aurelia, we decided that the academic year 1962–63 would suit us best. By that time we would be well settled in at Brooklyn; Whit would then be ten years old, an age when the experience would be meaningful and lasting; and Aurelia would have made some decisions about her own professional future that she had postponed to provide Whit the security and self-confidence he needed as long as the neighbors on New York Avenue and nearby streets remained unfriendly, and some even hostile.

The decision made and the departure date set, we booked passage to Southampton on the *Queen Mary*, sailing from New York on September 5, 1962. Our cabin was quite commodious, and it is well that it was, for we had invited several friends from the college as well as from the city to a champagne party we were giving just before the afternoon sailing. The

Queen Mary's magnificent public rooms and recreational parlors duly impressed Whit, and when Aurelia and I lounged in our deck chairs, he took walks around the deck. He even met a few youngsters with whom he became friendly. The experience was, on the whole, quite different from our first voyage in 1951, when the French line had humiliated us with their dining hall seating arrangements. Whatever else had changed in international race relations over the past decade, on the *Queen Mary* we discovered that we should judge our treatment on a case-by-case basis rather than make hasty assumptions about the treatment we might receive.

Before leaving New York, I had purchased a Mercedes-Benz automobile to be delivered at the Cunard pier in Southampton. I am proud to announce that despite the unfamiliar right-side steering wheel and the rain that greeted us on our arrival, within an hour or so of having packed the new car, we arrived safely in Cambridge. The first order of business was to get Whit settled in school. The Perse had been recommended by my friend Frank Thistlethwaite, the U.S. historian at St. John's College, and its headmaster welcomed Whit and placed him in the fifth form, the U.S. equivalent of somewhere between the sixth and seventh grades. It was an all-boys school, and as soon as he acquired his gray suit, short pants, purple and gray cap, and scarf, he was ready for his daily bicycle commute. Since The Perse was not so very far from where we lived, he did not, to our great relief, have to navigate the traffic through town. Soon, he was fully adjusted, playing soccer and cricket, and speaking English with a distinctly British accent!

The fall term, called Michelmas in the university calendar, was very busy. I lectured at a number of British universities, including Keele, Manchester, Birmingham, London, and Oxford. The range of topics was wide, but the focus was usually on the problem of race in America. Surely the most fascinating contemporary event in the United States was the effort of James Meredith to gain admission to the University of Mississippi that September. When we had arrived in England, the British papers were already covering that event. The English were astounded to learn that the application of one African American to be admitted to a tax-supported public university had created what was virtually a national crisis, involving the state government, the national guard, and the president of the United States. In defiance of a court order, the state of Mississippi had prevented Meredith from enrolling, appeasing the thousands of Mississippians affronted by the temerity of a black man seeking an education at an institution that was traditionally for whites only. When it became clear that Governor Ross Barnett's promise to president Kennedy to maintain order and see Meredith admitted was an empty one, the president first dispatched deputy marshals and eventually federalized National Guardsmen. By the time the rioting was controlled, two people were dead and many more were injured.

Shortly after my arrival I was invited by Richard Dimbleby, the anchor of the BBC's prime-time television show *Panorama*, to explain the Mississippi rioting, other forms of racial violence, and everything else happening in the United States regarding race relations, including the role of public officials such as the governors of Mississippi and Alabama. Meredith's effort was, I said, a serious challenge to the entire apparatus of segregation and discrimination, and the violent, at times vicious, response was a desperate effort to preserve an outmoded and antiquated system of privilege based on the specious foundation of race.

The previous spring, well before our departure to Britain, President Kennedy had appointed me to a three-year term on the Board of Foreign Scholarships. As the agency that oversaw all educational exchange programs under the Fulbright Act, it met at least four times per year, and I was expected to return to the United States for the fall meeting of the board, at which time I would be sworn in. I also was scheduled to lecture at the New School for Social Research on "The Centennial of Emancipation," which would be broadcast on a local radio station. There was not enough time in this whirlwind visit home to do all the things I wished to do. I spent a few hours at Brooklyn College greeting several close friends. The meeting of the Fulbright Board was impressive enough, with my old graduate school colleague Oscar Handlin presiding. I was sworn in and learned something of the scope of the board's activities.

I rushed back to Cambridge to resume my lectures in the midst of the Cuban missile crisis. President Kennedy had demanded that the Soviet Union remove its missiles from Cuba. The United States and the Soviet Union stood eyeball-to-eyeball even as I was flying back to Cambridge, leaving me to wonder if the plane would be blown out of the sky. Relieved when the crisis passed, Aurelia, Whit, and I—and I suspect much of the world—indulged ourselves with a small celebration.

During the year, our entertainment, dictated by our budget, was modest. Nevertheless, we saw a good deal of a few couples, some from the United States. On occasion, we gave large cocktail parties, in contrast to the sherry parties to which the English were accustomed. If we knew sufficiently far ahead, the party would coincide with the visit of friends. Thus, when Arthur Spingarn, one of the founders of the NAACP, visited us, we put on a rather large reception. In our own turn, we were honored by an invitation to Buckingham Palace and a garden party for the commonwealth ministers.

A more elaborate celebration awaited us at the end of the Michelmas term. Already, autumn in Cambridge had turned into winter, and although we had not suffered from the cold, we decided, at Oscar Handlin's suggestion, to observe the Christmas holidays in Morocco. Also at his suggestion, we made reservations at what was reputed to be one of Winston Churchill's favorite hotels, the Mamounia in Marrakech. The hotel had arranged for a companion for Whit, since children were not permitted at the black-tie gala on Christmas Eve. He had no objection, and he was more than compensated in subsequent days, for it was through his hotel companion that he met several boys and girls his own age with whom, and with their assistance, he could speak French. He repaid them by assisting them with their English. To this day he attributes this experience to the beginning of his subsequent career in international affairs and his fascination with and mastery of several foreign languages. All in all, we enjoyed ourselves tremendously, and as a surprise for Aurelia and Whit, I arranged for us to spend New Year's Eve in Paris.

The holiday in North Africa and France was almost enough, but not quite, to prepare us for the icy walks and frozen pipes that greeted us when we returned to Cambridge in early January. Soon, the Lent term had begun, and one had to focus on something other than the weather and bitter cold. I continued my lectures on the United States in the nineteenth century. I also continued to visit colleges and universities in Britain, with a swing up to Edinburgh and Glasgow, as well as visits to some so-called redbrick universities, such as Sussex and Southampton. Thanks to my friend Al Johnson, who had been at the University of Maryland when I was at Howard University and who was now in the American cultural affairs office at Bonn, I went in late January to Germany and lectured at Munich, Regensburg, Saarbrücken, and Cologne.

When I returned from Germany in late January, a letter from William H. McNeill, chair of the Department of History at the University of Chicago, was on my desk. McNeill informed me that there was an argument in his department that he hoped I could help him settle, and he wondered if he could come over to talk with me about the matter in person. I thought that it must be a serious problem if he wished to come all the way from Chicago to lay it before me, and I invited him to come whenever he pleased. I speculated on what it could be. Since my arrival at Brooklyn, I had acquired a reputation for putting out fires. Chicago, I feared, must be suffering a major conflagration to cause the department chair to arrive in Cambridge within a few days.

With the formalities over, I invited him to my rooms in college and asked him what his problem was. He replied that the department at Chicago was divided on the question of what I intended to do in the future. Some members were certain that I was about to leave the field and accept a high appointment in the Kennedy administration, a speculation based, no doubt, on my friendship with Kennedy adviser Arthur M. Schlesinger Jr. (I too had heard the rumor, but since I had not received any direct word, I dismissed it.) Other members insisted that my commitment to history was so deep that no offer, even from the president, could lure me away. Since his colleagues wished to invite me to join them, they would do so only if there was a chance I would remain in the field of history. After expressing my amazement that the department would be arguing about *my* future, I made it clear that under no circumstances did my plans involve a career outside the academy. I did not tell McNeill that in view of the fact that years ago I had been abused by my government during World War II and more recently used by it in ways that deeply disturbed me, I was not enamored of the possibility of some long-term invitation to work for it. I merely declared that I was deeply committed to historical research, writing, and teaching. That is where my future was, and that is where it would remain.

McNeill said that he could ask no more of me at that time. He expressed appreciation and returned to Chicago.

Almost by return mail, McNeill wrote that the department had voted to invite me to join it at my convenience as professor of American history. Even as I gave thought to the invitation, members of the department at Chicago began a letter-writing campaign to convince me to accept. Daniel Boorstin, Walter Johnson, Bernard Weisberger, and Richard Storr, among others, urged me to come and declared that I would never regret it. Soon began many agonizing hours and days before I made the decision to leave Brooklyn College.

Aurelia and I had discussed the matter far into the night following McNeill's visit. There was much to consider, including most especially how Whit would respond to such a change. The fact that he could, if we desired it, attend the famed Laboratory School at the University of Chicago meant he would have access to an excellent education. Aurelia was also certain that he would be far less likely to encounter the studied insults and humiliations in Chicago's Hyde Park that he had experienced in our Brooklyn neighborhood. Neither of us, however, were concerned over whether or not Whit would be able to make the adjustment to a new home, city, school, and circle of friends. Having witnessed the way he coped with the bullies and bigots on New York Avenue, we were confident he would manage the move happily.

The University of Chicago represented an opportunity never before extended to me, one that I had struggled and aimed for since the start of my academic career as a Harvard graduate student. It was a major research university, understood to be at the forefront of both teaching and scholarship, and it was the first such school from which I had ever received an invitation to join its permanent faculty. To be sure, several major institutions had invited me to visit for a summer or a semester, but the emphasis was always on visiting, after which I was to return from whence I came. With the possible exception of Hawaii, only Brooklyn had offered me indefinite tenure, an overture that was truly unprecedented at the time and which I felt a deep obligation to honor. But, as a scholar, I knew the resources and academic objectives of Chicago clearly outmatched those of Brooklyn.

Although I was becoming more favorably disposed to accept Chicago's invitation, I could not, would not, make up my mind until I discussed the matter with President Gideonse. After all, he had left the University of Chicago to become president of Brooklyn College. He was, therefore, in a unique position to advise me. When I told him of the invitation, he mused that the people at Chicago were smarter than he had thought they were. He added that while Chicago was a good place, nothing was too good for me, and finally, if I decided to go, I would go with his blessings. With that benediction, Aurelia and I decided to accept for the autumn of 1964.

When the word reached Chicago that I agreed to come, Walter Johnson wrote to me that they had celebrated. *Time* magazine carried a piece following the announcement of my move with the caption "Return of a Giant," a reference to the university, and listed the several major appointments that Chicago had made to indicate that it was climbing its way back to its former standing near the pinnacle of higher education.

Our remaining time in England was marked by a European tour, during which Whit was introduced to the artistic marvels of the Continent. I was introduced to fly-fishing, which was to join orchid cultivation as a lifelong passion. And most sadly, we all learned of Aurelia's father's critical illness.

When I was lecturing in Germany in late July, Aurelia received a letter from her mother informing her that her father's health was deteriorating. Aurelia and I decided that she should return to the States and proceed to her parents' home, where she could assist her mother in the care of her father. A railway mail clerk for many years, upon his retirement he had been content to remain at home in Goldsboro with virtually nothing to do. Soon, there was little that he *could* do. He fell ill with Parkinson's disease, and by the time Aurelia received word from her mother regarding his rapidly failing health, his near death, which would come in 1965, was clear. In her absence, Whit and I fended for ourselves over the remaining few weeks, closed the house, and made our way to the *Queen Elizabeth* for the return trip.

During our year in England, the struggle for civil rights proceeded with almost unabated heat back in the States. For years the NAACP had used "Free by '63" as a motto and rallying cry, and as 1963 dawned with only increased resistance to meaningful equality, confrontations became ever more common and violent. Among the more significant demonstrations was the early April march on Birmingham, Alabama, led by Martin Luther King and the Southern Christian Leadership Conference. Demands for fair employment opportunities, desegregated public facilities, and a plan for complete desegregation resulted in the arrest of twenty-five hundred demonstrators, including Dr. King. When police dogs and high-pressure hoses were used against marchers, rocks and bottles were hurled in defense. Soon it seemed the entire country was in racial tumult. Medgar Evers, the leader of the Mississippi NAACP, was assassinated by a rifle shot to his back in June of that year. Demonstrations, marches, and sit-ins were staged throughout the country, with crowds of more than twenty thousand gathering in Los Angeles and San Francisco. Even as President Kennedy and Congress debated a legislative response, the March on Washington for Jobs and Freedom was under way.

The March on Washington Movement had its origins in 1941, when A. Philip Randolph suggested a mass demonstration in the nation's capital to call attention to the numerous ways African Americans suffered discrimination in housing, employment, and other areas. That threat led President Franklin D. Roosevelt to issue an order against racial discrimination, particularly in war-related industries, and the move to march on the capital was temporarily quieted. Twenty years later, with real relief and real justice nowhere in sight, Randolph resurrected his March on Washington Movement. By this time, he was able to attract large numbers of leaders and organizations. The march was set for August 28, when Whit and I would be making the return trip to the States. Before we departed, however, the BBC asked me to assist the British public in understanding what was transpiring in the United States by appearing on a program to be called "The Briton's Guide to the March on Washington."

I assumed nothing regarding the understanding of the British people concerning racial problems in the United States, especially after learning over the course of the Mississippi crisis that they knew little and were generally misinformed. The BBC had film clips of the principals, such as Martin Luther King Jr., A. Philip Randolph, Malcolm X, and Ralph Abernathy, and I talked about each of them as well as others, such as Roy Wilkins, Whitney Young, Walter Reuther, and the person most responsible for the success of the march, Bayard Rustin. I pointed out that the struggle for equality in the United States seemed never-ending. The

United States was quite capable of taking the message of democracy and equality to various parts of the world but was pained beyond description whenever the challenge was confronted at home. I explained that it was the threat of a march during World War II that had forced President Roosevelt to issue an order requiring fair employment in defense industries. That success encouraged civil rights activists to envision a 1963 march as a force that would dramatize the continued plight of African Americans and, perhaps, bring about some significant results. I had no idea how many people would march on Washington, but I predicted that with all the enthusiastic support the effort was receiving, I would not be surprised if the marchers exceeded one hundred thousand, that they would come from every part of the country, and that it would be interracial and interfaith. Regarding the impact of the march, I was less sanguine. I could not imagine that it would result in significant legislation or far-reaching change of any sort.

After closing the house on Chaucer Road and making a journey to the West Country, where Whit could see the cathedral at Wells and the abbey at Bath, we went to London, where we said our farewells to the city as well as to our friends. Our year in England had come to a close. It had been an incredibly busy period, and a rich and rewarding one as well.

In our own way, our return to the United States at the end of the summer of 1963 was symbolic of the end of one chapter in my own odyssey as well as an end of an era for African Americans and the nation at large. On the day of the march on Washington, the day of our return, W.E.B. Du Bois passed away in Ghana. Later, I was asked to deliver the principal address at the memorial for him in Carnegie Hall. By then, I regarded Dr. Du Bois as a colleague, perhaps even a friend. Whatever his regard for me and my regard for him, his high standing among courageous spokesmen for justice was indisputable. I had spoken at his eightieth birthday dinner in New York in 1948, and at his ninetieth birthday reception, also in New York. In the earlier talk, I made reference to his opposition to the tyrannical leadership of Fayette Avery McKenzie at Fisk University in 1926, to his conflict with the leadership of the NAACP over its future in 1934, and to his matchless scholarship in history and sociology over the years. In the latter talk, I made reference to his heroic stand against his detractors during the McCarthy red scare years and to the remarkable and courageous position he took in the face of a variety of humiliating experiences, including an indictment and trial for the alleged crime of working for peace.

When I learned of his death, I reflected back to June 1960, when Dr. Du Bois and I received honorary degrees at Morgan State College in Baltimore. Since I had agreed to deliver the commencement address, I had the opportunity not only to speak to the graduates about their responsibility to society but also to say a word about the courageous and constructive career of Dr. Du Bois. I called their attention to what he meant to all of us, how indebted we were to him for his many contributions, and how important it was to express our appreciation even as the forces of reaction attempted to destroy him. When I had completed my address, Dr. Du Bois came over to me and told me how pleased he was with what I had said. That was the last time I would see him. Even though thirty-four years had passed since an awestruck Oklahoma eleven-year-old had gazed upon the great man for the first time, I was as awestruck in 1960 as I had been in 1926.

17

Points West

SHORTLY AFTER OUR RETURN from England, we began to give considerable attention to the matter of moving. We knew that we wanted to live in the vicinity of the University of Chicago, especially since we were familiar with the history of the neighborhood, Chicago's first suburb and among the very few to embrace integration early on, and the role of the university in promoting it. When my friends at the university asked about our housing preferences, we indicated that we were prepared to make a permanent move and that we wanted a home in the Hyde Park–Kenwood area. During the spring, my old friend and a longtime Chicago faculty member Dan Boorstin had informed us that Dean Alan Simpson was leaving the university to become president of Vassar College. Dan and his wife, Ruth, knew the Simpson house well and thought that it deserved our serious consideration. We went out to Chicago and visited with the Boorstins, toured the neighborhood of the university, and had a careful look at the Simpson house. An impressive Victorian built in 1893, it was in very good condition for a house of that vintage. It was also within walking distance of the university, on Blackstone Avenue, just around the corner from International House, home to an ambitious program begun in 1932 by John D. Rockefeller Jr. to promote cross-cultural understanding. When Whit claimed a room on the second floor as his own, there was nothing left to do except to decide that we liked it too! The house was in the hands of the university, and there was no question that we could have it if we wished, and at the most reasonable financial arrangements. Our only obligation, if we purchased it, was to make certain that the university had the first opportunity to reacquire it if and when we decided to sell. The entire transaction was pleasant and painless, in stark contrast with our Brooklyn experience.

Easily the most devastating and tragic experience of the fall of 1963 was the assassination of President John F. Kennedy, which occurred before our final transition to Chicago. Young people at Brooklyn College, as elsewhere, greatly admired the young, dynamic, and idealistic president, and regarded him as a leader whom they could trust. The news of his murder was brought to me when a student burst into the room in which I was holding my seminar and screamed, "What are we going to do?" I had no idea what she meant until, between sobs, she explained that the president was dead. That ended the formal class meeting, but the students remained with questions that were only variations on that of the student who had broken the news. The following days were characterized by planned and informal gatherings of students and members of the faculty, all of us attempting to make sense of something so senseless and irresponsible as the murder of this promising president.

The experience was made more poignant when I recalled that a White House aide was to call me the same afternoon Kennedy was shot to obtain a reply to the inquiry that I had received only the day before. The president had wished to know if I would accept his nominating me to be a member of the the U.S. delegation to the independence ceremonies in Zanzibar. When the first call came, I had hesitated. I had only recently returned from a year's absence in England and was all too soon leaving for Chicago. I asked the aide to re-call the following afternoon. The call, understandably, never came; it was at least ten days before an urgent request came from the White House asking me to accept the president's appointment and be prepared to leave the following day for Zanzibar, where independence ceremonies were just two days away. I accepted immediately, this clearly being a different overture from the government than the State Department's request years earlier that I go to Nigeria. Most obviously, I would be part of the official delegation, which had patently not been the case before. Second, I was happy to evidence my support for the outgoing Kennedy administration and encourage the new Johnson administration to continue the late president's commitment to using executive and federal authority to force intransigent segregationists to comply with the emerging body of civil rights law. It is fair to say that many African Americans mourned President Kennedy's murder as keenly as they had the four black children killed, just two months before the president, by a bomb that decimated the Sixteenth Street Baptist Church in Birmingham, Alabama, a known meeting place of civil rights leaders. I was not prepared, however, for how determined the new administration was to encourage me to forgo my scholarly career for a more direct involvement in world affairs.

On the flight to Zanzibar, Richard Fox, our escort from the Department of State, made it clear to me that he had been instructed by the department to use all his leisure moments to urge me to accept an embassy appointment from the new Johnson administration. I was flattered but also silently amused by the quiet but firm pressures applied to me to take a post in Europe. The proposal that I set aside research and teaching for some administrative post merely steeled my resolve to politely say no. By that time I knew that any service I would give to the United States, and I would do so often and with pleasure, would be brief stints such as the current one. Dick Fox soon realized that his was a futile task, and he eventually conveyed my refusal, as well as my personal good wishes, to the new president. It was a decision I never regretted. My ambition remained as I had described it to Dr. Shepard back in 1944, to be so dedicated a scholar and teacher that the entire profession, indeed the wider world, would take notice. And tangible evidence of my attaining that goal—twice now *The New York Times* had announced my new academic appointments—only further resolved me to continue in its pursuit. My decision made and accepted by Fox, I was free to focus exclusively on my role as a delegate and take notice of the many moving expressions of international sympathy the entire delegation received in recognition of our loss in the death of President Kennedy.

Beyond my commitments at the college and in the community, my work on the Board of Foreign Scholarships was becoming more demanding. Since, moreover, I had specific responsibilities for the Near East and South Asia, developments in India claimed my immediate attention. For some years, the branch of the Fulbright program in India had planned an American Studies Research Center in Hyderabad. By spring of 1964, the center was ready to open, and I was invited to deliver the inaugural address. I did so gladly, expressing the hope that the center would "create and perpetuate a community of cultural and educational friendship that will bind our two countries closer together." With scholars in attendance from various American universities as well as from Indian institutions of higher education, the inauguration of the center was an auspicious beginning of a new institution in a nation that only seventeen years earlier had become independent.

The spring of 1964 was a sad one. While I had many friends in New York City and at the college that made it difficult to leave, I continued to have reservations about the wider Brooklyn community and the college's near neighbors. Nothing like what had been accomplished in Chicago's Hyde Park, with the university often leading the way, had occurred in Brooklyn. I was particularly displeased with how Realtors took advantage of the college by advertising their homes as being especially attractive because they were "close to Brooklyn College," all the while actively avoiding any effort at integrating the neighborhood. In the student newspaper, *The Kingsman*, I pointed out it did not reflect well on the college when real estate agents took advantage of the location of their properties and then declined to offer them to any decent, honest, and reliable citizen, reserving them instead for persons who met the requirements of race, if no other. It was rather ironic that when we put our home up for sale, no African Americans showed any serious interest in purchasing it, and we sold it to a white couple who seemed as eager to move into the neighborhood as we had been several years earlier. I am certain that some of their new neighbors sighed with relief.

As a farewell gesture, Aurelia and I invited friends and colleagues to our home for an afternoon of food and drink. Those in attendance expressed their goodwill and affection as well as their unhappiness over our impending departure for the Midwest. Toward the end of the academic year, the college celebrated the twenty-fifth anniversary of Harry Gideonse's presidency with a luncheon. As the president responded to various expressions of esteem for all he had accomplished on behalf of the school, he asked me to come to the platform. I was dumbfounded and utterly unprepared. He thanked me for my years of service to the college and wished the Franklins well as we departed for Chicago. He then presented me with the Brooklyn College Medal of Honor, describing it as a rare recognition conferred only on persons who had made extraordinary contributions to the college. Happily, I was not required to make a response to this surprise honor, for it was one of the few instances when emotions robbed me of my senses.

During the previous year I had agreed with Aubrey Land, chairman of the Department of History at the University of Maryland, that I would teach there in the summer of 1964. I had many friends in the department and knew they were attempting to move the university's administration and student body forward in an effort to diversify all areas of the school. Despite the busy year and the impending move from Brooklyn to Chicago, I was determined to help. Our friends Sam and Marian Merrill had taken the initiative in trying to find housing for us, locating a home in Hyattsville owned by a professor of mathematics who would be spending the summer with his family in Berkeley. When Mrs. Virginia Reinhart, writing on behalf of her husband who was busy grading papers, described her house and neighborhood, she admitted frankly that all of her neighbors were white and "I am afraid that some of the southerners would ignore you, but most are very agreeable people." I did not reply that our experience in New York had prepared us for such possibilities. We agreed to rent their home.

There was a rumor that some of the neighbors so resented our temporary presence that they meant to demonstrate against us. When we arrived, members of the History Department were more apprehensive than we were, and they took turns the first day "standing watch" to make certain that we were not molested. And while Whit went ignored by the neighborhood children, presumably on the advice of their parents, the nearby city of Washington provided us with an abundance of old friends and diversions, such that he could not possibly have been affected by the snub of the local yokels.

On the whole, the Maryland experience was rewarding and worthwhile. Years later, during the period of student protests and uprisings over civil rights and the Vietnam War, I was invited back to receive an honorary degree. Many University of Maryland students urged me to reject the invitation. When I nevertheless accepted and appeared for the commencement, some of the students asked me why. Instead of coming there to be honored, they charged that I should instead be on their side. I told them that I had been on "that side" far longer than they and proceeded to describe my summer visit back in 1964, which briefly desegregated the faculty. They had never heard of my prior visit and were dumbfounded to learn that at an early date the university and faculty, however tentatively, had taken steps to promote integration.

Before we left Brooklyn, we had to face the question of making a final decision about a school for Whit in Chicago. Aurelia and I both believed in public schools as essentially democratic institutions as well as centers for the education and the socialization of the child; it would be difficult to abandon our support of them under any circumstances. At the same time, we recognized that our principles should not obstruct our providing Whit with the very best education available. There was no question that the Laboratory School of the University of Chicago would be difficult to surpass in any community. Consequently, we decided to enroll him there. At age twelve, he would be in what the Lab School called the prefreshman class, designed to rush students through early adolescence as quickly as possible and move them on into high school. To our surprise, this proved to be a wise maneuver. It also meant that Whit would complete his high school courses at the advanced age of sixteen! He made the adjustment well, loved being with students who were almost exactly his age, and the wisdom of our decision was soon apparent to all of us.

There was one other thing I was obliged to do immediately after moving to Chicago, and that was to go to Paris to participate in the first *Daedalus* Conference on Race sponsored by the American Academy of Arts and Sciences. Stephen R. Graubard was the editor of *Daedalus*, which would publish the papers presented in Paris, and the conference facilitator. Although the gathering was small, the participants came from many parts of the world, including Japan, Britain, Denmark, Holland, Brazil, South Africa, and the United States. We learned a great deal from each other, and for me there were three significant revelations: First, the Japanese made clear distinctions among themselves based on skin color; second, on the subcontinent, north Indians had a "vague prejudice" against south Indians because of their dark skin color; and third, in Brazil the lighter the skin, the better one's chances for rising on the social and economic ladder. Among the participants I met and with whom I became friendly in later years were Kenneth Little, Florestan Fernandes, Stephen Graubard, and Talcott Parsons. I readily agreed when Graubard asked me to serve as editor and to write an introduction for the volume that appeared as the spring 1967 issue of *Daedalus* and published in a hardcover volume, *Color and Race*, in 1968.

After we had settled finally in Chicago, my new colleagues proved as congenial and cooperative in real life as they had been in their letters and on the telephone. It also quickly became clear that I was going to enjoy the best teaching program that I had yet encountered. I couldn't have been more pleased; for my tastes, this was far better than any ambassador's post. On the quarter system, I taught two courses in the fall and two in the winter; in the spring I was in residence but only supervising reading and research, which meant that I need not remain in the city. In the summer I was out of residence. I was free, moreover, to shift around my teaching commitments as long as it did not create a hardship for the students or my colleagues. If a professor in the department was not in the college, it meant that he or she was not obliged to teach undergraduate courses. Consequently, if I chose not to teach in the college, I could confine myself exclusively to graduate courses.

Doing so, however, held limited appeal. As one who had always taught undergraduates and who believed that they were entitled to benefit from the experience and knowledge that senior professors possessed, I opted to teach a section of the undergraduate survey of American civilization, regularly teaching the portion dealing with the antebellum period through Reconstruction. Although this section usually had an enrollment of fifty to sixty undergraduates, we were not expected to use teaching assistants to grade papers or perform other chores. One year, when I was busy to the point of being overcommitted, I asked my research assistant to grade the midterm papers in my undergraduate course. He did a first-rate job, but the word spread that I did not grade my undergraduates' work. An advisory bulletin circulated by students the following year reported that although my lectures were satisfactory to the point of being not only learned but inspiring, Professor Franklin "does not grade his own papers." I announced quickly to the current class that it was most unusual for me to call on my research assistant to grade my papers and promised that it would not happen again. This was an example of Chicago's undergraduates demanding the best that the university had to offer, and I could only respect them for it.

Unfortunately, it was an arrangement that offered very limited opportunities for graduate students to experience lecturing to undergraduates or grading their papers. The result meant that Chicago's graduate students were at a disadvantage in the job market when competing with students from universities that had required them to teach sections of undergraduate courses. Most of our graduate students took pride in not having to be teaching assistants. At the same time, they had no teaching experience whatsoever upon receiving their doctorates, unless they had taken time out and taught in a college or secondary school. No less dedicated to graduate training than I was to undergraduate teaching, I decided to remedy this to the extent that I could. I devised a plan, with the approval of the dean of the college, to utilize the services of two or three of my own graduate students in my undergraduate course in American civilization.

At the beginning of term we planned the syllabus together. They attended all of my lectures, and I required each of them to prepare and deliver one lecture. I was present and took notes, along with the students. After the lecture, the other graduate students, who were also present, joined in discussing the lecture in detail. At midterm they prepared examination questions, and before giving them we discussed those as well. At times we decided that some of their questions were better than mine. After the students took the examination, each of the graduate students, along with me, graded all of the papers, compared the results, and then decided on each grade. We did the same thing for the final examination. Each graduate student was grateful for having had the opportunity to gain some teaching experience, and the dean was grateful for this innovative experiment.

Meanwhile, I was undertaking to provide a research experience that was rare among graduate students anywhere. During my first year at Chicago, Charles Lee, director of the archives at the University of South Carolina, chided those of us who were teaching the Reconstruction period at Northern universities for doing so with few if any primary sources.

Why would we not visit the archival sources in Southern states where, as in South Carolina, there were walls of manuscripts waiting for someone to show sufficient interest in them? He then laid down an open challenge to me and others: Come south and work in the region's archives.

I recalled Charles Lee's challenge as I planned the seminar for my third year at Chicago. Since I was already well acquainted with the archives in North Carolina, I decided to plan a trip for my seminar students to that state's Department of Archives and History. Before the term began I announced to interested students that during the first quarter we would be studying Reconstruction in North Carolina very intensively, using secondary sources and, where possible, primary sources that we could discover in the Chicago area. Additionally, the beginning of the second quarter we would visit North Carolina for two weeks. The dean even indicated that if any student found the trip to be beyond his or her budget, the university would provide the necessary funds. Since members of the seminar would have already decided on their research subjects well before the end of the first quarter, they would be able to begin serious archival work immediately, especially since I had notified the staff in Raleigh what each student's topic would be and sent the research topics to the curators of manuscripts at Duke University and the University of North Carolina. I had arranged with St. Augustine to house my two female students, while the five men would be at North Carolina State University.

At the beginning of our first working day, we spent the morning consulting with the staff of the North Carolina Department of Archives and History. I had known the director, Christopher C. Crittenden, since 1939, when I first visited the archives as a graduate student working on my dissertation. H. G. Jones, the archivist, proved equally supportive of our visit. Members of the staff discussed with each student the archive's relevant holdings. This was the first of several such seminars with the staff, and given the central importance of original research to the historical profession, these were among the most valuable experiences that the participating students had. Our friends at Chapel Hill and Durham offered similar cooperation, for which we were grateful. As a class, we usually had lunch and dinner together and also met several evenings each week. These regular meetings gave us an opportunity to exchange materials, discuss problems that arose, and suggest to each other possible ways of approaching the next stage of research.

Soon, the students knew intimately what was involved in getting to the heart of a scholarly problem, and quite early on I began to detect an air of confidence and a feeling of self-satisfaction among them. One student, working on "The Reception of the Fourteenth Amendment in North Carolina," began to talk quite confidently about the inadequacy of Joseph G. de Roulhac Hamilton's treatment of the subject, published in 1914. Another student, concerned with agricultural recovery in postwar North Carolina, complained that no historian—with the exception of him, of course—had given adequate attention to developments in the Piedmont. On the second day of our visit, I asked one student how he was doing. He replied that after reviewing the auspicious beginnings of the career of Jim Crow in the jails and cemeteries of Raleigh in 1866, he could assert with confidence, "I'm doing fine, but Professor C. Vann Woodward isn't doing very well." Vann's widely acclaimed book on Jim Crow argued that racial segregation began two decades later, an argument my student meant to, and eventually did, challenge.

The self-confidence and self-esteem of these emerging authorities on North Carolina history were bolstered considerably by the local attention they received. On the third day of our visit, the *Raleigh Times* devoted a half page with pictures to an article titled, "Chicago Students Sift North Carolina Historical Documents." Before the end of the week, the piece had appeared in more than a score of the state's afternoon daily papers. Other articles followed, and one of my unanticipated duties was to protect the students from reporters who wanted to write feature stories on them. Then there was the luncheon with Lieutenant Governor (and soon to be governor) Robert Scott. A measure of the effect of this heady, two-week-long experience was seen when one student was overheard saying, "Did you hear what I told Bob Scott about his state's educational needs!?"

As the students busied themselves with their own research, I remained busy performing my duties as impresario and "fixer." I was called on to make speeches at Shaw University and St. Augustine's College. I addressed the members of the archives staff on "What the Teaching Historian Looks for in a State Historical Agency." I also talked with local citizens' groups that were impressed with the newspaper coverage of our research adventure. In one case I was able to persuade a local resident that she should deposit her family papers, containing material on Reconstruction, in the state archives. I even talked about my own research before a group of graduate students from neighboring institutions at a dinner graciously hosted by Jones and Crittenden.

The opportunity afforded these seven students to go "beyond the water's edge," undertaking original research in a fashion reminiscent of my own tracking down of Edward Bellamy's widow and unpublished papers, formed the basis for the meaningful and even important essays they subsequently wrote. The members of the seminar were becoming true professionals, and they knew it. If there was any doubt, one had merely to witness their conduct upon their return to the University of Chicago. An African safari could hardly have been more proudly recounted, and archival finds were displayed with all the bluster of big-game trophies. And if the privileged seven were a bit difficult to live with, the many who had chosen to remain behind were infinitely more sober and even more teachable.

It would have been very rewarding if I could have repeated the undertaking each year, but my responsibilities at the university and elsewhere in subsequent years made it increasingly impossible.

18

The Uses of History

SHORTLY AFTER the appearance of *From Slavery to Freedom* in 1947, I began receiving invitations to write general summaries of the history and culture of African Americans. I accepted many, ranging from articles that appeared in scholarly anthologies and very popular encyclopedias to an eighth-grade American history text. I agreed to these and other assignments in the strongly held belief that historical ignorance abets racial ignorance, and an inescapable responsibility of the scholar is to advance publicly what has been learned in the private confines of research and scholarship. Throughout my life that responsibility never abated, though during the 1960s the passions and sense of possibility that so marked the decade imbued my efforts with particular enthusiasm. They did not, however, go unchallenged.

Fortunately, when I was still at Howard University, I had two experiences that prepared me for what was to come. Early in 1950, Richard Leopold and Arthur Link, both at Northwestern University, decided that it was important not only for students but for the lay public to have a book that raised all or most of the important questions Americans needed to confront when attempting to understand their own history. I had known Leopold since my Harvard days, when he served on my PhD final examination committee, and Arthur since my first teaching jobs in North Carolina. These longtime acquaintances had become my steadfast friends by the time I wrote *From Slavery to Freedom*, and the three of us had regular conversations about how best to project American history to our students. It was out of these discussions that they decided to edit a volume that came to be called *Problems in American History*.

Their approach would be similar to Arthur M. Schlesinger's single-authored *New Viewpoints in American History*, except that they would compile the knowledge and insights of twenty historians, each an authority in a given field. Thus, Merrill Jensen wrote on the Articles of Confederation and the Constitution of 1787, while Charles Sellers wrote on Jacksonian democracy. Kenneth Stampp wrote on the causes of the Civil War, and I wrote on Reconstruction. It was a great honor to be singled out as an authority on that dark period in American history, and with the hope of changing hearts and minds I gave it all that I had.

We used sources to illustrate and illuminate the points that we were making. Thus, at the end of my chapter, I presented the traditional interpretation of the period by James Ford Rhodes and the revisionist evaluation by W.E.B. Du Bois. The published volume was enthusiastically received, and four years later we prepared a second edition in which there were some new authors and some new interpretations. My piece remained essentially unchanged. Not only was I pleased with my contribution to *Problems in American History*, but the book's wide use rendered that effort among my most significant. I was, and remain, as proud of it as anything that I have ever written.

In June 1955, Walter Yust, an editor with *Encyclopaedia Britannica*, offered me an opportunity to speak to an even wider public. He informed me that for the next printing of that work they were planning to revise and reorganize the article on "Negro, The American." He wondered if I would accept the assignment, to run to ten thousand words, and indicated that I could collaborate with a colleague if I cared to. I accepted, knowing that the only information many people had on the Negro was through that encyclopedia. In my acceptance I indicated that I would very much like to have Rayford W. Logan, my colleague at Howard, as my coauthor. Logan, who was widely traveled and well acquainted with Europe and Africa, could provide information and perspective that I lacked. That stipulation was satisfactory with Yust, so Rayford and I proceeded to work on the article whose deadline was January 15, 1956. We divided up the subject as if it were a lengthy and long-range project. I would deal with most topics through Reconstruction, while he would deal with more recent matters. He would also focus on economic developments in general, while I would handle demographic changes and military history.

We completed the assignment and had it in the hands of the editors at *Encyclopedia Britannica* fully two weeks before the deadline. They commended us for the article and said that they were "proud indeed to be able to bring an article of this calibre to Britannica readers." It covered approximately nine pages, including an impressive bibliography for a piece of that length. No doubt galvanizing our effort was the pride Rayford and I felt on becoming the source of information for such a large readership.

For decades, of course, African Americans have attempted to provide the reading public with information about "the race" and its problems. This was particularly true when their opponents tried to denigrate them and claim that they had made no significant contributions to the growth and prosperity of the United States. Thus, in 1896, in the midst of Jim Crow justice and escalating lynch violence, a group of African Americans, imbued with race pride, published the *Afro-American Encyclopaedia: Thoughts, Sayings, and Doings of the Race*. Before the close of the century, J. W. Gibson and W. H. Crogman published their *The Remarkable Advancement of the Afro-American: Progress of a Race*. In the early twentieth century, African American authors were still attempting to demonstrate through their writings—sometimes polemical but always in earnest—that African Americans were as loyal, patriotic, and committed to the improvement of American society as anyone else. At Tuskegee Institute, Monroe N. Work, under the patronage of Booker T. Washington, began to issue in 1913 *The Negro Year Book*, summarizing, as he put it, "all the information available in regard to existing conditions." He brought it out for nine years and then began to devote most of his time and resources to his highly regarded *Bibliography of the Negro in Africa and America*, which was published in 1928.

In 1964 John P. Davis, who had become prominent as executive director of the National Negro Congress, began to feel that an effort to educate all Americans about African Americans would, in the long run, accomplish more than his congress, the Joint Committee on National Recovery, or the Southern Negro Youth Congress. In his position as editor of special publications for the Phelps-Stokes Fund, he used his resources and talents to "bring together in a single volume a reliable summary on the main aspects of Negro life in America, and to present [it] . . . in sufficient historical depth to provide the reader with a true perspective." *The American Negro Reference Book* was the result, covering virtually every aspect of African American life, present and past. It included Horace Mann Bond on "The Negro Scholar and Professional in America," Arna Bontemps on "The Negro Contribution to American Letters," Gordon Allport on "Prejudice and the Individual," and James Q. Wilson on "The Negro in American Politics: The Present." With subjects as disparate as jazz and agriculture and industrial employment covered by leading authorities, it can be said that Davis succeeded in bringing together a reliable summary of most of Negro life in America. I was privileged to write "A Brief History of the Negro in the United States," the opening piece.

Every generation of parents wishes to rewrite and reinterpret the nation's history so that their children will be able to understand it better and thus enhance their sense of informed citizenship. This was true in the 1950s, during the Korean War, and especially so in the 1960s during the Vietnam War. Parents sincerely believed that if their children had better textbooks and better teachers, especially in their civics and history courses, they would grow up to be better, more loyal citizens.

I could not quarrel with this general proposition, and that is why I found it exciting, even exhilarating, to visit high schools and middle schools and talk to students and their teachers. Each year I made it a point to accept at least a few invitations to speak to classes below the collegiate level. I found it a challenge not only to communicate with teenagers and preteenagers but also to familiarize myself with the study materials they presumably would use as the basis for the decisions they made about their society and themselves.

Over the course of several decades, I grew ever more familiar with the efforts of parents to influence the choice and use of textbooks in public schools. And while many parents felt that they were not capable of making judgments concerning, say, physics or chemistry, they readily reached quite firm judgments about history and civics texts. In some communities, parents, through the traditional organizations connected with their schools or through watchdog committees, scrutinized the civics and history textbooks to make certain that they contained no subversive materials, advocated patriotism, and reflected these parents' values, pure and simple. In time, a growing number of parents began to analyze civics and history textbooks to make certain that they did not advocate national, religious, or racial bigotry. In some communities, a veritable tug-of-war broke out between groups that advocated a more celebratory, which to them meant patriotic, past, and those that sought a more critical approach, encouraging a diversity of opinion and values in the belief that this would teach tolerance.

During the Vietnam War, which coincided with the onset of the civil rights revolution, groups on both sides of the ideological fence began to advocate changes in textbooks. In the midst of this debate, the California State Board of Education announced that the available textbooks did not adequately portray the role of minority groups in the nation's history. It soon issued a comprehensive set of guidelines for the treatment of ethnic and cultural minorities to be met by all texts submitted for state adoption. They were to be free of bias and prejudice and must accurately portray the participation of minority groups in American life.

In California, the history of the United States was taught in grades 5, 8, 11, and 12, and the state textbook commission adopted textbooks for each of those grades. In 1966, there was a call for a new textbook, which would adhere to the new guidelines, for grade 8. John and LaRee Caughey, long active in the effort to solve racial and community problems in Southern California, saw a unique opportunity to get a more inclusive understanding of American history taught throughout the state. John, a professor of history at the University of California at Los Angeles, asked me and Ernest May, his son-in-law and a professor at Harvard, to join him in writing an entirely new textbook for the eighth grade to be submitted to the California Textbook Commission. In the months that followed, the three of us exchanged views about the feasibility of such an undertaking, whether we could meet the deadline, and how much the public could take of what we had to offer. Despite the fact that we were all quite busy at our respective universities and with our numerous other commitments, we agreed the stakes were worth the risks and effort.

We had several advantages over our potential competitors. One was that we had LaRee who, although not a coauthor, was able to provide her enormous experience with not only California's history but also its citizens. Their approval, of course, would present the real challenge. Another was that we did not have a book to revise, and writing a book to meet the state's guidelines was infinitely easier than revising one. Meanwhile, we had fresh ideas and approaches for our book, which we would name *Land of the Free*.

We divided up the work, with Caughey taking the first third of the history of the United States, I the middle part, and May the final third. All chapters rotated among us, and each of us felt free to revise the other's work in any manner that we could defend. In the summer of 1965, Aurelia, Whit, and I went to California and lived with the Caugheys for several weeks. Ernest and Nancy May were also present, and working together we "broke the back" of our task. Well before the end of the academic year we had exchanged chapters, offered criticisms and suggestions to each other, and readied the manuscript for the publishers.

In California we placed it in the hands of Franklin Publications, which had experience in working with the State Board of Education and the Textbook Commission. Despite some early opposition from the state superintendent of education, Max Rafferty, and other highly placed persons, the Textbook Commission indicated that our book would be adopted if we made the revisions and corrections that a panel of experts recommended. We were not only willing but eager to consider and respond to the observations and criticisms of the state's experts and we felt confident that we could satisfy the panel. As professional historians, we were accustomed to submitting our manuscripts to publishers who would then send them out to peer readers. In this case, the panel, composed of Allan Nevins of the Huntington Library; Glenn Dumke, chancellor of the California State College System; and Charles Sellers, professor of history at the University of California, Berkeley, read our manuscript and issued a report that was searching and critical, but fair, containing numerous suggestions for improvement. We accepted the suggestions to the extent that we could, and after revising the manuscript, resubmitted it.

On December 9, 1966, the board reconfirmed the state's adoption of *Land of the Free*, and on January 20, 1967, the Curriculum Commission formally acknowledged that all revisions had been made, thus clearing the way for the book to be printed. Copies were placed in every public library in the state, where interested parents and citizens could read it and reach their own conclusions regarding its suitability for school use. It was a handsome book, copiously illustrated, with line drawings, paintings, primitive artwork, photographs, insets, poems, maps, charts, cartoons, patriotic symbols, study questions, lists of books for further study, and a usable index.

The book quickly became the target of virtually every right-wing group in the state. On May 13, a conservative professor at the University of Southern California called our book "slanted in the direction of the United Nations . . . militant groups, and unfriendly to the great majority." State Superintendent Max Rafferty declared that *Land of the Free* would require a "major salvage effort" before it would be fit for consumption in California's classrooms. On July 25, he issued a 218-page reproduction of letters his office had received questioning the book's adoption. In language remarkably similar, letter to letter, people objected to the book's favorable discussion of the United Nations and what they called derogatory statements about famous Americans, inadequate treatment of the nation's wars, and the favorable treatment of so-called radicals such as W.E.B. Du Bois.

In the spring of 1966, a twenty-four page pamphlet issued by a Pasadena-based group calling itself the *Land of the Free* Committee said the book "destroys pride in America's past, develops a guilt complex, mocks American justice, indoctrinates toward communism, is hostile to religious concepts, overemphasizes Negro participation in American history, projects negative thought models, criticizes business and free enterprise, plays politics, foments class hatred, slants and distorts facts, [and] promotes propaganda and poppycock." As though that were insufficient, the group also issued a filmstrip to be used in community and school board meetings.

The film *Education or Indoctrination?* was designed to frighten its viewers into action by implying that the book was a part of a Communist conspiracy to control the minds of American children. It carefully introduced each author in a fashion to ensure generating the maximum apprehension on the part of viewers. Thus, when I was introduced, a full picture of me filled the screen, my skin color alone being cause for serious concern if not alarm. That was followed immediately by a solemn reading of excerpts from the Communist Manifesto. The viewer was left to make his or her own connection. Other activities of the *Land of the Free* Committee included sending a motor caravan from Southern California to Sacramento to protest the book's use. It also placed women on picket lines at the entrances of state buildings in Los Angeles as well as Sacramento. Thus, they kept alive the movement to secure a reconsideration of the Textbook Commission's decision to adopt the book for statewide use. There can be no doubt that such tactics were somewhat effective. Many parents were persuaded of the book's supposedly evil intentions despite never having read it. I received numerous letters protesting our approach, interpretation, and conclusions.

Land of the Free had its own supporters, many of whom were quite enthusiastic. In *The Grade Teacher* for February 1967, the reviewer declared that "Patriotism takes precedence in this formidable (would you believe 658 pages?) history text, which in reality is rather interesting and lively. The text approaches past and present history in the United States from a prideful point of view and emphasizes preservation of our democratic way of life." Another reviewer called it "a solid, interesting and most worthwhile textbook which is a welcome addition to the junior high school field in Social Studies." A Mexican American member of the Los Angeles Board of Education said that "its honesty is outstanding, in that it tries to depict American history in an adult manner while couching what it says in language and concepts that a secondary student can understand."

In other parts of the country, teachers and school officials watched the showdown with interest. There was little hope that we could secure statewide adoptions in states where a conservative panel-review policy existed, such as in Texas. There was, however, the hope that Benziger, the company handling the book's national market, would be able to secure many local adoptions and have the book placed on the approved list of social studies materials for use in classrooms. In 1967, for example, the Philadelphia School Board approved the book for use in the eighth grade and bought five thousand copies for that purpose. It was used extensively in the Baltimore public schools, though it was never adopted citywide. And while many school boards approved it for use, it seldom received such enthusiastic endorsement that it became the book of choice for the eighth grade.

Meanwhile, the fight against the book continued in California, and the news of the opposition there impressed others who regarded the California experience as cautionary if not authoritative. One man in Southern California risked legal action by refusing to permit his daughter to be in the same room with *Land of the Free*. The town of Downey, California, refused to use the book even when threatened with action by the State Board of Education. As such stories spread, fewer and fewer public officials in other states were willing to run the risk of such negative exposure.

In 1968, *Land of the Free* gained a measure of notoriety when it not only landed on a list of 334 books cited in a survey of books that should be banned but was reported as such by *Time* magazine in its August 9 issue. This constant attack reduced any serious contention for a renewal of its adoption in California in 1971. Although we submitted a 1971 edition for consideration, it was ignored, and on April 30, 1979, John Caughey sent me what he feared would be my final royalty check. Accompanying it was a short note, in which he said, "We are grateful how you and the handful of participants pitched in to make [*Land of the Free*] such a glowing artifact. LaRee and I are sobered by the thought that through it we reached more readers than through all the rest of our writings. And there are other ways in which we can tote up what it has meant to us." I felt the same way, and I am certain that Ernest did too.

Textbooks are not the only means of communicating the past to a wide audience. Yet another way is through a pictorial history. This was true in the late nineteenth century when African Americans were desperate to defend themselves from the "calumnies and vilifications poured on our race by others" as one writer then put it. Despite limitations of the photographic industry, Thomas O. Fuller produced a work in 1933 that could honorably bear the title *Pictorial History of the American Negro*. I was in my second undergraduate year at Fisk when the volume appeared, and I believe that it was the subtitle that most impressed me: *A Story of Progress and Development Along Social, Political, Economic, Educational, and Spiritual Lines*.

Some thirty years later, Langston Hughes and Milton Meltzer brought out their *Pictorial History of the Negro in America*. Chronological in its structure, the work's principal objective was to give the reader a sense of the sweep of history, where African Americans came from, how they contributed, and how they have influenced and, in turn, have been influenced by their experience in the United States. Finally, the book aimed to show where their history was headed. The final edition boasted more than twelve hundred illustrations and reached a readership that suggested to other publishers that the genre was lucrative, indeed.

I do not know precisely when Time-Life Books became interested in publishing some kind of pictorial history of African Americans, but in 1968 editors there asked me to consider serving as the principal author of what they proposed to call *An Illustrated History of Black Americans*. They proposed a straightforward work of the finest photographs they could bring together with a first-rate historical commentary, for which I would be responsible. Time-Life Books had produced magnificent works with which I was familiar: *Life Library of Art*, *Great Ages of Man*, and *Life Library of Photography*. My interest was more than raised.

I was swayed in part by the tremendous influence that Time-Life Books, I hoped, could wield in persuading readers to buy *An Illustrated History of Black Americans*. I envisioned large advertisements as well as feature pieces in *Time* and *Life*. Such thoughts led to another hope: Was it possible that, at long last, Aurelia and I would have no more financial worries?

Having begun to think big, I was more than a little disappointed when the editors proposed to pay me a fee for my services in lieu of a royalty arrangement. With visions of long, long lines of buyers eagerly awaiting their turn to purchase a book for which I had been paid a pittance, I rejected the offer. I was adamant that I receive some royalty. Admitting that he had never dealt with such a stubborn author, my editor eventually relented. Having finally reached an amicable agreement, I began to work on the volume.

An Illustrated History of Black Americans was a significant departure from the pictorial histories that had preceded it. While the others were preoccupied with emphasizing achievements, our book was more concerned with the continuing struggle against racism and for civil rights. We did not emphasize personalities; instead, we emphasized the problems that African Americans had faced and how they had attempted to solve them. To be sure, from the antebellum years, there were likenesses of Harriet Tubman and Frederick Douglass, but there were many more of plantation workers and victims of brutality at the hands of slaveholders and overseers. Indeed, I made a point of including far more such pictures than one found in general history textbooks. In the chapters dealing with the post–Civil War years, there were images of leaders such as Booker T. Washington, W.E.B. Du Bois, Martin Luther King Jr., A. Philip Randolph, and Thurgood Marshall, but there were many more dealing with soldiers at war, workers in factories, protesters seeking justice, and men and women on relief. I grant that I amused myself by speculating how enraged the California opponents of *Land of the Free* would be if they ever scanned or even heard about the contents of this volume.

An Illustrated History of Black Americans did not have the spectacular bookstore and mail-order sales of which I had dreamed. Instead, it had a modest sale in the first few months, after which the demand for it declined sharply. Time-Life Books did little to promote it, about which I complained bitterly, and as a consequence they engaged an agency to help promote the book. When I learned that the agency was a black organization, I reminded the staff at Time-Life Books that they should be as interested in having the book find its way to such places as Westchester County as they were in getting it into Harlem. I continued to believe that Time-Life Books simply did not know how to market the book or had no interest in doing so. As long as its existence stated to the public that they were on the right side of "the struggle," they were content.

A very pleasant commitment that I made in 1969 was to deliver the commencement address at Whit's University High School. The years when these students were in middle school and high school were among the most turbulent and crucial of the twentieth century. The civil rights revolution was at high tide, Martin Luther King Jr. had been assassinated, the Democratic National Convention, held there in Chicago, had demonstrated the frailty of consensus and political tranquility. In many ways these were critical times, and all of the books with which I became involved during those years sought to convey some notion of the historical roots of those times, pride in the long struggle for justice, and hope for the future. In that talk I tried to distill some of the thoughts that I wished I could share with all high school students who were attempting to find their place in their world. I had every reason to give it my best effort, since Whit was in that class and would soon leave us for college.

Quite understandably, I had him in mind when I was writing down what I would say to his graduating class. On June 16, I delivered my talk, titled "Building Tomorrow's World." I reminded Whit and his classmates that their generation would take up where the previous generation had left off and that they would benefit from the successes and failures of their predecessors. "Each one of you," I told them, "will build your life—and this was true of your parents—on a foundation that was laid by those who have gone before you." I tried to make the point that in our world, we needed to cooperate without bending to the will of dictators or the smooth talk of hucksters, and that called for independence of thought and action. Remembering what Caughey, May, and I had tried to get across in *Land of the Free* and my other writings, I said, "As you go about your own work of study or play, remember that talents and gifts are widely distributed. Some of the rarest talents I have ever seen were possessed by peoples in India, Nigeria, and Hong Kong. Even if your talents and gifts seem quite ample, remember that there are others even among you who also possess them. Perhaps the wisest thing is to recognize that fact and seek cooperation with others . . . and if that fails proceed to do the best you can on your own."

I concluded by offering a challenge: "It may be trite, but it is also true to say that the world is virtually yours . . . What you will do with this precious commodity will depend on how you learn to care for your world *now*. It will need the care and attention that only truly educated men and women can provide. That care and attention represent the distillation of what you will learn. That learning then becomes not only knowledge but compassion, sensitivity, understanding and tolerance that will, in turn, make your responsibilities a great joy and your basic humanity the great good fortune of us all." The tumultuous years during which they had gone to Chicago's Lab School had amply demonstrated the extent of the responsibilities we all faced to achieve that end, and while without question much had been achieved, it had been at a cost, and even the victories appeared tenuous.

19

Students' Rights—Civil Rights

EVEN BEFORE WE MOVED to Chicago, students in colleges and professional schools were expressing their desire for greater involvement in the governance of their institutions and greater freedom in their personal lives. The desegregation of public schools in the 1950s and the legal assault on segregated higher education had encouraged all students to press for more "rights." Change was afoot and occurring at a seemingly fantastic pace. When we returned from England in 1963, it seemed that over the ten months we had been gone, the old order had changed. The year we moved to Chicago, 1964, was also the year the Civil Rights Bill had become law, and that changed forever, it seemed, most social relationships in this country. Without question, the Civil Rights Act was a landmark in the history of American race relations. It outlawed discrimination in employment, barred it in public accommodations, and forced the desegregation of public facilities and many public schools. But its passage and nationwide compliance were two separate considerations; absent federal enforcement, the act could prove as empty a promise as those made in the past, and it left untouched the numerous obstacles to black voting rights. Those facts left many of us even more determined to see to it that equality was not just the law but also meaningfully applied.

The ferment seemed to be almost everywhere, but nowhere more so than among young people. The summer of 1964 became known as Freedom Summer, during which thousands of predominantly younger volunteers conducted voter-registration drives in the South, an effort that famously costs the lives of three of them who were murdered by the Ku Klux Klan in Philadelphia, Mississippi, with local police complicity. That was only the most publicized act of vehement racist resistance on the part of Southern segregationists. By that summer's end, fifteen civil rights workers were dead and only twelve hundred black voters had been registered.

Throughout that fateful year, I was invited to many college and university campuses, and everywhere the students wanted to hear about the coming black revolution. When I did not speak on the civil rights revolution and its historical setting, the questions from the audience made it clear that I should have. Students themselves had assumed an active role in trying to transform the United States. What began in Greensboro, when students at historically black Agricultural and Technical College sat at a downtown lunch counter demanding to be served, was a wake-up call for young people everywhere, but particularly African Americans, to challenge long-held practices and laws that had relegated blacks to places of inferiority in virtually every aspect of life in America. They sat in white libraries, swam at white beaches, and challenged the old practices of segregation wherever they found them.

In response to the murder by police of Jimmie Lee Jackson, who was marching for civil rights, in February 1965, Martin Luther King Jr. and other civil rights leaders called for a march from Selma, Alabama, to the state capital in Montgomery. While crossing Pettus Bridge on March 7, just as they exited Selma, the marchers, their heads bowed in prayer, were viciously attacked by mounted state troopers armed with clubs and tear gas, all of which was aired on national television that evening. Public outrage followed. The televised image of law officers furiously beating bleeding African American marchers created an uproar: Demands for federal action flooded the White House, which was soon the site of a seven-hour sit-in by fourteen students, as Selma sympathy marches occurred across the country. King began difficult negotiations with the Johnson administration to stage an even larger march from Selma.

It was at this point that my colleague and the former chairman of our department at Chicago, Walter Johnson, suggested that historians should participate. Within a few days he and others had issued calls for historians to join the march, which some three thousand activists would start on March 21, to be joined by tens of thousands of supporters four days later outside Montgomery's city limits. Historians of the United States were the focus of his invitations, but others were welcome. Several of us from Chicago went, including Walter Johnson, Roger Shugg, Mark Haller, and myself. Other historians who came were C. Vann Woodward from Yale; Arthur Mann, of Smith College, who would join our department the following year; Bernard Weisberger, who had left Chicago for Rochester; John Caughey, John Higham, and Roger Daniels, who all traveled from UCLA; Samuel P. Hays, Pittsburgh; Rembert Patrick, Richard Hofstadter, and William Leuchtenburg, Columbia; Roger Hollingsworth, Wisconsin; Bradford Perkins, Michigan; Bennett Wall, Tulane; and forty or more other historians. The Chicago contingent flew down to Atlanta the day before the march. We were met by representatives of the Southern Christian Leadership Conference and were received in what I later came to know as the Delta Crown Room. We gave some interviews there, during which Woodward told a reporter that America was, in a sense, going through the final undoing of the work of the 1890s, when segregation was institutionalized as a legal system.

Those of us who gathered in Atlanta were taken in an SCLC bus to Tuskegee, where we were received by Luther Foster, president of Tuskegee Institute. It was en route to Tuskegee that the bus made a lurch around the corner and almost left the road. At that point, Richard Hofstadter stood and pleaded with the bus driver to be more careful: "If your driving leads to an accident that kills us all, you will set back the liberal interpretation of American history for a century!" At Tuskegee we were shown to our rooms, after which President Foster and his colleagues provided us with an excellent meal and wished us well in the following day's march. Following dinner, we were taken into Montgomery, where a premarch "rally" was already under way. There were speeches by Dr. King and other civil rights leaders, and music by well-known artists. Eventually, we returned to Tuskegee, where Arthur Mann, my roommate, and I talked far into the night.

The following morning of March 25 we were up early, had a very good breakfast at Tuskegee, and were off for the historic march from the out-skirts of the city, at St. Jude, to the capitol in downtown Montgomery. We had no banner indicating that we were historians, and our modesty precluded our proclaiming who we were. Nevertheless, as we were lining up, someone produced the side of a corrugated box on which was painted in crude lettering, "U.S. Historians." When by virtue of that impromptu sign someone recognized us as being historians, the order came down that since this was a historic event, we should be given a prominent place so that we could bear witness to the events about which historians would someday write. Thereupon we were ushered to a place in the line of march not too far from the leaders. Even from that vantage point, we were unable to see, except in the newspapers the following day, Dr. and Mrs. King, Reverend and Mrs. Abernathy, Ralph Bunche, and others walking on the front line.

The march down the narrow streets into the city was deeply discomforting. Locals were peering from narrow windows and partially closed curtains and blinds, and one could not be certain what they might do. Images of Bloody Sunday, as the March 7 carnage on Pettus Bridge became known, were uppermost in all of our minds. Our numbers, which were in the tens of thousands, the intense national scrutiny by then focused on the unfolding events, even President Johnson's explicit expression of support for the marchers could not erase from our thoughts the knowledge that for years such principled demonstrations had been met with terror, murder, and obstructed justice.

When we safely reached the capitol grounds, where the speeches were to be made, some historians, such as Vann Woodward and Rembert Patrick, who had not marched into the city, joined us. Within minutes, various white and black youths also joined the crowd, some of them back from their voting registration drives in various parts of the South. They looked weary, but in my eyes they were among the great heroes in the crusade to bring equality and democracy to the South. Between songs and cheering the crowd was prepared to hear such speakers as Martin Luther King Jr., who said that "no tide of racism can stop us," and Ralph Bunche, who apologized for having to speak from the steps of a state capitol over which waved the flag of the Confederacy. Before we had returned to Atlanta that evening, the Deep South had responded to this peaceful, principled demand that all Americans' rights be honored by saying, "Never," and by murdering Viola Liuzzo, a white woman from Detroit who had volunteered to transport marchers from Montgomery back to Selma. When Congress passed the sweeping federal Voting Rights Act later that year, the participants in the movement felt that they had accomplished something very important.

Before and after the Selma march, I watched with admiration as the young people, white and black, organized sit-ins, went on freedom rides, and defied the segregation laws until they were outlawed, at least theoretically, by the Civil Rights Act of 1964 and the Voting Rights Act, passed in August 1965, or just months after the march. I was especially proud of them when they pointed out that they were following in the footsteps of their ancestors who had fought the slave system and in this country's wars, sometimes at the same time. And when they urged whites and blacks to read and study the history of black people to better appreciate what they had done to make this country better, I and others sought to produce anthologies, encyclopedia entries, textbooks, and pictorial histories so that accurate depictions were available.

Meanwhile, my role in the department and in the university changed radically. In the spring of 1967, when I returned from one of my jaunts abroad in connection with my duties as a member of the Fulbright Board, I was informed that Edward Levi, the provost of the university, wished to see me. When I went to his office, he said that Bill McNeill was stepping down as chairman of the department. Levi then flatly declared that he wanted to appoint me chair. I was incredulous. I reminded him that I had served as a chair at Brooklyn College for eight years and was weary of administering a large department. He said that my experience made me most attractive to my colleagues at Chicago. Indeed, he told me that every member of the department had requested that I be their chair. I then complained about the time that it would take from my teaching and research. To every objection he had an answer. I could increase the number of my research assistants and decrease my teaching load from two courses to one. I proceeded to complain about the shabby appearance of the chairman's office. He suggested that I have it redecorated and purchase new furniture. Anticipating my next objection, he said I could retain the services of Margaret Fitzsimmons, who had become my secretary upon my arrival three years earlier and whose hire had been one of the conditions of my coming to Chicago. I told him that I would have to think it over and discuss it with my wife. I would give him my decision within a few weeks.

Aurelia had little enthusiasm for my becoming chair. She appreciated the fact that one of our considerations in coming to Chicago was that I would no longer have the administrative burdens that I had carried at Brooklyn. Indicating that she would nevertheless not attempt to persuade me one way or the other, she also swore to give me her usual support regardless of what I decided to do. Within days of my conversation with the provost, the word was out that I had been invited to become chairman of the department. People wondered why I hesitated, and one day I encountered Dan Boorstin at the entrance of the Social Science Building. I asked how he was and how the family was doing. He said that he was all right, but that Ruth was not doing too well. As I inquired further, he said that she had been sleeping poorly, kept awake by the thought that I might not become chairman. After further delaying my decision by weeks, I capitulated. The provost seemed immensely pleased.

A public announcement quickly followed, as though I just might change my mind, and it was heralded in the national press. That an African American would chair a first-tier university's department was news in 1967, and that stimulated a veritable flood of messages of congratulations from friends, acquaintances, and even strangers in many parts of the country.

I could not have become chairman at a more inauspicious moment. We had already begun to look at the role of students in the governance of the department, an effort that was progressing well. What we did not realize was that in a matter of months, if not weeks, our modest reforms would be swept up in a campuswide, indeed, a nationwide movement to transform the university into a center of activism whose goal, fueled by the widespread opposition to the war in Vietnam, was nothing less than the transformation of American society. With each passing day, the opposition to the war in Vietnam grew. By then, 485,000 American soldiers were stationed in Vietnam and antiwar sentiment deeply divided the country. President Lyndon Johnson was regarded in many quarters as an ogre who doggedly insisted on dragging the nation more and more deeply into the Asian quagmire. The year before, the Congress of Racial Equality declared the draft discriminatory and in 1967 Martin Luther King Jr. publicly denounced the war. The fight for civil rights and the movement to end the war grew increasingly intertwined.

Respect for law and order was breaking down, as many citizens felt that the federal government itself had little regard for the law. Nowhere was this manifested more dramatically than at the Democratic National Convention that met in Chicago in the summer of 1968. Many students from the university participated in various demonstrations protesting the war in Vietnam and joined in creating the disorders that caused investigators to declare that the local police were making war on the public. As clouds of tear gas rolled over crowds being advanced on by policemen in riot gear, the analogy seemed apt. Holed up in downtown hotels, young people poured buckets of trash and refuse down on the crowds below, and much of the spirit of outrage and confrontation so evident during the convention remained long after the delegates had left the city.

On every campus students sought a cause around which they could rally, and it need not be one of transcending significance. On one campus there was a furor over plans to revise the schedule of football games without consulting the students. At another college a group of students threatened to take over the administration building if they did not have a role in plans to revise the curriculum. At Chicago it was the fight over the reappointment of Marlene Dixon as assistant professor of sociology. Dixon, who also sat on the Committee on Human Development, was the flashpoint that precipitated the larger confrontation over the role of students in university governance. Some students, active in the radical women's liberation movement and the somewhat less radical Students for a Democratic Society, insisted that they should have equal voice with the faculty over hiring and rehiring. Any move not to rehire Dixon, they asserted, was a violation of their rights. An impasse followed, and when the students' demands were not accepted by nine a.m. on January 29, 1969, they vowed to take "militant action."

Meanwhile, John T. Wilson, the provost and dean of faculties, appointed a campuswide committee, chaired by Hanna Gray of the Department of History, to deal with the Dixon appointment as well as the larger issue regarding the role of students in the governance of the university. The Gray Committee approved the termination of Dixon but recom-

My sisters, Anne and Mozella, in the mid-1970s. My sisters were always supportive of my career; I suspect this photo was taken at an academic conference I was attending.

My mother-in-law, Bertha Whittington, joined us in Chicago after her husband's death. This picture of her was taken in the late 1970s.

Immediately following my first Jefferson Lecture, delivered in Washington, D.C., in 1976, I was surrounded by well-wishers, though not everyone approved of my frank discussion of race in America's history.

Here I am with Senator J. William Fulbright and fellow historians Anne Scott and C. Vann Woodward.

President Jimmy Carter appointed me to attend the 1980 UNESCO conference in Belgrade, Yugoslavia. President Ronald Reagan would cancel American membership the following year.

In 1981 Aurelia and I were again in Cambridge, Massachusetts, for another Harvard commencement. This time I was awarded an Honorary Doctor of Laws degree.

In December 1990, I was in Bellagio, Italy, for the Children's Defense Fund. I am sitting in the first row, third from the left.

Aurelia, Whit, and me visiting with Leopold S. Senghor,
President of Senegal, in 1981

Receiving the Spingarn Medal from Julius Chambers, former chief counsel of the NAACP
Legal Defense Fund and chancellor of N.C. Central University

Aurelia and I were thrilled in 1991 when Whit announced his engagement to Karen Roberts, who stands between Whit Aurelia.

Her father, Dr. James E. Roberts, being deceased, Karen asked that I give her away, a request that I was pleased to honor.

Whit's friend Bouna Ndiaye moved into our Durham home in 1983.

*Here I am at a Duke University event with
Whit and the Nobel laureate Toni Morrison.*
(CHRIS HILDRETH, DUKE UNIVERSITY PHOTOGRAPHY)

*I was photographed with the poet
Maya Angelou in Charlotte,
North Carolina, on the occasion
of my eighty-fifth birthday party.*

*My longtime secretary, dear friend, and otherwise
right-hand woman, Margaret Fitzsimmons,
joined me when I left the University of Chicago.*
(JIM WALLACE, DUKE UNIVERSITY PHOTOGRAPHY)

Chicago mayor Harold Washington, shown here with me in 1985, was one of several Chicago mayors with whom I worked over the years.

Signing copies of my biography of George Washington Williams at the Twelfth Baptist Church in Boston in 1985

On learning that I had been introduced to opera at Tulsa's segregated facilities, Joseph Volpe, general manager of the New York Metropolitan Opera, invited me to hear performances whenever I wished. Here I am with (left to right) Volpe, Denyce Graves, Eleanor Farrar, James Levine, and Plácido Domingo following a performance of Saint-Saëns's Samson and Delilah.

The Reverend Jesse Jackson and I view the centennial display of the Bill of Rights at the National Archives in 1987.

The writer Eudora Welty and me proudly displaying our Cleanth Brooks Medals, given to us by the Fellowship of Southern Writers

Walter Brown, Dean of the School of Education at N.C. Central University, and me in 1995 at a breakfast celebrating my eightieth birthday
(COURTESY OF THE DURHAM HERALD)

Alongside my dear friend Vernon Jordan, I received an honorary degree in 1981 from the University of Pennsylvania.

The musician Ray Charles and me at a 1993 White House reception celebrating our being awarded the Charles Frankel Medal

Aurelia holding one of our beloved orchids outside the greenhouse at our Durham, North Carolina, home

Aurelia and me at the celebration of her seventy-fifth birthday

ABOVE: *Receiving the Presidential Medal of Freedom, September 29, 1995*
(COURTESY OF THE CLINTON PRESIDENTIAL LIBRARY)
BELOW: *Lecturing at Vice President Al Gore's Seminar on Race in America,*
Washington, D.C., 1994 (OFFICIAL WHITE HOUSE PHOTOGRAPH)

Inside the Oval Office with President Clinton following the swearing-in of the first Advisory Board for the President's Initiative on Race (OFFICIAL WHITE HOUSE PHOTOGRAPH)

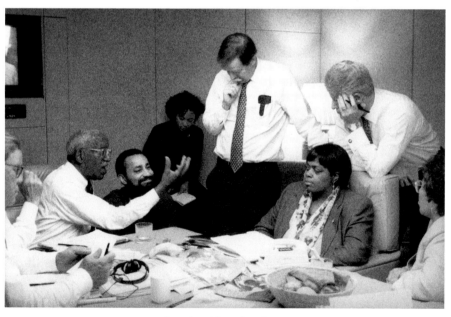

In June 1997, members of President Clinton's Initiative on Race used the time aboard Air Force One en route to San Diego and Clinton's formal announcement of our panel to discuss the problems and goals of the year ahead.
(OFFICIAL WHITE HOUSE PHOTOGRAPH)

*Sitting between President Clinton and Vice President Gore, I presided
at a Washington meeting of the President's Initiative on Race.*

In 1998 I joined Bishop Desmond Tutu in Senegal for several weeks to film the documentary Tutu and Franklin: A Journey Toward Peace, *in an effort to bring American and African students together to confront the legacy of slavery.*

I met with Rosa Parks at the White House at the final meeting of the President's Initiative on Race, September 1998.

Bill Cosby spoke at the opening of the Franklin Center at Duke in 2001. (LES TODD/DUKE UNIVERSITY PHOTOGRAPHY)

*With B. B. King
in 1977 at Yale
University, where we
both received
honorary degrees*
(WILLIAM FERRIS
COLLECTION,
UNC CHAPEL HILL
SOUTHERN FOLKLIFE
COLLECTION)

*Metropolitan opera star Leontyne Price and I received honorary
degrees from Harvard University in June 1981.*

I was taught to fish in Rentiesville, Oklahoma, by my mother, and it has become a lifelong passion. Here I am at Friday Creek, Alaska, after landing a thirty-two-pound king salmon.

mended a one-year extension of her position on the Committee on Human Development because the decision regarding her employment had been significantly delayed. The students who were supporting the Dixon reappointment called the Gray Committee's report a "whitewash" and urged students to go out on strike. Given the postconvention environment, more extreme measures seemed inevitable. At a mass meeting of students held on January 29, some 444 of them voted to resort to militant action, while 430 voted against. Later that same day, a second meeting of a smaller number of students voted to undertake a sit-in the following day in the administration building.

On January 30, the students began their sit-in. Edward Levi, who had succeeded George Beadle as president of the university the previous year, commented to me that occupying the administration building was the students' first big mistake. They would have done much better had they occupied the library or some of the laboratories. The operation of the university hardly depended on access to the administration building. He could still function as president in his living room or in his kitchen. The mounting frustration of the students could be seen in their conduct during the occupation. They poured ketchup into the typewriters and, among other things, called me to ask if it was true that the Chicago police were about to raid them. I replied that they were indulging in wishful thinking.

This was a period of soul-searching on the part of the faculty and administration of the university. Many members of the faculty issued statements that generally upheld the rights of students to make their views known but denied them any shared responsibility for the university's future. Richard Wade of the Department of History said that the fundamental issue raised by the sit-in was, of course, "the role of coercion in academic affairs. Those who value the life of the mind know that coercion undermines the processes of consent, rationality, and decency which alone make needed changes possible and enduring." Faculty members Morris Janowitz, Lloyd Fallers, Paul Meier, and Clifford Geertz reminded the sit-in participants that "all across the country and around the world universities lie crippled and dying because their faculties and students yielded to the illogic of the argument that the fight against war and injustice will somehow be aided by bringing free inquiry to a halt. 'End the war! Shut down the University!' they cry. How tragically absurd . . . When someone shouts at you 'Shut it down,' RESIST—not with your hands, but with your mind."

My own statement said, among other things, that I was very much disturbed by the fact that "some members of the University have renounced the rational approach to the solution of problems of the community and the University, however difficult. It is clear that in the resort to the seizure of a building, the ransacking of official files, and the effort to disrupt classes by noisome and juvenile antics, these members of the University community have rejected the very principles on which the University can have a healthy existence. In pursuing the present course of action, they have deliberately placed themselves beyond the pale . . . and in seeking amnesty under the circumstances, they have deliberately insisted that they enjoy an immunity to the higher learning that is the very hallmark of any seat of learning . . . And they insult the progeny of those early fighters for justice who have had the wisdom and grace, in our own time, to understand the difference between a great seat of learning and an ordinary public hustings."

The University of Chicago escaped the harrowing experience of violence and estrangement that some institutions went through. It was firm in its determination not to invite the police to handle the sit-in, but it was equally firm in its insistence that students who attempted to usurp the rights of others and to violate university governance by seizing and holding university property should be punished. When the students finally left the buildings they had occupied, they were brought to trial before the university's faculty-student discipline committee and suspended or expelled, depending on the severity of their offense.

The department experienced only one truly permanent injury. When students learned that Dan Boorstin had years earlier testified before the House Un-American Activities Committee and had not only confessed his own membership in a so-called Communist cell but had also given the names of others who were members of his group, they made copies of his testimony and placed them on the seats of students assembling for his next lecture. Dan did not mention the incident to me, but Ruth Boorstin came to my office with a copy of the sheet that had been distributed and inquired what I intended to do about it. I replied that I would not dignify this provocation by responding to it. President Levi shortly indicated to me that if I would agree, he would respond by appointing Boorstin to a distinguished service chair. I was delighted to concur. Thus, Dan became the Preston and Sterling Morton Distinguished Service Professor of History.

Although Dan was deeply appreciative of this recognition, he was hurt beyond healing, and when he was invited to become the director of the National Museum of History and Technology at the Smithsonian Institution, he accepted. Thus, the university lost its brightest star in the field of United States history. In 1975, President Gerald Ford appointed him librarian of Congress, a post that he filled with distinction until his retirement in 1987. Throughout it all, we remained close, personally and professionally, and I proudly served for several years on his Library of Congress Council of Scholars.

Confrontations on campus, however, were greatly overshadowed by national ones. The assassination of Martin Luther King Jr. in April 1968 was an event of seismic proportions that left no part of the country unaffected. Arthur and Sylvia Mann and Aurelia and I were having a meal at our favorite Chinese restaurant when we heard the news. For a moment I felt like the Brooklyn College student who, after the assassination of John F. Kennedy, burst into my classroom shouting, "What are we going to do?" What, indeed, could we do after King's death? The riots and other forms of violence that erupted in many places mirrored the apprehensions and impatience of the civil rights revolutionaries who took seriously King's declaration that "we have waited long enough." The day following his death, blacks admonished white motorists to "turn on your lights out of respect to Martin." And they usually did, if not out of respect, then surely for insurance against further violence.

It seemed that blacks who were impatient for change were at a crossroads. Some believed steadfastly in King's insistence that nonviolent demonstrations and boycotts would prove sufficient. Others, such as Black Power advocates and those in the Black Panthers, argued that history amply demonstrated that white people would never voluntarily concede equality to blacks. Blacks would have to fight for it, even if it meant taking to the streets and demanding "total liberty for black people or total destruction for America." Either racial repression would end, they insisted, or no one would enjoy peace and prosperity in the United States.

It was about this time that Knopf thought that we should consider publishing an updated edition of *From Slavery to Freedom*. I was quite willing to work on a third edition, but I reminded them that we had previously discussed the possibility of issuing it also in paperback. My editor's response was tepid, marked by his anxiety "to protect the market for the current hardcover edition." Then followed an escalating exchange of opinion, which I ended as follows: "I very much doubt that you are aware . . . that a new mood is rising which . . . could have a most deleterious effect on the sales of *From Slavery to Freedom* . . . At a time when the courses in Negro history are multiplying daily, and when the demand for cheap books is increasing, someone is going to come forward with a cheap, polemical book that will put us out of business . . . Meanwhile, you can continue to 'protect the market' for the hardcover edition, while the scores of people looking for a history of Negro Americans will turn to some other work."

Within a matter of weeks, the management at Knopf decided to allay my hysteria and publish the third edition in paperback. In September 1969, the first paperback edition of *From Slavery to Freedom* finally appeared, and purchasers snapped it up as though they had been waiting for it for years. Indeed, they had, for the book had first appeared more than twenty years earlier. My publishers, however, seemed not to understand what was happening. One had to be rather close to the civil rights movement to understand the great demand for a book that related the way the African American story was inextricably woven into the history of the United States. Consequently, the paperback of the third edition went rapidly into a second and a third printing. Soon, Knopf got the message that had eluded Time-Life.

I was surprised to discover the extent to which racial pride and sensitivity had increased immediately before and after King's death. Considerable numbers of African Americans turned their faces to Africa, adopting African or Islamic names and wearing African dress. It was their way of distancing themselves from the dominant trends and values in the United States. Malcolm X, who had criticized the March on Washington as a waste of time, underscored the importance of Africa in the lives of African Americans by visiting African countries and inviting more blacks to renounce Christianity, the religion of slavery, and embrace Islam, the true religion, he argued, of a free America.

African American women were asserting themselves as never before. I had noticed their deep involvement in the March on Washington, and the Selma march in which I participated. At both events they were present in abundant numbers, associating themselves not only with the male leadership but with all the women, white and black, whose presence I noticed during the Selma march and in the civil rights movement's infrastructure. The names of certain black women leaders approached household familiarity. Barbara Jordan from Texas, Shirley Chisholm of New York, and Eleanor Holmes Norton of Washington were just some of the more articulate and energetic leaders who had an impact on developments.

I was happiest about the growing civic involvement of African Americans, particularly in the political process. Following the passage of the Voting Rights Act in 1965, the first reaction of blacks was an increased sense of empowerment, and they seemed to develop a growing appreciation for the effective exercise of their voting rights. Those of us who were alive to witness it still bitterly resented the secession of white Southerners from the Democratic National Convention in 1948 because the party saw fit to take a stand in favor of civil rights, and we well knew that it would require the active participation of truly enfranchised African Americans to offset the retreat of those same Southerners into the Republican Party in subsequent years. By the time King was assassinated, the growing political strength of blacks, primarily in the Democratic Party, was apparent, and they were beginning to elect considerable numbers of blacks to public office. There were blacks on local school boards and county commissions, in the office of mayors, in state legislatures, and in the Congress. I cheered the election of blacks to Congress, not only in New York and Illinois but in California, Virginia, South Carolina, and several other Southern states. Times were changing, although not at a sufficiently rapid pace for those of us who had been impatient for change for so many years.

In other parts of the country, student unrest continued, with some violence here and there. Students at Cornell rattled their sabers and their rifles, to the dismay of others, while at Kent State in Ohio and Jackson State in Mississippi, students gave their lives in the spring of 1970 protesting an "unjust war" abroad and numerous inequities at home.

Surely the saddest and most tragic realization for me was how the spirit of change cut several different ways, and sometimes with unconstructive, even tragic, consequences. As students across the country were standing up for their rights, some defined those rights in ever stranger ways. At Fisk, of all places, some students were involved in some of the shoddiest activities imaginable, all done in the name of students' rights and civil rights. Resting on the false claim that Fisk University was a black university, they became resolved to clear it of all white personnel, including teachers, staff members, and the few white students who were there. Among their first moves was to burn the automobile of my friend and early mentor, Theodore Currier, presumably to let him know that they were "dead serious" about ridding the university of any and all white people. The next thing they did was to demand that he leave Fisk immediately, for there was no place, they reportedly said, "for a white man at a black university." They gave him until sundown to leave the campus.

He called me, as he often did when he wanted to talk through a problem, and asked what he should do. As an ardent pacifist and one who did not wish some tragedy to befall him or Fisk, I suggested that he go to a hotel until things cooled off. He considered the suggestion, and then reminded me that he had already been at Fisk for forty years, representing the investment of a lifetime. Then he added, somewhat plaintively, that Fisk belonged to every generation of faculty who had taught there and every generation of students who had studied there. It belonged to him, he concluded, more than it belonged to the vandals who had burned his automobile or the students who now demanded that he leave. He resolved to stand his ground in the passionate belief that he would save Fisk from those who would destroy him and, in the process, the institution itself. Hearing his commitment, I felt ashamed for suggesting that he withdraw even temporarily. I also felt ashamed for those Fisk students who were so ignorant regarding what he had invested in the university and in them. Currier believed that people's character and intellectual muscle could be exercised and strengthened. He had witnessed the truth of this in himself, and he had spent his life trying to improve both qualities in others. Certainly, he had done so for me. And it is among my fonder hopes that when the threats subsided and the protests ceased, Currier realized how integral his courage and his contribution were to Fisk and the accomplishments of the many students he influenced.

20

Town and Gown and Beyond

I N THE SPRING OF 1970, President Levi reluctantly allowed me to
conclude my term as chair of the department after the agreed-to
three years were up. I at once felt as though a heavy burden had been
lifted from my shoulders. I had spent the past decade with one eye out for
the straw that would break my back. All the while buffeted by national
events—the high points surrounding the passage of the Civil Rights Act
and Voting Rights Act, and the low points of confrontation and violence,
most jarringly the assassinations of President Kennedy in 1963 and Martin
Luther King Jr. and Robert Kennedy in 1968—my professional life and
personal life marched on. Again and again my help and participation were
requested and again and again I found it hard to say no. This was particularly true when the request permitted me to exercise influence over an intersection of scholarship and policy. Such opportunities arose with
increasing regularity, involving a range of international, national, and local organizations. Well before I was corralled into becoming department
chair, my activities on behalf of the Board of Foreign Scholarships were
consuming more of my time. I served on the board's Committee on Africa
and the Near East, and in the spring of 1964, I went out for brief visits to
Tehran, New Delhi, Hyderabad, Bombay, and Cairo. By next spring, I
was returning to the Near East, spending nearly a month traveling in

Greece, Turkey, Iran, and Egypt. In each country, I talked with embassy personnel, members of the staff of the United States Information Service, educators, members of the binational commissions, staff personnel of the commissions, and grantees. This is the pattern I would follow in all of my visits on behalf of the Board of Foreign Scholarships. The experience was invaluable in getting a better view both of the strengths and weaknesses of each nation's program of educational exchange. In some countries new universities were springing up both to fill a need and to offset the conservatism of the older universities, whose enormous influence could be undermined only by the establishment of new and competing institutions. While older universities continued to take in lecturers under the auspices of the Fulbright program, they often had no intention of utilizing their services fully. Meanwhile, the newer institutions were clamoring for Fulbright professors, eager to be able to claim that they were a part of the globalization of education and learning.

One of the problems I saw in my 1965 visit to the Near East was the rather heavy hand of American officials as they administered the Fulbright program and their inability always to remember its unique binational character. Yet another problem was the coordination of the Fulbright program with the Peace Corps educational program. The resulting redundancy often created scheduling conflicts and the cancellation of not one course but both courses. I called such problems to the attention of the board, urging it to be alert to the ways it could encourage the binational commissions to attempt to solve them.

In March 1966, I was again traveling throughout the Near East and South Asia—Iraq, Lebanon, Syria, Israel, Cyprus, Ceylon, and India—and by September of that year I was elected chairman of the Board of Foreign Scholarships. A great honor, it was also an awesome challenge. I made my first visit as chairman and as a member of the subcommittee for Europe in the spring of 1967, visiting England, the Netherlands, Belgium, Germany, France, Italy, and Spain. I was impressed repeatedly with the widespread interest in and admiration for the program of educational exchange between the United States and those several countries. I was no less impressed with the widespread anxiety I encountered as our European Fulbright partners struggled to reconcile the bold and imaginative programs incorporated in the new International Education Act with substantial reductions in levels of educational exchange in virtually all the countries. Ranging from U.S. ambassadors to members of the commission secretariats, there was an air of uneasiness and doubt that was easily discernible but not easily dispelled. Even as they recognized the obvious and inevitable redirection of resources caused by the Vietnam War, they pointed to the importance of continuing and strengthening the traditional relationships between the United States and its friends in Europe.

In 1969, I was invited to participate in the exhibit called "Education—USA" scheduled to tour the Soviet Union in 1970. I was unable, because of my winter teaching schedule, to participate in the Leningrad and Moscow segments of the exhibit, but I would be able to catch up with it in Tashkent. Consequently, just as my duties as chair were winding down, Aurelia and I departed Chicago on March 13, 1970, arriving in Leningrad, via London and Helsinki, the following day. After excessive red tape and other inconveniences, we made it through customs and immigration and got to our hotel before midnight. We were finally settled in the Europeiskaya Hotel and had two days of rest and sightseeing. Following some memorable, and not so memorable, sightseeing in Leningrad and Moscow, we completed our journey to Tashkent, where members of the staff of "Education—USA" briefed us not only about what was expected of me at the exhibit but also about how we should conduct ourselves away from the exhibit. They were almost certain that our room was bugged and suggested that if we wished to discuss anything pertaining to the exhibit or even personal matters, we should go outside. Sure enough, when we sought to move our room, given its noisy location just above the hotel entrance, we were refused with the empty excuse that nothing could be done. Also, although locals might befriend me, they would not, could not, visit us in our hotel. And it went without saying that whenever we left the hotel, we were required to surrender our key to a hall maid who was stationed at a desk near the elevator. We had visions of her rummaging through our room in our absence.

It was my duty to make myself available during the exhibit to answer questions relating to educational matters within my purview, participate in seminars and meetings with Soviet educators and officials, and schedule hours in the library for informal discussions with Soviet citizens. I appeared almost every day in the early afternoon to answer questions posed by people attending the exhibit. Within a day or two, I noticed several individuals who appeared regularly with questions they wanted me to answer. In such cases, I would indicate that I was pleased to see them back. Questions ranged from how rich I was to how many blacks had been lynched the previous year. It was never entirely clear if these questions were set ahead of time or authentically spontaneous.

We took advantage of what leisure time we had to visit various parts of Tashkent and to extend our visit to nearby places, such as Bukhara and Samarkand, a place I had wanted to see since I studied geography in the eighth grade. We were especially interested in the vast cotton fields that reminded us of the cotton kingdom in the American South. One did not have to travel in the Soviet Union to be fascinated by the people and their ways. Once, as we were leaving the Hotel Tashkent, I took a picture of the traffic officer who sat in a box above the intersection directing traffic. The moment I snapped the picture and before I could close my camera, I heard a shrill whistle. I saw that it was from the policeman with a look of stern admonition on his face. As I mused at the possibility that the remainder of my days would now be spent in Siberia, I approached the officer. He asked me if I had taken his picture. I confessed that I had. He then whipped out his card in the same way that he directed traffic and ordered me to send one to him! I thanked him and promised that I would.

Living in the Soviet Union for three weeks was tedious, and even departing had its problems. From Tashkent, we were to journey to Karachi before going on to Tehran, Istanbul, Athens, and Zagreb. The U.S. officials in Tashkent informed me that I would need a cholera shot before proceeding to Pakistan. Aurelia already had hers, but I did not. The officials arranged for me to get it at the Tashkent hospital. When I arrived with my interpreter, a man was waiting at the gate to escort me to the office of the chief physician. He greeted me, welcomed me, and offered me coffee and fruit. In due course, he summoned a physician who would give me the immunization. I was surprised that my physician was a large blonde woman whose very countenance and bearing bespoke efficiency. She took me to her office, where she gave me the shot.

When Aurelia and I arrived in Karachi at midnight and got settled finally in the Intercontinental Hotel, we had a celebration: hot showers and a few sips of vodka we had brought from Tashkent. There followed a whirlwind tour of the Near East, my first in no official capacity, and then it was back to Chicago and my newly reduced departmental duties. I suffered no illusion that things were going to slow down. Some of my heaviest local responsibilities were only then coming into view.

My sporadic friendship with the mayor of Chicago, Richard J. Daley, eventually resulted in his appointing me to the board of the Chicago Public Library. My experience on the board put me in touch not only with some of the finest colleagues with whom I had the pleasure of serving but also with some of the most remarkable professional librarians that I have met anywhere. I even attended the meetings of the American Library Association as often as I could, and on occasion Aurelia—now the retired librarian—would go with me.

In Chicago I held membership in three clubs that gave me an opportunity to meet a variety of citizens, many of whom were well connected and quite influential. Early in my tenure at the university, I was invited to join the Commercial Club, an old organization composed primarily of business and professional leaders. Among them was Otto Kerner, former governor of Illinois and currently a member of the Fourth Circuit of the United States Court of Appeals. Another was Jay Pritzker. If someone was sitting next to me, Jay would ask him to move over so that he could sit beside me. We would then talk about all sorts of things during the meal. I did not know that his family owned and managed the Hyatt hotels until the day he asked me to suggest some literate, intelligent young African Americans who could be employed by the hotels. I put him in touch with some people in personnel at Fisk University, from which he was able to engage the services of a considerable number of young people. Once when Aurelia and I were arriving in California, we encountered Jay in the San Francisco Airport. He asked me where were staying, and I replied that we had reservations at the Hyatt on Union Square, of course. When we arrived, the hotel's general manager had us escorted to a very elaborate suite on the top floor.

Shortly after I arrived in Chicago I was also invited to become a member of the Wayfarers Club, the principal purpose of which was to see to it that its members had a relaxing good time at the monthly meetings. The membership was made up of businessmen, public officials, and a larger proportion of educators than had been the case of the Commercial Club. A big feature was the annual meeting, held in June, when the club elected officers, presented names of proposed new members, and adjourned to box seats in Wrigley Field for the annual attendance at a baseball game between the Cubs and some unworthy rival that was bitterly denounced by the Wayfarers.

My relations with Fisk, my alma mater, reached a new level during our years in Chicago, perhaps because of the lively, energetic Fisk Alumni Club there. I had been active even during my graduate student days, for there was a healthy contingent of Fiskites in the vicinity of Boston. In Chicago, the support of Fisk took on a new meaning, and Aurelia and I became more ardent supporters of Fisk than ever before. I had been in much closer touch with developments at Fisk from the time I was elected to its Board of Trustees in 1947, first to represent the alumni and after six years in that capacity as a board member at large until I resigned in 1984. It was during my Chicago years that I served as chair of the board, 1966–73, and was deeply involved in the operations of the institution.

I was never pleased with the meager support that Fisk received from Nashville's white community, and when I became chair of the board, I learned firsthand just how little financial support our neighbors "across town" actually gave Fisk. Our major resource was our history and, at times, they seemed to begrudge us that. Rumor had it that there was bitter resentment that the remarkable multimillion-dollar Alfred Stieglitz art collection, donated by Georgia O'Keeffe, was housed at Fisk. When I was chair and we were building a new dormitory, primarily with federal funds, we learned that due to a mix-up it would be about six months before we would receive the $1 million due us from Washington. At that point, several Nashville bankers became quite actively interested in how we would manage the payroll and meet other expenses in connection with the construction project for the ensuing six months. Two of them came to Chicago to discuss the matter with me. I indicated to them that somehow we would survive. They returned to Nashville without my having indicated what my strategy would be.

Through the Commercial Club, the university, and other connections, I had met several bankers who, I thought, just might help Fisk at this point. I decided to take up the matter with Robert Abboud, president of the First National Bank of Chicago. When I called on him, he received me cordially and listened attentively to what I said about Fisk and the Nashville community. I then told him that I wanted to borrow $1 million, which would be repaid in six months. He said that, of course, his bank would be pleased to lend us the money under the conditions I outlined. He reminded me that long after this episode was over, Fisk would still have to live with its neighbors, and he did not wish to do anything to drive a wedge between Fisk and the community. I assured him that what caused the university's strained relations with its near neighbors was of long duration and nothing he could do would influence it one way or another. That said, I expressed my gratitude not only for his willingness to let us have the money but also for his advice and counsel.

One morning in the spring of 1972, I encountered a man who was looking for my university office. He was Charles Brown, president of the Illinois Bell Telephone Company. He was there to invite me to become a member of the board. I was shocked and flattered, and after he explained the work of the board I agreed to serve. Initially, my education into the telephone business took the form of a series of briefings about all areas of the company's business. These took place over almost two months and covered everything from operations to the legal environment in which Illinois Bell operated. Thereafter, the regular monthly board meetings plus luncheons and conferences with the company's principal officers as well as management reports were the means by which board members kept themselves abreast of the business.

I was placed on the committee on public policy, which made recommendations not only regarding charitable contributions that the company should make, such as donations to sickle-cell anemia and the Chicago Symphony, but personnel matters as well. In that role I felt free to look into company policy regarding employment and promotions.

This interest was replicated during my work on the board of the Chicago Museum of Science and Industry. As in the case of Illinois Bell, I took the opportunity, as a member of the board, to press for a clear policy that would ensure equality of opportunity in evaluation and promotion. In 1971, I called for the museum to conduct a "summary of the present racial composition of the staff" and suggested that it could best be done "by a breakdown of departments and a further breakdown of the number in supervisory or other capacities." The very exercise itself had the effect of raising the consciousness of the senior staff regarding equal employment opportunities.

This experience was repeated yet again in my capacity as a member of the Board of Directors of the Orchestral Association, the governing arm of the Chicago Symphony. My most serious problem with the Orchestral Association was that the symphony was all-white, and there seemed to be little that I could do about it. While I repeatedly pointed out the absence of blacks in the symphony, my amateur's grasp of how to judge a musician's talents routinely kept me from being able to champion an individual African American musician seeking a position. Though never able to refute the conclusion that an individual artist did not measure up, I always found suspect the impossibility of locating a single black musician up to par.

These activities in Chicago and beyond were the backdrop for my own work at the university and particularly with my students, both graduate and undergraduate. Neither ever went neglected; indeed, they were at the very center of my professional life and would remain so.

When I look back on the years when I was supervising more than thirty doctoral dissertations, I am reminded of a remark I made in jest when I was introducing one of my outstanding PhD students, Loren Schweninger, at a reception. At the time, he and I were collaborating on *Runaway Slaves: Rebels on the Plantation*, which would be published the following year. The hostess wondered if that was the first time that we had been coauthors. Before Loren could reply, I spoke up and told her that it was not, that we had collaborated on his dissertation! It was only after everyone laughed that I realized just what I had implied.

What I really meant was that I worked with my students so carefully and so consistently that I felt completely engaged in what they were doing. I read several drafts of their dissertations, and I made innumerable suggestions for revision. I felt so involved that I came to view my teaching and their learning as a true collaboration. It was the only way I knew to bring out the best in them. To one of my students whose dissertation was almost first rate but could have been even better, I wrote, "I have now read your manuscript quite thoroughly for the second time. It shows improvement, although I must confess that I wish that you had taken more time and given more thought to some of the observations and criticisms I made the first time around. I am afraid that you must once more go through the manuscript, page by page, and take into account the corrections I have made and the questions I have raised." I do not doubt that my recommendation elicited a groan from the student, but I am equally certain that the manuscript was greatly improved after he heeded my advice.

I never regarded myself as a severe taskmaster, and I do not believe that my students so regarded me. My continued association with most of them and their countless expressions of gratitude and esteem persuade me that the spirit of collaboration was mutual. That most of my doctoral students have remained professionally connected with the field of history, not only by teaching in colleges and universities but also by serving as archival administrators at national and state levels, has meant that they continue to maintain contact with me and with one another. I have always taken immense pride in their accomplishments, most especially their commitment to the highest standards of scholarship. In 1991 they returned the favor in a commensurate fashion. When a group of them published that year a volume of essays in my honor titled *The Facts of Reconstruction* they were quick to point out that it was not a Festschrift, "at least not in the conventional sense." The work was not only to "honor Franklin," but to "engage him as well," and indeed in their thoughtful, critical essays, my previous scholarship was engaged marvelously.

Reading that book distinctly recalled for me a moment toward the end of my tenure as president of the American Historical Association in 1979. My doctoral students then gave me a luncheon in New York at which they presented me with a bound volume of handwritten tributes. I was deeply moved, and whenever I reread their letters I am left to only hope that I in fact exerted in some measure the influence over their development as scholars that they attribute to me. Ever since Ted Currier so decidedly directed my life toward history and scholarship I knew that I too would strive to mentor another generation of scholars. Such tangible evidence as given me in 1979 and in 1991 that I had accomplished that goal pleased me more than all of my honorary degrees. Many of my students came to Durham in 1995 to celebrate my eightieth birthday and again in 1997 to observe the fiftieth anniversary of the publication of *From Slavery to Freedom*. Both occasions gave me further opportunity to reflect on the doctorates I have trained and the even greater number of undergraduate students

I have had the privilege of teaching in colleges and universities both in the United States and around the world. Not only did I consistently ask much of my students, but they consistently asked much of me; it is my fond hope that they thrilled to the challenge as much as I did, for nothing has so quickened my intellectual life than the pleasures of the classroom and the tasks of teaching.

Over the course of my academic career, I have noted that one way of avoiding leadership roles is to remain inactive in the organizations of which one is a member. I have always been unable to be passive, and perhaps that is why I have been "rewarded" with additional responsibility. That was true in all the organizations where I ended up as president—the American Studies Association, the Southern Historical Association, the Organization of American Historians, Phi Beta Kappa—and was particularly true in the American Historical Association. Over and over again, I served on the latter's committees, read and discussed papers, chaired sessions at annual meetings, and sat on the executive council for two three-year terms, once as chair. When I was president of the Organization of American Historians, a former student whom I had taught at Howard University complained to me of the small number of African Americans I had selected to serve on committees and to participate in sessions at the OAH's annual meetings. I reminded him that under the constitution, only *members* could serve on committees and that he was ineligible because he was not a member. My point was simple: Membership was the necessary first step to address any such criticism. I wanted him also to understand that a central objective of my leadership of whatever organization I belonged to was to see to it that it was inclusive and welcoming to any and all persons qualified.

21

Family Matters

HEN WHIT WENT TO STANFORD in the fall of 1969, Aurelia and I were determined to maintain close family ties. Aurelia went out on parents' weekend each year, and I would visit him whenever I was on the West Coast. He made the adjustment admirably, while we slowly adjusted to his absence. Stanford was not immune to the turbulent roiling so many colleges and universities experienced throughout America during these years. Nor were Stanford students without their violent impulses, and we were appalled when we learned that Whit's fellow students were smashing windows by the scores if not hundreds and committing other acts of violence. We were relieved that the situation never got out of hand and were always pleased to learn that Whit was neither implicated in anything illegal nor injured by the behavior of others.

As Whit entered college, I could not fail to think of my own and Aurelia's collegiate experience or even those of my parents. My father found his life's partner in college, as did I. He had to work throughout his college days, as did I. While I did not confront the campus unrest that Whit encountered, there was in my time the legally sanctioned racist climate pervading college life. Those differences granted, however, it was remarkable how similar the mid-twentieth century was to the situation a half century earlier. Much had changed. Yet to a scholar's eye, in so many ways the old order had not. In 1969 more than four hundred thousand American soldiers remained in Vietnam, their average age nineteen, and an estimated 80 percent of them the sons of the poor and working classes. For those with means and connections, the draft could be evaded through deferments, medical exemptions, or—the preferred choice of many politicians in the wings—appointments to the National Guard and reserve units. Everywhere a rising militancy—among feminists, students, Mexican Americans, Native Americans, and particularly blacks—was met by an ever more conservative reaction. Whit had gone off to college on the heels of Richard M. Nixon's 1968 presidential election on a "law and order" campaign that, Nixon claimed, stood upon a groundswell of support from the "great majority of Americans, the forgotten Americans, the non-shouters, the nondemonstrators." Nixon could not have made it clearer that he intended to rule over an America populated by an "us" and a "them." While the anxieties of Whit's time might seem to pale in comparison to the stark segregation and Jim Crow realities that Aurelia and I had faced as undergraduates at Fisk, we did not minimize the divisiveness and apprehensions that were so much a part of Whit's life as he pursued his studies. We made every attempt to follow developments at Stanford, but even with our visits and our regular telephone conversations, we felt strangely out of touch, which amplified our anxieties.

Aurelia and I fretted that in our anxiety to protect him from the rather hostile environment in Brooklyn and to some extent in Chicago—once a profiling campus police officer questioned his presence at the home of a friend just across the street from where we lived—we had somehow left him unprepared for the turmoil of Stanford. I also wondered whether my periodic trips abroad or to some other part of the country deprived him of the parental security that a father could provide. Yet even in the midst of my busiest years, I had never permitted my own work to interfere with conversations with him whenever we were together. The example of my father, who did precisely the same thing with me, suggested that I was for once doing the right thing.

My greatest moment of soul-searching came when Aurelia and I went on a jaunt to central and southeastern Europe in the summer of 1970 with a couple from Washington. Whit encouraged us to make the trip, assuring us that he would be quite all right, working in the Neighborhood Youth

Corps on Chicago's west side. It was a long commute from Hyde Park, and he seemed a bit apprehensive about the gangs in that part of the city who were in turf fights with one another, but he was having a wonderful time and insisted that we not worry. We had completed about two-thirds of our journey when we received a cable from Aurelia's brother-in-law saying that Whit was in the hospital. When we called him from Zagreb, he said that we should not interrupt our trip, that Whit would "pull through it" all right, whatever that meant. We informed him that we would be in Chicago the following day.

The trip across the Atlantic was excruciating. I could neither sleep nor relax; I couldn't eat or drink. In such circumstances, I did not know whether to admire Aurelia or upbraid her for falling asleep. Regardless, she awoke refreshed and ready for the next day, while I was so overcome with fatigue that only my body's excessive adrenaline got me through the next twenty-four hours. Upon our arrival we called Whit from the airport. To our great relief he said that he was feeling better. His malady had been diagnosed as a ruptured appendix, with resulting peritonitis. Later in the summer, after the infection had cleared up, Whit returned to the hospital for a routine appendectomy. Perhaps he believed that we continued to have some anxiety about his health. Thus, one morning at sunrise, he came to our bedroom and sat on the side of the bed and said quite calmly that he wanted us to know that he was healthy again and that everything would be all right. By this time it was characteristic of him to show concern for us and, at the same time, assure us that he could take care of himself. Though a parent's concern for his child never entirely dissipates, I spied in his bearing and tone that morning that he was his own person and fully in command of his choices and decisions.

Whit did not make the mistake that I had made when I was in college. From the start it was clear that he did not intend to follow in the footsteps of his father. Perhaps he interpreted my own struggles to find decent employment and decent housing among decent people as somehow related to the teaching profession. He never said as much, and it is possible to speculate that his silence on the subject could be interpreted as being unappreciative, to say nothing of not admiring what I was attempting to do for all of us and how I went about it. He never gave me cause to entertain such ideas and that I indulged them no doubt reflected my own fears. I refrained from giving him advice about what to choose as a major, how to select an adviser, or how to navigate the treacherous waters of the undergraduate curriculum. I had sufficient confidence in Stanford, in the members of the faculty whom I knew, and in Whit to believe that he would get along without my interference. Once he decided on his own to major in anthropology, I discussed his academic future with his dean, James Gibbs, and his adviser, St. Clair Drake, both anthropologists. I was certain he was on the right track.

By the end of the summer, Whit had indeed fully recovered from his appendectomy and returned to Stanford for his junior year. After he settled down to major in anthropology, he began to think about postgraduate years. He seemed to think that it would be good to use his French, and he began to talk about looking into the influence of French culture on the colonies in Francophone Africa. We encouraged him, there being no question that he was proficient in the language. He had camped with French boys in Yugoslavia when he was still in high school, and he had spent a summer in Martinique studying the French and African intellectuals who had developed the concept of Negritude. At the end of his junior year, he decided to visit West Africa and spend considerable time in Senegal. From that point on, it was clear what his interests would be.

Whit's senior year went smoothly, and we looked forward to one of the biggest events in our lives—the college graduation of our only offspring. Grandmother Whittington would be the senior member of the family to attend, followed by Sister (Mozella) and Waldo. Anne, my younger sister, would also attend the graduation and accompany Aurelia's mother on the return trip. I could not help thinking of the graduation days of Aurelia and me, when only our mothers were able to attend because our fathers could not finance the trips for themselves *and* their wives. We felt downright affluent when we compared our situation in 1973 with theirs in 1935. Much more important was the fact that in Palo Alto there were two generations of college graduates ready to welcome Whit into the family of educated men and women, which was something of which many European American families could not boast. And we all were leading constructive lives and contributing to the well-being of their communities. Buck was deceased, but he had been a school principal. Sister was a veteran elementary school teacher, and Anne, a graduate of the Howard University

School of Social Work, was an inspector with the Washington Metropolitan Police Department. In the absence of the deceased patriarchs, my attorney father and Aurelia's postal service father, we were faring somewhat better than most Americans, and at this commencement it was something of which we were all proud.

It is not too much to say that Whit's graduation from Stanford was more than an academic festival; for us it was a time of family reunion and celebration. For the first time it was possible not only to consider our twenty-year-old Whit an adult but to see him in his own element as an adult. He now had his own automobile, which we gave him at the beginning of his senior year, after he had three bicycles stolen from him. So armed, he assumed full responsibility during commencement festivities for setting the schedule, transporting and guiding us around Stanford and Palo Alto, and he seemed to enjoy it thoroughly. Very early on Aurelia and I had deliberately decided to practice a thoroughgoing restraint when it came to Whit's collegiate experience, and we did not interfere in his life at Stanford or in the decisions he was called on to make while there. We were available if he wished for our advice, but we did not intrude. Over the four years we watched his progress from Chicago, we saw consistent evidence that he was navigating his undergraduate responsibilities successfully, and during those days surrounding his being awarded his diploma we saw even clearer evidence that he had taken seriously his responsibilities as an adult. I noted the immense pride that Aurelia took in his reaching maturity, and she seemed satisfied that the numerous sacrifices she had made, most particularly regarding her own career, to maintain close contact with him as he grew up and went to school in Brooklyn and Chicago had been well worth it.

What I did not tell Whit until the time of his graduation was that I had received a Guggenheim Fellowship to spend the next year at the Center for Advanced Study in the Behavioral Sciences at Palo Alto. He congratulated me and said matter-of-factly that he had just about decided to spend the following year in Palo Alto taking some courses that he had missed during his undergraduate years. Consequently, we all looked forward to spending much time together.

At the end of the summer, prior to Whit's returning to Stanford for his postgraduate year, Rafael Loisson, Whit's French "brother," came to

Chicago for a visit. Rafael and Whit had been close friends since 1967, when Whit spent the summer in the Loisson household in Compiègne, France, to learn about life there and to improve his language skills. At the beginning of his visit, Rafael joined Whit, who was working with anthropologists at the University of Chicago in connection with the International Congress of Anthropological and Ethnological Sciences. Whit was thrilled to be working with such luminaries as Margaret Mead, Clifford Geertz, and Sol Tax, while Rafael was excited to be assisting in the translation from English to French, and vice versa. It was the beginning of Whit's achieving true bilingual fluency, which would be of great benefit to him in later years.

We would all be going to the West Coast in September 1973: Rafael accompanying Whit as he went for his postgraduate year at Stanford, and Aurelia and I for our long-anticipated year at the center. We had rented the home of Alan Mann on Mayfield Avenue in Palo Alto, which we found comfortable and convenient. The center, located in the hills south of town, proved to be an ideal place to complete my book on Southern travelers in the North. Aurelia settled into a round of activities with members of the faculty at Stanford and wives of fellows at the center. After a few days of visiting various parts of California, Rafael returned to France, and Whit enrolled in several courses in anthropology and African studies at the university.

The year went very well for all of us. I settled into my work with ease. I had brought my voluminous notes on Southern travelers with me, and what research materials I needed I could secure through either the library at Stanford or the library staff at the center. The fellows that year were an interesting lot, and I learned much from them at lunch, in private conversations, and in the talks that they gave concerning their work.

Having witnessed Whit's maturity, we wanted to be certain that we treated him as an adult and that he realized that we regarded him as such. Thus, after having him in our Palo Alto home for a few days, we suggested that he find an apartment of his own, which he was delighted to do. To be sure, we continued to take advantage of the fact that after four years of being separated by half a continent we could now see each other frequently, and he visited us several times each week. By then Whit was already an accomplished cook who prepared his own meals regularly, which was an additional reason to welcome him over once in a while to join us in preparing a meal together, just as had been our habit in Chicago. We also had a great deal to catch up on. Since I had made a point of not prying into his academic experiences while Whit was an undergraduate, I was delighted during that year to have him share with Aurelia and me what he had learned as a student, articulate where his interests lay, and begin to sketch what his plans for the future were. He was enjoying his courses and talked regularly about going to graduate school. Primarily we enjoyed each other's company, taking short trips together, going to orchid ranges, of which there were many in that part of California, and going to San Francisco to enjoy the numerous attractions of the big city.

The well-being of the family, so tangibly felt during our summer together in California, bespoke the end consequences of so many things so long in progress in all our lives. By 1973, I could honestly reflect that my ambition long ago stated to Dr. Shepard had been in some substantial measure fulfilled. The University of Chicago was so replete with academic talent that no one single professor could claim his reputation might stand synonymous for the school's, but every meaningful benchmark of scholarly attainment I had hoped for decades ago I could now claim to have substantially achieved. Despite the truth of that, however, I hardly felt complacent.

Over the past decades my achievements as a scholar had run parallel with and at times directly intersected with the nation's evolving race relations. But it was increasingly evident by the early 1970s that America's commitment to realizing true racial equality and race-blind justice might be reaching its high tide. President Nixon had been reelected by a landslide in 1972, with the Democratic contender, George McGovern, being found too liberal even for many traditional Democrats. And as has happened all too often in history, economic woes bolstered the forces of reaction. Starting in 1970, American unemployment began to rise, productivity to decline; in 1971 the dollar fell to its lowest level since 1949 and the United States posted its first trade deficit. A full-blown energy crisis set off by the decision of the Organization of Petroleum Exporting Countries (OPEC) in 1973 to embargo oil to the United States delivered a shock to the American economy and its sense of security. The forces of deindustrialization and what would be termed stagflation—inflation combined with unemployment—were afoot. And everywhere, the sense of possibility that had marked the late 1950s and early 1960s, and had fueled hopes and imaginations thereafter, was beginning to dim.

At the end of the year Whit joined us in Chicago and announced his plans to go to Senegal for a year before making a definitive decision about graduate studies. He thought that after a year he would be better able to pursue his objective of concentrating on some aspect of the role of France in Senegalese culture and civilization. We thought it an excellent idea and we pledged our support in every way possible. He made his plans to leave in the early autumn of 1974. Although I was attending a meeting in Philadelphia at the time of his scheduled departure, I left the meeting and went to New York to see him off. It was an emotional goodbye, but not what it would have been had we known what was to come. Whit would not be returning in one year but in eight, so profoundly taken was he with what he encountered in Senegal.

22

Reaching a Larger American Public

THE OPENING YEARS of the 1970s would provide a unique opportunity for me to speak to a wider American audience. In previous years I had addressed audiences regarding the intractable problem of race in the United States in many countries in virtually every part of the world: at the Salzburg Seminar in 1951 and 1958; at Cambridge University in 1954 and in the year of my Pitt Professorship there, 1962–63; in Australia in 1960; and in numerous countries in Europe, Africa, and Asia. Perhaps, with the beginning of a new decade, my fellow Americans were ready to have me share with them my views on the subject. Certainly, opportunities to do so came to me with far greater regularity. It could have been because they wished some diversion from Watergate, Vietnam, or the ups and downs of the economy. Regardless, I was ready. I had honed my views and skills in my "sideshow appearances" and was now ready for the "main tent."

The lecture opportunities that would come to me in the 1970s were hardly the first major public lectures I delivered in the United States. At Howard University, in December 1961, I had delivered the eighth annual Sidney Hillman Lectures. Choosing as my subject federal enforcement of civil rights, I spoke on "The Unfinished Beginning," "The Long, Dark

Night," and "The Threshold of Equality." In those lectures, given in Rankin Chapel before overflow audiences of more than five hundred, I discussed the rather unsuccessful post–Civil War attempts by the federal government to define and promote the enjoyment of civil rights by all citizens. Then I traced and examined the failure of these first efforts and the subsequent decline of interest on the part of the federal government in enforcing a constantly diminishing area of civil rights. Finally, I described and sought to explain the significant enlargement and more vigorous effort to enforce civil rights in the 1950s.

Much had changed since my Hillman lectures. But the changes were all too often merely cosmetic rather than fundamental. De jure racism had fallen, only to be replaced by de facto racism. The resistance to any significant modification of the age-old patterns of race relations seemed only to increase with every suggestion of real change. Some communities closed their public schools rather than desegregate them. Other communities left their public schools open but placed their white children in "Christian" academies or other private schools, at times receiving camouflaged public support to do so. Provisions for public housing, which greatly benefited lower-income African Americans, were often followed by the retreat of whites to the suburbs and a deterioration of public services supporting the neighborhoods where housing had been built. In many places in various parts of the country, the resistance to any changes in the old pattern of race relations was vigorous and, at times, violent.

During the academic year 1971–72, Louisiana State University invited me to give its esteemed Walter Lynwood Fleming Lectures, the publication of which was assured by the Louisiana State University Press. I agreed to offer them during the second week of April and selected as my subject Southern travelers in the antebellum North. This gave me an opportunity not only to display my scholarship to a largely all-white audience but also to indicate that an African American scholar could work in the mainstream of American history rather than be confined exclusively to subjects dealing with African Americans. During a year of research I had observed the intense interest of antebellum white Southerners in the cultural, social, educational, and business life in the North, and they seemed to enjoy visiting the region. Not only did they visit the North, but they sent their sons to be educated at West Point, the Naval Academy, and the region's "better colleges," such as Princeton, Yale, and Harvard. Some even sent their daughters North for "finishing."

My interest was not so much in what Southerners saw as how they reacted to what they saw. I sought to show that the antebellum South was not the feudal society so much recent scholarship claimed, but very much a part of a national American society and economy. What was more, it wished to be even more so, and this desire could not coexist with what other historians asserted was the region's firm conviction that it had no wish to emulate the North. If anything, their Northern travels persuaded Southerners that in pursuit of this greater national comity, their own way of life deserved defense, not condemnation, especially where race was concerned. Intentionally drawing parallels to the contemporary South, I underscored that these antebellum Southerners had no difficulty viewing themselves as both very much a part of the larger American society and at the same time living a unique, even superior way of life that should be understood, accepted, and appreciated.

In April 1973, Aurelia and I were in Argentina, where I was delivering the Lincoln Lectures commemorating the twenty-fifth anniversary of the Fulbright program. It was there that I received a cable from President Edward Levi telling me that I had been selected by a committee, which had canvassed the entire University of Chicago faculty for nominations, to deliver the first Nora and Edward Ryerson Lecture, which was to honor Edward Ryerson, a trustee of the university for forty-eight years, and his wife. Long interested in public policy issues, I decided to speak on "The Historian and Public Policy." Since I was already on a Guggenheim Fellowship at the center in Palo Alto, I easily set aside the time to prepare the lecture. I drew not only on the experience of historians in other fields but also on my own work in *Lyman Johnson v. the University of Kentucky* and *Brown v. Board of Education* to show how a historian could effectively influence the way legislatures and courts addressed society's problems. "It is the function of the historian," I said, "to keep before the people . . . the different lines of action they have taken, the several, often complicated reasons for such action . . . and to point to the defects and deficiencies when they exist." As the servant of the past, I concluded, the historian was a reliable source of information and strength on which to base a policy that looked toward the future.

The lecture was broadcast over some five hundred radio stations and was printed and reprinted several times by the university. I also delivered the lecture, more or less unchanged, before alumni groups and in East Asia as a part of the Fulbright-Lincoln Lectures.

Yet another invitation came in the fall of 1973, this one from Daniel Patrick Moynihan, the United States ambassador to India, whom I had met earlier at the University of Chicago. He had established what he called The Ambassador's Lecture in New Delhi, to which he invited about two hundred of the most influential citizens of India to hear an American scholar expound on some aspect of American public or foreign policy. Having heard of the arguments I presented in my Ryerson Lecture, he was convinced that such a statement could have a profound influence on American-Indian relations. Pat, who seemed to know everything, knew that I had no teaching duties during that year, and so he asked me to come and speak. I agreed, announcing my talk to be "American Scholars and Their Government."

Just before I left for New Delhi, I received a cable from Moynihan informing me that he had been called to Washington "to explain the P.L. 480 rupee agreement to three or four Congressional committees that would be considering it in early February." Since his invitation to me was personal, he gave me the opportunity to decline or postpone my visit. Too many arrangements had been made for me to drop out at such a late date, so I decided to keep to the agreed schedule.

From the time I arrived in New Delhi from Hyderabad, I was caught up in a whirl of official activities. In Pat Moynihan's absence, his wife, Liz, graciously assumed full responsibility for my welfare. She gave a dinner for me at Roosevelt House, the embassy residence, and arranged for me to see the Presidential Gardens. Prominent Indians and friends in the city invited me to other activities. My principal responsibility, however, was to deliver my lecture at the India International Center.

The audience, presided over by my old friend Jim Roach, the cultural attaché, was large and attentive. I discussed the historical evolution of big government, indicating how the early view of national political leadership was of a president who was self-made and largely independent. This, in turn, encouraged Americans to regard the president as all-knowing, even all-powerful, and capable of acting unilaterally. As a matter of fact, that was seldom if ever the case, and as government grew and became more complex, it was less and less the case. Indeed, governmental bureaucracy grew because the responsibilities of government grew enormously, and consequently the president became more and more dependent on specialists to assist him in managing the state. This led, inevitably, to the employment of an increasing number of scholars, heading up certain agencies and advising the president. The danger lay in an excessive reliance on people whose focus was so narrow that they failed to see the larger picture. Were that to occur, the scholar might dictate policy rather than more appropriately advise in its formulation. To be sure, the scholar was indispensable to our complex political structure, but politicians and public servants were necessary to make certain that constraints ensured the correct use of the expert's training and talents.

More and more, whether in Chicago or New Delhi, I felt an expectation to make some pronouncement about the role of the scholar in society. As someone who had repeatedly bridged that divide, I was not uncomfortable with the request. Indeed, I began to feel that I had a duty to speak out in matters affecting the scholar and, in turn, in matters affecting the larger community. As this instinct pushed me closer to the role of an activist, I made a greater effort to distinguish between activism, with all of its possibilities, and implementation, which might push me into the quite different arena of policy enforcement.

In February 1975, I received a letter from Ronald Berman, chairman of the National Endowment for the Humanities, informing me that the NEH had voted to invite me to be the fifth Jefferson Lecturer in the Humanities. I was, of course, greatly honored and accepted with pleasure. This invitation placed me in the company of Lionel Trilling, Erik Erikson, Robert Penn Warren, and Paul Freund, the four previous Jefferson Lecturers. To the pressure of such august company was added the fact that the year of my lecture was the bicentennial of the Declaration of Independence, an appropriate time to say something about the declaration's author whose name also graced the endowment's lectureship. I would not, of course, focus merely on Jefferson, but rather I intended to be fair to him and, at the same time, do justice to the period in which he was a key player.

I decided to deliver a sufficient number of lectures to give some indication that they were national in thrust and significance. Instead of merely one lecture in Washington, as my predecessors had done, I would give at least three: one in Washington, another in Chicago, and a final one in San Francisco. Press coverage, even before the lectures were delivered, was extensive. Upon my arrival in Washington for the first lecture, there was a full press conference in the offices of the National Endowment, with major representation from the print and broadcast media. There was to be similar coverage in Chicago and San Francisco.

In Washington's Constitution Hall, I delivered the first lecture before a crowd of approximately three thousand. With the general subject for the three lectures given as "Racial Equality in America," the Washington segment was called "The Dream Deferred." In it I said that for three centuries, black people had aspired to the equality for which all Americans fought and died during the American Revolution. In those early struggles for independence and sovereignty, blacks had had to plead for an opportunity to fight for their country. I also voiced the opinion that it was most unfortunate that in its final draft, the Declaration of Independence said nothing about the widespread practice of trading in human flesh and holding human beings in perpetual bondage. I could not avoid the observation that Jefferson's antipathy toward slavery never reached the point of freeing his own slaves or using his enormous prestige to oppose the peculiar institution "unequivocally in word or deed." In this he had hardly been unique, of course. Once patriots gained their own freedom from Britain, they were overwhelmingly unwilling to extend that freedom to their slaves. Even worse, the ideology of the revolutionary movement did not extend to blacks, whether slave or free. The new dispensation did not permit them to vote, hold office, or serve in the military as equals. Even in the nation's new capital, free blacks were reminded of their degraded position as they were ineligible to be mayor, sit on the board of aldermen or the common council, or vote, the franchise being restricted to white males.

In discussing Jefferson, I reviewed not only his ambivalent attitude toward slavery but also his self-serving doubts about the intellectual honesty of blacks. When Benjamin Banneker, the African American astronomer and mathematician, sent Jefferson a copy of his almanac, he was blunt enough to recommend that Jefferson "and all others . . . wean yourselves from those narrow prejudices which you have imbibed." Jefferson, meanwhile, was indiscreet enough to write his friend Joel Barlow, impugning

Banneker's work as "not without suspicion" of having received the assistance of his white friend Andrew Ellicott. Jefferson's first reaction to the poems of Phillis Wheatley, the black servant who had dedicated poems to the Reverend George Whitfield and George Washington, was that they had been written "under her name," that in any case she was not a poet, and finally that "of all men I am the last who should undertake to decide as to the merits of poetry."

I concluded the lecture by observing that, whether it was in the struggle for independence from Britain or in the fight for equal opportunity in the middle of the twentieth century, the dream for blacks was always deferred. What, I asked, happens to a dream deferred? Quoting from Langston Hughes's poem, I answered, "Maybe it just sags like a heavy load. *Or does it explode?*"

The lecture was followed by a black-tie dinner in the Pan American Union Building's Hall of Americas. There were many out-of-town guests, including my sister Mozella and her husband, Waldo Jones. (My sister Anne, who lived in Washington, was there too of course). President Edward Levi of the University of Chicago and his wife, Kate, led a considerable contingent from the university. The mayor of the city, Walter Washington, and his wife, Bennetta, were present, as were some members of Congress. The national media, of course, were there in force.

That night and after, the lecture drew mixed reactions. Some believed that I should not have criticized Jefferson in a lecture named in his honor. Those who were perhaps equivocal about its contents found it "interesting." Among the unequivocal were the authors of several letters calling me unspeakable names. One writer said that America's great mistake was bringing blacks out of Africa in the first place, since they did not appreciate the white man's efforts and could not assimilate satisfactorily anyway. A large number of those in attendance, however, later praised me for what I had said. And some of the letters I received provided sufficient praise to persuade me that, controversy notwithstanding, I should continue in the same vein.

On May 5 I delivered the second lecture, "The Old Order Changeth Not." Approximately one thousand people came to Prudential Hall in downtown Chicago to hear my talk. I reviewed the nation's racial problems, beginning in 1820. I pointed out that racism so permeated nineteenth-century American society that even those who spoke out against slavery had frequently barred black people from membership in their antislavery societies. Over that extended century, whenever and wherever the matter arose, the nature and urgency of the problem, the underlying assumptions made about it, and the difficulties thrown in the way of resolving it satisfactorily, were amazingly similar.

I spoke of the conflict, dominated by race, that led to the Civil War and of the postwar era, again dominated by race. The argument that blacks were inferior to whites thoroughly informed the debate over the black man's place in a free society both before and after the Civil War. In 1865, President Lincoln hoped that the two races could "gradually lift themselves out of their old relation to each other and both come out better prepared for the new." It was a forlorn hope.

In the last four decades of the nineteenth century, nothing occurred to challenge the principle of racial inequality. In the North, whites were eager to return to "business as usual," while in the South they were willing to admit that slavery was dead but not that Congress had the power to enforce principles and practices of equality for the former slaves. Gradually, the position of black people in the United States reached what Rayford W. Logan has called "the nadir," when the betrayal of the Negro was complete, accompanied not only by bloody race riots but also by the most remarkable display of racial arrogance, bigotry, and inequality that the country had ever witnessed. Worse still, the doctrine of "separate but equal," set forth in *Plessy v. Ferguson*, provided constitutional support for segregation, discrimination, and humiliation. The old order had indeed not changed! I concluded the lecture by quoting from the poem "Copper Sun" by Countee Cullen, whose last lines read: "So in the dark we hide the heart that bleeds, / And wait, and tend our agonizing needs."

Despite the fact that I spoke of some of the darkest days in the history of the country, nothing in the second lecture struck as raw a nerve as the first lecture did. Perhaps because no historical figure mentioned was comparable to Jefferson, who enjoyed virtual beatification. Following that first lecture, someone had written to warn me that whatever I might say was all right as long as I did not speak unkindly of "his" Jefferson.

The second lecture was again followed by a black-tie dinner, this time at the Mid-America Club and attended by about two hundred people.

Chicago was, of course, home turf, and Aurelia and I enjoyed ourselves immensely. At the end of the dinner, Ronald Berman; Lawrence Towner, director of the Newberry Library; and Frederick Burkhardt spoke. Also present and speaking were Frank Thompson, of the U.S. House of Representatives, and David Matthews, secretary of health, education and welfare. The big surprise of the evening, however, was the presentation to me by Carolyn Moore of the *Phalaenopsis John Hope Franklin*, an orchid that had been bred by Hermann Pigors, owner of Oak Hill Gardens, and registered in my name. I was rendered practically speechless.

The show then moved to San Francisco on May 26 for the third and final lecture, which was to be delivered in the grand ballroom of the Fairmont Hotel. It was titled "Equality Indivisible." In it I sought to indicate the major areas of American life where the problem of racial equality was essentially "the story of the struggle to divide a privilege or a right whose indivisibility would become more and more apparent." For example, in the political sphere, the practice of excluding Negroes from the franchise had become a fine art as well as a nearly perfected practice until the passage of the Voting Rights Act in 1964. The picture was virtually the same in employment, housing, social services, education, public accommodations—wherever whites and blacks came into contact with each other.

It was not until after World War II that America began to pay attention to black protests and the strong indictment made by President Truman's 1947 Committee on Civil Rights. A decade after the Truman Committee had completed its task, Congress had created the Commission on Civil Rights, which was followed in 1964 by the Civil Rights Act and, in the following year, by the Voting Rights Act. The latter two acts led to dramatic increases in the number of black voters and ultimately black elected public officials. By this time, moreover, the courts had become more responsive. In case after case involving education, housing, transportation, civil rights, and voting, the federal judiciary handed down a series of decisions that greatly encouraged black Americans as well as all Americans seeking racial equality.

In my concluding statement I said that it is difficult to imagine or to assess what the experience of three centuries of inequality had done to American Negroes. In the eighteenth century, they had witnessed the shaping of a revolutionary doctrine of equality that was deliberately and systematically denied to them even as they fought to secure it for all white Americans. In the nineteenth century, they witnessed the tortured justification of racial inequality on the basis of doctrines that were as widely accepted as they were bizarre. In the twentieth century, they participated to incremental advantage in two world wars fought against the twin evils of totalitarianism and racism. I concluded by pointing out that more than anything else, Americans need to recognize that equality is indeed indivisible. We must abandon the futile policy of trying to divide it and adhere to the policy of sharing it.

In keeping with how I had ended the two previous lectures, I quoted from A. W. Thomas:

Then speed the day and haste the hour,
Break down the barriers, gain the power
To use the land and sail the sea,
To hold the tools, unchecked and free . . .
Be free! Set free!
Democracy! Democracy!

Even before heading off for San Francisco, I was deep into conversations with the University of Chicago Press about publishing the Jefferson Lectures. Since the press had copies of all three lectures before I delivered them, and since there were very few revisions I wished to make and the text proved to need little editing, *Racial Equality in America* was promptly published in October 1976. In addition, the lectures were broadcast over National Public Radio, with commentaries on other radio stations, and were the subject of numerous newspaper editorials. The coverage was, perhaps, as much as or more than the National Endowment had anticipated. Nathan Kroll, a distinguished musician in his own right, assumed the unenviable task of taping all the lectures and preparing them for distribution as well as for a permanent record.

Through the Jefferson Lectures, I had given Americans an opportunity to reflect on the history of race relations over some three centuries. It was not a pretty picture, but I believe it was both fair and accurate. I was flattered when my audience praised me, but I was not distressed when they disagreed with what I said. I had had an opportunity to share my views widely, and for that I was appreciative. Meanwhile, listeners and readers would, I hoped, reflect on America's distant and immediate past.

Now was an ideal time for national reflections. Nixon had been relieved of his duties as president in 1974, the Vietnam War had raged, virtually out of hand, until the last American troops left in 1973, and most recently Boston had yet again erupted into riots over court-ordered busing. On the one hand, by the time the nation was observing its bicentennial, some Americans were satisfied that the racial climate had improved. After all, blacks were gaining power in city halls, in state legislatures, and even in the halls of Congress. The rawest racial violence, such as preceded the Voting Rights Act, had receded. Yet, one wondered if it was the calm preceding a storm.

23

Winding Down—Somewhat

O F ALL THE YEARS of my life, 1976 was, without question, the
very busiest. To a full teaching schedule, I had, of course, added
the time-consuming, three-part Jefferson Lectures. Even before
those lectures, I gave several public addresses in various universities and
cities: Fort Lauderdale; Beaumont, Texas; and Boston, to name a few. I
had also accepted an invitation to participate in the University of Pennsylvania's second annual Spring Symposium on African American Studies to
be held in March. I was by then far enough along in my research on the pioneer African American historian George W. Williams that I spoke on the
subject, and I was greatly encouraged by my audience's response. I also
spoke that month to a group of young black and white civic, educational,
and professional leaders calling themselves the Chicago Forum, who
wished to hear a different view of the bicentennial from what was generally set forth. In April, I went to the Los Angeles Valley College to lecture
again on Williams. May found me delivering the Solomon Fuller Lecture
at the annual meeting of the American Psychiatric Association. In June I
spoke at the annual dinner of the Chicago University chapter of Phi Beta
Kappa, and a few days later I was off to Springfield, Illinois, to discuss the
history of discrimination in employment and the role of the federal gov-

ernment in eliminating violations under the Equal Employment Opportunity Commission before the state Bureau of Manpower Development. In July, Aurelia and I went to Trinidad and Tobago for two lectures, returning in time for the annual National Urban League conference in Boston.

Shortly after the fall term began, I was off again. In October, I accepted an invitation to lecture at Sacramento State University. I was invited by the Ethnic Studies Center there to give a lecture that I had given before, "Toward a Second American Revolution," which, with variations, turned out to be my signature lecture for the bicentennial year. A few days later I repeated it at De Anza College in Cupertino, California.

I reminded my audiences that neither the American Revolution nor the so-called Second Reconstruction had extended the fundamental protections and rights to African Americans that they claimed to extend. "When a group of people three thousand miles away becomes immersed in conflict, for whatever reason, this nation has on numerous occasions found constitutional and legal justifications for intervening and providing guns, tanks, and all kinds of sophisticated weaponry. But when a Negro family moves into a Chicago suburb such as Cicero or Berwyn or some other so-called white section of the city—any city—we as a nation experience constitutional and legal paralysis. And there are no guns or tanks or even a squad car to protect that family from the barbarians who view blacks as a menace to their civilization." I then pointed out that despite the American revolutionaries' early reluctance to use blacks in the patriot army, George Washington finally relented, perhaps out of desperation, and sent them into battle. Consequently, a German soldier remarked in 1778 that "no regiment is to be seen in which there are not Negroes in abundance; and among them are able-bodied, strong, and brave fellows." That blacks had bled for the birth of the nation yet had enjoyed none of the resulting liberties was proof enough that our founding fathers had no deep and abiding interest in any meaningful idea of freedom.

In concluding, I said, "We need a new declaration, a declaration in favor of the rights of all men . . . We need a new commitment to a more perfect union, one in which some are not more equal than others. We need a new adherence to the principles of equality. We need a new American Revolution that will create a new ideology of comradeship in the great enterprise of building a society in which every man and woman can face tomorrow unencumbered by the burdens of the past or the prejudices of the present. This calls for a revolution in the heart and soul of every American. That is what the first American Revolution did not have . . . This is what the New American Revolution must have."

During that busy year, radio and television claimed some of my attention. In February I appeared on the *Today* show and talked about African American history. In April I participated in another television show, *Perspectives*, and in May, to observe the thirtieth anniversary of the Fulbright program, I taped a radio program, "Conversations at Chicago," with a group of Fulbright alumni. There were, moreover, radio and television interviews in connection with the Jefferson Lectures in all three cities where I spoke.

My services to the national government also continued. In July 1976, President Gerald Ford appointed me to a six-year term on the National Council on the Humanities. Among many other duties and responsibilities, the council selected the Jefferson lecturer; it was to be my privilege to participate in the selection of my successor.

I was sixty-one in 1976 and working at full tilt. Yet even then I began to perceive, somewhat dimly, that I could not keep up this pace indefinitely. Indeed, although I thoroughly enjoyed what I was doing and even felt that I was simultaneously making a contribution to the field of history and to the public discourse on race as never before, it became increasingly clear that I might accomplish even more if I adopted a somewhat slower pace. My energy was undiminished and I had no desire to rest on laurels, but I also sensed a need for a change.

The entire Franklin family enjoyed the city of Chicago, admiring it especially for a vitality apparent even to the most insensitive visitor. So memorably captured by Carl Sandburg and a host of others, that vigor was as real when we lived there as at any time in the city's past. It could be seen in the way the city recovered from natural disasters, most memorable for us being the blizzard of 1967. It could be seen in the civic spirit so apparent in virtually every local organization. I saw it manifested over and over again in the Commercial Club, where banker after banker and merchant after merchant provided yet another vision for a "New Chicago" with a confidence that, in itself, was awe-inspiring.

We loved the city and the university, and we thoroughly enjoyed them to the fullest. But there was *the weather*! Having lived in relatively warm climates all of our lives, Aurelia and I did not complain of Chicago's hot summers. The spring and autumn months were lovely. What we could not accustom ourselves to were the winters. I was in North Carolina during the blizzard of 1967, but I clearly remember Whit's response when I called to see how the family was managing and made the suggestion that the bird feeders in the backyard should be kept full so that the birds would not be deprived. He replied that they could not even open the back door because the snow had them blocked in.

It was Chicago's consistently bitter winter weather that made life for us there so trying. I have always suspected that Whit's choice of Stanford had much to do with California's mild climate. After Aurelia's mother came to live with us, she virtually hibernated during the winter months. Aurelia seemed to endure the cold weather better than the rest of us, but toleration is a far cry from enjoyment.

I had no intention whatsoever of leaving the university before the retirement age of sixty-five. By the same token, I had no intention of remaining after that. For several years I had watched colleagues who were approaching sixty-five go to their mailboxes with the hopes that they would discover an extension of their contracts beyond the mandatory retirement age, and I was not pleased at their silent supplication. I had hoped that I would be prepared, psychologically and financially, to leave when my time came in 1980. Consequently, when President Levi and the Board of Trustees did in fact offer me an unsought extension, complete with a heartfelt request that I not turn them down, I was so flattered that I felt compelled to accept. The moment I did so, however, I regretted it and began to wonder how I could politely break the agreement.

In 1978 I experienced my first real health challenge. In the spring of that year, I noticed an increasing overall weakness that I could not explain. One day, when I continued to feel so weak that I feared that I would faint, I decided to consult my physician, Dr. Quentin Young. He took one look at me, checked my pulse and blood pressure, and decided that I should go directly from his office to Michael Reese Hospital, where I was received curbside by an orderly with a wheelchair. Dr. Young was certain that I was losing blood at a rapid rate, and he ordered transfusions immediately. The examinations confirmed what he suspected, that I had an ulcer, serious enough to require a week's hospital stay. It was sobering to have my first hospital experience at age sixty-three. Dr. Young and his colleagues had no difficulty in persuading me that in order to recover fully I should change my diet and significantly reduce all stress-generating activities. I obeyed their orders and returned to robust health in due course. Nevertheless, the experience stiffened my resolve to retire at sixty-five.

I spent much of my time during the next several years searching for the best way to leave the university gracefully. In January and February 1979, the winter was as fierce as any that I could remember. One morning when I went out to get the paper from the porch, I saw only the tops of automobiles parked on the street. It would be days before the street was cleared of snow. Several days later, when I again went to the porch to retrieve the newspaper, I began to navigate the icy first step and before I knew what was happening I had slipped and landed on the sidewalk! By that time I was prepared to stand my ground against any counterarguments over the necessity of our leaving the Windy City.

When I took up the matter with Aurelia, she wanted to know only when we should start packing, especially after I told her that I truly wished to return to North Carolina. She was certain that her mother would be happy to see us move to *her* home state; although she had been born in Pittsburgh, she had lived in North Carolina for more than fifty years. When we communicated our plans to Whit, still in Senegal, he did not regret our leaving Chicago's weather, but he could not understand why we wanted to live in Durham. Convincing Whit of the wisdom of our choice, however, was secondary to explaining my decision to the university's president, Hanna Gray, who had replaced Edward Levi in 1978.

Toward the end of April 1979, I summoned sufficient courage to write to Hanna, asking her to relieve me of my agreement, made with Edward Levi in 1975, to hold the John Matthews Manly Professorship until 1983. I told her that my recent illness had forced me to confront mortality in a way that I had never done before. "There are several research and writing projects that I desperately wish to complete," I said, "and I need more time than I could possibly have here, where I am persuaded—as you well know—that professors should *not* be part-time." I referred to our Hyde

Park home as one of the loveliest in the area, but a three-story Victorian town house was not an abode in which to grow old. "What we want at this stage are fewer stairs and a bit more space, and a somewhat less rigorous climate."

Following her receipt of my letter, Hanna and I had several long talks. When she saw how determined I was, she relented and we agreed that formally I would take a leave of absence for two years, understanding that I would retire at the end of that time. "I don't know what we, or the University, will be like without you," she wrote after the decision was reached, "and I hope you know what your presence has meant to us, and the University, not only in terms of the distinctive and extraordinary contribution and service you have brought to this institution, but also through the wisdom and character and exemplary humanity which you radiate." She concluded with the personal observation, "And I hope you also know what a joy it is to be your colleague, and how very grateful I have been for that over the years, as now."

In April 1979, I visited the National Humanities Center in Durham to speak at the dedication of its newly constructed building. A private, not-for-profit institute dedicated to the importance of the humanities in American society, the center is literally one of a kind in this country. I commended the supporters of the center for the vision they displayed in providing a place where the humanities would be studied in much the same way that the social sciences and hard sciences were studied elsewhere. The future of the nation would be secure, I asserted, if this was an indication of the great respect and commitment that even a segment of our society held for the liberal arts. During that visit, Charles Frankel, who was to be in charge of the newly opened center, and I discussed my coming there following my retirement, with him urging me to do so. Since I was determined to leave Chicago, the Mellon Senior Fellowship that he dangled before me was attractive indeed. I delayed my final agreement until I had an opportunity to discuss it with Aurelia, but within a month Frankel and I "shook hands" over the telephone. In that I was to receive an honorary degree from UNC Chapel Hill in just two days, we made plans to meet locally and finalize the details.

Aurelia and I were met at the Raleigh-Durham airport by our longtime friend John R. Larkins, director of Negro Welfare in North Carolina. He was to take us to the National Humanities Center. Sadly, he first had to greet us with truly shocking news. Robbers had murdered our friends the Frankels in their Westchester, New York, home the day before. As all of us wrestled with our sudden grief, we went through the exercise of affirming the arrangements I had made previously with Frankel. I would be a senior Mellon fellow for two years, with a third year to be mutually determined during the second year. I would have two rooms, and my full-time secretary, Margaret Fitzsimmons, would be retained at the salary she was receiving when she left the University of Chicago. We did not remain long at the center, and after the ceremonies at Chapel Hill ended, we returned to Chicago. Despite the shock over our friends' utterly unexpected deaths, we remained firm in the belief that our decision to move to North Carolina was a wise one.

The word was soon out that 1979–80 would be my final year at the University of Chicago. My time became even less my own. There were those who were determined to extract the last bit of service and energy out of me while I was still at the university and, as it happened, still president of the American Historical Association. I got a running start in the spring of 1979, during the observances of the twenty-fifth anniversary of *Brown v. Board of Education*. On May 17, the actual anniversary day, Aurelia and I attended a White House reception commemorating the anniversary. We were warmly greeted by President and Mrs. Carter, whom we had met earlier at a state dinner for President Daniel Arap Moi of Kenya. I had also been associated with President Carter shortly after his inauguration, when he appointed me to his Advisory Board on Ambassadorial Appointments. It was at that point that I began to admire him greatly. His insistence that people representing the United States in foreign countries should have done more to earn that responsibility than contribute a portion of their fortunes to a political victory was revolutionary. Once more I congratulated him for this wisdom and foresight and expressed the hope that his successors would follow his lead. (Incidentally, as of 2005, none of them had done so.)

Without question, my most demanding task as president of the American Historical Association entailed visiting the People's Republic of China. Since 1949, the United States and Communist China had not experienced normal diplomatic relations. With the collapse of the latter's so-called Cultural Revolution in 1976, however, the two countries began to encourage better, more open communications with each other. An early result of those efforts was the decision to establish an agency in China and one in the United States to facilitate an exchange of ideas and scholars. So it was that the Chinese Scientific and Technical Association authorized the World History Research Institute of the Chinese Academy of Social Sciences to extend an invitation to me to lecture in the People's Republic in the autumn of 1979. I was encouraged to lecture both on the state of historical research and writing in the United States and more broadly on what had been happening in American historiography since 1949. I accepted the invitation with pleasure and in late October flew from Chicago to Tokyo, eventually arriving at the airport in China's capital, Peking, where I received a very warm welcome from representatives of Peking University, the World History Institute, and the Bureau of Foreign Affairs.

I delivered the first of four lectures in Peking at the International Club. More than one hundred people, including several from universities and provinces outside Peking, heard me speak on "Recent Trends in Historiography in the United States." While someone translated my comments at the end of each paragraph, I was pleasantly surprised to discover that a considerable number of the listeners understood English. At the end of the lecture, the questions and comments lasted for more than a half hour, and it was quite clear to me that interest in United States history was high. The audience's curiosity was also clearly not expressed for form's sake. Their interest was substantial and their willingness to pursue a line of argument more than evident. Several of my listeners expressed their desire to talk to me further, and I told them that I would be delighted to do so. Following the formal end of lectures, crowds lingered as individuals came up to ask questions, and when it could be arranged I met with people outside of the lecture halls.

On November 1, I lectured on "Historians and the Black Movement." Whereas previously, questions had been confined to matters of historiography and fields of history, the questions that followed this lecture revealed my listeners' intense interest in the American government's racial policy and radical or deviant facets of the black movement such as the Black Panthers and the Black Muslims. Equally notable was what they did not ask me about, namely, the NAACP, the Urban League, or even the Southern Christian Leadership Conference. I warned them that they would get a better picture of African American aspirations as well as organizational activities if they broadened their canvass to include a wider variety of civic, religious, and fraternal groups. Unable to answer all of the questions within the allotted time, I promised to continue the discussion with anyone who wished to see me following the close of the meeting.

I gave the final lecture on "Historians and the United States Bicentennial." I traced briefly the way historians took note of national anniversaries in the United States and how observances gave us an opportunity to review our history from new and different perspectives. It was well received, and afterward I answered questions left over from the previous lecture as well as those raised by the current lecture.

Although I saw some sights and attended some cultural exhibitions in between lectures, my sightseeing in Peking came afterward, by which time I was pleased to play the tourist. The people, the Great Wall, and the meals were all impressive. Indeed, the latter were notable for their frank interest in America and their willingness to discuss the recent history of Communist China and even be critical of it. All of this was in marked contrast to what I had encountered during my visit to Soviet Russia in 1970. Thus, it was with nearly no time to rest that I was off for my scheduled lecture tour to other parts of this magnificent country.

As had been the case in Peking, I had sent the lectures to Wuhan, my next stop, so that they could be translated in advance. For my first lecture, "Recent Trends in Historiography in the United States," the crowd of about 150 welcomed me warmly. A lively session of questions and discussion followed my talk, during which my listeners made clear their desire to know more about the New Left School, made up of historians and other scholars who were critical of American society and who viewed it from a socialist or communist perspective. I replied that the New Left School was not very new and not very left. They also asked about American interest in Marxism and other Marxist-influenced interpretations of history. Growing more specific, they requested factual data regarding slavery, the role of blacks in the nation's wars, and more about the methods of the Schlesinger Sr. type of social historian in contrast to the more recent social historians.

I gave my second and final lecture in Wuhan on November 15 on "Historians and the Black Movement." The questions were, on the whole, good, but after a series of questions about William Z. Foster, Malcolm X, and the Black Panthers, I commented that some members of the audience were understandably interested in such people and should continue to learn more about them. I warned them, however, that if they studied those persons exclusively, they would run the risk of knowing very little about what had been happening to African Americans since World War II.

I soon had the chance to expand on this point. One morning, the vice chairman of Wuhan University's Department of History, the director of the American History Research Group, and two of his young colleagues together with my interpreter, Zhang Yu-jiu, called on me; for more than three hours we discussed African American history. Most of their questions centered on the period from 1945 to the Black Power movement in the late '60s. I pointed out that arguably the most seminal civil rights leader, Martin Luther King Jr., had been assassinated in 1968, and that the most dramatic objectives achieved were the passage of the Civil Rights Act of 1964 and the Voting Rights Act of 1965. Thereafter, the character of the movement had changed as a new set of objectives, primarily economic, became more sharply defined. Achieving these objectives called not so much for demonstrations as for negotiation, mediation, and focused challenges to government and private-sector employment policies, for one example.

I made the point that the civil rights movement was not dead but quite different. We talked about the Black Belt and the concept of the Negro population as a colony, a view against which I argued; about their understanding of King's assertion that the United States should reform itself by adopting the principles of communism and socialism (news to me!); and the current state of political power among blacks. I was struck by the fact that while they knew even the obscure utterances of black radicals, such as Angela Davis, they were not aware that the mayors of Atlanta and New Orleans were African American.

I believe that I learned at least as much from the Chinese scholars about the twists and turns American historiography can take as they did from the information and interpretations I gave them. I was amazed to dis-

cover from their inquiries that they knew a great deal about Herbert
Aptheker but very little about the Negro History Movement and such
larger-than-life characters as Carter G. Woodson, Charles Wesley, and
Rayford Logan. The knew a great deal about W.E.B. Du Bois, but only as
a critic of the U.S. government. They were particularly familiar with the
famous episode resulting in the seizure of his passport, namely, his visit to
the People's Republic of China in 1959. But they knew almost nothing
about the rise of black studies in the United States, already in 1979 a major
addition to the curriculum of many American colleges and universities.

I told them as clearly and as forcefully as I could that to truly understand recent African American history they should watch political developments. I mentioned the election of black mayors in American cities,
large and small, and pointed at the national increase in the number of
blacks on school boards, in state legislatures, and even in the lower house
of Congress. America's racial picture was not rosy, but one needed the
facts, which many of them lacked, in order to make an appraisal of just
how cloudy it was. It was also personally painful to see how far my Chinese colleagues were from what I valued as the professional scholar's ethos
of a catholic interest in and studied objectivity before the facts. I could
only hope that in due course they would be able to achieve a broad understanding and appreciation for every facet of the ongoing African American
struggle for equality and tolerance so long wanting in the American spirit
as well as in American practice. Scholarship has without question a role to
play in the steady advance of respect for our universal human dignity, requiring open and free inquiry and a commitment to unbiased teaching and
training. It is the profession's finest calling, a point I undertook to make in
Canton, my final stop before leaving China.

My thinking on the state of historical studies and professionalism was
no doubt influenced in some measure by the death of my friend, mentor,
and earnest advocate, Ted Currier. On July 29, 1979, Currier had called
me from his home in Maine, wondering when I would be arriving for my
annual visit. I would be there in about two weeks, I said; delighted, he responded by saying he was looking forward to seeing me more than ever.
The following morning, I received a call from our mutual friends, Allen
and Maryetta Maxwell. At that moment, I knew. I said to them, "Don't tell
me!" "Yes," they replied. I asked when it had happened. They said that

when they had gone to pick him up to take him to see his physician, they had found him cold, a severe look on his face. He had passed away, presumably during the night, sometime after talking with me. They knew that I would come as soon as I could, not only because he was my dearest friend but also because I was to be the administrator of his estate. I flew up the following day.

Currier had spent forty-five years at Fisk, during which he had profoundly influenced hundreds of students. Most of the time, he was the only person teaching history, thereby saving the institution many thousands of dollars but also assuring his enormous influence over the entire student body. His reward was the large number of prominent and influential citizens, across all walks of life, who had found early inspiration in his classroom. As a young professor he had the energy and the interest to pursue research and writing as well as teaching. Yet he spurned lucrative offers from publishers and invitations to teach elsewhere because of his deep commitment to his work at Fisk, which for him had become the only meaningful life. He had given it literally everything he had.

Those of us who studied with him marveled at his mastery of the several fields he covered in his teaching. One hour he would be deeply involved in the problems of Russia's Peter the Great, and in the very next hour he would be expounding on the nuances that marked the differences among the republics of nineteenth-century Latin America. One day he would be concerned with the defects in the machinery of international peacekeeping agencies, and later that same day he would lead his students through a searching and critical analysis of the *Federalist Papers*. Important in his role as teacher was his manifestation of a profound confidence in the student's capacity to grow toward an intellectual maturity where he or she could perform at the very highest level. It could surprise others, but it did not surprise him, that one of his students became solicitor general of the United States, another became general counsel for General Motors, and that many others were successful lawyers, historians, and public servants. When he sent me to Harvard in 1935 with money he borrowed from a Nashville bank, there was no intimation that my intellectual experience in graduate school would differ in any significant way from what I already had enjoyed at Fisk. And he was right, for nothing at Harvard surpassed the intellectual rigor to which I had been exposed in his classes. His belief, moreover, in honesty, integrity, high professional standards, and loyalty to ethical principles and supporting institutions was the hallmark of his academic statesmanship.

Although I had much to do and much to think about, my experience in China gave me ample opportunity to think about Ted Currier and what he meant not only to me but to the very ideal of true and dedicated scholarship. If the profession of history had wandered off the path, as I felt that some practitioners in China and the United States gave evidence of, Ted Currier was, to me, a perfect and poignant example of one man who utterly fulfilled the ethos of research, teaching, scholarship, and a profound participation in civic life, through the lives he inspired and changed. I would miss him terribly.

That final year at Chicago, I was invited to deliver several spring commencement addresses, but without question the most meaningful was the one I gave at the University of Chicago on the eve of my departure. The preceding November, Hanna Gray had invited me to be the speaker at the spring convocation on June 13 and 14, 1980. Since most members of the university community knew that I was retiring at the end of the spring term, perhaps they regarded this final address of mine as something of a valedictory. I certainly did, and I put much time and thought into the twelve and a half minutes that Hanna had allowed me.

My subject was "Clio's Vision," and I began by pointing out that Hesiod, the Greek poet, referred to Clio, the muse of history, as the "proclaimer." Customarily concerned with the past, Clio was known for looking backward, not forward. However, as one of her proclaimers for more than forty years, and as a historian taking leave of his formal teaching responsibilities, on this occasion I would dare to think of Clio as having a vision of the future. This might even be fitting, since Clio had not proved very successful in teaching us the lessons of the past.

"Two centuries ago," I began, "we . . . fought a war for independence and freedom, but we did so while holding fast to human bondage, which was infinitely worse and more despicable than any form of political subordination . . . We hobbled through the ensuing seventy-five years getting deeper into an impossible rationalization for the maintenance of slavery. In expanding our territory in the middle of the nineteenth century, we despoiled the rights of our neighbor to the south and created a legacy of distrust and suspicion that has clouded the relations of the two countries from that day to this." I went on to point out that in the twentieth century we fought the First World War to make the world safe for democracy, and in its wake there emerged some of the most inhumane practices the world has ever seen, in the form of Italian fascism and German Nazism. A generation later we fought another war to preserve the Four Freedoms, but at that war's end we witnessed the suppression of personal and religious freedom in many places, most notably Stalinism abroad and McCarthyism at home.

I would be the first to admit, I said, that some good was emerging. Organizations and individuals sought to assist the helpless and the powerless, while some governments sought to mete out justice and economic resources. I would hope that Clio, resting firmly on her vast knowledge of the past, might state clearly and unequivocally the implications of past events for the future. She might point out that the deeds that nations and peoples commit in the name of civilization are, as often as not, misdeeds, and the scars of the misdeeds often have virtual permanence. History was replete with examples. "When one nation enslaves another people for the ostensible purpose of civilizing them, that nation merely reveals its own barbarity and invites the eternal wrath of the enslaved. When one nation assists another in gaining its independence and then is the first to exploit the fledgling nation, not only were the older nation's motives devoid of altruism, but its future unhappy relations with the new nation had already been predetermined by its crude and selfish conduct. When a nation's armed forces attack and bomb an innocent people in the name of . . . outflanking some formidable enemy, it invites the scorn of the victims as well as the bystanders."

I suggested that Clio must watch with interest, even distress, as she observes the world's refusal to heed the lessons of history. "Over and over again she has recounted with pain how and why the peoples of the world have, on occasion, acted more like lower animals than human beings . . . It is about time that we took a careful look at what I call Clio's vision of the future, her view of the consequences that will inevitably flow from our experiences and activities in the past and present. From where Clio sits the vision of the future is not bright . . . She invites the Classes of 1980 not to wring their hands in despair or to make simple gestures of apology . . . but to be as active as it is humanly possible to be in attacking and solving the problems of our time. For example, the volcano of Mount St. Helens is beyond our capacity to control. The time bombs of our so-called inner cities were built by man, and he has both the power and resources to dismantle them. He only needs the will!"

Increasingly, however, I feared that not only was the will lacking but an uglier, more cynical use of history was at work. Following Ronald Reagan's nomination as the Republican Party's 1980 presidential candidate, he and his handlers made the calculated decision to stage his first campaign speech in Philadelphia, Mississippi. It was a town almost exclusively significant as the place where three civil rights activists—Andrew Goodman, Michael Schwerner, and James Chaney—were murdered in 1964 by police-protected Ku Klux Klan members. Far from decrying this dispicable event, Reagan picked this town, of all places, to voice his support for states' rights, by then the well-established code for a candidate's willingness to turn a blind eye to local racism. Whatever else my retirement would bring, I was certain of one thing: it could not entail any complacency in America's ongoing struggle for civil rights and race-blind equality.

24

A Whole New Life

WE DID NOT BEGIN PACKING for our departure the moment that Hanna Gray gave me the green light, but we did begin thinking seriously about what moving entailed. We would need a home large enough to have essentially two master bedrooms, since we insisted that Aurelia's mother be as comfortable as we would be. We also wanted grounds spacious enough on which to build our "dream" greenhouse for our now substantial orchid collection. And we would need large public rooms to accommodate the kind of entertaining to which we had grown accustomed. Realizing how selective our needs had become, we resolved to go to Durham and see what was available.

We flew down for a long weekend in January 1980, staying with Eva and Charles Ray, who were delighted that we were planning to move nearby. Once settled, we contacted Kelly Matherly, a local real estate broker, who already had several homes lined up for us to see. With six or even eight months before having to move, we were not prepared to take just anything, a resolve made greater by the fact that Durham, being more welcoming than Brooklyn, offered greater choice. I was also prepared to be less flexible since my means were somewhat greater. Consequently, we turned down everything that Kelly showed us. One place had a green-house, another a very comfortable master bedroom, but neither had a bedroom suitable for Grandmother's use. We went up and down streets, looking at one unsatisfactory house after another.

We were already conceding that our first foray into Durham real estate had been a failure when, in the midst of a party Bob Durden, a Duke University history professor and old friend, was giving for us, Bob ventured the opinion that we should consider the home of John Blackburn, the former chancellor and economics professor who had taken an early retirement and had already left the city. The house was not yet on the open market, and indeed Blackburn's wife and children would not vacate the house until early summer, when the school year ended. It was also quite likely too large for us, he feared. Nevertheless, he thought we should have a look at it, and Kelly Matherly agreed.

Sunday morning, Kelly took us to see the Blackburn home in the Rockwood section of the city. As we pulled into the driveway, Aurelia turned to me and said that she was already impressed. It was a Williamsburg Colonial brick with green shutters sitting back from the street on more than an acre of wooded land. It had five bedrooms and five bathrooms, and two bedrooms had bathrooms attached, thus giving us what we had been looking for. All its other features, including a finished basement and an attic with dormer windows, pleased us immensely. We made an offer to Mrs. Blackburn, and she was prepared to accept it as soon as she had discussed the matter with her husband. He proved agreeable, and without further discussion we had settled on a home in Durham.

We returned in the spring, settled with the Blackburns, and arranged for the construction of the only missing piece—a large greenhouse, seventeen feet by twenty-four feet. My hope was it would be ready to receive our orchids when we moved permanently that summer.

Since we did not dare subject Aurelia's mother to a two-day automobile trip, she and Aurelia flew down to Durham in early July and lived with Charles Ray's sister and her husband, Flora and John Gray. I had the responsibility of seeing that the furniture was loaded onto the moving van, closing the Chicago house, renting a truck in which to transport the orchids, and engaging my research assistant, Patrick Thompson, to drive that truck while I drove our car. Despite temperatures in the nineties, the flowers survived the trip. We arrived in Durham the afternoon of June 9, 1980, and set off for 208 Pineview Road.

Alas, we could not find it. We inquired at shops and filling stations and were given specific directions, but after two hours we gave up and went to where Aurelia and her mother were staying. Aurelia was happy to see us and said that obviously we had read her note. I replied that I had not seen the note. She said that she had left it at the house. I countered that we had not seen the house, fully admitting that we could not find it. She was greatly amused and immediately took us to our elusive destination. The greenhouse, as the note reported, had not been completed, but the young men who were building it had constructed some temporary shelving on the screened-in porch, where Patrick and I placed the orchids. In another week I was able to place them in their new home with humidifiers, heaters when needed, and running water.

Somewhat to our surprise, our neighbors welcomed us most cordially. We were the only African Americans on the street and, indeed, in the neighborhood. One physician across the way came over with his wife, two children, their maid, flowers, and a pie. They wondered what they could do to help us settle in. Our next-door neighbor on one side called within a day or so just to welcome us into the community. The neighbor on the other side, a young accountant living alone, came to greet us and wanted to know where we stood on the wisteria "problem." When we told him that we were against its unbridled aggression, he grasped our hands, exclaiming that he was pleased we were in the fight together! An elderly man several houses away came to call and brought flowers. He greatly admired one of the orchids that was in bloom, and when he died a few days later, I called on his family, taking that orchid with me.

To my great delight, my longtime secretary, Margaret Fitzsimmons, had agreed to move to Durham and continue her work with me. Margaret arrived later in the summer and, because she was more of an old family friend than a working colleague, made Durham feel even more our home. Toward the end of the summer, Margaret and I had our quarters at the National Humanities Center and she was able to settle not only into her own apartment but into her work as well. Our daily routine entailed my picking her up and driving the twenty minutes out to the National Humanities Center located in Research Triangle Park. The midday meal proved an excellent time for me to become acquainted with other fellows. Many of us were at last having the opportunity to write the books and articles that we had long been planning. They were a lively group, and in many cases I was already familiar with their work and often with them personally. Fellows with similar interests often conducted informal seminars, and since I was writing the biography of George Washington Williams, I invited people who had some interest in biographical writing to meet and discuss our experiences in working in that genre.

Aurelia and I had scarcely settled into our new home when we had a heartwarming visit from Whit. We sincerely believed that he came at that particular time to see if we had taken leave of our senses in deciding to move to Durham. He was soon pleased with our commodious home and evidenced a dawning appreciation of the local cosmopolitanism. While planning his birthday dinner, we indicated that we would eat out and asked what kind of food he would like. He wondered if there were any Chinese restaurants in Durham. I countered by asking him what region of China and what cuisine he would prefer. He was certain that I was responding in jest. When he said that he would prefer Szechwan, I told him that I would reserve a table in a restaurant that specialized in that cuisine. Following that exchange and the consequent dinner, he was persuaded that we would be able to survive in Durham.

Despite the fact that I was enjoying my life as a scholar, there were the usual demands on my time. Even before I could get settled in at the center, I had to journey to Minneapolis for a meeting of the United States Commission on Public Diplomacy to which I had been named by President Carter. By that time President Carter had also nominated me to be a member of the delegation to the twenty-first general conference of the United Nations Educational, Scientific, and Cultural Organization in Belgrade, Yugoslavia, which was scheduled to run from September 23 to October 28, 1980. Other members of the delegation included Ambassador Robin Duke of New York, who would act as chair of the delegation; Barbara Newell of our UNESCO office in Paris, who would be our vice chair; Elie Abel of Stanford's Department of Journalism; and John Fobes, chair of the U.S. National Commission for UNESCO. There were also five alternates, four senior advisers, and thirteen advisers. The delegates were invited to a briefing on September 16 at the Department of State, and there would be a second briefing in Belgrade on the day before the opening of the conference. Although our nominations technically had to be confirmed by the

Senate, no hearings were held and aside from a rather elaborate financial disclosure report that I was required to fill out—twice—my confirmation was routine.

During the briefings in Washington and Belgrade, it became clear to me that the major issue of concern to the United States was control over the dissemination of information within other countries, particularly those in the Soviet bloc as well as most of the third world. Control over information was regarded as central to influencing political developments but also manipulating scientific and cultural knowledge. The debate that would develop in Belgrade was over the New World Information Order, described in an advisory report written by the foreign minister of Ireland, Seán MacBride, and his colleagues. Its aim was to correct a perceived imbalance in communication and information resources favoring the industrial countries. The official position of the United States was to be wary of any suggestions that tended to place communications and information beyond its control.

Two things very much impressed me during the conference. One was the flurry of activity that accompanied the arrival of one American media mogul after another. He might be from radio, television, or print journalism, and he was generally there for only a few hours or a day, but his presence was widely known not only among the Americans at the conference but among all the delegates. They were there, it was inferred, to make certain that the New World Information Order did not work against their interests. What also impressed me was the hostility toward the American delegation on the part of delegates from economically disadvantaged countries. It became obvious that they immediately suspected that our policies were detrimental to their interests and should be opposed, often even before we had a chance to clearly articulate them. I shall never forget the hostility displayed by a member of the delegation from Benin when I merely sought to become acquainted with her. The fact that I was a member of the American delegation was enough to dictate her attitude toward me.

The American delegation met each morning for a briefing, to digest any communications that had come from the Department of State, and to try to make sense of what was transpiring at the conference. Then we were off to our various assignments. I was a member of Commission I, which dealt with problems of education. Two things became quickly apparent. No matter what the commission was, it ended up debating some aspect of the New World Information Order. And second, I was having an ever dimmer view of the spirit in which the United States was participating.

At the conclusion of the conference, I bluntly shared my observations with the chair of our delegation and some key persons in the Department of State. Our delegation had been inexperienced; we were conscientious and hardworking, but that did not compensate for the lack of high-level government and private-sector participants. That the undersecretary of state had flown in for two days (though I never saw him) was insufficient. What we needed either on the delegation or in a consultative capacity were people of real standing and expertise from the Departments of State and Education. Many delegations had ministers of culture and/or ministers of education who were there at the opening and remained for varying periods of time. We had no one of comparable status.

Indeed, we had been in Belgrade for a week and already engaged in some acrimonious debate before the Senate even got around to confirming us! I also pointed out that the half-day briefing in Washington and the briefings each morning in Belgrade were not nearly enough. We had received no position papers before we arrived in Belgrade; the morning directives cabled from Washington were sometimes hysterical, sometimes vague, and always cryptic. We had no overall strategy or set of proposals to which other delegations could react, and so instead we were always responding to the resolutions offered by the Soviets and their satellites.

More than once, I expressed my distress over our accommodations. The rooms assigned to us were more like cells in which one's arms could touch both walls at the same time. This was more than personal pique. Our accommodations and facilities precluded our entertaining even one guest. It was hard not to infer from all of this the low regard our government had for the principles and purposes of UNESCO. And, indeed, three years later President Reagan would take the United States out of UNESCO altogether.

I could not resist the thought that, perhaps, as the countries of the world evolved, becoming more modern and sophisticated, the United States still persisted in the notion that it could take them lightly, as though neither they nor the times had changed. The acrimony and suspicion with which some of them viewed us and the persistence of our attitude of condescension toward them indicated to me that we were not aware of the profound transformations taking place in many parts of the world. If these changes did not always indicate the acquisition of power, they marked an alteration in the attitude of nations toward power. America, I sadly concluded, had not adjusted to these new realities.

Upon my return from Belgrade, I immersed myself in my biography of George Washington Williams. There was a steady barrage of distractions, however, and none more pleasant than my delivering the convocation address at the fiftieth anniversary of Brooklyn College. It was a great homecoming for me and a magnificent opportunity to express my affection for the college and to take notice of the changes that had occurred since I was there. In my address I referred to the fact that with open enrollment set to begin, the college would have a larger number of blacks and Hispanics matriculating, and I cautioned my former colleagues not to be disturbed. I pointed out that when Brooklyn College was half its present age, it was engaged in a special educational enterprise that no longer characterized its work. The college was not only older, it was different. "This need not mean that its standards are lower but that its reach is greater. This need not mean that its work is less important but that its clientele is more diverse. This need not mean that its impact is diminished but that its influence is broader. As it has taken on these new characteristics, it moves a bit closer to the goal of equalizing opportunity in higher education." I couldn't have been prouder of what they were about to attempt.

I soon had yet further opportunity to reflect on change, speaking not only to the broadened mandate of schools like Brooklyn College but also to some of the wider concerns my involvement with UNESCO brought to light. The occasion was the Mordecai W. Johnson Memorial Lecture at Howard University, which I delivered on January 23, 1981.

The Mordecai Johnson Lecture was an important event not only in the history of the university over which Johnson presided from 1926 until his retirement in 1960, but also in its significance to the Washington, D.C., community and nation. The first Johnson lecturer was Benjamin Mays, former dean of the School of Religion at Howard and later president of Morehouse College. The second was Dean Rusk, former president of the

Rockefeller Foundation and secretary of state to presidents Kennedy and Johnson; and the third was John W. Davis, lifelong friend of Dr. Johnson and for many years the president of West Virginia State College. The lecture incorporated a dinner to which numerous Washingtonians, including officials of the United States government, were invited. It offered a platform from which to make a statement on a matter of importance to the university and to the nation, and I strove to rise to the occasion.

My subject was "Higher Education and the World Community." I referred to historically black institutions as America's multiracial and multicultural pioneers. "Whether the institution had a conscious and deliberate plan, such as Hampton Institute, to provide education for Negroes, Indians, and Hawaiians, or a less overt arrangement, such as Howard, to educate all who cared to come, black colleges and universities early became models for the training of persons of the most diverse racial, cultural, or even national backgrounds. There was no presumption at such institutions that barriers to learning . . . existed or that education was not an effective instrument for solving the most difficult problems imaginable." Such institutions, I argued, were essentially optimistic, expressing through their curriculum, their faculty, and their students a belief in their mission to improve the individual and to improve the human condition, anywhere and everywhere. Few other organizations in this country during the nineteenth and early twentieth centuries had attempted this.

Indeed, many of them had policies of social exclusion, racial segregation, and quotas for certain ethnic or religious groups. Such considerations, of course, would have been ridiculous at institutions committed to the education of former slaves. "They could logically and consistently function only if they believed in the educability of everyone and in the power of education to transform the social order." Some of them quite early began to welcome foreign students. Within a few years of its founding, Howard University, for example, had welcomed students from Japan, China, several African countries, and the West Indies.

Within the twentieth century, I pointed out, higher education in the United States had grown exponentially, and support for it at every level had grown to keep pace with college and university enrollments that expanded by more than 300 percent in the two decades ending in 1980 alone. One would have thought that with such demand and support, we would have the utmost confidence that higher education would play an important role in solving at least some of the major problems that beset the nation and the world. Yet this was not the case. While America's catalog of scientific, cultural, and educational achievements is long and rightly celebrated, Americans nevertheless do not seem to believe that we can commandeer the talents and resources to tackle our domestic problems in human relations "or when we confront those problems that bedevil the world community." We are good at providing services for peoples around the world when they encounter earthquakes, floods, famines, pestilence, and other disasters. On occasion, we will commit military and economic assistance, although quite often only on a quid pro quo basis. Offering solace for souls, American missionaries have even taken their religion to the various peoples they serve.

"It is when we seek to establish educational relationships or to use education to build a common vehicle for communicating with other peoples that we seem less effective." As an example, I called attention to our program in the field of international educational and cultural exchange, the Fulbright program. It formed the centerpiece of our educational outreach efforts and was thirty years old. Under its auspices, thousands of students, teachers, and researchers had gone to other countries, and their counterparts had come to America. Since I was on the Fulbright board for nine years and served as a Fulbright lecturer in many parts of the world, I was in a special position to appreciate the possible influence of such an institution on the peaceful relations of the peoples of the world. Unfortunately, the program was hampered, at times, by budget cuts or threats of cuts, because it was often regarded as expendable. I then gave two examples of the manner in which our role in the world community was injured by clumsiness or indifference. One was the cavalier way Congress had treated nominees for the U.S. Advisory Commission on Public Diplomacy. Although their appointment required congressional approval, their membership on the commission was not of sufficient importance for the appropriate Senate committee to bother to hold hearings, or for the members of the committee to inform themselves of the work of the commission or the fitness of the proposed members. The other example was the role of the United States in the work of UNESCO. Regarding the lack of knowledge on the part of members of the Senate concerning that international body, I expressed the hope that it was not as bad as the story, doubtless apocryphal, of a senator attending a State Department reception honoring U.S. ambassadors on home leave suggested. Introduced to our ambassador to UNESCO, one senator, it was claimed, remarked, "Now, *that* is a brave little country."

Our institutions of higher education could in fact play a leadership role in shaping a better world, a role pioneered by America's historically all-black colleges. "If they have been, through the years, multi-racial, multi-cultural, and even multi-national institutions, they doubtless are in a better position to search for new and better ways than armed conflict for settling disputes . . . The very presence of foreign students and faculty, in an atmosphere that assumed their common humanity and their equality, tends to raise significantly the consciousness about international matters on the part of those who had never ventured beyond the shores of this country." I pointed out how the curriculum at Howard University reflected the desire that its students have some impact on world developments. How much greater might the impact be if universities in this country and abroad shared students, experiments, and experiences. In the long run, I argued, such sharing would do more to assure peace and prosperity in the world than the billions poured into the arms race.

I took no small amount of pride from the fact that I continued to do my part. In 1981, shortly after delivering the Johnson Lecture at Howard University, Aurelia and I had gone to Sierra Leone and Senegal under the auspices of the Advisory Commission on Public Diplomacy. In the former country I gave two lectures and several interviews with the local press, and in Senegal enjoyed the hospitality of various officials as well as members of the U.S. embassy staff. We had visited Senegal three times in the past to see Whit, then teaching in that country, but this time I had been invited to observe the centennial of the establishment of the first U.S. consular office there. My program in Senegal was full but not crowded, and I enjoyed many informal conversations with local students and professors. I was impressed with the much larger number of Senegalese who spoke English than I had remembered from previous visits, and Aurelia and I explained it to ourselves by observing that Whit was now the director of the English-language program at the U.S. Cultural Center. Although I had excellent interpreters at my lectures, I was well aware of the fact that many of my listeners understood me as I spoke, for they reacted to my remarks even before the interpreter had put them into French.

One of the highlights in all of our visits was a call on President Léopold S. Senghor, the first president of Senegal and generally regarded as the father of the country. He was also highly respected in France, from which his nation had gained its independence. After all, as a member of the French Chamber of Deputies he had been responsible for the wording of the French Constitution following World War II. For this and other contributions, he was later elected to the French Academy. On this visit, he was as cordial and charming as ever, especially to Aurelia, as he received us in his home that was, in every way, a fitting residence for a former president. Knowing that I did not speak French, he usually spoke to me in English, but now he had to confess that since leaving office he had failed to keep up with that language. He hoped, therefore, that I would forgive him if he spoke in French. I replied that as long as my son was willing to translate, it would be quite acceptable to me.

Our conversation was, as usual, wide ranging and covered subjects from Senegalese politics to French literature to American race problems and my writings. He was pleased that a French translation of *From Slavery to Freedom* was coming out shortly, and I expressed gratitude for the role that I knew he had played in promoting its translation. At one point, as Whit spoke to him in French to clarify a point that he was making, he paused to tell Whit that his French was "elegant." I was immediately struck by the fact that President Senghor had made a point of conveying that compliment to Whit in English. I had no doubt what he intended by that gesture: He wanted to be certain that Whit's less linguistically talented parents were aware of the president's appreciation of their son's skill. I treasured this acknowledgment of Whit's talent, for in it I saw evidence of all that Whit had accomplished during his long stay in Senegal. While the eight years Whit had been outside the United States had been difficult for me and Aurelia, straining our long-held belief that our best course as parents was to allow Whit to pursue his own course in his own way, we knew that things were again about to change. Whit would return to America in 1982 and enter the graduate school of Johns Hopkins School of Advanced International Study. Suffice it to say, both Aurelia and I were immensely pleased with his decision.

Unfortunately, we could not remain in Senegal long, nor could we do more than pay brief visits to our friends in London before we were back in Durham on March 22. I had already agreed to deliver the 1981 James W. Richard Lectures at the University of Virginia, arguably the most important lecture sponsored by that institution. Even though at the time I was fast at work on my biography of George W. Williams, I already had another idea I wished to address.

I intended to take on those apologists for slavery who even in the 1980s still insisted that slaves had been happy and, indicative of this, never truly rebelled against the institution. Far from being a conspiracy of silence, these articulators of the belief in contented slaves were all too clearly and vocally evolving into the individuals who would insist in 2000 that African Americans not only did not need an apology from the descendants of former slaveholders and the most egregious perpetrators of Jim Crow violence, but were trifling and lazy and deserved no consideration of redress in the twenty-first century. I sought to speak to them in the Richard Lectures. If they had not read my critique of Coulter published in the 1950s or my own delineation of slavery, Reconstruction, and Jim Crow in numerous editions of *From Slavery to Freedom*, I would, yet again, call their attention to the barbarism of slavery.

The first lecture, "Dissidents in the 'Conscript Army,'" was delivered on March 24, two days after our return from Senegal. The second, "The Runaway as Dissident," was given on March 26; and the final lecture, "Profile of the Runaway," was delivered on March 31. With an abundance of documentary evidence, I sought to settle, once and for all time, the absurdity and falsity of the claim that slaves were content. Many slaves were restless, conniving, and determined to throw off the yoke, and given that slave owners knew this for certain, it was high time that their descendants and apologists were also, finally, made aware of it.

Thanksgiving 1982 was very special. Whit, weary from his graduate studies and looking toward a respite, arrived in time to assist in the kitchen. He also announced that he had invited a friend from Senegal who was stranded because the college to which he had been recruited as an undergraduate was closing for a week during the holidays; he had no place to go and was wondering what he should do. Whit invited him to come to our house, and we welcomed him warmly. He was Bouna Ndiaye, whom Whit had met when he had attended Whit's English class at the American Cultural Center in Dakar. Bouna subsequently became president of the English-speaking group, and that threw him and Whit together regularly. They had stayed in touch ever since, and when over that Thanksgiving it became clear that Bouna had grown restless at his current college, I raised, after discussing the matter with Aurelia and with Whit, the possibility of Bouna attending North Carolina Central University and coming to live with us. Whit thought it a great idea, especially since we had plenty of room and Bouna could be helpful in many ways. Bouna, briefly speechless, recovered and happily accepted the invitation. After he had secured his transcript and a release from his current classes, I went with him to North Carolina Central University to assist him with his registration. Duly admitted, he quickly settled into his room in our home.

Even as my home life was being enriched by Bouna's presence, I was participating ever more directly in trying to encourage a more enlightened national conversation on race. The roots of one important effort trace back to when I was in New York late in 1979 on the occasion of my presidency of the American Historical Association. Kenneth Clark dropped into my suite to resume a discussion that we had begun several years earlier with Ira Reid, Ralph Ellison, Saunders Redding, and a few others on what we should do about the plight of African Americans in American society. We concluded that without making any claim whatever to assuming the role of the "talented tenth," we should be able to say something, even if that proved nothing more than a description of the contemporary situation of African Americans and a call for them to make resolutions to chart a new course for the future. We resolved to take our ideas to Eddie Williams and the Joint Center for Political Studies, seeking assistance to give our thoughts some structure and substance. Eddie liked the idea and, with his vice president, Eleanor Farrar, began to formulate a plan, including seeking persons of similar interests and objectives as well as support for the organization that we envisioned. They were able not only to get the latter but lined up people who were willing to meet and exchange views on what we were proposing. Meanwhile, Ken Clark and I wrote a piece that

was to form the basis for discussion at a conference that would bring together about twenty-four people primarily from education and the professions.

After tracing the roller-coaster adventures of African Americans in the
years following World War II, Clark and I credited the struggles to
achieve equality to Supreme Court decisions such as *Brown* and to congressional legislation such as the Civil Rights Act and the Voting Rights
Act. Even so, the future continued to be uncertain. "It is difficult to be optimistic about the future of blacks in American society," we said. "Resolution of the complex and intractable racial problems confronting us today
will depend . . . on many factors beyond the control of blacks: inflation,
general economic conditions, urban fiscal crises, international relations,
the energy crisis, and the willingness of the majority to understand the
need to fulfill the promises of the United States Constitution." That was
all the more reason, we concluded, for a group to come together, review
the situation, and develop some strategies and methods to deal with the
complex racial realities of the day.

The Joint Center called a stellar group of conferees together at the
Rockefeller Conference Center in Tarrytown, New York, on July 29,
1980, for two days of discussion. Calling itself the Committee on Policy
for Racial Justice, the group issued other papers in subsequent years, including "A Policy Framework for Racial Justice" (1983) and "Visions of a
Better Way: A Black Appraisal of Public Schooling" (1989). These papers
enjoyed a wide circulation, and I like to believe that they had some influence on public policy. Perhaps most tangible, many members of the group
went on to occupy positions where they could influence policy, whether
that proved to be in the president's cabinet, at other levels of government,
or in the private sector.

25

A Duke Affair

I WAS DETERMINED to complete the first draft of my biography of George Washington Williams in my second fellowship year at the center, despite all distractions. As usual, I did not lack them. In May 1981, I was invited to give the commencement address at Booker T. Washington High School in Tulsa; since it was the fiftieth anniversary of my graduation, it was a unique honor. It was also a homecoming, of sorts, and Aurelia and I enjoyed ourselves tremendously. That same spring I was invited to receive an honorary degree from the University of Pennsylvania, at which my old and good friend Vernon Jordan delivered the commencement address. Vernon had been the executive officer of the National Urban League before joining one of the leading law firms in Washington.

During the previous year, in the course of a conversation, Vernon Jordan sought to compare his experiences receiving an honorary degree from Harvard with my own. I confessed that I had not received an honorary degree from Harvard and that to my knowledge no African American scholar ever had unless he wished to count Booker T. Washington's honorary MA in 1896. Jordan could hardly believe it. He threatened not to acknowledge that Harvard had so honored him unless and until it also honored African American men and women in education, the arts, and similar fields.

Not many months later I received a letter from the president of Harvard University inviting me to accept an honorary degree on the occasion of the fortieth anniversary of my receiving the doctorate in history from the university. I accepted, all the while wondering over the serendipitous timing of the overture, and Aurelia and I went to Cambridge in June 1981 for the exercises. As had been true in 1936, when Harvard awarded me my MA, and in 1941, when I received my PhD, the Harvard commencement was a curious combination of formality and informality. Some platform guests, as well as graduates, wore grand academic attire, while others wore ordinary, everyday clothing. The ceremony was likewise a combination of rowdiness and simplicity. Among my fellow honorees were Leontyne Price, Ansel Adams, Cyrus Vance, and Jorge Luis Borges. University President Derek Bok and his wife, Sissela, lived up to their reputation of being gracious and thoughtful hosts, presiding over the exercises in a manner appropriate for the leader of the nation's oldest institution of higher education.

Amid these pleasant interruptions to my progress on George Washington Williams, I was also being courted. Even before we moved to Durham, Bob Durden, in his role as chairman of the Department of History at Duke, had sounded out my interest in teaching one course per year or per semester. Though flattered, I nevertheless made clear my preference for confining my continuing activities to the work that I had laid out for myself at the center. That would be sufficient for the time being, especially since I was far behind in my writing. Duke, however, would not relent. Soon, Dick Watson became the university's principal agitator. Born within a week of each other, we had long regarded ourselves as twins and felt especially close. He raised the idea of my teaching at Duke on several occasions, and I brushed it aside, arguing that I was already retired and there was not much left in me. He argued to the contrary, insisting that many at Duke felt as he did. I pointed out that I had only three years left before Duke's mandatory retirement at seventy. He insisted that it was my seniority and broad experience that recommended me.

Out of the blue I received a letter from the provost, William Bevan, inviting me to accept the position of James B. Duke Professor of History. This was Duke's highest professorship, and although there were several in the university, no one in the Department of History had ever held one, and no African American had ever held an endowed chair at Duke. Bill Bevan and his wife, Dottie, invited Aurelia and me to dinner at their home in Forest Hills, to which he had also invited Dick Watson, Bob Durden, and Ernestine Friedl, dean of arts and sciences and the James B. Duke Professor of Anthropology. They put no pressure on me whatever, but by the time the evening was over I was prepared to accept their offer, a decision Aurelia heartily approved of.

With only three years left before retirement, I would not take on any doctoral students or involve myself deeply in graduate written and oral examinations. Instead, I would offer two courses per semester: a lecture course or a colloquium and a seminar, both of which would be centered on the history of the South. The university agreed to employ Margaret Fitzsimmons as my full-time secretary and to provide us a newly redecorated three-room suite in the East Duke building on East Campus. I was scheduled to assume my responsibilities in the fall of 1982.

At the center I worked furiously to complete the draft of my biography of George Washington Williams. Realizing that I would perhaps never again enjoy the leisure of writing full-time, I made the most of it, in spite of continued commitments.

Near the end of my tenure at the National Humanities Center, I participated in two memorable activities that meant a great deal to me personally. One was the commemoration of the twenty-eighth anniversary of *Brown v. Board of Education*. By 1982, the number of living participants in the historic case was gradually dwindling, and although my role was central to neither the planning nor the argument, those planning the event decided that as a historian, I could place my recollections in context. The principal observance in 1982 was in New York on May 20, at the National Civil Rights Institute. At the time, Julius Chambers was president and William T. Coleman was chairman of the NAACP Legal Defense Fund. The honored guests were the nine students who had desegregated the high school in Little Rock in 1957 and their adviser, Daisy Bates. Three years after the decision in *Brown*, the Little Rock students, by their courage, showed what it took to make the decision a reality. Sadly, what they accomplished in Little Rock had not yet been achieved in many parts of the country, North and South.

I made the most of my final summer at the center, completing the first draft of the Williams biography and sharing it with friends and colleagues for a thorough and critical reading. Completion of this work seemed to be the end of a long journey that had begun forty years earlier. I had become interested in Williams when I was just beginning to consider writing a history of African Americans. Here was a man, born free in western Pennsylvania in 1849, who had already written such a history in the 1880s, with no training as a historian and little formal education. Yet he persevered not only in the writing of history but in the pursuit of other interests, such as tracing and criticizing the Belgian conquest of the Congo. I admired him greatly, and over the years I must admit that I came to identify with him. Writing his biography had become not only my longest pursuit of a subject but my favorite pastime, and as I reached the conclusion of one of my most exciting and satisfying forays into the field of history I was in equal measure elated and saddened.

Since we had already lived in Durham for two years, we did not have the usual problems of adjusting to a new community when I began my teaching duties at Duke in the autumn of 1982. Very soon I felt welcomed into the extended "Duke family," including its undergraduates. They were an unusual lot. Already, Duke was regarded as a "hot college," and gaining admission was a prize to which many thousands aspired each year. Only a fraction of the applicants were admitted, and they were among the best students to be found anywhere. But their intellectual ability far exceeded their intellectual dedication. Indeed, they seemed to enjoy their reputation of being laid back and none too studious, although this was clearly a pose designed to preserve a reputation. When I handed out the syllabus in my lecture course, one of the students asked, with disarming innocence, if I really expected them to read all that I assigned. I replied, to his feigned dismay, that in fact I expected them to read far beyond what was listed on the syllabus. I believe that many of them did, although they would never admit to it.

When I met my colloquium, composed of ten students, I called attention to the fact that the final meeting would be held over dinner at our home and that my wife wanted me to tell them how much we looked forward to seeing them there. At that point one of the students slumped in his seat as if mortally wounded. I asked him what was wrong. With an all-knowing tone in his voice he asked me if I did not realize that on December 5, the date scheduled for the dinner, the Duke basketball team would be playing the University of Virginia. I replied, quite as all-knowing, that I could not see how that had anything to do with the class. After some further consternation, another member of the colloquium wondered if the class and meal could be held an hour earlier, which would make it possible for those interested to be finished before game time. Wishing to be flexible, I agreed.

The class proved to be of great interest to the students, and I had the distinct impression that several of them were reading far beyond what was on the syllabus. On the final day of class, the members found their way to our home and were greeted warmly by Aurelia, a glowing fire in the living room fireplace, and enticing aromas from the kitchen. The discussion was lively, and soon it was time for dinner, after which they could rush off to the game. At the end of the meal, when I reminded them of the time, they seemed to ignore what I had said. They were in the midst of a discussion, and it was obvious that not one of them wished to leave. They remained at our home for several hours, and as the evening came to an end, I had the feeling that at least on this occasion the discussions at a colloquium had proved more important than the outcome of a basketball game.

Duke University, no pioneer in the admission of Africa American students or the employment of black faculty, was by the time that I accepted its job offer seeking to redress both. I assume that my own recruitment to Duke reflected, in part, that effort. Although it was never suggested that I teach African American history or be involved in black studies, early on I was invited to become a member of the President's Council on Black Affairs, to which I had been recommended by the Executive Committee of the Academic Council. It was composed of fifteen people: faculty, administrators, students, and Duke trustees. The president of the university usually presided at the monthly meetings and indicated by both his presence and his participation that he was very much interested in enhancing the role of African Americans in the life of the university. When President Terry Sanford was absent, William Griffiths, the vice president for student affairs, presided. The meetings addressed directly the status of recruitment of black students and faculty, and it was obvious that Duke was willing and eager to improve its record.

Surely one of the most widely discussed and, perhaps, most successful recruiting of an African American scholar was when Stanley Fish, chair of the Department of English, recruited Henry Louis Gates Jr. A former member of the faculties of Yale and Cornell, with a doctorate from Cambridge, Gates was both remarkably able and disarmingly charming. I keenly recall, however, how Fish got Gates off to a bad start. When Gates visited Duke, Fish gave a luncheon for him to which he invited only black faculty, and when they assembled, he withdrew, leaving the group all-black. It was an awkward situation, and I was embarrassed. I could not imagine that Fish, a distinguished scholar and chair of the department, would think that black faculty would feel comfortable only in the presence of blacks or that they could speak frankly about Duke if only blacks were present. I certainly never expected anyone at Duke, and certainly not a white department chair, to sponsor the equivalent of a Jim Crow luncheon. I sent Fish a note informing him that this was the very first time since I had left the region in the 1940s that I had experienced segregation at Duke. Despite this gaff, Gates accepted Duke's offer, only to be then met by expressions of disgust on the part of some members of the faculty who believed that his salary was much higher than it actually was and that he received favors from the administration, which was not the case. After a two-year stint at Duke, Gates left for Harvard, where he has lived happily ever since.

Even more difficult was the recruitment of black students, especially when the competition among the colleges for top-ranking students was so keen. Duke's administration, in an effort to gain some advantage over its competitors, employed recruiters of black students for the college and the graduate school. This proved to be a highly successful strategy, especially when the recruiters were able to put together attractive scholarship packages. Even so, there remained considerable fluctuation in the number of black students enrolling from year to year. Consequently, the effort to recruit as many eligible black students as possible was unceasing. Employing a range of efforts to render Duke attractive to those candidates, to which I was happy to contribute, by 2003 the university led the nation's major research universities in the successful recruitment of African American faculty and students.

My three years in the Department of History at Duke passed quickly, and when I reached the mandatory retirement age of seventy, in 1985, I was more than ready to enter the ranks of retired persons. Alas, it was not to be. I had already been approached by the legal scholar Walter Dellinger about joining him and William Leuchtenburg, the celebrated political historian at the University of North Carolina and an old friend of mine, in offering a course in American constitutional history at the Duke Law School. We would take turns, with Dellinger offering the first third of the course down to 1820; I would offer the middle third of the course down to the end of the nineteenth century; and Leuchtenburg would address the twentieth century. We were free to attend each other's lectures, and we would collaborate in preparing the final examination. I had never taught in a professional school, although I had occasionally attended lectures at Harvard Law School, and we agreed that instead of the Socratic method common to law schools, we would lecture with the understanding that students could interrupt and raise questions at any point. Too exciting an opportunity for me to forgo, I signed on.

I could not have anticipated that teaching in the law school would be so stimulating. If I was inclined to imagine that what I had taught for some fifty years could go unchallenged, my law school students disabused me of that inclination. The questions they raised were so different from the ones to which I had grown accustomed that they forced me to look at the incidents and materials in an entirely new way. If I discussed the facts in the Dred Scott case as I had always done, the law school students bored in on the whole question of property, and the differences not only between the laws affecting persons in Missouri and the territories, but also between property, say, in general and property in persons. The course became so popular that it was generally oversubscribed, and we attempted to control the enrollment by placing it in a room that would not accommodate more than eighty students. When students persisted in demanding admission, we declared that it was open only to third-year students. Even today I encounter individuals who complain that they were denied the opportunity to take the course because we had changed the rules of admission.

Easily the most exciting experience of the 1980s was the publication of my biography of George Washington Williams in 1985. In so many ways it was my most creative undertaking. Indeed, when I set out to write the biography of Williams, virtually nothing was known about him except that he had written in 1882 a two-volume *History of the Negro Race in America*.

I was determined to re-create him to the best of my ability. Virtually nothing was known of him when I began to stalk him in 1945. For almost forty years I scoured three continents searching for materials to illuminate certain aspects of his life. I went from Boston to California, from England to Belgium, from the Congo to Egypt following his trail, tracing it wherever it led, and I was gratified with what I found. There always seemed to be gaps I was attempting to fill and connections I wished to make. It was only when I began to repeat the research and rediscover the same things that I realized that I had found all that I could. A deep sense of satisfaction settled over me as I realized that I had re-created a historical character through my own energy, imagination, and determination. Though I had closed out the biographical series I had edited for the University of Chicago Press, and for which the book had long ago been intended, the press wished to publish it as an independent volume. I was all too pleased to have them do so.

When *George Washington Williams: A Biography* appeared in the spring of 1985, it was widely and favorably reviewed. Having lived with the research and the writing of this book for so very many years, I was pleased to read reviews calling it a "superb biography" and its appearance "a major publishing event." When John Blassingame of Yale proclaimed it "an extraordinary accomplishment . . . a model biography," I was thrilled. Nominated for the Pulitzer Prize in 1985, it was acknowledged as the runner-up. It also won the Clarence Holte Literary Award, presented by David Dinkins, the 106th mayor of New York City and the very first African American elected to that office.

On the morning following the Holte Award in New York City, Aurelia and I emerged from our hotel to take a taxi to the airport for the return trip to Durham. After we worked our way to the head of the line of impatient travelers, five successive taxis drove up and, seeing us as their prospective customers, drove off. Presumably they were in search of a better, which almost certainly meant whiter, fare. The doorman confessed his inability to engage a taxi for us and sent us to the airport in a hotel limousine.

During my tenure at the law school, my physician, Dr. Charles Johnson, a pioneer African American member of Duke's medical center and faculty, discovered through a routine semiannual examination that my blood count was extremely low, a diagnosis a hematologist quickly confirmed. He recommended several weeks of regular dosages of iron, after which he could determine whether I needed further treatment. I told him that my wife and I would be in Brazil for several weeks. He had no objection to my going but admonished me to take the iron tablets regularly, and when I returned he would see if my blood count had improved.

Upon our return I went to see him; despite tablets, my blood count had not changed. A gastroenterologist eventually pronounced that I had a malignancy in my stomach. From that point on, things moved rapidly. Dr. Johnson sent me to see a surgeon, Dr. Onye Akwari. As I waited outside his office, Dr. David Sebasto, chair of the Department of Surgery and whom I knew as a James B. Duke professor, came by and wondered what I was doing up there. When I told him about the diagnosis and said that Akwari was my surgeon, he said that I could not possibly be in better hands. That was indeed reassuring, particularly when Dr. Akwari announced that his plan was to operate the following morning.

The operation, performed on October 29, 1987, was successful, and the first person I saw in the recovery room was Walter Dellinger leaning over my bed, wondering, I surmised, if I was breathing. Later, I had painless chemotherapy and, in due course, resumed my normal activities. Still later, Dr. Akwari, with whom I had cultivated a close friendship, told me that my physical condition favored a rapid recovery, thanks to my regular program of exercise and diet under the supervision of the Duke Center for Living.

The year 1987 was also marked by President Ronald Reagan's nomination of Judge Robert Bork of the United States Court of Appeals and former professor in the Yale Law School to the United States Supreme Court. A controversial figure who had freely expressed his views on a variety of public issues, his nomination was enthusiastically supported by some and vigorously opposed by others. I was disturbed by many of the public positions he had taken, especially his criticism, for example, of the Civil Rights Act. My colleagues at the law school were equally critical of him. Bill Leuchtenburg thought that Bork came late and grudgingly to the more enlightened positions he endorsed during his nomination testimony, positions he had earlier opposed. Dellinger, who had been Bork's law student at Yale, admired his intellect but was highly critical of his legal positions on many matters. We decided to seek to testify before the Senate Judiciary Committee in opposition to Judge Bork's nomination.

Our request was granted, and on September 23, 1987, we appeared before the committee. With Senator Joseph Biden of Delaware in the chair, I led off. I told the committee how important this opportunity to express my misgivings over Bork's nomination was to me personally because of my support of certain legislation that I had reason to believe Judge Bork might oppose. I told of being put off the train when I was a child because my family had sat in the "wrong" coach. After telling of other experiences with segregation and discrimination, I told how I had joined the fight to rid our country of all forms of segregation and discrimination. Then I referred to Judge Bork's remarks about the Civil Rights Act. I shuddered to think that were he on the Court in a case involving that law, he could very well join the group that would strike it down.

Dellinger and Leuchtenburg were both eloquent in their testimony, and I believe that collectively we made a good impression. Our testimony was praised by some members of the committee, such as Chairman Biden and Senators Patrick Leahy and Edward Kennedy. Senators Orrin Hatch and Arlen Specter were gracious if unbending in their support of Bork. Senator Alan Simpson was snide and graceless in his reaction to our testimony. After first enjoining us to evidence greater respect for those members of Congress who years ago had voted against the Civil Rights Act, he then warned us that if we succeeded in defeating Judge Bork's nomination to the court we would not have another similar opportunity when the next nominee came around. His first comment stunned me; his second jarred me to challenge him. I interrupted the senator to ask pointedly if the committee would hold hearings on the next candidate. When he answered in the affirmative, I assured him that we would be there to express our views on that candidate too. Senator Strom Thurmond merely said that had we been there earlier in the day to hear the testimony of Chief Justice Warren Burger we would have heard "the whole truth and nothing but the truth." Most of the senators asked pertinent and searching questions, and for our part, we did our best to answer them candidly.

For an appeals court judge and Yale professor to be rejected by the Senate Judiciary Committee in a nine-to-five vote was an ignominious defeat, and that would provide the backdrop for future fights over judicial nominations. While Bork supporters would insist that his defeat in 1987 was the result of a "campaign of distortion," supporters of Clarence Thomas would claim that his victory in 1991 was despite the "high-tech lynching" that sought to derail his nomination. By then it was clear that the political ramifications of the Bork defeat were so powerful as to have influenced attitudes toward future debates regarding the composition of the federal judiciary, especially the Supreme Court. And the politicizing of the courts meant a further politicizing of the struggle against racism and bias. Those who wanted a judiciary that would follow in the footsteps of the Warren Court and reach decisions favorable to the improvement of race relations, decisions that *Brown* anticipated, would be ever more at loggerheads with those who regarded *Brown* as a social catastrophe. I watched with mounting dismay as the latter gained the ascendancy, encouraging a more restrained judiciary.

In 1991, I was invited to speak before the Senate Judiciary Committee when it was holding hearings on the nomination of Clarence Thomas. I respectfully declined, for it appeared to me that a favorable decision on Thomas was a foregone conclusion. Nevertheless, I followed his nomination with interest and some dread. As I read of the committee's sessions, in which some of its members extolled natural rights and the virtues of being on the conservative, strict-constructionist side of everything, and how virtuous Thomas was in his beliefs and actions, I realized that nothing I or anyone else might have said or done would have changed the outcome. I did nevertheless express my opposition to the Thomas nomination to the NAACP and in an op-ed piece in *The New York Times*. The "Negro" seat on the Supreme Court, so recently vacated by Thurgood Marshall, would shortly be "bleached white" by Thomas.

The entire nomination process in 1991 was a painful reminder of the nation's evident nonconversation about race and an indication of how much the discourse had deteriorated and how bleak the future looked. Thomas's nomination was a sad capstone to the late 1970s and early '80s. This brace of years were not happy times for those of us who had hoped for so much a decade or two earlier. It seemed clear from all indicators available to me that there were hard times ahead on the racial front.

26

Matters of Life and Death

EVEN BEFORE I CEASED TEACHING in Duke's Department of History, I began to sense that some things were coming to an end. In March 1983, Anne, the younger of my two sisters, passed away, and I felt as though I had lost a twin. We were fewer than thirteen months apart in age, had been classmates through high school, and went off to college together. She had an interesting and rewarding career as an inspector in the District of Columbia's Metropolitan Police. She enjoyed her work, and after retirement delighted in traveling and being with her family and friends. During our years at Howard, Anne and Aurelia had become close friends, more like sisters than in-laws, and when Whit returned from Senegal and entered graduate school in Washington, she was delighted to have him close by. It did not last long, for in the spring of the first year of his return, she suffered cardiac arrest and passed away. Her funeral was at her church in Washington, after which we took her to Tulsa for burial in the family plot at the Booker T. Washington Cemetery.

In October 1983, Aurelia and I went to Europe, as much to divert ourselves from family matters as to attend a conference of historians in Florence. It was on this trip that Aurelia experienced difficulty in getting around because of arthritis in both knees. Still the "trooper" that my father had insisted she was, Aurelia never complained. But when we returned to

Durham, we consulted with our neighbor and friend, the orthopedic surgeon Richard Bruch, who concluded that knee replacement was in order. She and I both agreed. He made the first replacement in October 1983 and the second one in August 1985. It was during Aurelia's recovery from the first operation that we learned she had breast cancer requiring a full mastectomy, which was performed in August 1984. She recovered, thankfully, from all three procedures, even postponing the second knee replacement until we had celebrated the fiftieth anniversary of our graduation from Fisk.

How different things were in 1985 from the time that we entered Fisk as freshmen. Whereas in 1931 I had been so terrified by the treatment I had received from a bus clerk that I seldom visited downtown Nashville during my years as a student, for our fiftieth anniversary Aurelia and I engaged a large suite at the now long desegregated Hermitage Hotel. Here we entertained all of our returning classmates with a champagne brunch. While time and World War II had taken their toll, more than twenty out of our original class of seventy-five returned for the golden anniversary. To my chagrin, I learned the truth of the adage that there is no more accurate a mirror than the reacquaintance of an old friend. When I asked Aurelia to identify one woman particularly ill-treated by time, she merely said that she was the same person I had tried to date in 1933! Thereafter, I did not seek her assistance in identifying our classmates.

The following year I suffered the loss of Mozella. Sister's confidence in me had been boundless, and she fancied herself as inheriting our mother's strong belief that I could achieve something really worthwhile. She truly loved her husband, and she worshiped her son, Waldo II, but there was adequate room in her big heart for others. She regularly followed my career and work, wished to be present whenever and wherever an honor came to me, and enjoyed my being president of the American Historical Association more than anyone; she always felt that she was a stand-in for our mother, who passed away in 1936. When, therefore, Waldo called me one morning in April 1986, to tell me that Sister, who had always seemed larger than life, had died suddenly from an aneurysm, I was grief stricken. After Aurelia and I went to Tulsa for her funeral and then witnessed her burial in the family plot, I felt that the family as I had known it had come to an end.

Meanwhile, Bouna had graduated with high honors from North Carolina Central University and had won a full scholarship to the International University of Japan. He won high honors there, too, graduating in 1989. Aurelia and I journeyed to Japan to congratulate him at his commencement and to cheer him on. Immediately, he was employed by Coopers and Lybrand in West Africa, where he would remain until he rejoined us in Durham in 1996.

Aurelia would lose her mother in February 1992. We were visiting Nassau, in the Bahamas, when our Durham housekeeper, Juanita Roberts, called us to say that Grandmother, as she was affectionately called, was not eating. Mrs. Roberts had also grown apprehensive about her general condition. We were unable to reach our primary care physician, Dr. Johnson, so we called Dr. Akwari, our surgeon. He was not in, but Anne Akwari, his wife, also a physician, said that she would be pleased to go and look in on Grandmother. She did, and promptly placed her in the Duke Medical Center, informing Dr. Johnson that she had done so. The latter then called to assure us that he was keeping vigil. We volunteered to return at once, but he said that there was no need and that he would keep us informed. Two days later, he called and said that she had passed away quietly.

We immediately returned to Durham, arranged a memorial for her, then took her to Goldsboro, where we had a graveside service to which many old friends came to pay their last respects. At age 102 she was buried beside her beloved husband. Despite our early difficulties, when she had worked to prevent my marrying her daughter, she and I came to have a loving relationship, and over the more than two decades that Grandmother lived with us, she was truly a part of the family. I not only respected her but cared for her as if she were my own mother, and I loved her as devotedly. Unable to come for the memorial and unable to arrange for a memorial in his mosque, Bouna had a Mass said for her in the local Catholic church in Dakar.

For some time, Beverly Jarrett, then editor-in-chief at the Louisiana State University Press, had suggested that I collect some of my essays and publish them. When I realized that Margaret Fitzsimmons would soon observe twenty-five years of working with me, I found a compelling incentive for complying with Beverly's suggestion: I would dedicate the volume to Margaret. Intent on its being a surprise, this book became one of the few publishing projects for which Margaret did not lend a helping hand.

The more I worked on the volume, the more I became persuaded that it could have some real value, bringing together as it would some of the more important statements I had made over the past fifty years. One of the difficulties I had was in selecting just twenty-seven essays out of more than one hundred and then organizing them in a way that made sense. What galvanized my efforts was my hope that this book would give me another opportunity to place before the general public some thoughts and arguments that I had advanced over decades of active work, as a scholar, educator, and writer.

Race and History, as we titled the book, was widely and well received. Dan Carter of Emory University wrote, "These essays are examples of first-rate scholarship. Even when treading his way through the most treacherous issue of American life, race, Franklin is a model for us all: diligent and ingenious in uncovering sources and then scrupulous in the use of primary materials. To read this collection is to be reminded of just how important John Hope Franklin has been in the historical profession." My old friend C. Vann Woodward called it "engagingly forthright, unpretentious, and richly informative . . . This is a book packed full of hard truths that needed saying. It is our good fortune that they are said so well and in a voice that carries such authority." The comments of scholar Drew Gilpin Faust were notable for putting a finger on what had for so long inspired my professional aspirations: "In an era when many scholars in the humanities and social sciences are questioning whether it is possible to identify any foundations for truth or scholarly objectivity, John Hope Franklin offers a compelling case for continuing to struggle toward these goals. Both his life and his work represent a commitment to learning as an important way to 'bear witness' in a society that he, perhaps better than any American scholar alive today, knows to be far from perfect. His faith and his achievement cannot but serve as witness and inspiration to all of us privileged to be engaged with him in the historical enterprise." But none of this praise matched my joy at Margaret's expression of surprised gratitude when I handed the work to her on her birthday.

Shortly after that memorable event, Aurelia and I celebrated our fiftieth wedding anniversary. Many years earlier we had concluded, on our first visit to Brazil, that we wanted to spend our golden wedding anniversary in Rio de Janeiro and Salvador. We shared the event and the trip with our dear friends Harold and Lucille Pinkett, always ready for an adventure. The entire journey was a joyous one, characterized by leisure, the festive nature of the cities visited, our celebratory mood, and the pleasure of the Pinketts' company.

For me, it was also an occasion to confess to myself and to Aurelia how very fortunate I was to have her as my closest friend for almost sixty years and my wife for a half century. As I looked back over that stretch of decades, I could truly say that there was never a time when she uttered one word of doubt about what we should do with our lives. Her support of me in all my endeavors was more than I deserved, and at this point in our marriage, I wanted to indicate in every way possible my gratitude for her unselfish support. Though I had struggled to give her every opportunity to see what I had seen and to enjoy the things to which, thanks to her, I had been exposed, how could I ever thank her enough? Not only was this our golden anniversary, it was another chance to express my admiration, appreciation, and love for "Old Gold," as Ted Currier always called Aurelia.

By now Beverly Jarrett had departed Louisiana State University Press to assume the directorship of the University of Missouri Press but that did not mean she had tired of finding things for me to do. At her urging, the University of Missouri committee in charge of the Paul Anthony Brick Lectures invited me to deliver these in 1992, with their publication timed for the following year. I accepted. These three talks, delivered over two days, April 30 and May 1, before large and attentive audiences, were inspired by the assertion of W.E.B. Du Bois that the problem of the twentieth century would be the problem of the color line. There was nothing prescient in the fact that the lectures were delivered against the backdrop of the Los Angeles riot that had followed the not-guilty verdict by an all-white jury in Simi Valley of the four white Los Angeles policemen who had been caught on videotape beating Rodney King. Given the longstanding nature of the problem, all I could claim was sad coincidence.

I opened the first lecture by updating Du Bois's famous statement: The problem of the twenty-first century, I said, would likewise be the problem of the color line. I argued that by any standard of measurement or evaluation, the problem had not been solved in the twentieth century and thus it remained a burden for the next. Tragically, this simply meant that the pattern remained unchanged. The eighteenth century had bequeathed the problem to the nineteenth, as had the nineteenth century done to its successor. By the time that Du Bois died in 1963, an optimist had reason for hope. The United States armed forces had been desegregated, the United States Supreme Court had outlawed segregation in the public schools, and new civil rights and voting rights laws were in the offing. Blacks began to climb the corporate ladder, and they were breaking new ground in the public sector. But there were persistent signs that the national commitment to truly and forthrightly address the problem was less than complete or sincere.

I then described what could well be called the ensuing slippage in our commitment to the elimination of the color line. The "New Beginning" that was to characterize the Reagan administration contributed significantly to a climate that tolerated racism and, indeed, encouraged policies and measures that denied equal opportunity and equal treatment. Reagan's appointment of Clarence Thomas to head the Equal Employment Opportunity Commission was indicative: With Thomas at the helm, the backlog of complaints grew from thirty thousand to more than sixty thousand. Small wonder that such a stellar performance would merit his appointment to the District of Columbia Court of Appeals and eventually to the United States Supreme Court. Surely the fact that 90 percent of America's blacks voted for Reagan's opponents in 1980 and 1984 conveyed how they felt. The New Beginning about which Reagan boasted was a false start as far as African Americans were concerned.

In the remaining two lectures, I pursued the argument that the color line was alive and well at the close of the twentieth century. The 1896 claim of Justice John Marshal Harlan in *Plessy* that the constitution was color-blind did not make it so. Even in Harlan's time, many states codified in law the parameters within which blacks could conduct themselves. Race itself was ever more carefully defined. Virginia's law of 1879 defined a Negro as one possessing one-fourth or more of Negro blood. Fearing that some blacks would slip through the genetic cracks and be viewed as white, the law was amended several times so that by 1930, it declared that any person in which there is "ascertainable any Negro blood shall be deemed and taken to be a colored person." Worse still, two world wars merely indicated to blacks that whatever the nation's victories, their status would not be significantly improved. Small wonder that Du Bois became more and more discouraged, even depressed, to the point that he gave up on his native land and became an expatriate, going into exile in Ghana, where he spent the remaining years of his life. For him the color line had become unbreachable.

This was not a problem of yesteryear or even yesterday; the color line was flourishing at the end of the twentieth century. Schools that had some prospect of desegregating after 1954 were in the process of resegregating in 1990. It was the same in housing, employment, and virtually every phase of life where the races had some contact. The color line thrives, I argued, because people who live with it have been desensitized to its significance, and it comes to permeate our thinking and our actions. I concluded my final lecture by saying that what we needed so desperately was the assumption of responsibility at the highest levels in the public and private sectors to eliminate the uglier aspects of the color line. Only that rededication to the centuries-old problem might give us a healthier, happier, even gentler society. Then I issued a call for Americans to take some "first steps" to face up to their past in order to move positively toward erasing the color line in the future.

"We need to recognize it for what it is and not explain it away, excuse it, or justify it," I said. "We should make a good faith effort to turn our history around so that we can see it in front of us, so that we can avoid doing what we have done for so long. If we do that, whites will discover that African Americans possess the same human qualities that other Americans possess, and African Americans will discover that white Americans are capable of the most sublime expressions of human conduct of which all human beings are capable. Then, we need to do everything possible to emphasize the positive qualities that all of us have, qualities which we have never utilized to the fullest, but which we must utilize if we are to solve the problem of the color line in the twenty-first century."

I dedicated *The Color Line*, as the book that was drawn from these lectures was called, to Mary Frances Berry, "Courageous Fighter Against the Color Line." From one of her offices, either at the United States Civil Rights Commission, of which she was chair, or at the University of Pennsylvania, where she was Geraldine R. Segal Professor of American Social

Thought, she called to tell me that she was both speechless and grateful. Of all the reviews this slender volume received, none meant more to me than the one in which Thomas Davis concluded by saying, "Anyone interested in understanding or improving America needs to read this powerful little book."

In 1991 I became involved in a public professional argument with one of my best friends, C. Vann Woodward, resulting from a review of Dinesh D'Souza's *Illiberal Education: The Politics of Race and Sex on Campus* in *The New York Review of Books*. A 1978 immigrant from Calcutta, D'Souza attended Dartmouth College and plunged into conservative politics even before graduating. As editor of *The Dartmouth Review*, he unapologetically embraced the right wing in the columns of that undergraduate paper, and he continued to do so as a Reagan White House Fellow and at the American Enterprise Institute. Soon, he was involved in studying the politics and culture of six universities about which he would write: Berkeley, Stanford, Howard, Michigan, Duke, and Harvard. D'Souza argued that minority recruitment at universities was corrosive to liberal education and even fostered racial differences. He was vigorously opposed to the special treatment that institutions of higher education extended to minority groups. He also viewed with a jaundiced eye perceived challenges to academic freedom and the "wild" suggestions for curriculum reform at the universities about which he wrote. He, of course, said nothing about the preferential treatment that whites in general had enjoyed for centuries or about the corrosive effects on higher education of giving preference to the children of alumni and wealthy donors.

Woodward, while sensitive to D'Souza's conservative views, expressed surprise that Eugene Genovese and Robert Bork, individuals he seemed to believe to be ideological polar opposites, had praised the book, as had others "from all points across the political spectrum." This was the first statement in the Woodward review that caused me to wonder just what my friend meant. Did he truly believe D'Souza's analysis was objectively unbiased? I was not at all surprised that the book won praise from Genovese and Bork, for I had never thought that Genovese was as left wing as many gave him credit for being, and I, of course, had testified before the Senate Judiciary Committee regarding my views on Bork's conservative positions. But it was D'Souza's snide remarks about the universities bowing to black students' demands for changes in the curriculum and Woodward's reaction to those remarks, that caused me to respond publicly to the review. Specifically, it was Woodward's account of what was transpiring at Duke with which I took issue. "Duke's plunge into the mainstream of academic fashions stressed star faculty appointments in several fields," Woodward wrote. "On the black side it made a fine start by recruiting John Hope Franklin, the best historian in his field, for the last years of his teaching career." It seemed clear to me that by "his field," Woodward was referring to black studies or, more specifically, to black history. He proceeded to describe Duke as being intimidated by those who seemed to want to increase the number of black faculty at any cost. Thus, the university's stated commitment to have at least one minority professor in each department by 1993. "Not a racist school, Duke—not anymore." Perhaps most troubling of all was that Vann Woodward, my very dear friend for forty years, had written the review without consulting me about the terms under which I had joined Duke's faculty, what I knew of its recruitment initiatives, or what subject I taught there.

He had accepted, uncritically, D'Souza's description and interpretation of what was transpiring at Duke without checking with any of his many friends who actually taught there. Consequently, I felt compelled to tell my side of the story to the editor of *The New York Review of Books*. "While one is tempted to re-examine D'Souza's work and Woodward's review of it, I shall confine my comments to Woodward's use of the work to expatiate on the evolution of black studies as an area of intellectual inquiry and discourse." Regarding Duke's plunge into the mainstream of academic fashions, "Your readers should know that I was not recruited to teach black studies, if Woodward was referring to that when he calls me 'The best in his field.' As the James B. Duke Professor of History I was free to teach whatever I wished. Not having taught African American history in 25 years only because I chose to 'integrate' white and African American history of the South, I taught a colloquium on the History of the South and, later, the Constitutional History of the United States. I have no way of knowing how Mr. D'Souza's views of Duke would have been affected by a discussion with me. He made an appointment with me on two different occasions, and he broke both of them without explanation or apology."

It was Woodward's "best in his field" comment that especially and personally grated. African American scholars have repeatedly been cast or pushed into the field of black studies even when they were not inclined to go that route. I gave as examples Charles H. Wesley's being denied the opportunity to write a dissertation at Harvard on the collapse of the Confederacy, the subject being deemed more appropriate for a white man; my being invited in a Harvard seminar to write on Booker T. Washington when I expressed a desire to write on Lyman Abbott; and the distinguished historian, a Southerner, who had read my manuscript for the Harvard University Press and wondered why they were interested in publishing a book on *The Militant South* unless it was the particular wish to have "a Negro view of the South."

Vann Woodward, of course, was not unaware of this problem. Indeed, in his review he quoted from my own essay, "The Dilemma of the American Negro Scholar," in which I said, "Negro scholarship had foundered on the rocks of racism. It had been devoured by principles of separation and segregation. It had become the victim of the view that there was some 'mystique' about Negro studies, similar to the view that there was some 'mystique' about Negro spirituals which required a person to possess a black skin in order to sing them. This was not scholarship; it was folklore, it was voodoo." I hoped, however, that the *Review* would reproduce a longer quote from that essay in my letter, especially since *Race and History* had never been reviewed in *The New York Review*, as indeed had none of my books. I wished my letter to provide the proper context for why I had made the argument: namely, when black scholars went into black studies, it frequently was not by choice "but by white racism that dictated the nature of scholarship, as it did in virtually all other aspects of American life."

In his reply, Woodward seemed a bit stunned. "John Hope Franklin must have got up on the wrong side of the bed the day he wrote his letter," he began. Then, recovering his poise while taking on a slightly patronizing air, he continued, "It does not sound like him. I have always counted on him as an anchor of sanity in whatever storm we happened to be caught. I have reason to expect that of him. Our relations go back more than forty years and include repeated defiance of the racial code to which we were both born when it was at its worst, he in Oklahoma, I in Arkansas . . . And now here is John Hope who wonders what Woodward meant by describing him as the 'best in his field.' " Woodward insisted that he had meant by this simply that Franklin was the best "in any field of history he cultivated." But context was *everything*, and when Woodward described me as the "best in his field," he was talking to the point that D'Souza was making regarding black studies. If I misunderstood him, as my reply to the review indicated, I was full of apology. But Vann and I necessarily viewed the world through different lenses, felt nuances with differing degrees of acuity. If he viewed the Civil Rights Act and the Voting Rights Act as signal victories, to me they were mere tenuous toeholds that could slip away at any moment, as indeed they seemed to be doing even as we exchanged letters. As D'Souza's book reminded me, no matter which side of the bed I chose to wake up on, I would still be a black man in a racially divisive America.

Later, at our next face-to-face meeting, Woodward and I expressed thanks that the public dispute had no lasting effect on our personal regard and mutual esteem for each other. At our last encounter, in 1999, at the meeting of the Southern Historical Association, we sought a private corner, away from his public and mine, where we could talk privately and reminisce about the culture wars and racial wars we had fought together. We recalled my talk at his seminar at Johns Hopkins in 1948 and his coup in placing me on the program of the Southern Historical Association the following year, and how I became president of that association twenty years later. We recalled the fights with Southern hotels in the 1940s and 1950s when they resisted making accommodations for African Americans. We remembered his winning the so-called triple crown as president, successively, of the three major historical associations, and how I followed him to that pinnacle a few years later. We remembered that I had read the first draft of his University of Virginia Richard Lectures, had urged him to deliver them as written, and how they made their mark when they were published as *The Strange Career of Jim Crow*. We recollected that he had delivered the first annual John Hope Franklin Lecture at Adelphi University in 1986. All the while we were unaware, of course, that this would be our last encounter.

27

Honorable Mention

I HAVE NEVER SOUGHT public recognition or rewards in connection with my work. For me it has always been sufficient to earn the respect and support of my peers, without any plaudits from those on the sidelines. If an institution favored me with an honorary degree, for example, I regarded it as a recognition by my counterparts at that institution who wished to call attention to the praiseworthy efforts that a friend and fellow scholar, researcher, and educator had made. I continued to believe that up until 1978, when I was selected for a niche in the Oklahoma Hall of Fame. None of my fellow inductees were historians or even connected with educational institutions. They were primarily from the fields of business, politics, public service, and philanthropy. Throughout the 1980s and '90s, I was overwhelmed with varying degrees of public attention and awards for my accomplishments, all of them meaningful, some particularly so.

Recognitions I received were more likely to be at colleges or universities where I was invited to "show my wares" in the form of a lecture or to participate in some scholarly enterprise. Thus, in 1987 I was invited to give a series of lectures at the University of Washington, and while there, I received the Bunn Award from the Seattle Public Library, where I gave yet another lecture, "African American History: The Search for Authority."

An even better honor mixed with pleasure was Aurelia's and my visit to Europe in 1988, during which I lectured at the University of Göttingen, visited former students and colleagues and longtime friends, making sure that there was also time for some theater in London, where we saw, among other things, August Wilson's *Fences*.

My peregrinations and commitments made it impossible to accept in person one of the awards that I cherished most. I was made a founding member of the Fellowship of Southern Writers. Louis Rubin of the Department of English at the University of North Carolina at Chapel Hill had taken the initiative in establishing the organization, and among my fellow founding members were such well-known Southerners as Ralph Ellison, William Styron, Robert Penn Warren, Eudora Welty, C. Vann Woodward, Elizabeth Spencer, Reynolds Price, and Ernest J. Gaines. The first step the organization took to recognize achievement was the establishment of the Cleanth Brooks Medal for Distinguished Achievement in Southern Letters. To my astonishment, the committee selected me as its first recipient. Unfortunately, I was unable to attend the fellowship's meeting in Chattanooga, where the award was made, because it conflicted with a long-standing commitment to speak at the annual meeting of the Organization of American Historians. Cleanth Brooks, still thriving at Yale in 1989, wrote to congratulate me and was gracious enough to say that when the name of the medal is "coupled with your name, I have no doubt about which of the two names is being enhanced."

In July 1990, I went to Chicago, where I had been invited to deliver the Fourth of July Oration at the Chicago Historical Society. That summer the society's principal exhibit dealt with the themes laid down by Abraham Lincoln in his "House Divided" speech in 1858, and I decided to wrestle with the same, speaking on the subject "Who Divided This House?" I pointed out that perhaps the situation would have been happier in 1858 had the founding fathers in 1787 anticipated the dire consequences of trying to build a house half slave and half free. At issue was less the fact that the founding fathers, and the generations that immediately followed them, had failed to work adequately to address the problems they were bequeathing the future, than that they were much too comfortable with the status quo. The glaring need to reconcile their institutions with the social and philosophical positions that they assumed proved far too easy to ignore. "There was too little self-criticism, too much inclination to accept things as they were and to postpone dealing with the hard problems. It was this postponement that put Lincoln's generation in a bind and that led to the tragic events of the eighteen-sixties." I concluded by pointing out that the responsibility of our generation was to "face up to our staggering problems now and not to put them off for some unknowing, innocent generation to which it will cost infinitely more to solve."

Early in 1990 I went to San Francisco to deliver the Mathew O. Tobriner Memorial Lecture at the Hastings Law School. Tobriner had been a justice on the Supreme Court of California, and his friends and relatives established the lectureship as a permanent memorial to him and his life's work. Hastings, in downtown San Francisco, is the "other" law school of the University of California. Located in the Tenderloin section of the city, it attracts more working-class and mature students than does Boalt Hall School of Law located on the campus in Berkeley.

For the lecture, I addressed a problem that had recently been decided before the United States Supreme Court. It involved the treatment of an African American woman, Brenda Patterson, who worked for a credit union in Winston-Salem, North Carolina. Employed as a teller and file clerk coordinator, she was subjected not only to the requirement that she perform menial duties not required of her equivalent white counterparts but also to harassment and racial slurs, even from her supervisor. Her job was rendered virtually unbearable. When she was terminated ten years after her initial employment in 1972, she sued for damages arising from mental anguish and emotional distress. She also sought reimbursement of her attorney's fees. Citing a wealth of evidence, she claimed that the actions of her employer were "willful, wanton, intentional, malicious, and in total disregard" of her rights and in violation of section 1981 of Title 42 of the United States Code.

When the case of *Patterson v. McClean Credit Union* reached the United States Supreme Court, Patterson's plea was supported by sixty-five members of the U.S. Senate and 118 members of the U.S. House of Representatives, 40 civil rights organizations, a group of historians, and numerous professional groups, including the American Bar Association, the National Bar Association, the Lawyers' Committee for Civil Rights Under Law, and the NAACP. After hearing oral arguments, Justice Anthony Kennedy, speaking for the majority, ruled against Patterson, claiming that the right to make contracts "does not extend to conduct by the employer *after* the contract has been established, including breach of the terms of the contract or imposition of discriminatory working conditions." As far as harassment was concerned, Justice Kennedy declared that the petitioner was not entitled to relief under the statute. If it was any consolation, he said that the conduct of which the petitioner complained was actionable under the "more expansive reach of Title VII of the Civil Rights Act of 1964." In his dissent, Justice Brennan said that the Court had ignored "powerful historical evidence about the Reconstruction Congress' concerns . . . bolstering its parsimonious rendering by reference to a statute enacted nearly a century after Section 1981 and plainly not intended to affect its reach." Lamenting the decision, I concluded my lecture by observing that it was a pity lawmakers in 1866 had been more attentive to the rights of freedmen than the current Court was to the rights of black Americans in 1989.

Indeed, I struggled to understand how the highest court in the land could tolerate the violation of a statute enacted by the Congress of the United States in 1866 to protect the rights of freedmen. One hundred twenty-three years later, despite the overwhelming support of civil rights groups and a majority of the Senate, a lone African American woman could find no relief from the humiliating conditions imposed on her by her employer. Even as I received ever more attention and praise for what I had accomplished over the past five decades, I grew ever more disquieted by the mounting evidence that there continued to be significant slippage in the status of African Americans in the United States.

In December 1990, I joined a group from the Children's Defense Fund that was planning a conference at the Rockefeller Foundation Conference Center at Bellagio, Italy. The CDF had been founded by Marian Wright Edelman in response to the widely acknowledged plight of thousands of black children who were abused, neglected, starved, and in many other respects in need of attention. Marian had asked Dorothy Height, president of the National Council of Negro Women, and me to cochair the meeting. The group was charged with moving children to the top of the priority list of the black agenda and to forge a new and concerted national and local effort on behalf of black children and youth. Among the twenty-two attending the meeting were James Forbes of New York's Riverside Church, the noted child psychiatrist James Comer, the philosopher Cornel West, and Angela Glover Blackwell of CDF. In curious juxtiposition to the problem we had convened to address, we conferred for four days in one of the loveliest settings I had ever seen.

I missed some of the discussion, for I had been asked to draft a manifesto setting forth the hopes of the group. It read in part: "Our desires and hopes for our children are reasonable to the point of modesty, but we wish no less and no more for them than we wish for every child in every land. We want them to grow up with healthy bodies and healthy minds, in a drug-free society, with ample tools for engaging in critical thinking and making sound judgments. We want them to have every opportunity to achieve success in school and to understand fully the world of work, what is involved in acquiring marketable skills, and how important it is to make a significant contribution to that world. We want our children to learn that the greatest success lies not so much in amassing a fortune as in having a concern for others and in recovering and preserving the tradition of selfless service to family and community. We want them to appreciate fully the artistic, moral, and spiritual values that will bring to them much of their heritage of the past and make it possible to pass these on to their successors. We want them to have an understanding and appreciation for family, for their own rich heritage derived from their African forebears as well as their American experience, the kind of understanding that will simultaneously provide them with roots and wings." The document concluded, "We pledge ourselves to do everything humanly possible to strengthen the black family, save black children through succor as well as love, and to improve and modernize our schools in order to enhance significantly their chances for educational and life success. In this gigantic task we shall utilize to the fullest the resources of parents, children, and the general public."

In succeeding years the manifesto has been a centerpiece for the work of the Children's Defense Fund, both in its national program and in the numerous activities that it conducts at Haley Farm near Knoxville, Tennessee. At a typical summer program, it holds seminars for young adult leaders, classes for children fortunate enough to qualify or be invited, and recreational activities for everyone present. The CDF's copyrighted motto, "Leave No Child Behind," has become the watchword for a nationwide movement to strengthen every activity and institution affecting children wherever they happen to be.

In the midst of all this activity, my own child, Whit, remarked that he was in love. I congratulated him and asked with whom. When he answered that it was Karen Roberts, I responded that I remembered that she was his best friend. He said that she was not only his best friend but the person he intended to marry. Aurelia and I were delighted.

As they made their plans, they wanted two favors from me. One was that they wished to marry at the Cosmos Club in Washington, D.C., which as a member I could easily arrange. The other was that since Karen's father, Dr. James E. Roberts, a prominent Washington gynecologist and a member of the Howard medical staff, was deceased, she wished me to give her away. Her mother, Sylvesta, already in a nursing facility, would be present, as would Aurelia, with no official roles, but both were pleased to see their children "settling down." Bouna could not miss the occasion, so he flew in from Dakar. About fifty guests witnessed the ceremony, which was followed by a champagne reception marked by an abundance of food and beautiful music. That evening the newlyweds left for a honeymoon in Brazil, and upon their return they settled down in their home in Silver Spring, Maryland, where they have lived ever since.

Overshadowing my joy was my sad realization of Aurelia's worsening condition. Several years earlier she had been suspected of having Alzheimer's disease, and we determined immediately to give as little ground to its inexorable progress as possible, refusing to curtail our joint activities for as long as proved practical. These included our regular visits to St. Petersburg, Florida, where we would take a condominium for six or eight weeks, visit with our friends in the city, and participate in the activities at the Academy of Senior Professionals at Eckerd College, where I would give a few lectures. Then we would join Harold and Lucille Pinkett on a Caribbean cruise. We continued that routine even after it became clear that Aurelia was in the early stages of the disease. Later, when she became a participant in an experiment with a trial medication, we did not allow it to interfere with our travels. She took the medication as instructed, and in St. Petersburg, Nassau, or wherever, we would go to a hospital once per week so that Aurelia could have a blood sample drawn and sent by air to the appropriate laboratory.

On one of those visits out of the country, however, I was frightened almost to the point of sheer panic. We were in Nassau with the Pinketts, with whom we had adjoining rooms. Aurelia and Lucille were chatting in the Pinketts' room, while Harold and I were sitting on its balcony. After a while I left the balcony and asked Lucille where Aurelia was. She replied that she had just gone over to our room. With a premonition of worry, I rushed through the door, calling out to her. She obviously was not there or in the bathroom. As I ran into the hall, a maid asked me if I was looking for someone. When I identified Aurelia, the maid pointed in the direction that she had gone. I dashed around the corner just as Aurelia was entering the elevator. I called out to her and she stepped back into the hall, as the elevator doors closed behind her. I asked her where she was going and she replied that she was looking for us, even though she had just left Lucille in the room where Harold and I were sitting on the balcony. Here, I realized, was another indication of the progress of her illness and a jarring indication of what lay ahead.

Soon after that we traveled to San Diego for a reunion of Aurelia's library school classmates. I doubt that many of them realized that Aurelia was ill. We made no public announcement of her illness, but if anyone inquired we would tell him or her of the disability. We also went to Alaska on a cruise that did not involve our getting off the ship except in Juneau, where we disembarked to visit a clinic so that Aurelia could have her blood drawn.

On that Alaskan trip, and especially when we visited Aurelia's best friend, Pat Withner, in Bellingham, Washington, I had time to think about what the accomplishments of the past decades had meant to the two of us and of Aurelia's role in giving me a wonderful, meaningful life. Throughout my career, she was aware of the challenges, opportunities, and sacrifices required of us both, and her selflessness had been essential to my and Whit's achievements. If anything stood out of all the wonderful qualities she exhibited, it was the quiet dignity with which she faced the racist laws and culture that battered us and bore down so unfairly on our son. I could reminisce about our lives together and could truly say that I owed much of whatever success I enjoyed to her strong and consistent support at every stage of my life.

Back in Durham, at the suggestion of the staff at the Memory Disorders Clinic, I joined an Alzheimer's support group. Without question, it was good to exchange views with others undergoing similar experiences, and there was real worth in the factual information learned. One thing I discovered was that the disease could affect *anyone* regardless of background, education, or experience. In the group were businessmen, college professors, and persons from all walks of life, all brought down by one of the cruelest maladies known. One thing I also learned from caregivers was what to expect as the disease progressed. There were patients who were no longer able to walk, talk, or even swallow. A grim future faced us.

Soon, Aurelia experienced difficulty walking. I thought it had to do with the fact that both her knees had been replaced. I took her back to our orthopedic surgeon, our neighbor and friend Richard Bruch, who had performed the surgery. After he assured us that everything was as it should be, I had an electrically operated chair installed for our stairway to the second floor, to relieve Aurelia of having to negotiate the steps. All too soon, however, she was unable to operate the chair without assistance. Since she could no longer walk easily and was no longer able to drive, she was now confined to our home unless I took her out.

Believing it important that she remain in contact with other people, I looked into the possibility of placing her somewhere for a part of the day. I learned that there was an adult day-care center at Durham's local Unitarian Universalist Association. It was intended for people who for whatever reason would otherwise be left alone at home when their spouses, children, or caregivers could not be available. They were pleased to have Aurelia join them, and soon she was doing so for a half day each day, which I thought was sufficient, especially since our housekeeper, Juanita Roberts, could look after her when I was away from home. Consequently, beginning in 1994 our trusted driver, George Faulk, would come for Aurelia each day just before noon and drive her to the center, where she would have lunch. She would remain there until about five p.m., at which time I would call for her and take her home. If I were held up or out of town, Mr. Faulk would do so. For the time being that proved a satisfactory arrangement. Somewhere in the recesses of my mind and heart, I realized that at some future point Aurelia would require more care, but the brace of friends and help who allowed us to maintain our new routines permitted us to adhere to our decision to give grudgingly to her condition and permitted me to meet most of my commitments even as I strove to meet Aurelia's changed circumstances.

During the last week of October 1992, I received a call from a member of the advance team of Governor Bill Clinton, who was in the final weeks of his run for the presidency. The person informed me that the Clinton campaign would be coming to Durham the following day, and Governor Clinton wondered if it would be possible for him to meet me. I indicated my willingness and then arranged to be at North Carolina Central University where the governor was to speak at a rally. The next day the governor was more than two hours late, a habit of his for which he was to become well-known. Upon his arrival, I was instructed to meet him at the bus, where he would come after he had spoken and "worked the crowd."

At the end of the rally, my friend Walter Dellinger and I dutifully went to the bus for our rendezvous with the Clinton party. The first to arrive was Al Gore with one of his daughters. As we began to introduce ourselves, he assured us that he knew who we were, whereupon he explained to his daughter who I was, adding emphatically that she should never forget that she had met me. Then Hillary Clinton arrived with her daughter, and I inquired of Chelsea's foot, which she had recently injured. She seemed immensely pleased that even during the campaign someone was interested in her well-bring. At that point the governor finally arrived and expressed gratitude for my willingness to meet with him. Mrs. Clinton and Mrs. Gore were likewise gracious in expressing their appreciation, and we all entered into a discussion regarding the origins of civilization and other arcane subjects, but no politics. By the time someone announced that the Gore-Clinton entourage would, once again, be late for its next appointment and must leave at once, we had all taken the measure of the other. At minimum, I knew for a certainty for whom I would vote come November.

The next time I heard from Clinton, he had been in the presidency for more than six months. He had appointed the president of the University of Pennsylvania, Sheldon Hackney, to be director of the National Endowment for the Humanities. In turn, the endowment indicated that the president had approved me to be one of the recipients of the Charles Frankel Humanities Award for 1993. Other recipients would be the Puerto Rican anthropologist Ricardo Algeria; my one-time colleague and boss Hanna Gray, former president of the University of Chicago; Andrew Heiskell, former chairman of Time, Inc.; the writer William Styron; and Laurel Ulrich, a historian at the University of New Hampshire.

My visit to Washington to receive the award was a most happy one. The first item on the agenda was a luncheon at the offices of the National Endowment, presided over by Sheldon Hackney, at which I spoke about my current research on runaway slaves. The awards were presented on the south lawn of the White House, at which time the first lady opened the proceedings and then introduced President Clinton. He handed each recipient his or her award, making appropriate remarks as he did so. In the evening, we were guests at a black-tie dinner at the White House. I noted that I now could tick off the third administration that had invited Aurelia and me to the White House, the others being the administrations of Johnson and Carter. Sadly, this time I had come alone, as I would on the ensuing visits over the next several years. The Clintons were understanding, friendly, and informal, and my esteem for both of them increased.

It was inevitable that in due course I would reach my eightieth birthday, but it was not inevitable that it would be marked by the notice my friends took of it. First, Whit and Karen put on a big celebration at our home for friends and relatives. Then, Duke University invited David Levering Lewis to deliver a lecture, "Race, History, and John Hope Franklin," to a capacity audience at the Reynolds Theater at Duke. With a deftness that Lewis shares with few others, he traced my career almost from the beginning, placing each of my major pieces of writing into some meaningful context. Late in the lecture he said, "Looking back on your career . . . one can espy a trajectory arcing in the later years out of history into law and public policy and now, it appears, into the privilege of prophecy. Your latest book, *The Color Line: Legacy for the 21st Century*, might be said to be inspired by Santayana's well-worn premonition about the past and his student Du Bois's repeatedly invoked admonition about the future." In closing, Lewis said, "We honor ourselves in praising you, and I close with a paraphrase of a soldierly saying: Old historians never die, they just make history."

Lewis's lecture was followed by a reception to which the entire audience was invited and by a birthday dinner attended by more than one hundred guests. Nearly overwhelmed by warm remarks and greetings, I nevertheless managed to arise at the appropriate occasion and deliver "Reflections of an Octogenarian."

After thanking the president, provost, and others responsible for the festivities, I pointed out how irresponsible it would be for one to wait until his eightieth birthday to say something important in order to win praise for being a wise old man. Regardless, a particular age, I conceded, does not bring any special gift, prescience, or wisdom. "Whether one is 40 or 80, the magic is in the transforming power to see and understand, to give evidence of mature thought and reflection which, in turn flows from emotional, psychological, and intellectual maturity." I then spoke of the duty and responsibility of any person at any age to do everything possible to make life better for the least among us. "One of the privileges of old age," I said, "is to be able to speak even outrageously about what is wrong with our society and what should be done about it . . . I hope that I am not among those who would yield to profligacy and prodigality in order to make a dramatic and flourishing point. I wish to be counted among those, not yet sages, perhaps, who want their peers, even the world, to know that they have done all they could to make this place . . . a place of decent habitation where men and women, boys and girls, can find that pervasive peace and prosperity that will abide among them now and forever."

In the spring of 1995 we reached yet another benchmark, the sixtieth anniversary of our graduation from Fisk University. Aurelia, whose condition had further deteriorated, could not go to Nashville, but I went and joined the small number of our classmates who came for the reunion. One of the sad things about going to such events is how they remind one of the inevitability of the grim reaper's role. By this time Aurelia's illness had reached the point that she was unable to travel, and even had she been able to do so, her cognition was such that her presence would have been meaningless. She would not have known she was in Nashville, and her resulting confusion would have bordered on cruelty. We had been back for our fiftieth reunion, and it was a much happier occasion. Now, barely a handful of the class of 1935 had returned. We chatted about old times, especially about friends who had passed away, were infirm, or remained incommunicado. Perhaps the most joyous moment for me was the alumni banquet. It was at that gathering that I was named the outstanding living alumnus. The citation read, "To John Hope Franklin, '35, Scholar, Historian,

Teacher, Orchidologist, Writer, Distinguished Son of Fisk University, First Recipient of the W.E.B. Du Bois Lifetime Achievement Award." Since it came from my alma mater, I cherished it all the more.

Later that year, I received two honors that were among the most important that I had ever received or, indeed, that I could imagine ever receiving. One was the Spingarn Award, presented each year at the annual meeting of the NAACP for "the highest and noblest achievement of an American Negro." The medal was first awarded in 1915, the year I was born, and John Hope, for whom I was named, received it posthumously in 1936. The 1995 meeting was held in Minneapolis, and it was the first time that a woman, Myrlie Evers-Williams, the widow of Medgar Evers, presided over the organization. Julius Chambers presented the medal, saying of me, "Not only has he reconstructed America's sordid racial history, but he has a secure place in history for his input and research in the landmark . . . case, *Brown v. Board of Education*." Then, in an extravagant flourish, he added that Franklin's research "ranks him equally with the lawyers in that case." By the time the presentations were over, I could add little and deny much, and so restricted myself to noting that from the beginning the NAACP had been fighting to obtain a level playing field for every person, and I added that the awards and prizes that it bestowed on people like me must be coupled "with a continued commitment to fight to improve the lot of the disadvantaged."

I was utterly speechless when I received a call from the White House in the early summer of 1995 informing me that President Clinton intended to present me with the Presidential Medal of Freedom. The ceremony was postponed for two days because of the president's efforts to bring together the disputants in the Middle East's continuing crisis, but on the evening before the delayed ceremony I gave a dinner for a small group of friends at the Cosmos Club. It was during our stroll through the club that a white woman called me out, presented me with her coat check, and ordered me to bring her coat. I patiently told her that if she would present her coat to a uniformed attendant, "and all of the club attendants were in uniform," perhaps she could get her coat.

The ceremony was finally held on the morning of September 29 in the East Room of the White House. Among the twelve recipients were two other African Americans, Leon Higginbotham of the United States Court of Appeals and William T. Coleman, former secretary of transportation. Also being awarded medals were C. Everett Koop, the former surgeon general; Frank M. Johnson of the U.S. District Court; and Joan Ganz Cooney of the Children's Television Workshop. In presenting me with my medal, President Clinton was most generous, saying that Franklin "looks history straight in the face and tells it like it is." He even recounted my experience riding on the train from Greensboro to Durham in 1945, when the black passengers were crowded into a half coach, while a half dozen white passengers were left to occupy a full coach. The president loved telling a story, and he told this one with pleasure. He recounted how the conductor, when challenged over this self-evident inequality, had stuck to the letter of the Jim Crow law. He was unable to move the more comfortable white passengers, despite the fact that they were German prisoners of war. Even in the very face of the demise of Nazism, those African American passengers remained victims of American racism. That evening, Vernon and Ann Jordan gave a gala dinner for me and my guests at their home in Washington. My satisfaction and excitement on receiving the nation's highest civilian award remains to this day.

28

___

One America

THE FIRST CLEAR INDICATION I had that the Clinton administration was thinking seriously about a new approach to the problem of race came from the vice president, Al Gore. To be sure, the president had appointed more African American members to his cabinet—four—than any other president. And there were numerous African Americans on the staffs of the president and the vice president. But when Vice President Gore called me and proposed that he hold several seminar-type meetings at his home to discuss race, to which would be invited a number of people in the government as well as the private sector, I realized that a more deliberate consideration was in the works. The vice president proposed that he and his wife, Tipper, would convene the group and I would introduce the subject, outline its parameters, and lead the discussion.

The vice president planned three informal dinners in which race in America would be discussed. They were scheduled for February 6, 16, and 21, 1994, and in each case the seven o'clock meal was to be followed by a discussion that would conclude at ten-thirty.

On the first evening, the guiding question was, "What does race mean to us as Americans?" On the second, the subject was, "What do we want the future of race relations in America to be?" The final discussion confronted was, "How do we get there from here?" Each night the guest list was different. Among those I clearly recall were Senator Bill Bradley and Secretary of Commerce Ron Brown. I also remember the participation of Henry Cisneros, Lani Guinier, Henry Louis Gates, William Julius Wilson, Maggie Williams, Lawrence Fuchs, Stanley Crouch, and Jesse Jackson. The discussions were lively and serious without being somber, and over the course of them I discovered that the vice president was far from the wooden character with no sense of humor that the media so frequently described him as.

The passionate conviction so evident in Gore's speeches given during the months leading up to the 2004 presidential election was amply evident during those evenings at his home. He was intensely serious about the problem of race. His reactions to his experience as head of the national delegation sent to observe the inauguration of Nelson Mandela as president of South Africa was indicative. He had felt "overpowered by the countless images of the people of South Africa—images of the struggle for freedom at long last victorious, of the boundless joy at finally knowing that hope *is* alive, and of the goodness of the human spirit that allowed this turning point in history to take place on a day as peaceful as it was beautiful." Perhaps his South African experience helped inspire the speech that he made in observance of Martin Luther King Day in Atlanta in 1998. On that occasion, I flew down with him on Air Force Two, and as he boarded the plane he handed me the text of his speech, asking for my reactions. After I had read it, he sought me out well before we landed. My reaction, which drew a laugh from us both, was, "When will you be ordained?" It was a highly charged fire-and-brimstone speech, worthy of a Billy Sunday or a Billy Graham.

On the first evening of the "Gore seminars," I sought to answer the question regarding the meaning of race in America by touching on a few low points in the nation's history, including the clause in the Constitution that counted slaves as three-fifths of a person, the Dred Scott decision that stated categorically that residing on free soil did not confer freedom on a black person, and the provisions in several state constitutions defining a Negro as a person with even a small amount of "Negro blood" in his or her veins. On the second evening I described a hypothetical society, quite different from ours, in which race was irrelevant, and on the third I suggested some steps we could take toward reaching that goal. There was never any lack of lively discussions and penetrating observations. Even working collectively we did not answer all of the questions raised, but at the conclusion of the third and final gathering we all agreed that the federal government should take the initiative in promoting a dialogue on race and in keeping the matter before the general public for the indefinite future.

I had no notion then that the task of keeping the matter before the general public would devolve, in part, on me. When President Clinton asked me in the spring of 1997 to chair the advisory board to the President's Initiative on Race, I struggled over whether to accept the request. I delayed my reply until I could discuss the matter with our family physician and Whit and Karen. Tragically, Aurelia was no longer capable of participating in formulating a reply, and this was painful indeed. She was by then in a nursing home, and although I saw her daily, the steady deterioration of her memory meant that my visits with her were increasingly more for my benefit than for hers.

Neither Whit and Karen nor Dr. Johnson could find any valid reason why I should decline, so I accepted an assignment whose difficulty I could not fathom until I was well into the task. Nothing, however, could detract from the excitement of receiving a presidential appointment and meeting the people who would be my colleagues on the board. With the naïveté that always accompanies optimism, we were embarking, with the full support of the executive office, on a sincere effort to confront and further erase the color line in America.

The board consisted of two women and five men: two African Americans, one Mexican American, one Korean American, and three European Americans. The members were William Winter, former governor of Mississippi; Linda Chavez-Thompson, executive vice president of the AFL-CIO; Thomas Kean, president of Drew University and former governor of New Jersey; Angela Oh, Los Angeles attorney and former special counsel to the Assembly Special Committee on the Los Angeles Crisis; Robert Thomas, executive vice president for marketing of Republic Industries and former president and CEO of Nissan Motor Corporation; and Suzan D. Johnson Cook, former White House fellow and senior pastor of the Bronx Christian Fellowship. We met each other in the Oval Office on June 12, 1997, where the president personally thanked us for accepting the assignment and went over very roughly what he wanted us to do in the ensuing year. He hoped that we would spark a serious dialogue on race and, on the basis of that dialogue and other findings, make recommendations to him for action. Following its conference with the president, the advisory board answered questions raised by the press that awaited our emergence from the Oval Office. The formal announcement of the board, its members, and its purpose would be made the following day.

That was when President Clinton was scheduled to deliver the commencement address at the University of California at San Diego, and since he would speak on the subject of race and would announce the appointment of the president's advisory board on race, we were invited to accompany him on Air Force One.

Back in 1963 I had flown on Air Force One when President Johnson sent it to retrieve the delegations to the independence ceremonies at Zanzibar and Kenya, but the president himself was not aboard. Clinton's presence on the plane made all the difference. It was a delightful trip, with plenty of good food and fellowship, and it provided a golden opportunity for the members of the board to become acquainted. I had met only one of the board members previously: Governor Thomas Kean, who had looked me up in North Carolina at the suggestion of his brother Robert with whom I served on the Fisk University Board of Trustees. In the comfortable confines of the plane, it was easy to get to know the other members, and we made the most of our time together, which included President Clinton joining in our discussions, especially since federal law made it impossible for us to meet privately as a board once we had been sworn into office.

President Clinton was at his best the following day as he addressed the university graduates. He told them that they would take their places as citizens of the great American community "at a truly golden moment for America. The Cold War is over and freedom is now ascendant around the globe . . . Our economy is the healthiest in a generation and the strongest in the world. Our culture, our science, our technology promise unimagined advances and exciting new careers. Our social problems, from crime to poverty, are finally bending to our efforts." Work remained, however, especially in the area of race. As I listened to the president speak, I vividly recalled Du Bois's gloomy prediction in 1903 that the problem of the twentieth century would be the problem of the color line, and while so much had been accomplished since then, so much remained yet to be done. It was the president's habit to ask select people to read his speeches in draft before he delivered them, and a phrase from the version I had read on the way to San Diego leapt to mind as he spoke: It was time for the post–Martin Luther King generation to finally shoulder its fair burden in this struggle. Listening to him now address the graduating class, when President Clinton noted how threatened many Americans were at the prospect of a frank confrontation with race, I heard confirmation of my own fears that for far too long the forces driving the nation toward truly color-blind equality had been losing rather than gaining ground. I took strength, however, in Clinton's determination that "now is the time we should learn together, talk together, and act together to build one America." Sitting before that array of hopeful graduates, I wholeheartedly concurred when Clinton proclaimed how much we all have to gain "from an America where we finally take responsibility for all our children so that they, at last, can be judged as Martin Luther King hoped, 'Not by the color of their skin, but by the content of their character.' "

"What is it we must do?" President Clinton asked. "For four and a half years now, I have worked to prepare America for the twenty-first century with a strategy of opportunity for all, responsibility from all, and an American community of all our citizens. To succeed in each of these areas, we must deal with the realities and the perceptions affecting all racial groups in America."

He then spoke to many of the opportunities and challenges that faced all Americans, particularly education, economic security, and professional advancement. Knowing full well that he was delivering his speech in a state that had recently voted to repeal affirmative action, the president acknowledged how for centuries white Americans had enjoyed the benefits of "one hundred percent affirmative action" and that there was "a public interest" in having "young people sit side-by-side with people of many different backgrounds." Demanding accountability from every American, that the benefits of the economic boom extend to all, and that at minimum those members of Congress who had publicly denounced affirmative action at least provide the funds necessary so that the Equal Employment Opportunity Commission (confronting a shameful backlog of discrimination cases) could effectively apply the law of the land, President Clinton then turned to the hopes and goals of his Initiative on Race.

"Over the coming year I want to lead the American people in a great and unprecedented conversation about race." After naming the members of the initiative's advisory panel, he enumerated his expectations: "I want this panel to help educate Americans about the facts surrounding issues of race, to promote a dialogue in every community of the land to confront and work through these issues, to recruit and encourage leadership at all levels to help breach racial divides, and to find, develop, and recommend how to implement concrete solutions to our problems—solutions that will involve all of us in government, business, communities, and as individual citizens." As chair of that panel, I knew that I had just heard the president enunciate the broad extent of my mandate.

"Emotions may be rubbed raw," the president presciently warned, "but we must begin." Admonishing America and the panel, Clinton proclaimed, "if ten years from now people can look back and see that this year of honest dialogue and concerted action helped to lift the heavy burden of race from our children's future, we will have given a precious gift to America." In the days ahead I would recall that admonishment, just as I would recall the president's hopeful conclusion:

> More than thirty years ago, at the high tide of the civil rights movement, the Kerner Commission said we were becoming two Americas, one white, one black, separate and unequal. Today, we face a different choice: will we become not two, but many Americas, separate, unequal and isolated? Or will we draw strength from all our people and our ancient faith in the quality of human dignity, to become the world's first truly multiracial democracy? That is the unfinished work of our time, to lift the burden of race and redeem the promise of America.

Almost immediately, all across the country, the president's speech was quoted, discussed, praised, and criticized. Some felt that it was high time that the leadership in the United States took the initiative in calling for the nation to confront its race problem. Some felt that there was no need to stir up feelings about race and that in doing so the president ensured that only long-suppressed animosities would become a part of the so-called national dialogue. Also there was speculation regarding precisely what role the advisory board would play, despite the fact that the president had spelled out very clearly the goals of his race initiative, which were also the goals of the advisory board: to articulate his administration's vision of racial conciliation; to help educate the nation about the facts surrounding the issue of race; to promote a constructive dialogue and confront and work through the difficult issues surrounding race; to recruit and encourage leadership at all levels to help bridge racial divides; and to find, develop, and implement solutions in critical areas such as education, economic opportunity, housing, health care, crime, and the administration of justice.

The advisory board was to meet at least once per month in various parts of the country. We would additionally meet, as individuals or in groups smaller than the full board, with organizations or communities that welcomed our contribution to their role in the search for common ground on the matter of race. The president would also keep his promise to hold town meetings, a format of which he was fond and in which he excelled. The format that we adopted for our monthly meetings was usually broken into three parts: first, to discuss among ourselves our plans and strategies for carrying out our mandate; second, to invite specialists to address some aspect of the problem on which we and the general public needed to be informed; and finally, to invite members of the audience to express their views on the subject or subjects with which we were dealing.

Long before the advisory board's first meeting on August 15, 1997, the White House had appointed Judith Winston, former general counsel and former undersecretary of the Department of Education, as the board's executive director, and she in turn had by that time appointed more than twenty people to the board's staff. The board and Judy were sworn in by the president's chief of staff, Erskine Bowles, before our first meeting, and thereafter we were ready for business. At that first meeting I made some brief opening remarks, titled "Let the Dialogue Begin." I summarized some of the things that the president had said in his San Diego speech, including his view of the role of the advisory board in his plan for One America. The problem we faced was immense and entrenched, and a constructive dialogue was our foremost goal, rather than formulating some programmatic solution.

It is remarkable how many people had their own view of the role of the advisory board on race regardless of how clearly the president or board members defined it. When one man of Hispanic background learned that I lived in Durham, he drove from his New Jersey home to mine to tell me about the loss of his office job at a college, expressing his certainty that it was due to discrimination of some sort. He pleaded with me to take up the matter with the administrators at his institution and thereby assist him in reclaiming his position. I told him that we were not empowered to do what the Equal Employment Opportunity Commission was created to do. Unhappy with my reply, he said that he thought that the advisory board had been created to take care of some of the backlog of the EEOC, which had ballooned to such an extent that few had any hope of getting relief. Others attended the meetings of the board with the apparent expectation of airing their grievances and in hopes of an immediate solution. Others, having no confidence in the process or in the ability of the board to do anything at all, attended the meetings to embarrass its proceedings and the president, or merely to ensure that nothing was accomplished.

By early September 1997, the advisory board had developed a work plan, including the schedule of monthly meetings of the full board, meetings of board subcommittees, activities of individual board members, and the coordination of the board's work through its executive director and her staff. My own tasks outlined within this plan could safely be described as sufficient to fill all of my waking hours for the next twelve months. For example, during July, our first full month of work, I met and had dinner with the Congressional Black Caucus; dinner with Bob Thomas and Jerry Florence of Nissan Motors; an interview for the *AARP Bulletin*; an address before a joint session of the North Carolina General Assembly and lunch with that state's Governor James Hunt and some members of the General Assembly; interviews with reporters from the *Chapel Hill News*, the *Norfolk Journal and Guide*, and *The Boston Globe*; and a live radio interview on WVON in Chicago. In addition, I received, digested, and attempted to respond to numerous telephone calls from interested citizens as well as a regular flow of information from the Executive Office Building, where our staff offices were located.

Given this schedule, I worked to make sure everything I did had as national a focus as possible. For example, when I spoke to the joint session of the General Assembly of the State of North Carolina, I took it as an opportunity to speak to the state legislatures throughout the country. To be sure, I said things to my own legislators that would not apply to the lawmakers in other states, but most of what I said about the importance of giving due attention to racial and ethnic problems was as applicable to California or New York as it was to North Carolina. I reminded the legislators of their responsibility to make certain that young people, regardless of race, would have ample opportunity to reach the highest pinnacle in education that their abilities permitted. And I added that once they were educated, America's youth should not be shackled by prejudicial actions on the part of our citizens that would obstruct in any way their reaching their chosen goals in life.

Surely, in some ways, the most exciting of the regular meetings of the advisory board took place in September, when both the president and the vice president attended and personally participated in the deliberations. It was the meeting at which we were giving particular attention to problems of accessibility of education to all children and in what ways their opportunities could be more fully realized. Both President Clinton and Vice President Gore actively entered into the discussions, contributing their opinions and their considerable energy. At one point President Clinton referred to the schools in Fairfax, Virginia, as an example of what could be regarded as an ideal educational experience. He understood that there were more than a hundred languages represented in the schools of the county, and his enthusiasm over what was transpiring there directly caused the board to decide to hold its October meeting in Annandale, Fairfax County, Virginia.

Instead of regarding the visit by the president and vice president as an expression of their deep interest in the work that the board was doing, some observers went so far as to claim that they had attended the meeting in order to give some oversight to a "rudderless" board that did not know which direction to take. Other critics then, and later, claimed that this visit merely reflected what was an insufficient degree of exchange between the board and the president's office. For its part, the board felt honored and flattered that these extremely busy men took time out to meet with us, and I never failed to view it as anything other than what it was—a public indication of their support of the problem with which the board was wrestling.

At a time when there was broad general disapproval on the part of so many that any good-faith effort to deal with the nation's most intractable problem was under way, it was important that notice be taken at the very highest level of government that the problem deserved the nation's serious attention.

Even before the board held its first meeting and on the day following the president's speech in San Diego, criticism of the president's vision for One America began to take shape. On June 15, 1997, an op-ed piece by Speaker of the House Newt Gingrich and Ward Connerly, a regent of the University of California and avowed anti–affirmative action advocate, appeared in *The New York Times*. They bemoaned the fact that the president's speech was a missed opportunity to address the real problems affecting education, poverty, and race discrimination. There was little indication, they claimed, that the advisory board included anyone "who will critically examine the impact of racial preferences on society . . . We wish he could have laid out a plan for real education reform that would produce genuine equality of opportunity for all." It was remarkable that these two comrades-in-arms felt they knew precisely what the views of each member of the advisory board were regarding "racial preferences" and their impact on society. This sort of quasi-pietistic, politically motivated criticism was only the beginning of what became a concerted effort to undermine the position the advisory board took on virtually any matter that came before it.

Also following President Clinton's San Diego speech, *The New York Times* published an editorial praising the president for taking on such a difficult task, concluding that if the speech succeeded in starting a nationwide discussion of race, affirmative action, and diversity, "it could be remembered as a turning point for him and the country. Let the conversation proceed." Steven Holmes, a reporter for *The Times*, was assigned to cover the activities of the advisory board. By September he was reporting that the group had gotten off to a "slow start and has been criticized for not representing a sufficient diversity of political opinion." He complained that it had held "only one meeting, in mid-July," which had been taken up by a "wandering" discussion of the many issues and institutions the board might examine, including "enforcement of civil rights laws, the criminal justice system, education, environmental racism, health services, and racism." The discussion to which Holmes referred was the board's efforts to establish the parameters and scope of its work, yet it had been the scope of the discussion rather than the problem had most impressed Holmes. That the board had held meetings of subcommittees in August instead of its "monthly" meeting, and had held another full board meeting in September was neatly overshadowed by his charge of inactivity. He also claimed in that September 28 article that the board had not yet filled the twenty-five to thirty staff jobs that the White House had approved. I can only say that at least twenty of the jobs had been filled by the time that Holmes interviewed me, and the staff had already sufficiently bonded by then to be celebrating the birthday of one of its colleagues.

Following Holmes's article, I wrote a letter to the editor pointing out that before Holmes interviewed me, the staff was virtually complete and that he had misunderstood the board's discussion of plans for the future as "wandering." The editor chose not to print my letter or reply to it, setting a pattern. It was to become increasingly clear to me that some channels for a national dialogue were foreclosed.

In late September, the advisory board accompanied President Clinton to Little Rock, Arkansas, to observe the fortieth anniversary of the desegregation of Central High School. The president called attention to the work of the board, expressing his satisfaction and gratitude for all that it was doing. Later, we accompanied him to a town meeting in Akron, Ohio. It was a wide-ranging, freewheeling session that, at times, proved quite amusing, with the president obviously relishing his role as a debater with others on the panel, such as Abigail Thernstrom, who vigorously denounced affirmative action in all its forms, while the president defended it, using the rise of Colin Powell to the top of the ladder in the military establishment as a prime example of the way affirmative action was intended to work.

On another occasion we accompanied Clinton to Pittsburgh, Pennsylvania, for the annual meeting of the NAACP, where he spoke to a large and enthusiastic audience. As he boarded Air Force One en route, he handed me his speech and said that before we landed he wanted my opinion of it. Unfortunately, he was unable to seek me out over the course of the flight, for which, when we disembarked, he apologized. He went on to say that the speech he had handed me was not up to his standards and that he had worked on it during the entire trip. When he delivered it, I knew that he was reworking it even as he spoke; I had a copy of the updated draft, and what he was saying was, in so many ways, different from the version I had before me. My comment to myself as I listened to him was that it was most unfortunate that he did not have the time to write all of his speeches, for he was a first-rate writer, better than many of those whose responsibility it was to draft his addresses.

After the board's meeting in Fairfax County, Virginia, in December 1997, Stephen Holmes reported that it had been sharply criticized for "failing at previous meetings to solicit the views of conservatives and opponents of affirmative action," though he noted that "it went out of its way to hear a diversity of views" when it met in this Virginia suburb of Washington. Among these were those expressed by an old friend of mine, the conservative William J. Bennett, former secretary of education, and Lisa Keegan, superintendent of Arizona Public Instruction. Their inclusion in the meeting, however, was less as a response to specific criticism as it was of a piece with the board's larger mandate: encouraging conversation about race at all levels.

Early in the life of the board, we learned that our meetings could be characterized not only by dialogues and exchanges of one kind or another but also by fireworks, verbal explosions, and sometimes worse. At the Fairfax meeting, for example, a white separatist took the floor to argue that blacks and other minorities, because of genetics, were less intelligent than whites and that they were bent on destroying America. Another resident of Fairfax County interrupted the session to accuse the board of ignoring the interests of whites. No opinion was foreclosed, so long as the standing rules of order were observed. I ruled the latter Fairfax commentator, for instance, out of order on two counts: that he needed to be recognized by the chair (otherwise the meeting would have quickly deteriorated into a disorderly shouting match) and that we had already set aside a time, later in the meeting, for public participation when he could speak freely.

At the meeting in Denver, held some months later and attended by an enormous crowd, two people were to speak on the way race had adversely affected their own careers. Federico Peña, the former mayor of Denver and then secretary of energy in the Clinton cabinet, spoke of his own experiences as a Hispanic. I was to follow him in talking about my experiences as an African American. After Mayor Wellington Webb's words of welcome, Secretary Peña spoke. The audience was not completely quiet, but it was not disorderly. However, when I arose, the audience became unruly, even rude. Whenever I began, a considerable portion of the audience shouted me down. Various board members and guests seated on the platform attempted to regain order, yet whenever they succeeded and I began to talk, the audience again simply refused to listen. I eventually gave up, holding to the view that if the audience did not wish to hear me, I did not wish to speak. The need for dialogue was rarely so evident in its inability to occur at all.

When I learned that the crowd that shouted me down consisted largely of Native Americans, I could hardly believe it. Later, I was told that Judy Winston and some members of the advisory board had met with a group of Native Americans even as I was arriving in the city. Running late, I had not even been able to register at the hotel but went immediately to the meeting. As a consequence, I was unable to canvass the room personally as was my usual habit. Everyone was initially cordial, and we brought them up-to-date on what we were doing in behalf of Native Americans. One of the first appointments to the staff was Laura Harris, the daughter of LaDonna and former U.S. Senator Fred Harris, widely respected Native Americans, as a senior consultant on American Indian Nation issues. In March 1998, Bambi Kraus, a Tlingit, joined the staff to strengthen our outreach effort and to assist further in dealing with American Indian Nation issues. Under the circumstances, I thought that Native Americans had reason to feel included and that their concerns were represented. Later, I learned what the problem was.

A rumor had circulated through the Native American community that I had *prevented* the president from appointing a Native American to the advisory board because it might interfere with my plans to keep the attention of the board and the president focused on the problems of African Americans. I was amazed that anyone could believe that I had such influence over the president, but any Native American who shared in such speculation was indulging in sheer fantasy. As a native Oklahoman, with strains of both Choctaw and Chickasaw ancestry coursing through my veins, I could not imagine being a party to any such machinations.

As we went about our duties, holding board meetings not unlike a traveling road show, we convened in various parts of the country: Phoenix, Arizona; College Park, Maryland; San Francisco, California; and Boston, Massachusetts, were high points on the tour. We encountered a variety of reactions everywhere we went, including sentiments that were strongly critical of the board's efforts, though nothing quite like the Denver experience. Indeed, everywhere we went our primary goal was achieved: A dialogue of some sort on race ensued. I was especially heartened by reports that at the local level, enterprising citizens had assumed responsibility not only for engaging in conversations about race but also for creating groups and agencies that sought to reach certain objectives that they had set for themselves. Numerous examples come to mind. When I visited the YWCA in Winston-Salem, North Carolina to deliver a lunchtime speech, I discovered that someone had included in the price of admission the rule that each attendee bring a guest who was of a different race. I later learned that this small local effort sparked a number of lasting friendships. In Seattle, several neighborhood groups had taken the initiative to make certain that all racial and ethnic groups living in their communities became a part of a program designed to encourage a discussion of racial problems with a view of finding solutions for them.

Reports of such activities occurring all over the country came to the offices of the advisory board, and they were so impressive that Judith Winston and her staff began to compile them. They were published in January 1999 as *Pathways to One America in the 21st Century: Promising Practices for Racial Reconciliation* and distributed by the White House. In a foreword to the work, Albert Camarillo, director of the Stanford Center for Comparative Studies in Race and Ethnicity, said, "Among the most valuable activities by President Clinton's Initiative on Race was the identification of 'Promising Practices for Racial Reconciliation.' Across America groups of concerned and committed people are working effectively to facilitate constructive dialogues and to establish opportunities to bridge racial and ethnic divides." The volume listed all kinds of initiatives in this important work undertaken by groups working at the local as well as the national levels. They ranged from Common Bonds Diversity Training in Austin, Texas, to the Multicultural Institute of Downey, California, to the ALANA (African, Latino, Asian, Native, and American) of Brattleboro, Vermont.

Board member Angela Oh captured the sentiments of us all when she said, "The work of the President's Initiative on Race has just begun. There is no silver bullet or quick fix. This is about long haul commitment that must be made by all sectors of society. Moreover, it is local leadership that will transform the talk into reality. These promising practices represent the kind of leadership that envisions a future in which racial and ethnic divides can be overcome in the pursuit of leading our Nation closer to its highest aspirations." The staff also created and distributed a "dialogue kit" to teach groups and individuals how to set up community meetings to discuss racial problems and find solutions.

It is not possible for me to count the speeches, comments, and interviews that I gave while chair of the president's advisory board on race or measure the consequences, good or ill, of our relentless pursuit of a national dialogue on race. Throughout the entire life of the board, I reminded myself of the admonishment President Clinton delivered to America in San Diego, just as the board's work was commencing: There was no more precious gift our generation could present to future generations than to lift from them the heavy burden of race. This was not a problem to be fixed by the board; at best the board could help delineate its contours and point to solutions. This was not a problem to be fixed by a president; several presidents with courage equal to Clinton's had struggled to confront American racism, and each had advanced the cause of equality incrementally. The problem of race in America has been, and continues to be, an American problem, and the conversation the board began was, and remains, the means to a national solution. Regrettably, those facts did not become the story reported.

29

A Conversation Stalled

IRONICALLY, FROM THE BEGINNING, the advisory board to the President's Initiative on Race experienced a problem of communication. Not among its members, certainly not with the president, nor even in the sometimes contentious exchanges had at meetings and submeetings of the board. From the time that the op-ed by Ward Connerly and Newt Gingrich appeared in *The New York Times* the day after the announcement of the president's creation of the advisory board, to the board's disbanding in September 1998, the communications industry reported what it wished to report and not what actually transpired. From the outset, it was clear that the media defined "conversation" on race as a "debate." If there were no fireworks, that was clear evidence that nothing of importance was being accomplished. If there were, then necessarily something was amiss. Confrontation became the litmus test for meaningful dialogue. The board was criticized for not having one or more members opposed to affirmative action. Presumably, starker disagreements among board members would have been beneficial. Similarly, the board meeting "wandered" or "floundered" if it failed to hotly debate some subject. It was widely and inaccurately reported that I had said that conservatives would not be invited to the meetings because they had nothing to contribute. I denied this numerous times and repeatedly sent corrective letters to editors who had attributed such a statement to me. None of them printed my letters. Newspapers such as the *Chicago Tribune*, which sent no reporter to attend board meetings, accepted as fact *The Times* reportage and decried my supposed misconduct.

The consequences were lamentable. For example, the *Chicago Tribune* excoriated me for conducting what it described as a "one-sided dialogue," inaccurately reporting that I had steadfastly opposed the participation of any anti–affirmative action advocates. Adopting a tone of knowing indignation, the *Tribune* article read, "What a tragedy! What a tragedy! What an inglorious way for Franklin to cap a distinguished scholarly career— covering his ears, in effect, to avoid hearing opinions he disagrees with." The sad fact was that the *Tribune* never sought to confirm with me what I had or had not said. Instead, it quoted *The New York Times*, whose reporter willfully and regularly distorted my positions. That every meeting of the board included a period during which individuals were allowed to say anything they wished and that many took full advantage of the opportunity escaped the *Tribune*'s imbalanced coverage.

I was briefly hopeful that an invitation from the chair of the program committee of the American Society of Newspaper Editors to address a plenary session of its annual meeting in Washington might offer an opportunity for a dialogue with the media. And, indeed, I could hardly make my way to the ballroom where the session was to be held because of the enormous crowds in the hallways. Alas, when I arrived, only the chairman who had invited me and a few others awaited me. We delayed my address for a few minutes, during which time a few more drifted in. However, when the chairman of the session called the meeting to order, there were fewer than a hundred people out of the several thousand attending the annual meeting who came to hear a discussion on "One America: The President's Initiative on Race." Some came out of curiosity but did not participate in the discussion following my talk. Others were most interested and had many questions and observations. But this was promising only in a spirit of what might have been. The chair of the committee was obviously disappointed that so few editors and reporters had attended the session, later writing me a letter of apology for taking time out of my busy schedule to talk about a matter that was obviously of quite limited interest to the members of America's fourth estate.

If the Monica Lewinsky affair did not distract the advisory board, its work, or even as far as I could tell the interest and support of the president, it was one more excuse the communications industry seized upon to the detriment of the advisory board's claim that it was indeed fulfilling its mandate. The work of the board alone, however important, simply could not claim the full attention of the media. That the color line had damned the country for centuries, that national initiatives to confront the problem had been all too rare, and that the board was in fact encouraging the very conversation it was charged with, could not compete with a media more interested in digging up whatever it could to fan interest in events so obviously ephemeral in comparison. It could be Whitewater or it could be Lewinsky, but the story that occupied their attention certainly was not the entrenched problem the president's advisory board on race had been convened to address.

We did not wait until the end of our tenure to make recommendations to the president. Indeed, shortly after we began our work, we indicated to Clinton what we thought he should do in specific areas of social or racial needs. In the fall of 1997, I talked with Dan Glickman, the secretary of agriculture, and told him that we had discussed with representatives of the National Black Farmers Association the Department of Agriculture's alleged discrimination against them, which in fact had a long history. He said that he was aware of the problem and that the department was handling it to the satisfaction of the aggrieved farmers. Even so, we also mentioned the allegations to the president, who said that the problem was high on his agenda. When we called for a clear-cut public policy on housing equity, both the president and the Secretary of Housing and Urban Development Andrew Cuomo acceded to our request to crack down on housing discrimination. We requested that the president increase funding for the Office of Equal Employment Opportunity, and he did. Franklin Raines, the director of the budget, was so proud of this accomplishment that he came to me on a social occasion at the White House and indicated that what we had requested was in the budget for the next fiscal year.

Perhaps because I wrote to the president regularly to inform him of the board's activities, rather than flying in to Washington to meet with him, some reporters drew the inference that I had no personal contact with Clinton. "For his entire year as chairman," wrote a reporter for *The Boston*

Globe, "Franklin never met face-to-face with Clinton." This was, of course, stunningly inaccurate. Once again, the reporter never asked me whether or not I had met the president "face-to-face." I do not know if the reporter checked with the White House to see if I had ever visited the Oval Office; had he done so, he would have learned that I had called on the president more than once. By then I had traveled with him on Air Force One more than a half dozen times, and I had met him "face-to-face" on most of those flights. I wonder if the reporter had checked the telephone log. Although I grant these were not "face-to-face" encounters, nevertheless, the president and I talked on the telephone numerous times. Had the *Globe*'s reporter bothered to inquire, I could have recounted Clinton's saying to me quite early in the life of the advisory board that he was as near to me as my telephone and that I could see him anytime, an overly generous offer of which I did not take advantage.

Knowing the president's directives, meeting with him was secondary to encouraging a national conversation on race. In addition to the regular monthly meetings of the advisory board, there were numerous meetings and other activities sponsored by the board. There were, for example, corporate leader forums, each hosted by a member of the advisory board; religious leader forums; and meetings with American Indian tribal governments. In addition, there were some 275 other board events and activities, not including the 38 town hall–like "conversations" held in various parts of the country or the campus week of dialogues held at more than 575 colleges and universities. There were also 41 statewide days of dialogue in which state governors participated.

In our report to President Clinton after our final meeting on September 18, 1998, we told him of the wide-ranging activities of the board. We did not claim credit for all that had transpired in the country designed to promote better race relations, such as the Human Relations Foundation of Chicago, which had been established in 1990, or the Fulfillment Fund of Los Angeles, which had been created in 1977. We did, however, point to these and similar institutions as models to be admired and replicated whenever and wherever feasible.

We made several recommendations with a view to continuing the effort to achieve One America. In each of the areas cited for improvement, we concluded that the most effective way to achieve the goals of equality and justice was to seek broad community cooperation. We proposed a President's Council for One America, composed of people from the public and private sectors who would come together to work for the common goal of racial equity. We called on the president to summon the leaders in each sector of American life and secure from them commitments to work diligently to assume responsibility within their areas of influence for taking genuine steps to achieve the goal of One America. To that end we suggested that the president summon to the White House leaders in the administration of justice, in the economic sector, in religion, in welfare, and so on in an effort to secure their promise to move as rapidly as possible toward the goal of greater racial equality and justice. These and other proposals, set forth in quite specific terms, appeared in our final report, *One America in the 21st Century: Forging a New Future*.

The media was no more friendly to the board's final report than it had been to the board. One newspaper called it "a wide-ranging diffuse chronicle of the 15-month effort to begin a national discussion about race." It presented few surprises, the reviewer claimed, instead reflecting the difficulties inherent in the problem the board was organized to address. Another said that President Clinton "had hoped to carve out his place in history as the president who bridged America's great racial divide. But a slow start by his advisory panel and controversy over the panel's political makeup, not to mention the distraction of the growing sex scandal in Washington, reduced bold ambition to . . . cautious rhetoric."

I was eighty-two when I chaired the board, am ninety as I write this, and I can honestly reflect back on America's long unfortunate history of race relations, from Jim Crow to the present. And, were it not so tragic in consequence, I could find laughable the notion that the problems faced by the board were preeminently the Lewinsky scandal or any perceived political bias on the board itself. The difficulties faced when anyone anywhere in America attempts a concerted effort to ameliorate the baleful results of centuries of de jure and de facto racism are profound. None of which is aided by an unfortunate short-sightedness on the part of the national press that too often forestalls rather than furthers the needed national conversation.

Long after the board ceased to exist, President Clinton was following up on our suggestions. For example, several months after the board was dissolved, the president invited to the White House more than a dozen state attorneys general, Attorney General Janet Reno, including several members of her staff, and at least fifty practicing attorneys from large, medium-size, and small firms. As was his practice, he sent me an invitation. The lawyers met among themselves for several hours and then came together with the president and several former members of his advisory board. At that point, the attorneys from the public and private sectors pledged themselves to work more energetically to achieve a more equitable system of justice and to increase their pro bono work on behalf of the poor.

In a similar effort, the president convened at the White House a large and representative group of religious leaders, including Catholics, Protestants, Jews, Muslims, and Buddhists, as well as leaders of other faiths. They first met among themselves and then came to the East Room of the White House and declared to the president that regardless of religious differences, they were in agreement that racial discrimination in any form whatsoever was a sin. They pledged to use all resources at their command to see to it that their respective groups, as well as all others with whom they had any contact, would work to eliminate all forms of discrimination. Many of the clerics gave personal accounts of their own experiences with racism and the seriousness of their determination to take on the demon of racial discrimination and defeat it.

In retrospect, it was clear that the president's San Diego speech, daring as it was in a time of comparative racial peace, divided the country into two major groups—those who thought that he should let "sleeping dogs lie" and those who thought that some national attention to the nation's oldest social problem was long overdue. There were those, moreover, who thought that the board should deliver much more than it was capable of delivering and expected it to wield more power than it actually had. Some believed that the board should have devoted its attention to getting the federal government to apologize for slavery and to have a definitive discussion of affirmative action, even though its mandate incorporated no such dictate. We were criticized because every board member presumably believed in affirmative action, though, so far as I know, that was never a prerequisite for appointment to the board.

Christopher Edley Jr., the Harvard Law School professor and adviser to both the president and to the advisory board on race, sought to correct some of the misunderstandings and misperceptions about the board's work. At one point the president described the board as a useful teaching tool for the country and said that he hoped its efforts would be more visible. But, of course, the board's visibility depended on the willingness of the media to render it visible. This is not to say that the board was ignored; far from it. Nor did the media utterly fail to attempt the historical contextualization of the problem of race in America, spurred to do so, it would seem, by the very existence of the board.

Easily the most ambitious response to the president's initiative on race was *The New York Times*'s series of articles, extending over several weeks, called "How Race Is Lived in America." It would win wide attention as well as a Pulitzer Prize. The articles touched on many aspects of living with race in this country, including the problem of bridging the divide among minorities. In its editorial of June 4, 2000, introducing the series, the editor boasted, "In a way, without deliberately trying to, the people who populate these stories provide the uncomfortably candid conversation about race that Mr. Clinton sought but never got." In response, I wrote the editor, stating, "Perhaps you do not know of the results of the efforts of the President's Initiative on Race in this regard." I then listed the numerous events, activities, community-based initiatives, etc., that resulted from the board's efforts, noting in conclusion that "perhaps the least successful was my effort to initiate a dialogue with the members of the American Society of Newspaper Editors at their annual meeting in 1998, when fewer than one hundred members attended the general session where I spoke." The editor declined to publish my letter, as he had declined to publish any of the several letters that I sent to him to correct his reporter's distortions during the time that I was chair of the president's advisory board on race.

One of the most constructive contributions of the media to the national conversation we were charged with encouraging was the week-long series of editorials in *The Philadelphia Inquirer* beginning on January 17, 1999. The first was on Prejudice, followed by Education, Urban Revitalization, Affirmative Action, Civil Rights Enforcement, Civic Dialogue, and What You Can Do. It encouraged its readers to declare zero tolerance for racism, insist that the schools celebrate the roles of diverse groups in the nation's life, support companies and organizations committed to racial inclusion, break the silence on racism, and teach our children the importance of tolerance.

Perhaps the "soaring goals" of the advisory board on race had not been reached by its dissolution, as *The Washington Post* claimed when commenting on the conclusion of the board's work. But it could be argued successfully, I think, that the nation's consciousness regarding the importance as well as the gravity of the race problem was raised considerably by what the board attempted and by what its members accomplished. And if the energies of the hecklers on the sidelines could have been transformed into constructive support for the efforts of those who worked to improve the racial climate, and if the media had been willing to give appropriate visibility to the board and its work, we might well have advanced the course of racial relations even more than we did.

30

In Sickness and in Health

EVEN AS I BECAME DEEPLY INVOLVED in the work of the president's advisory board on race, there were other activities that I could not neglect. One of them was a documentary film. Stanley Zuckerman, a retired foreign service officer with an enormous amount of experience in communications, conceived the idea of presenting on public television the career patterns of several individuals who were, in his opinion, sufficiently interesting to appeal to the general public. They were the architect I. M. Pei, Elie Wiesel, the Holocaust survivor and Nobel laureate, and myself. I became his lead-off project, and the hour-long program, eventually titled *First Person Singular*, was taped over several months in several venues.

Happily, my presence before the camera was not too demanding, for the emphasis was on informality. It was pleasant to return to such places as Rentiesville, Tulsa, and Washington, D.C., for the filming. Everyone was most cooperative, and it was a joy to work with Zuckerman and his colleagues. The finished film had its premiere in the spring of 1997 and was presented several times over the PBS network as well as independent television stations.

Duke University was already expressing in several ways its appreciation for what I had done and was doing on behalf of the college. Most notable was President Nannerl Keohane's request for permission to have an oil portrait of me painted and hung in the Gothic Reading Room of the University's Perkins Library. Keohane made it clear that her question was more in the manner of a command, and so a committee was formed and the African American artist Simmie Knox commissioned to undertake the task. He was delighted to do so, and in March 1997, President Keohane unveiled the portrait before a throng of invited guests. In it I am standing, holding a copy of the seventh edition of *From Slavery to Freedom*, and the Presidential Medal of Freedom is clearly visible on my lapel. On a stand nearby, Knox painted an orchid, the *Phalaenopsis John Hope Franklin*. And, most meaningful for me, on a desk beside me is a framed photograph of Aurelia.

Long before I had been able to do so, if indeed I ever truly did, Whit and Karen came to the conclusion that Aurelia needed more care than I could provide her at our home. On their visits from Washington, which became more frequent in the 1990s, and without my knowledge, they began looking into alternative possibilities. In the summer of 1995, they confronted me with the assertion that I could not care for Aurelia alone, that she needed professional attention, and that although I was doing everything I could for her, it was not helping her all that much while it was taking a very heavy toll on me. They invited me to join them in a tour of the nursing homes they had already looked into and encouraged me to explore others if the ones they had visited did not prove to be satisfactory. It was with the greatest reluctance that I joined in the search for what I regarded as a grim sentence for my beloved companion of fifty-five years.

We decided to place Aurelia in a nursing home five or six miles from our home in Durham. We moved her into a private room there on October 23, 1995. Even as we packed her things, I was unable to tell her that she would be moving out of our home. If she had said that she did not wish to go, I simply would not have had the will to insist. Nor, for the same reason, could I tell her that she would never be returning. Whit, Karen, and I attempted to make her new room as comfortable and as much like our home as possible. We took my Harvard chair that she had given me when I graduated, a Turkish rug that she and I had purchased in Istanbul, several treasured paintings, some family photographs, and a bulletin board on which to post events in our lives and the world outside the nursing home.

I kept fresh flowers in her room at all times. We also put a radio and television set in her room and hoped that she would continue to enjoy the music to which we had always listened. And for the first time in my life, I wished that we had become television addicts, so that watching shows would be familiar to her.

In the beginning I visited Aurelia twice every day. That was an ambitious undertaking. As I completed one visit I was already preparing for the next. It proved a grueling schedule that permitted little else and took not just an emotional but a physical toll on me. Soon I reduced my visits to one per day, at times in the morning and at other times in the afternoon. I avoided night visits as well as mealtimes. She was soon unable to feed herself, and I could neither bear to do it nor see others feed her.

Aurelia was always delighted to see me, and she expressed her pleasure not only with a warm smile but also with appropriate comments. However, it became clear to me over time that she was not aware that I had been there earlier that day or that I had not been there for four or five days, if I had been traveling. This relieved me of some of the guilt that accompanied my rare long absences. I do not believe I could have undertaken the demands of President Clinton's appointment without knowing that Aurelia was both looked after and also increasingly in her own world.

Even as my responsibilities for the President's Initiative on Race began to subside, other projects seemed to crowd in on me. At some point in 1998, the editorial staff of the Raleigh *News and Observer* decided that I should be named that newspaper's "Tar-Heel of the Year." Two reporters, Laurie Willis and Geoff Edgers, were assigned to cover my activities and conduct in-depth interviews with me, which formed the basis for the feature story that ran on Sunday, December 27, 1998. Flatteringly, it covered my entire career, from birth through my work on the president's advisory board on race, arguing that in my professional life I had "always sought to dispassionately render a portrait of black and white." This is the story, they said, that I had taken around the world, "to Argentina, Australia, England, Germany, Japan, Norway, and Russia." Somehow, seeing it in print brought home just how busy I had been, most particularly in the last year. "In just the past six weeks," the article noted, "he has huddled with Bishop Desmond Tutu in Senegal, been honored by the NAACP Legal Defense Fund in New York City, and given a keynote address at the National Communication Association in New York. All this only weeks after completing 15 months as chairman of President Clinton's advisory board on race."

My recent work with Bishop Tutu had been especially gratifying, perhaps in part because of my sense that a national conversation on race was only a partial solution to the problem. I had sensed it earlier, when Aurelia, Whit, and I made an extensive trip through Africa in 1981, beginning in Senegal and going through Ghana, Liberia, The Gold Coast, Zambia, Zaire, and Kenya. Whit, well into his career at the Smithsonian Institution, joined with Camille Cosby and Renée Poussaint, who had been planning a feature educational film on race and the burden of its history. The focus of the film would be three groups of teenagers from South Africa, Senegal, and the United States brought together to spend a week in Senegal. During that time they would be filmed getting acquainted and talking about the ways slavery had placed a burden on the society in which they lived and how it even now continued to affect almost everything that transpired around them. The bishop and I had been invited to spend time with the young people, counseling them and assisting them in sorting out their own differing experiences and opinions.

Senegal was an ideal setting for such an adventure. The young people were able to visit a seventeenth- and eighteenth-century slave house and vividly come to understand what it meant for people, many as young as themselves, to be condemned to a lifetime of servitude far away from family, home, and culture. And against the backdrop of an island where slavery's impact was still a vibrant memory, they also discovered how much cultural baggage they brought with them. Nothing was more instructive than watching these young men and women grappling with their own assumptions as they confronted and sought to understand peoples from other places and backgrounds. Bishop Tutu and I served as facilitators of these exchanges, as well as, we hoped, "sages" who could make observations, call attention to problems, and point the twenty-one young people toward the frank conversation about race that necessarily must precede efforts toward solutions. The result was a film called *Tutu and Franklin: A Journey Towards Peace*, which had its first showing in the United States at the Smithsonian Institution in February 2001 and a South Africa premiere a month later.

The humanity I watched emerge in Senegal among those youthful strangers was all too sadly lacking back in Durham. That Aurelia's nursing home was a for-profit organization became clear quite early in her stay there. The company operated more than a score of nursing homes, and the extent of the profits could be seen in the lavish manner in which the company's owners lived, with their stables of thoroughbred horses, private planes, and warehouses of supplies that they maintained in pursuit of reduced costs. Shamefully, this did not translate into a deeper dedication to service. At the end of Aurelia's second month at the home, I noticed that they were charging me for medication that she was not receiving. They were also billing me for laundry service they did not provide. Since our longtime housekeeper was doing her laundry, which would provide some feeling that we were involved in her day-to-day care, I was especially pained by this revelation.

We soon began to miss items from Aurelia's closet. One day it might be a dress or a skirt, another time it would be a blouse or some underwear. Such losses were particularly disheartening given the obvious vulnerability of a patient in a nursing home. I removed her engagement ring and replaced it with a less expensive one. This seemed to be an invitation to looters. Within a matter of days, the new ring had disappeared. I was not only furious but overcome with a feeling of helplessness, as I realized that my options were minimal. I made the expected and ineffectual protests, knowing that there was no guarantee that she would fare any better at another institution. Regardless, this option seemed unrealistic and, in fact, cruel to the person least deserving of further suffering. One could not move a patient around like a piece on a chessboard. We decided to keep Aurelia where she was and assume greater responsibility for her day-to-day care.

As Aurelia's health declined and as she became more helpless, I became more anxious about maintaining her health in the areas where it had not deteriorated. As problems with chewing and swallowing became more evident, I made a point of taking every precaution, for example, against tooth decay and gum disease. I had a dentist go to the nursing home and clean her teeth, which he was willing to do for a substantial fee. In view of the fact that she already had glaucoma, I made certain that our ophthalmologist saw her regularly. Dr. Dwight Perry was mercifully reasonable in the bills he charged for looking after Aurelia's eyes.

In view of her popularity and the number of contacts she had built up over the years, Aurelia had surprisingly few visitors. I could not hold it against those who did not, for one reason or another, drop in and see her. People are busy, and many are squeamish about visiting the ill and the institutions for the helpless or the aged. Those who did, however, were a tremendous comfort and help. My friend Walter Brown frequently accompanied me when I visited. Some of my former students, Genna Rae McNeill, for example, were frequent visitors, as were Loren and Pat Schweninger from Greensboro. When North Carolina Central and Duke recognized the fiftieth anniversary of *From Slavery to Freedom*, the celebration attracted large numbers of friends and former students, many of whom took time out from anniversary events to see her. She was as gracious as ever. The visits of Whit and Karen were so regular and so frequent that they could almost be referred to as commuters.

Shortly after Aurelia went to the nursing home, Whit and Karen, ever concerned about my own well-being, suggested that I ask Bouna, who was not especially happy with his job in Senegal and wished to return to the United States, to move into the house with me. Soon, we put the necessary machinery in motion. He secured a position with his alma mater, North Carolina Central University, and returned to the States and 208 Pineview Road. He often went to the nursing home with or without me and was as devoted to Aurelia as he would have been to his own mother.

My travels and commitments abated considerably with the conclusion of the work of the president's advisory board on race and the end of filming of *Tutu and Franklin*. To be sure, there were other public responsibilities, but I could and did spend more time with Aurelia. Then, in late January, I noticed that she was experiencing some respiratory difficulty. I called this to the attention of the home's nurses and aides, who had all failed to notice it. Since there was by this time no resident physician, as had been the case when she originally moved there, presumably for cost-saving reasons, I asked the attendant to call one to examine her.

Aurelia had a cold which, due to her weakened condition, she could not handle. Once again, I began to visit her twice a day, remaining longer than usual. I felt utterly helpless as I watched her steady decline. I was scheduled to give the Zora Neale Hurston Lecture at Eatonville, Florida, later that week. I canceled that engagement and soon began a constant vigil. Our relatively new friends, Lois and T. J. Anderson, who had recently retired from Tufts University to live in Chapel Hill, were visiting her regularly. On Wednesday, January 27, 1999, the 121st anniversary of my mother's birth, I left Aurelia's bedside as Lois and T.J. came to visit her. Earlier that day Genna Rae McNeill had visited her and brought primroses. I intended to go home, get some rest, take a shower, and return for what could clearly be Aurelia's final hours.

Shortly before I left home to return, the head nurse called to inform me that Aurelia had quietly passed away at nine-thirty p.m. I called Whit to inform him that he no longer had a mother, and he said that he and Karen would be down the following day. Bouna was out at a concert, so I called Walter Brown to inform him and to ask him to go to the nursing home with me. Then I called the Cremation Society of North Carolina.

As Walter and I arrived at the nursing home, a sense of relief came over me. I was not at all sad, for I realized that Aurelia had undergone an ordeal that no merciful person could have wished on anyone. As I went into her room to see her, she had a look of complete serenity, which pleased me very much. I told the nurse that the people from the crematory would arrive shortly and that I did not want anything done to her room. I especially enjoined them not to remove anything before my son, his wife, Bouna, and I arrived to collect her things the following day. Their final indignity would be to ignore that explicit request.

The family went to Raleigh on Thursday afternoon to visit the crematory and to say good-bye to Aurelia. The attendants were kind and thoughtful, and we were grateful for their solicitude.

Aurelia and I had long ago agreed that upon our deaths there would be "no mourning at the bar" and that there would be no formal services of remembrance. Those who loved us would need no organized memorial and certainly no burial ceremony. For our friends and acquaintances, I reissued with a foreword, titled "From the Survivor," the piece we had written together, shortly after our fiftieth wedding anniversary, which we called "For Better, For Worse." In it we celebrated our love and described how we had sustained it over more than fifty years of marriage. Our life together was our most meaningful memorial to one another.

Per our wishes, her ashes were scattered in a place or places unknown to us. Many, many people, memorably including President Clinton, called to privately convey their condolences, but the only public recognition of her passing was the premier performance in April 1999 of T. J. Anderson's *Aurelia, In Memoriam*, for solo violin, which Karen, Whit, Bouna, and I attended with friends at the National Humanities Center. Meanwhile, I established in her memory the Aurelia Franklin Scholarship Fund at Fisk University. Instead of placing flowers on a grave, I make an annual contribution to the fund. In that way, some young, motivated student will receive the support for his or her promising future in memory of a young and promising alumna who contributed so much not only professionally but for posterity through her family and through the many whose lives she touched in so many ways.

Epilogue

Through a Looking Glass

ALTHOUGH I WAS NOT AWARE OF IT at the time, certain events during the first decade of my life had a profound impact not only on me but on the nation and the world. World War I, the first armed conflict of such global magnitude, illustrated just how far the United States would go to ensure that peoples in every part of the world might enjoy freedom and democracy. Yet it pursued those ideals with a racially segregated military force that made a mockery of the very values that President Woodrow Wilson proclaimed. Second, when Attorney General A. A. Palmer in the early 1920s raided offices and private homes in search of communists and other so-called terrorists, he showed little or no regard for the civil liberties of ordinary citizens. Nothing more clearly demonstrated how easily prejudice and expediency could dispense with political principles. Third, the early-twentieth-century race riots in Chicago, Washington, East St. Louis, Elaine, Omaha, Tulsa, Rosewood, and elsewhere showed American hypocrisy at its very worst. Here was damning evidence of just how far white America would go to quarantine the United States from the "virus" of racial equality all the while mouthing platitudes about saving the world for democracy. The Tulsa riot deprived me of my father for almost five years, and it was only on account of my strong parents and strong family ties that its long-term effect on me was not nearly as devastating as it might have been.

These were extraordinary experiences for a child to have before his tenth birthday. Although I was not even fully aware of them at the time, they would affect me for years to come. Indeed, such experiences in the American race jungle, some large and impersonal, some immediate and deeply personal, have touched me throughout my life and in more ways than I can count. Some of them I was instantly aware of; others I have only gradually come to understand and appreciate.

I regret to say that in this bright, beautiful, and bountiful country, the specter of race has been ever present. In a country whose founding was not only predicated in large measure on race but also on a profound commitment to the exploitation of one race by another, it could hardly have been otherwise. For ninety years I have felt the consequences. It was inconceivably cruel for a blind white woman to humiliate me simply because I was a twelve-year-old black Boy Scout trying to help her across a busy street. My fear as a sixteen-year-old college freshman when confronted by a white ticket agent incensed at my recommending how he could make change for a large bill arose from the same cause as my terror at nineteen when threatened with being lynched. In my early years there was never a moment in any contact I had with white people that I was not reminded that society as a whole had sentenced me to abject humiliation for the sole reason that I was not white. Small wonder that some black boys and girls, having no one else to blame for the cruel disadvantage of being black, have grown to maturity hating themselves.

Happily for me, my parents always insisted that race was irrelevant as far as one's personal development was concerned. They even taught me to believe that I could be, as they then articulated it, the first Negro president of the United States; if as a youth I had tongue in cheek when I declared my intent of realizing that ambition, it had the effect of establishing a measure of self-confidence that permitted me to pursue more realistic goals, if only more realistic by matter of degree.

I was a sophomore in college before I met a white man who treated me as his social and intellectual equal. It was my relationship with Theodore S. Currier, along with the self-confidence my parents instilled in me, that gave me the determination to reach any height to which my ability and energy could take me. Even this white man, who became my mentor, major professor, and closest friend, was sufficiently realistic to understand that American society would resist every effort I would make to be acknowledged as a scholar on an equal footing with my white counterparts. Neither Ted nor I could anticipate in the 1930s how much the racial climate in America might change, but we could even then determine that I would acquire the skills to become a leader in my own universe that would not be racially defined. That is what that white friend set out to have me achieve. He would provide me with the richest experiences possible and prepare me for the most rigorous training that existed in higher education in general and United States history in particular.

None of us, not even my prescient white professor, foresaw the forces beyond our control that would eventually send young black scholars up the professional ladder. There was the slow, halting move by white scholars to give the appearance of their being willing to countenance some scholarly advances by African Americans. As if they were on some kind of intellectual and academic probation, black scholars were invited to appear on the programs of learned societies, to teach during a summer session or for a single visiting semester at some of the major colleges and universities, to submit the occasional article for publication in refereed journals, the occasional monograph for consideration by a university press.

Even so, timing was everything, or almost. Many in the generation of African American scholars who preceded me were every bit as qualified as any in my generation. Yet, the learned societies, the university presses, and the faculties of so-called mainstream universities never paid much attention to such distinguished post–World War I African American scholars as Rayford W. Logan, E. Franklin Frazier, Alain Locke, or Sterling Brown, all faculty at Howard University. Even so, the works of these and other African American scholars prepared the learned professions for what would come later. Nor can one overlook the persistent and successful legal battles that forced higher education to accept black students before *Brown v. Board of Education* chipped away at the fortification that finally fell to the relentless attacks of Thurgood Marshall and the NAACP Legal Defense Fund.

I was an early beneficiary of the liberal forces that opened up the learned professions, especially in the field of history. I never entertained the thought that the gates opened exclusively for me and throughout my career, I assumed some responsibility for keeping them ajar for others. While I never considered my own appointments as "token" gestures, I also knew that they did not open wide the gates. My colleagues at Brooklyn College and the University of Chicago were so full of self-congratulations for having persuaded their institutions to invite me to join them that I generally focused my efforts on *other* departments and *other* institutions, urging them to take their first steps in the experiment of diversifying their faculties. In due course, and not many years later, African Americans were receiving regular appointments at several historically white colleges and universities; and they were moving up to leadership roles in the learned and professional societies.

From the very beginning of my own involvement in the academy, the goal I sought was to be a scholar with credentials as impeccable as I could achieve. At the same time I was determined to be as active as I could in the fight to eradicate the stain of racism that clouded American intellectual and academic life even as it poisoned other aspects of American society. Both challenges were formidable. While I set out to advance my professional career on the basis of the highest standards of scholarship, I also used that scholarship to expose the hypocrisy underlying so much of American social and race relations. It never ceased being a risky feat of tightrope walking, but I always believed that if I could use my knowledge and training to improve society it was incumbent on me to make the attempt. Thus, in addition to teaching and writing, I served as an expert witness in cases designed to end segregation in education, most memorably at the behest of Thurgood Marshall, and I marched in Montgomery to make common cause with those who sought in other ways to destroy racial hatred and bigotry.

Another early-twentieth-century event that profoundly influenced me was the Spanish influenza pandemic of 1918, which laid its cruel hand on me and taught the world the importance of approaching such threats on a global rather than on a local or national basis. As a young scholar I recognized that intellectual pursuits similarly should know no geographical boundaries. From the time that I lectured at the Salzburg Seminar in American Studies in Austria in 1951 I cultivated interests and connections in many parts of the world. Serving as Pitt Professor in Cambridge University in 1962–63 and participating in a variety of scholarly activities on every continent, including Australia and New Zealand, and the translation of my books into European and Asian languages have been liberating for me. These experiences, together with my lengthy tenure on the Fulbright Board, have determined the way in which I look at the world today. It is a world in which language barriers can and must be breached and where common ground among peoples can be found if only we are willing to look for it.

It is a world in which the United States cannot boast of having the most commendable record of equality and civil rights for all. In the instances where this country's role has been the most influential, in Liberia and Haiti—both black nations, one in the Old World the other in the New—America's record can hardly be described as other than sordid. I am moved to wonder if America's experiences in the nineteenth and twentieth centuries with such nations have influenced its policies toward darker peoples in the twenty-first century. Does this history have something to do with the way we have lagged behind even our promises to do something significant to relieve the suffering in Africa related to malaria and AIDS? In any given year, as we make claims to the world concerning our compassion for the oppressed, more Africans die of malaria and AIDS than there were deaths in the tsunami of 2004.

All of us should reflect on the role African Americans have played in compelling this country to live up to its professed ideals. By insisting on fighting in the War of Independence when they clearly were not wanted, blacks reminded the founding fathers that the American Revolution should bring a better life to *all* Americans. Black warriors in the Civil War pursued the same course, as did the black men and women who served during World Wars I and II. By the time of the civil rights movement following the Second World War, black and white American citizens resorted to a variety of actions to force a confrontation between the values the nation liked to profess and its stark failure to adhere to them. The remarkable struggles, sacrifices, courage, and bravery of activists ranging from Fred Shuttlesworth and Fannie Lou Hamer to Martin Luther King Jr. and Rosa Parks forced Americans to envision a world *beyond race*, and showed how far activists were willing to go and, indeed, were compelled to go in order to realize the dream of equality.

The victories of the civil rights era did not wipe away three centuries of slavery, degradation, segregation, and discrimination. President Lyndon Johnson said at Howard University in 1965 that the battle for civil rights looked toward not just "freedom but opportunity . . . not just equality as a right and theory, but equality as a fact and equality as a result." Stating the goal no more ensured its being achieved than did passing legislation. As if the president of the United States had not spoken and acted in signing the Civil Rights Act and the Voting Rights Act, even after these became laws of the land, racial disturbances reappeared in new, virulent forms, thus dimming the optimism that the legislative and executive actions had seemed to promise.

In the ninety years that I have observed the human condition I have attempted diligently to understand the foibles and peculiarities of my fellows, especially my fellow Americans. There have been times when I was on the verge of giving up, when I doubted that I would ever gain more than a glimmer of insight that would encourage me to persist in my quest. I looked around me—at my contemporaries and fellow sufferers. There they were, many of them privileged all their lives, who had little or no interest in the well-being of their fellows. When many of them met their underprivileged, underserved compatriots, some in poor health, they would pass on the other side of the street. Too many were indifferent, insensitive, even uncaring to take notice of the disadvantaged among them.

The longer I live the more I am inclined to question the capability of the human race to be consistent in its judgment and unswerving in its commitment to lofty, constructive principles. We point with pride to the historic congressional legislation and Supreme Court decisions against racial discrimination. But racial discrimination and even racial segregation continue in blatant as well as subtle forms. Racial imbalance in the schools, described now as reflecting parental "preferences" rather than inequity, persists in every part of the country. The glass ceiling is very much intact when African Americans seek employment or promotion on the basis of skills and proficiency. Discrimination in housing continues not only in so-called upper-class neighborhoods but in low-income neighborhoods as well. Indeed, low-income neighborhoods where the majority of African Americans live are without the agencies and organizations that encourage ambition and nurture lofty goals. In such areas, reform is more a verbal expression than a committed goal.

All too often we tend to take notice of our progress toward economic justice and equality by pointing to the few African Americans who have reached the top in the communications industry and to the very small numbers in the powerful investment firms and merchandise establishments. At this point it is well to remember our history. In the antebellum years, when the vast majority of black people were in slavery, some blacks were free and a few even held slaves. In the post-Reconstruction years, there were a few powerful black educators and even a few well-to-do blacks in business and the professions. But they were not a portent of better days or even a promise of a brighter future. We are compelled to ask if these were the exceptions that prove the rule. Might such variations from the norm serve the purpose of ensuring that there is sufficient "sway" in America's still-racist structure to provide the "give" necessary to protect that structure against the winds that could, without that "give," destroy it?

I believe a much more accurate measure of American progress toward justice and fairness is in the number of young adult African American men detained in various stages of the criminal justice system as opposed to those in, say, higher education. What does the fact that in 2001 there were more young black men in jails and penitentiaries than in college say for the direction in which our society is moving? Surely, a much more accurate appraisal of our commitment to race-blind economic opportunity can be made by ascertaining the extent to which African American workers are proportionally retained in the face of increasing competition with other minorities at home and the outsourcing of jobs abroad.

We cannot have a healthy and wholesome society as long as the young black male is alienated. He has never enjoyed an equal opportunity in the nation's history. In slavery he was suspected of and often, regardless of evidence and certainly without due process, hideously punished for misconduct ranging from malingering to stealing to sexual assault. In freedom avenues of justice did not improve and he had little opportunity for self-development. During the years of Reconstruction the newly freed father was more anxious to educate his daughters and place them in positions beyond the reach of white men who, all too often with cause, were suspected of being sexual predators. With this in mind, my maternal grandfather sent all of his daughters, including my mother, and none of his sons to college. Meanwhile, it was only because the white headmistress of the preparatory school in the Indian Territory saw much promise in my father that she insisted my paternal grandfather send him to college. Thus my father became the only educated male among his siblings.

Several generations of young African American men with little or no education became sharecroppers, peons, day laborers, or, if they were fortunate, factory workers in the industrial North. Consequently, the black family was off to an unhealthy start, and the black male was saddled with burdens for which he was ill-prepared. In times of economic stringency, he quickly lost his job, and his limited training and meager resources made it extremely difficult for him to cope with any economic downturn.

Small wonder that many young black men, frustrated and discouraged, entered the underground economy and set out to develop a way of life, a culture of their own. State and local governments dragged them farther down by criminalizing the cheaper forms of narcotics while easing penalties for the possession of the more expensive forms. Rejected in the economic sphere of the larger community and alienated from the larger social arena, they saw no reason to conform in conduct, habits, dress, or any other way. Increasingly, the legitimate areas to which they were attracted and where they were readily accepted were certain musical pursuits and professional athletics, particularly football, basketball, and baseball. In both fields a limited few became successful. Indeed, those who became wealthy established impossible goals for most of their peers, thus adding to their frustrations and encouraging further misconduct. I have come to regard most of these success stories as millionaire wastrels, spending their fortunes on huge mansions and custom-built automobiles, with little thought of their fellows in the ghettos, from which many of them came.

I have had these angry, disappointing musings challenged. I recall in particular the letter I received from basketball star and Duke graduate Grant Hill of the Orlando Magic requesting me to write a foreword to the catalogue of his collection of African American art, titled *Something of Our*

Own. The collection was shortly to begin a nationwide tour and with the catalogue was intended to inspire youth to set for themselves ambitious goals. I was happy to comply, of course. But one swallow does not make a spring. There are not yet sufficient numbers of Grant Hills in athletics, art, social welfare, big-brother movements, and education to contribute significantly to the transformation of our society for the better.

I demand the same of all privileged Americans, black or white. Most have manifested little or no interest in the well-being of their fellows. All too often they are indifferent, insensitive, and uncaring. At times, presumably stricken by conscience, they contribute a few dollars to some cause with which they are scarcely familiar, when a few precious hours of their time and talent could more directly inspire and encourage some vulnerable youth to pursue his or her studies more diligently. In particular, black professionals—physicians, lawyers, engineers, those in business, teachers, and others—could do much to rescue young African Americans from the brink of dismal failure if only they would be willing to take the time.

The rehabilitation and redirection of young black males is not the sole responsibility of their more advantaged senior brethren. After all, our society as a whole and the fate of the least among us are inextricably woven together. And our entire social system bears the special responsibility for the current plight of these young people who, in a very real way, may be regarded as a metaphor for the ills of our society and the problems we face. It was the nation's slave policy, even before it was a nation, that sealed their fate and the fate of the nation. It was the nation's erection of an apartheid society after slavery that made them pariahs of the land, thus hanging a chain of dishonesty and hypocrisy around the nation's neck. It was a national economic policy that withheld from them opportunities to train for jobs requiring technical skills and special responsibilities that modern America could provide. In so doing, the nation deprived itself of much-needed manpower and condemned this group that had played such a valiant role in building the nation to the lowest possible place in the social order to become a burden and a drag on the progress and well-being of the nation. And it was national policy that permitted its citizens to badger them, goad them, and humiliate them to the point that they could not be easily reached. But they *must* be reached, through legislation, goodwill, understanding, and compassion. The test of an advanced society is not in how many millionaires it can produce, but in how many law-abiding, hardworking, highly respected, and self-respecting loyal citizens it can produce. The success of such a venture is a measure of the success of our national enterprise.

Index

Note: JHF throughout the index refers to John Hope Franklin.